I0759500

Pāṇini's Perfect Rule

Pāṇini's Perfect Rule

A Modern Solution to an Ancient Problem in Sanskrit Grammar

Rishi Rajpopat

Harvard University Press
Cambridge, Massachusetts
London, England
2025

Printed in the United States of America
First printing

EU GPSR Authorised Representative
LOGOS EUROPE, 9 rue Nicolas Poussin, 17000, LA ROCHELLE, France
E-mail: Contact@logoseurope.eu

Library of Congress Cataloging-in-Publication Data
Names: Rajpopat, Rishi, 1995– author.
Title: Pāṇini's perfect rule : a modern solution to an ancient problem in Sanskrit grammar / Rishi Rajpopat.
Description: Cambridge, Massachusetts ; London, England : Harvard University Press, 2025. | Includes bibliographical references and index. | English; some words and phrases in Sanskrit. | Summary: "Linguist Rishi Rajpopat solves an ancient puzzle, showing that Pāṇini's Sanskrit grammar is self-sufficient. Centuries of commentators, having misunderstood it, created tools to overcome its supposed flaws, but to no avail. By reinterpreting some key Pāṇinian rules, Rajpopat shows that the language machine is in fact entirely free of such glitches."— Provided by publisher.
Identifiers: LCCN 2025018926 (print) | LCCN 2025018927 (ebook) | ISBN 9780674297647 (hardback) | ISBN 9780674302228 (epub) | ISBN 9780674302235 (pdf)
Subjects: LCSH: Pāṇini. Aṣṭādhyāyī | Sanskrit language—Grammar. | Computational linguistics. | Sanskrit language—Grammar—History.
Classification: LCC PK519 .R35 2025 (print) | LCC PK519 (ebook)
LC record available at https://lccn.loc.gov/2025018926

LC ebook record available at https://lccn.loc.gov/2025

CONTENTS

Preface vii

CHAPTER ONE: The Existing Understanding of Rule Conflict 1
- 1.1 Metarules in the Pāṇinian Grammatical Tradition 4
- 1.2 The Traditional View on Rule Conflict 7
- 1.3 Modern Perspectives on the Functioning of the *Aṣṭādhyāyī* 14
- 1.4 Modern Scholarship on 1.4.2 18
- 1.5 My View 22
- 1.6 Road Map for the Rest of the Book 23

CHAPTER TWO: A Novel Approach to Pāṇini's Grammar 25
- 2.1 Two Types of Operational Rule Interaction 25
- 2.2 Solutions for Type 1 (Same Operand Interaction (SOI)) and Type 2 (Different Operand Interaction (DOI)) 26
- 2.3 Evidence for My Interpretation of *Para* 27
- 2.4 A Key Difference between SOI and DOI 30
- 2.5 Pāṇinian and Post-Pāṇinian Approaches to Derivations 32
- 2.6 Traditional Solutions 37
- 2.7 Examples of DOI—Nominal Inflection 40
- 2.8 Examples of SOI—Nominal Inflection 54

CHAPTER THREE: Examples of Derived-Base Inflection 69
- 3.1 DOI 69
- 3.2 SOI 80

CHAPTER FOUR: Examples of Finite Verbs and Primary Derivatives 82
- 4.1 *Aṅgādhikāra* 82
- 4.2 Examples of Application of 1.4.13 and 6.4.1 84
- 4.3 Examples of DOI 92
- 4.4 Examples of SOI 100

CHAPTER FIVE: Situating Examples Within and Outside 1.4.2's Ambit 105
- 5.1 Selection of Examples 105
- 5.2 Distribution of Examples 107

5.3 Challenges to My Interpretation of 1.4.2 111
5.4 Some Clarifications about SSRI 116
5.5 Vedic and Accentuation Rules 121
5.6 Conflicts between *Antaraṅga* and *Bahiraṅga* Rules 125
5.7 Some Thoughts on the *Siddha* Principle 131
5.8 How and Why Pāṇini Composed 1.4.2 136
5.9 Conflicts between Pairs of *Saṁjñā* or *Paribhāṣā* Rules 141

CHAPTER SIX: Asiddha(vat) and 1.4.2 **152**
6.1 Traditional Views on *Asiddha* and *Asiddhavat* 152
6.2 My Interpretation of These Three Rules 154

CHAPTER SEVEN: The Evolution of Conflict Resolution Tools in the Pāṇinian Tradition 177
7.1 Kātyāyana on 1.4.2 177
7.2 Kātyāyana on *Nitya* 179
7.3 Kātyāyana on *Antaraṅga-Bahiraṅga* 188
7.4 Style and Attitude 192
7.5 Summary of Traditional Developments 193

CHAPTER EIGHT: Pāṇinian Studies and Other Disciplines **198**
8.1 The Philosophy of Pāṇinian Studies 198
8.2 Pāṇinian Computational Linguistics 202
8.3 Pāṇini and Computational Theory 206
8.4 Pāṇini and Theoretical Phonology 210
8.5 Concluding Remarks 213

Postface: Responding to the Reception 215

Appendix A: Tables of Concordance 219
Appendix B: List of Sūtras Containing the Term *Para* 221
Appendix C: More Examples of DOI Conflict 223
Notes 245
Bibliography 263
Acknowledgments 273
Index 275

PREFACE

Pāṇini, who is thought to have lived around 350 BCE in the northwestern part of the Indian subcontinent, is credited with composing the *Aṣṭādhyāyī*, which Leonard Bloomfield has quite rightly described as 'one of the greatest monuments of human intelligence'. Pāṇini's grammar, which packs the entire structure of Sanskrit into about four thousand concise rules, is celebrated by not only linguists and Indologists but intellectuals across the disciplinary spectrum for its elegance and ambition. It envisions language as a self-governing system and presents it to us as such—in the form of a unique derivational grammar. This grammar has been designed in such a way that one would expect it to function like a machine that receives a grammatical input, namely bases and affixes, and then churns out fully formed, grammatically correct words without any subjective, that is, human intervention whatsoever. As one can imagine, this makes Pāṇini's grammar extremely germane and interesting for those working in language modeling and computation. But how well does his language machine hold up to contemporary scrutiny? In this book, I attempt to answer exactly this question. But before I do that, I must tell the story of how I ended up attempting to answer it in the first place.

In India, students who pursue graduate work in Sanskrit studies generally come from traditional, often Brahmin families and, more importantly, have bachelor degrees in Sanskrit. They are likely to have spent time in Sanskritized environments, memorizing hundreds of *śloka*s and prayers in Sanskrit. While they were doing all that, I was reading novels and philosophical works, training to crack math problems, and earning a BA in economics, all of which I thought made me a rather unusual candidate for conducting research on Pāṇinian grammar. In hindsight, this is exactly what helped me arrive at the research findings I was able to produce.

Having studied Sanskrit in secondary school, I complemented my undergraduate studies by learning Pāṇini's grammar from a retired professor. I was studying Pāṇini's rules using the *Kaumudī* method, which rearranges his rules in a way that allows pupils to focus on individual derivations. The main book we were using would mention certain important *vārttika*s for each rule, while the Hindi, Gujarati, and Marathi commentaries would also mention what I later realized were post-Pāṇinian *paribhāṣā*s and excerpts from the *Mahābhāṣya* and the *Kāśikā*. I felt that the tradition was exhaustive and thorough, asked probing questions, and undertook surprisingly detailed investigations, which left a very positive impression, at least initially. For a question like 'How do we resolve rule conflict?', the tradition had pages upon pages, entire books even, to offer in response. The novice that I was, I felt overwhelmed, impressed, and awestruck upon encountering such voluminous and technically dense material. I felt as though I was staring at a sea of rich knowledge, unnavigable in one lifetime and worthy of respect.

However, whilst I was getting familiarized with the tradition, I was also simultaneously getting disillusioned with it. At first, I readily assimilated conflict-resolution tools like *nitya* and *antaraṅga* into my mental system of Pāṇinian grammar without giving it too much thought. But as I stumbled upon more and more instances of rule conflict, I realized these tools were not being consistently applied and that, very often, even when applied, they were not giving correct outcomes. As I started expressing my frustration over this, my teacher introduced me gradually to the world of post-Pāṇinian *paribhāṣā*s 'metarules', which basically contained tens of exceptions to the main metarules teaching these tools. Basically, every time there was a problem, post-Pāṇinian commentators produced yet another agonizing metarule. With no end to this madness in sight, I contemplated quitting the study of Pāṇini's grammar altogether on several occasions. But every time I did that, the joy of performing Pāṇinian derivations, of witnessing the magic of systematic rule application, would draw me back.

It is during this period that I realized that I had to understand Pāṇini's rules, which I was convinced were very sophisticated, on my own terms, without the influence of the tradition. I took certain steps to put this into effect. Until then, I had been used to looking at Pāṇinian rules mainly in the *Kaumudī* order. I decided to change this and started studying them in their original order, without discontinuing my *Kaumudī* studies. I also started reading secondary literature to understand what had already been written on the subject and was relieved to find that scholars like Joshi and Kiparsky had already been thinking about simplifying traditional conflict-resolution procedures—a goal that I shared with them. But I was interested in more than just simplification. I had begun to ask certain key questions that would go on to inform my doctoral research: Is it possible to resolve rule conflict purely on the basis of what Pāṇini has taught us, that is, without taking into account any post-Pāṇinian tools? And is it possible to view Pāṇini's grammar as a closed, self-governing machine that always produces grammatically correct words? There was only one way to find out: I would have to get my hands dirty, perform derivations, and look for patterns.

In retrospect, I think all the experiences and training I had had so far were helping me in one way or another. I remember feeling like I was in a Dan Brown novel unravelling some kind of mystery. This kept me on my toes and gave me the incentive I needed to push ahead: I was enthusiastic and excited to uncover the next, looming twist in my own Pāṇinian nailbiter.

My mathematical training played a crucial role in directing my research: I was able to think about each derivation as a cumulation of distinct steps not unlike mathematical proofs wherein one applies different axioms step-by-step or solving equations wherein one performs various operations step-by-step. In mathematics, correctly understanding and applying formulae, principles, and axioms always leads to the correct answer. Likewise, I thought, if Pāṇini's grammar is indeed mechanistic, then the only reason we are not getting grammatically correct forms is our incorrect interpretation and subsequent misapplication of at least some of his key metarules, which run the entire system. Therefore, I concluded that I had to find and reinterpret those rules.

Being an outsider to the traditional world of Pāṇinian studies proved immensely helpful: I had not inherited any set frameworks of conceptualizing Pāṇini's grammar and felt free to use the lens of my own intellectual experiences for this purpose. This allowed me to explore well beyond what the tradition had established for itself, to approach the problem with an open mind, to liberally consider all kinds of possibilities. Unlike traditional scholars, who operate in a highly hierarchical culture of respect and honour, I did not have to worry about the consequences of disagreeing with Kātyāyana and Patañjali, the two earliest commentators on Pāṇini's grammar, on such major issues.

Almost a year into my PhD at Cambridge, having made little if any progress, I thought it would be a good idea to break the monotony, disinvest from the research question, and then return to work, feeling healthy and rejuvenated, having recovered from all the stress. I have noticed that doing this allows me to approach the subject in a fresh, novel, invigorated manner. So, I took a month off to do the simple things that I enjoy: swimming, cycling, cooking, meeting friends, and so on. Thanks to my maternal grandfather, meditation has been an integral part of my life, and I spent a lot of time meditating during that one month. Then, upon returning to work after that much-needed revitalizing respite, I started flipping the pages of the book that was at the top of the pile on my desk. I had written several derivations in it.

Within minutes, I started observing certain patterns. To my utter disbelief, almost effortlessly, I had just discovered the actual meaning of '1.4.2'. That was my very own eureka moment. The rest is history: I spent about two or three more years figuring out other, related things and writing my doctoral thesis, at the heart of which is the Pāṇinian rule 1.4.2, which reads: *vipratiṣedhe paraṁ kāryam. Vipratiṣedhe* means 'in the event of conflict or opposition', *kāryaṁ* 'operation, task', and *paraṁ* 'that which comes later'. Thus, the rule means: In the event of conflict or opposition between two or more rules, the operation that comes later than the rest should be performed. But 'that comes later' in what sense or context? The tradition had interpreted *paraṁ* to mean that which comes later going from top to bottom in the traditional order of rules, whereas I argue in this book that it means that which comes later going from left to right in a word.

What was wrong with the traditional version though? And what difference does the new interpretation make? Because 1.4.2 deals with conflicts between two or more simultaneously applicable rules of which one must be chosen, as you can imagine, it plays a very important role in the functioning of Pāṇini's grammatical apparatus. There are countless instances of rule conflict that simply cannot be resolved without the help of 1.4.2. Since the tradition misunderstood such an important rule, it is not surprising that they started facing many serious problems in running the Pāṇinian machine. Put differently, very often, if one accepts the traditional interpretation of 1.4.2, one gets a grammatically incorrect form at the end of the derivation.

Instead of reconsidering their interpretation of 1.4.2, traditional scholars smuggled several new concepts into Pāṇini's system and added dozens of metarules to it—not to mention the various additional axioms regularly invoked by them from various commentaries. This converted Pāṇini's elegant grammatical machine into a nightmarishly complex, intractable system that kept getting worse rather than better every time traditional scholars sought to add more material to it or to make changes to the original Pāṇinian infrastructure.

In this book, I discuss what I have discovered to be the actual meaning of 1.4.2 and show how accepting this correct meaning automatically eliminates all the rule-conflict-related problems that traditional scholars have been struggling with for centuries. I show that Pāṇini's grammar is self-sufficient and that the umpteen changes made to the Pāṇinian system by post-Pāṇinian scholars are neither useful nor necessary. One of the most important implications of this finding is how remarkably simple it has now become to teach Pāṇini's grammar to the computer as one integrated system—rather than in bits and pieces! All one has to do is teach the computer the correct meaning of 1.4.2—without having to teach the hundreds of metarules created by traditional scholars to block or override the application of 1.4.2 to certain types of rule conflicts.

This book demonstrates that works of genius are stamped with simplicity, efficiency, and brilliance and tampering with them without fully understanding them can create complicated problems that take millennia to solve. I hope it will also act not only as a technical introduction to my novel interpretation of Pāṇini's grammar but also as an interesting illustration of the manner in which time and tradition influence our understanding of ancient treatises and how we can recover lost wisdom from such texts using lateral thinking.

Pāṇini's Perfect Rule

CHAPTER ONE

The Existing Understanding of Rule Conflict

Pāṇini's *Aṣṭādhyāyī* has been a mystery not only because of how laconic his rules are but also because we know very little, if anything, about Pāṇini. According to the existing Western consensus, Pāṇini composed the *Aṣṭādhyāyī* around 350 BCE in *Śālātura*, which is in the northwestern part of the Indian subcontinent (Cardona 1976, 267–68). I say 'composed' and not 'wrote' because scholars disagree on whether he used the aid of writing to create his grammar. In recent times, Vergiani (2020) has presented strong arguments in favour of the proposition that Pāṇini did use written means to put together his magnum opus. Writing or not, it is known that, just as happened with the Vedas, the *Aṣṭādhyāyī* too was orally transmitted from one generation to the next.

About Pāṇini, Upinder Singh writes: 'little is known about Panini's life. He was a Brahmana and seems to have belonged to a place called Shalatura in Gandhara country in the northwest. The Chinese pilgrim Xuanzang visited Shalatura in the 7th century CE. He mentions a statue of Panini standing in the town and tells us that its children pursued the study of grammar and held the great grammarian in high esteem. The 19th century archaeologist Alexander Cunningham suggested the identification of ancient Shalatura with Lahur, a town four miles northwest of Ohind, close to the confluence of the Kabul and Indus rivers' (Singh 2008, 258).

Given the scant historical record, we have to rely on Pāṇini's rules almost exclusively to understand him better. And although they are brief, and therefore to some extent elusive, they are about four thousand in number, which means that we have several opportunities to understand each rule in the context of other related rules.

The *Aṣṭādhyāyī* is a *samāhāra* 'collection' of *aṣṭa*(*n*) 'eight' *adhyāya*s 'books', hence the name *Aṣṭa-adhyāy*(*a*)-*ī*. Each book of the *Aṣṭādhyāyī* has four *pāda*s 'chapters' that are made up of *sūtra*s 'rules'. The *Aṣṭādhyāyī* is a comprehensive grammar of the Sanskrit language as known to its author Pāṇini. It stands out for doing more than merely describing its object language: the *Aṣṭādhyāyī* is a full-fledged machine that helps one construct grammatically correct Sanskrit words and sentences through a step-by-step derivation[1] process. In the *Aṣṭādhyāyī*, Pāṇini does not give us a general introduction to his work, nor does he discuss the theoretical principles that have been used to construct his *sūtra*s. He conveys whatever has to be said through his *sūtra*s alone.

The first two books are mainly composed of *saṁjñā sūtra*s 'definition rules' and *paribhāṣā sūtra*s 'metarules'.[2] The remaining books mainly consist of *vidhi sūtra*s 'operational rules'. Books three to five teach the addition of both inflectional and derivational affixes to bases. Book three teaches the addition of various affixes to verbal roots and stems, and books four and five teach the addition of different affixes to nominal stems. Books six, seven, and eight teach various morphophonological operations that should be performed on both bases and affixes. Different kinds of rules from multiple books are required to derive a word using Pāṇini's method.

To truly understand the *Aṣṭādhyāyī*, one needs to familiarize oneself with the methodology used by Pāṇini to compose and arrange rules in his work. Pāṇini's style is not entirely self-evident, and one faces challenges at multiple levels when attempting to unravel the enigma that is the *Aṣṭādhyāyī*. Firstly, it is not easy to determine the exact meanings of Pāṇini's rules because the *sūtra* style in which they are composed is very concise and compact. Much information is often packed into a few words, thereby making it considerably difficult to comprehend their exact purport. Take, for example, 6.1.9 *sanyaṅoḥ*. The word *sanyaṅoḥ* simply means 'ending in/before *saN* and *yaṄ*'. But considered with words that are *anuvṛtta* 'continued' from previous rules, this rule actually teaches that a verbal base,[3] which has not undergone reduplication, undergoes reduplication in the presence of affixes *saN*[4] and *yaṄ*, that is, the desiderative and intensive markers, respectively.[5] The question about whether *sanyaṅoḥ* is a genitive dual or a locative dual is a crucial one and has important implications for how we conceptualize *prakriyā* 'the (derivational) procedure' (Cardona 1997, xvii; Kiparsky 1982, 85–86).

Secondly, to make sense of any given rule, it is essential to take into account the contents of preceding rules. This is because Pāṇini uses a device called *anuvṛtti* 'continuation into the following rules' to economically express his observations: to understand the complete and correct meaning of a rule, certain words from preceding *sūtra*s may need to be borrowed into that rule by *anuvṛtti*. But there is no universal convention as to which terms are supposed to or can become *anuvṛtta* 'continued' into a certain rule. For example, consider 1.1.33 *prathamacaramatayālpārdhakatipayanemāś ca*, which teaches that certain words are called *sarvanāman*. But it is difficult to determine whether or not the words from the previous rule 1.1.32 *vibhāṣā jasi* should be continued into this rule. If they are continued into 1.1.33, then this would restrict 1.1.33 only to those cases where these stems are followed by the nominative plural affix *Jas* and would also make 1.1.33 optional (Bloomfield 1927, 61–70).

Thirdly, even after the meaning of the rule has been understood, it does not become patently obvious how to use it. This is because Pāṇini's rules are placed together on the basis of topical and functional categories and not according to the derivations in which they participate.[6] Thus, one cannot easily ascertain the order in which rules apply or select the step at which they become applicable. For example, consider the rule 3.1.33 *syatāsī lṛluṭoḥ*, which teaches that the affixes *sya* and *tāsI* should be added to the left of *LṚ* (*LṚṬ* and *LṚṄ*) and *LUṬ*, respectively. But the question that has troubled both traditional and modern scholars is: Should and can this rule apply before the *lakāra*s are replaced with finite verb endings (3.4.77 *lasya*; 3.4.78 *tip-tas-jhi*...[7]) (Roodbergen 1991, 293–99)?

Fourthly, after one has come to a conclusion about where to apply a given rule, one is often faced with situations in which two rules become applicable at the same step. In many such cases, one rule blocks the other, or both rules block each other. This is called 'rule conflict'. According to the tradition, a metarule taught by Pāṇini, namely 1.4.2 *vipratiṣedhe paraṁ kāryam*, addresses this issue. However, it seems unable to give the right answer when applied to certain cases of conflict—when applied in accordance with the traditional interpretation.

We can conclude that the *Aṣṭādhyāyī* is a very sophisticated grammar and that to operate its grammatical machine we have to understand it at multiple levels. What would an early grammarian or linguist have done to interpret the *Aṣṭādhyāyī* independently? With negligible access to any commentary on the text, and with limited or no guidance of a teacher well versed in the *Aṣṭādhyāyī*, a scholar would have taken notes for himself in order to comprehend, analyse, and corroborate the teachings of the *Aṣṭādhyāyī*. He would have started by paraphrasing the contents of the *Aṣṭādhyāyī* to establish what they mean exactly, both independently and in the context of the preceding rules.

To ensure that he had understood such a complex grammar correctly, or to confirm that the grammar accurately describes the structure of the language, a scholar would have tried to verify the validity and accuracy of different rules against spoken language or attested literature. He would have gradually developed his own ideas about where rules should apply and how derivations should proceed. He would have noticed how rules interact amongst themselves and would have come up with ways to classify and deal with such interactions. He would also have suggested certain changes to these rules to make them more precise, to help them better characterize their object language, and/or to help them function more consistently with other rules within the Pāṇinian system.

This is presumably what happened in the Indian grammatical tradition when Kātyāyana understood the meanings and functions of Pāṇinian rules on the basis of his independent study of the *Aṣṭādhyāyī*.[8] Then as a teacher, he also taught them to his pupils, using his notes on the *Aṣṭādhyāyī* as pedagogical aid. His students taught the *Aṣṭādhyāyī* to their students using Kātyāyana's work and also commented on Kātyāyana's writings, thereby sharing their own opinions, interpretations, and analyses with their students and readers. Successive generations participated in this process of knowledge processing, production, and transmission, thereby giving birth to the Pāṇinian grammatical tradition.

The texts of the Pāṇinian grammatical tradition have played a dominant role in influencing and shaping our understanding of and opinions about the *Aṣṭādhyāyī*. They also give us significant insights into the evolution of different ideas in the Pāṇinian tradition. Below I introduce the texts that I shall refer to in the rest of the book and briefly discuss the history of the Pāṇinian tradition with special reference to metarules.

1.1 Metarules in the Pāṇinian Grammatical Tradition

Early grammatical thought in the Indian subcontinent, as represented by the works called *Prātiśākhya*s, was intended to assist the recitation of Vedas by explaining the pronunciation of accents and dissolution of *sandhi*s. The *Prātiśākhya*s' objective was merely descriptive, that is, to make grammatical observations and offer clarifications where necessary. But a number of independent and full-fledged grammars emerged subsequently that sought to 'derive' language rather than simply 'describe' it: they built mechanistic systems that perform various operations on bases and affixes in order to produce correct word forms and, using these fully derived words, to construct meaningful sentences.

While Pāṇini himself mentions many of his predecessors in his *sūtra*s, the *Aṣṭādhyāyī* remains the oldest surviving derivational grammar of Sanskrit. Composing such a grammar required Pāṇini to meticulously design every aspect of the derivational procedure, which explains why Pāṇini made significant efforts in formulating his *paribhāṣā sūtra*s 'metarules'. These metarules play a pivotal role in the correct interpretation and application of *vidhi sūtra*s 'operation rules' at every step of the derivation, thereby ensuring that the derivational machine produces the grammatically correct output.

Given the *Aṣṭādhyāyī*'s remarkable exhaustiveness and accuracy, it is not surprising that Kātyāyana, around 250 BCE, undertook a systematic analysis of what must have been for him an unprecedented and extraordinary treatise (Cardona 1976, 267–68). Kātyāyana recorded his thoughts and findings in the form of *vārttika*s, which are short statements seeking to explain, examine, criticize, and sometimes integrate Pāṇini's rules with additions. Without overlooking the more specific and individual aspects of the grammar, Kātyāyana sought to develop a broad perspective about the functioning of the *Aṣṭādhyāyī* as an integrated machine. This involved interpreting the metarules of Pāṇini's grammar, providing examples and counterexamples to determine their verity, and composing new metarules to help the Pāṇinian system run even more smoothly.

Around 150 BCE, Patañjali wrote the *Mahābhāṣya*, which is a commentary on Kātyāyana's *vārttikas*.[9] It records the arguments and counterarguments that must have transpired between Patañjali and his pupils about the contents of the *vārttika*s. Sharma writes:

> The *Mahābhāṣya* of Patañjali is regarded as the second most important grammatical text after the *Aṣṭādhyāyī*. As has been stated, its aim is the presentation of *vyākhyāna* 'exposition' of the *sūtra*s of Pāṇini. It is claimed (Sarma 1968:53) that Patañjali commented upon 1,701 sutras in addition to *atha śabdānuśāsanam* and eight *Śivasūtras*. He classified the *Mahābhāṣya* into 85 *āhnika*s

> 'day-sessions' with the first being generally known as *Paspaśāhnika* (*Paspaśā*) 'introductory day-session'. The order of selected *sūtra*s follows the Pāṇinian order. A *bhāṣya* discussion is rendered as a dialogue or structured argument where a *vārttika* or a statement from Patañjali serves as *pratīka*. After a paraphrase of a *vārttika* is presented, the discussion illustrates and evaluates it by means of arguments supported by examples and counterexamples. The tradition recognizes three participants in the discussion: the student (*śiṣya*), teacher's aide (*ācāryadeśīya*) and teacher (*acārya*). The tradition also makes references to a participant who knows only part of the truth (*ekadeśin*) and another who offers the final view (*siddhāntin*). It is to be remembered here that identifying the statements of these participants is often difficult. (Sharma 1987, 9)

Like Kātyāyana, Patañjali too approached the *Aṣṭādhyāyī* with his independent perspective about its derivational system and skilfully wove Kātyāyana's *vārttika*s into his own presentation of the Pāṇinian machine. In doing so, he both established his independent interpretation of Pāṇini's and Kātyāyana's metarules and wrote new metarules to afford us greater clarity to the *Aṣṭādhyāyī*'s derivational procedure.

In the course of time, some Pāṇinīyas took it upon themselves to compile and comment on all such metarules from Patañjali's *Mahābhāṣya*. They also came up with new metarules to fill the knowledge gaps that they thought existed in the tradition. They came to be known as *paribhāṣākāra*s 'authors of *paribhāṣā*s', and the literature composed by them as *paribhāṣā* literature. *Paribhāṣā* texts have been written over many centuries—from around (or soon after) Patañjali's time, if not before him, to the eighteenth century (Abhyankar 1967, 12). Among the *paribhāṣā* texts of the Pāṇinian tradition, the most popularly studied, quoted, and commented upon in modern times is the relatively recent *Paribhāṣenduśekhara* of Nāgeśa Bhaṭṭa, which was written in the eighteenth century.

A rich tradition of *paribhāṣā* literature has long existed in other schools of Sanskrit grammar too (e.g., *Kātantra, Haima, Cāndra*).[10] Both Pāṇinian and non-Pāṇinian *paribhāṣākāra*s were especially interested in certain topics, for example, rule conflict. In Nāgeśa's work, the section containing *paribhāṣā*s 38 to 70 deals exclusively with rule conflict and is thus called *bādhabīja*

(Abhyankar 1967, 12). Similarly, in the *Kātantra* system, *paribhāṣā sūtras* are actually divided into *balābala sutras* 'metarules dealing with comparison of rule strength' and others that do not deal with this topic (Abhyankar 1967, 3). A significant exchange of ideas took place between Pāṇinian and non-Pāṇinian traditions due to mutual borrowing of *paribhāṣās*.

Circa seventh century CE, Jayāditya and Vāmana wrote the *Kāśikā*, which consists of *vṛttis* on each rule.[11] A *vṛtti* paraphrases the rule, teaches metarules that help us correctly apply that rule, gives examples of its application, and justifies the existence of each word of that rule. *Vṛttis* borrow a significant proportion of their contents from Patañjali's *Mahābhāṣya*. They are unique in that they do not comprise new metarules; yet by quoting some metarules from Patañjali's *Mahābhāṣya* and ignoring others, they present an evolved perspective about the mechanistic aspects of Pāṇinian derivations—often quite different from Patañjali's.

Lastly, let us talk about *Kaumudī* texts, which explicitly envision the *Aṣṭādhyāyī* as a grammatical machine. The *Kaumudī* tradition, which began in the fifteenth century with Rāmacandra's *Prakriyākaumudī*,[12] reorders the *sūtras* of the *Aṣṭādhyāyī* to reflect their derivational roles: in any *Kaumudī* text, a rule is introduced when the first derivation involving it is taught. The *Kaumudī* texts first introduce *saṁjñā* and *paribhāṣā* rules, then teach *sandhi* rules, then introduce nominal and verbal inflections in the order in which forms appear in paradigms, and then teach derivatives and compounds. The most celebrated text in this genre is Bhaṭṭojī Dīkṣita's *Siddhāntakaumudī*, written in the seventeenth century.[13] By reordering the *Aṣṭādhyāyī*'s rules, the *Kaumudī* not only gives us a glimpse of how Pāṇini's derivational mechanism actually works, but also tells us which metarules apply where and how these metarules enable us to perform derivations uniformly.

Even though the traditional texts discussed above broadly agree on most derivational technicalities, they present different perspectives on the nature and characteristics of the machine.

1.2 The Traditional View on Rule Conflict

As will be shown in chapter 7, the views of the tradition have gradually evolved on the topic of rule conflict. But here, I shall introduce the topic by outlining those ideas on rule conflict that today's traditional scholars hold true. To achieve this, I will present the views of the *Kāśikā* and *paribhāṣā* texts on this topic. 1.4.2 *vipratiṣedhe paraṁ kāryam* is the only metarule in the *Aṣṭādhyāyī* that explicitly deals with rule conflict. Here is Vasu's English translation of the rule 1.4.2 of the *Aṣṭādhyāyī*, which is in keeping with the *Kāśikā*'s interpretation: 'when rules of equal force prohibit each other, then the last in the order herein given is to take effect'.

On this rule, the *Kāśikā* says, representing the traditional interpretation of 1.4.2:

> *virodho vipratiṣedhaḥ. yatra dvau prasaṅgāv anyārthāv ekasmin yugapat prāpnutaḥ sa tulyabalavirodho vipratiṣedhaḥ. tasmin vipratiṣedhe paraṁ kāryaṁ bhavati. utsargāpavādanityānityāntaraṅgabahiraṅgeṣu tulyabalatā nāstīti nāyam asya yogasya viṣayaḥ, balavataiva tatra bhavitavyam. apravṛttau paryāyeṇa vā pravṛttau prāptāyāṁ vacanam ārabhyate.*

> The word *vipratiṣedha* means 'conflict'. When two operations that can be applied at other sites become simultaneously applicable at one [and the same site], this is called a conflict of equal strength or *vipratiṣedha*. In the event of *vipratiṣedha*, the rule that comes later [in the serial order of the *Aṣṭādhyāyī*] prevails.[14] A general rule (*utsarga*) and its exception (*apavāda*), or a *nitya* rule and an *anitya* rule, or an *antaraṅga* and a *bahiraṅga* rule, are not rules of equal strength. These pairs do not fall under the jurisdiction of this rule. In these cases, the stronger rule wins. When both rules are unable to apply, or when they are only able to apply alternatively, this rule comes into play. (my translation)

Then the *Kāśikā* gives us an example:

> *ato dīrgho yañi supi cety asyāvakāśaḥ. vṛkṣābhyāṁ plakṣābhyāṁ bahuvacane jhaly et ity asyāvakāśaḥ vṛkṣeṣu plakṣeṣu ihobhayaṁ prāpnoti. vṛkṣebhyaḥ plakṣebhyaḥ iti. paraṁ bhavati vipratiṣedhena.*

This is explained by Vasu as follows:

> As an example of rules of equal force, see 7.3.102 and 7.3.103. The first rule declares, when a case-affix beginning with a letter of *yaÑ pratyāhāra* follows, the long vowel is substituted for the final of an inflective base ending in a short *a*. As *vr̥kṣa* + *bhyām* = *vr̥kṣābhyām*. The next rule declares:- When a plural case-affix beginning with a letter [of] *jhaL pratyāhāra* follows, *e* is the substitute for the final *a* of an inflective base. As *vr̥kṣa* + *su* = *vr̥kṣeṣu*. But when the plural case-affix *bhyas* follows, what rule are we to apply? For the letter[15] *bha* belongs both to *pratyahāras yaÑ* and *jhaL*. Are we to lengthen the short *a* or substitute *e*? The present *sūtra* gives the reply, *e* is to be substituted because 7.3.103 ordaining *e* follows next to 7.3.102. Thus, *vr̥kṣa* + *bhyaḥ* = *vr̥kṣebhyaḥ*.[16]

The *Kāśikā* teaches us that when two conflicting rules are not of equal force, 1.4.2 is not applicable to the conflict between them. The *paribhāṣā* tradition throws light on conflicts between rules that are not of equal strength:

1. Between a *nitya* and an *anitya* operation, a *nitya* rule is more powerful. *Nityānityayor nityo vidhir balavān* (*Paribhāṣā* 118, *Vyāḍiparibhāṣāpāṭha*).[17]
2. Between an *antaraṅga* and a *bahiraṅga* operation, an *antaraṅga* operation is more powerful. *Antaraṅgabahiraṅgayor antaraṅgo vidhir balīyān* (*Paribhāṣā* 115, *Vyāḍiparibhāṣāpāṭha*).[18]
3. Between an *apavāda* and an *utsarga* operation, an *apavāda* operation is more powerful. *Utsargāpavādayor apavādavidhir balavān* (*Paribhāṣā* 85, *Bhojaparibhāṣāsūtra*).

The more powerful rule wins. The following *paribhāṣā*, which has been popularized by the *Paribhāṣenduśekhara*, creates a hierarchy of importance amongst four tools of rule conflict resolution, namely *paratva*, *nityatva*, *antaraṅgatva*, and *apavādatva*[19]: *pūrva-para-nitya-antaraṅga-apavādānām uttarottaraṁ balīyaḥ* (Pbh 38, *Paribhāṣenduśekhara*). We have already mentioned this *paribhāṣā* before. Below I will clarify its implications.

Paribhāṣā 38 of the *Paribhāṣenduśekhara* says that a *para sūtra* is stronger than a *pūrva sūtra*; a *nitya sūtra* is stronger than a *para sūtra*; an *antaraṅga sūtra* is stronger than a *nitya sūtra*; and an *apavāda sūtra* is stronger than an *antaraṅga sūtra*. In practical terms, this translates into the following procedure.

First try establishing the relationship taught in step 1:

1. *apavāda* > *utsarga*: an *apavāda sūtra* 'exception rule' is more powerful than and wins when competing with an *utsarga sūtra* 'general rule'.

   If and only if this step does not yield the correct result, try establishing the relationship taught in step 2:
2. *antaraṅga* > *bahiraṅga*[20]: an *antaraṅga sūtra* is more powerful than and wins when competing with a *bahiraṅga sūtra*.

   If and only if this step does not yield the correct result, try establishing the relationship taught in step 3:
3. *nitya* > *anitya*: a *nitya* rule is more powerful than and wins when competing with an *anitya* rule.

   If and only if this step does not yield the correct result, apply 1.4.2 *vipratiṣedhe paraṁ kāryam*, which we call step 4 here:
4. *para* > *pūrva*: a *para sūtra* (a later rule in the *Aṣṭādhyāyī*'s serial order) is more powerful than and wins when competing with a *pūrva sūtra* (which appears before the *para sūtra*).

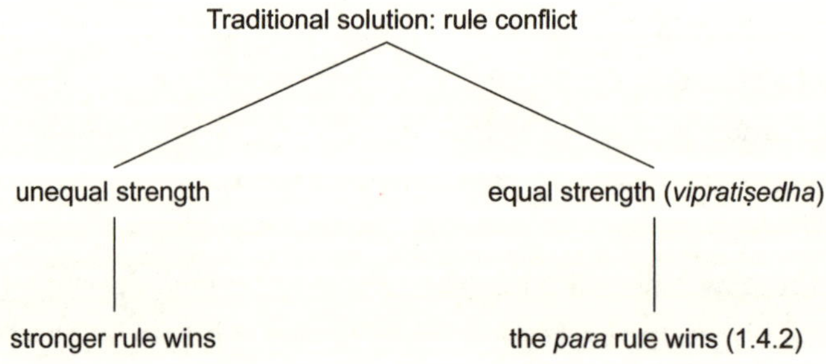

Let us look at 1.4.2 *vipratiṣedhe paraṁ kāryam* again. Pāṇini does not explain the meaning of *vipratiṣedha* in the *Aṣṭādhyāyī*. The *Kāśikā* claims that *vipratiṣedha* means *tulyabalavirodha* 'conflict between two equally powerful rules'. This is a plausible assumption because, in Sanskrit literature, the term has been used to mean 'the opposition of two courses of action which are equally important, the conflict of two even-matched interests'.[21] But which conflicts qualify as *tulyabala* 'having equal strength'? The *Kāśikā* says that rule pairs that are not *nitya-anitya, antaraṅga-bahiraṅga,* or *apavāda-utsarga* are *tulyabala* 'having equal strength'.

Let us try to understand why the tradition felt the need to come up with these tools. According to the tradition, *para* in 1.4.2 means 'the rule that appears after another in the serial order of the *Aṣṭādhyāyī*'. Thus, in the case of a *vipratiṣedha* 'conflict' between two rules, the operation prescribed by the later rule should prevail. However, if one assumes that any rule conflict can be called *vipratiṣedha* and therefore applies 1.4.2 uniformly to every instance of such a conflict, in many cases one gets the wrong answer at the end of the derivation. To avoid this, the tradition has come up with tools like *nitya, antaraṅga,* and *apavāda,* which I will discuss with examples below. I will then show how these tools have been integrated by the Pāṇinīyas into their approach to the *Aṣṭādhyāyī.*

Let us start with *tud,* a sixth-class root that can take both *parasmaipada* 'active' and *ātmanepada* 'middle' endings. When deriving its present third-person singular form, two rules become applicable at the step *tud* + *tiP.* One is 7.3.86 *pugantalaghūpadhasya ca* (*sārvadhātukārdhadhātukayoḥ guṇaḥ*),[22] which teaches that the penultimate light vowel *iK* (*i, u, ṛ, ḷ*) is replaced with *guṇa* (*a, e, o*) when followed by a *sārvadhātuka* or *ārdhadhātuka* affix. The other is 3.1.77 *tudādibhyaḥ śaḥ* (*sārvadhātuke kartari*), which teaches the addition of affix *Śa* after roots belonging to the class starting with *tud* in the *Dhātupāṭha,* when the root is followed by a *sārvadhātuka* affix in an active construction. Note that since 7.3.86 comes after 3.1.77 in the serial order of the *Aṣṭādhyāyī,* according to the traditional understanding of 1.4.2 it should win, but applying 7.3.86 would give the wrong answer: *tod* + *tiP* (7.3.86) → *tod* + *Śa* + *tiP* (3.1.77) → **todati.*[23]

Notice that 3.1.77 is applicable after 7.3.86 applies, as seen in the derivation above. On the other hand, if 3.1.77 applies first, we get: *tud* + *Śa* + *tiP.* Since *Śa* is marked with a *Ś*, it is *sārvadhātuka* by 3.4.113 *tiṅśit sārvadhātukam,* and being a *sārvadhātuka,* which is not marked with a *P*, it is treated as if marked by *Ṅ* by 1.2.4 *sārvadhātukam apit* (*ṅit*). By 1.1.5 *kṅiti ca* (*na iko guṇavṛddhī*), the *guṇa* replacement of *u* in *tud* by 7.3.86 is no longer possible. So 7.3.86 is not applicable once 3.1.77 has applied.

Thus, 3.1.77 and 7.3.86 are *nitya* and *anitya*, respectively. If the *nitya* rule, that is, 3.1.77 wins, we get: *tud* + *Śa* + *tiP* (3.1.77) → *tudati*, which is the correct answer. In this example, relying on *paratva* gives the wrong answer, but using *nityatva* gives the right answer. We shall come back to this after we look at a few more examples.

Consider the next example: to derive *syona* 'a sack, something stitched', *na* is added to *siv* 'to sew, stitch': *siv* + *na* (3.3.1 *uṇādayo bahulam*).[24] Firstly, by 6.4.19[25] *chvoḥ śūḍ anunāsike ca* (*kvijhaloḥ kṅiti*), *v* of *siv* is replaced with *ū*: (*siū*) + *na*. Now, two rules are simultaneously applicable here: 6.1.77 *iko yaṇ aci*, which is caused by *ū* and prescribes the replacement of *i* with *y*, and 7.3.86 *pugantalaghūpadhasya ca*, which is caused by *na* and prescribes the replacement of *i* of *si* with its corresponding *guṇa* (i.e., *e*). Since 7.3.86 comes after 6.1.77 in the serial order of the *Aṣṭādhyāyī*, by 1.4.2 it should win. But applying 7.3.86 gives us the wrong answer.

According to the *Paribhāṣenduśekhara*, '*antaraṅga* is [a rule] the causes [of the application] of which lie within [or before] the sum of the causes of a *bahiraṅga* rule'. So, in the case of *siū* + *na*, *ū*, the cause of 6.1.77, lies before (i.e., to the left of) *na*, the cause of 7.3.86. Thus, 6.1.77 is *antaraṅga* whereas 7.3.86 is *bahiraṅga*. Using the *antaraṅgatva* tool, 6.1.77 wins. We get *syū* + *na* → *syo* + *na* (*sārvadhātukārdhadhātukayoḥ*) → *syona*, which is the correct answer. Relying on *paratva* gives the wrong answer, while using *antaraṅgatva* gives the right answer.

Let us look at one more example. Two rules, namely 1.4.16 *siti ca* (*padam*) and 1.4.18 *yaci bham* (*svādiṣv asarvanāmasthāne*), lie in the *ekā saṁjñā* section (1.4.1 *ā kaḍārād ekā saṁjñā*). 1.4.1 teaches that up to 2.2.38 *kaḍārāḥ karmadhāraye*, any item can take only one *saṁjñā* 'technical designation'. 1.4.16 *siti ca* (*padam*) teaches that an item is called *pada* when an affix marked with *S* follows, and 1.4.18 *yaci bham* (*svādiṣv asarvanāmasthāne*) teaches that an item is called *bha* when a *y*- or vowel-initial, non-*sarvanāmasthāna* affix belonging to the class starting with *sU* follows. Consider the example *ūrṇā* + *yuS*.[26] Here, *ūrṇā* can potentially take two *saṁjñās*: *pada* by 1.4.16 and *bha* by 1.4.18. However, since both rules lie within the jurisdiction of 1.4.1, *ūrṇā* can take only one of the two *saṁjñās*. By 1.4.2, the *para* rule, that is, 1.4.18, should win. But if *ūrṇā* takes the *bha saṁjñā*, then *ā* of *ūrṇā* gets deleted by 6.4.148 *yasyeti ca* (*bhasya lopaḥ taddhite*), which teaches that the final *i* or *a* (both short and long) of an item, which is termed *bha*, are deleted when followed by an *ī* or a *taddhita* affix. This gives us the wrong *taddhita* stem **ūrṇyu*. The *Kāśikā* says that 1.4.16 is an *apavāda* of 1.4.18, without justifying this claim.[27] If the *apavādatva* tool is used, 1.4.16 wins, which gives the correct stem *ūrṇāyu*. Using *paratva* gives the wrong answer, while using *apavādatva* gives the right answer.

In all three examples discussed above, using *paratva* gives the wrong answer, but using *nityatva*, *antaraṅgatva*, and *apavādatva*,respectively, leads to the correct answer. Below, I present an abridged version of how I think the current method of solving rule conflict has gradually evolved. Having realized that treating all rule conflicts as *vipratiṣedha* and applying 1.4.2 uniformly to every instance of such a conflict gives the wrong answer in many cases, the Pāṇinīyas:

1. claimed that they found *jñāpaka*s 'hints or clues' in Pāṇini's *sūtra*s, which authorised them to devise new tools like *nityatva, antaraṅgatva, anavakāśatva,* and so on for the purpose of solving rule conflicts;
2. restricted the jurisdiction of rule 1.4.2 by declaring that *vipratiṣedha* implies only *tulyabala* conflicts, that is, conflicts between equally powerful rules; and
3. declared that rule pairs like *nitya-anitya*, *antaraṅga-bahiraṅga*, and *anavakāśa-sāvakāśa* were to be called *atulyabala* 'not equally powerful'.

This allowed them to exclude the *atulyabala* rule pairs, namely *nitya-anitya, antaraṅga-bahiraṅga*, and so on, from the jurisdiction of 1.4.2, thereby containing the problems caused by their interpretation of 1.4.2 to a smaller number of cases. Gradually, the Pāṇinīyas also constructed the hierarchy taught in *paribhāṣā* 38 of the *Paribhāṣenduśekhara* above to determine which tool takes precedence over which other tools.

However, these post-Pāṇinian tools are not without flaws, and to compensate for them, umpteen other *paribhāṣā*s have been written by Pāṇinīyas. Many of these *paribhāṣā*s address very specific cases[28] or even single examples of conflict, thereby defeating the entire purpose of writing metarules, which is to arrive at broad generalizations that can govern the application of and interactions amongst the whole body of rules. And even after this, the Pāṇinīyas are not able to solve every case of conflict correctly: every time they falter, they find one tortuous explanation or another to justify that 'exception'.

I do not think that all *paribhāṣās* taught by the Pāṇinīyas should be rejected. Many post-Pāṇinian *paribhāṣās* accurately capture how the Pāṇinian machine functions, and thus they are of great importance to us. They are mostly descriptive in nature and make insightful observations about the *Aṣṭādhyāyī*. However, we also find post-Pāṇinian *paribhāṣās* that teach us tools for rule conflict resolution, such as *nityatva* and *antaraṅgatva*, which Pāṇini would certainly not have left unstated if he actually wanted to teach them and which impose post-Pāṇinian ideas onto the *Aṣṭādhyāyī*. Thus, the validity of this set of *paribhāṣās* is questionable.

1.3 Modern Perspectives on the Functioning of the *Aṣṭādhyāyī*

Before we explore how modern scholarship perceives the *Aṣṭādhyāyī*, let us very briefly consider what the tradition and more specifically Kātyāyana and Patañjali say about the meaning and purpose of *vyākaraṇa*. In *vārttika* (vt.) 14 of the *Paspaśāhnika* (Mbh I.12.15), Kātyāyana says: *lakṣyalakṣaṇe vyākaraṇam* 'grammar [stands for the combination of] *lakṣya,* that is, words [and sentences]' and *lakṣaṇa* 'rules'. This is true of any grammar, not just the *Aṣṭādhyāyī*. But does the *Aṣṭādhyāyī* have certain mechanistic properties that set it apart from conventional grammars? Below, we will look at modern perspectives on this topic. But first, let us consider a traditional perspective. According to Patañjali (Mbh I.1.14), *vyākaraṇa* serves several purposes, expressed as *rakṣohāgamalaghvasandehāḥ*: *rakṣā* (protection of the Vedas), *ūha* (adapting inflected forms in Vedic mantras as required during rituals), *āgama* (following Vedic injunctions), *laghu* (brevity, that is, ease of learning the language), and *asandeha* (resolution of doubts). These certainly are some of the factors that must have motivated Pāṇini to write his grammar. But was Pāṇini also aiming to build a somewhat mechanistic model for deriving Sanskrit words (and, subsequently, sentences)? Let us look at what modern scholarship tells us about topics like rule conflict and order of rule application in Pāṇinian derivations and, therefore, about the status of the *Aṣṭādhyāyī* as a 'machine'.

Let us start by looking at Bronkhorst's work on this topic. Bronkhorst (2004) shows that Patañjali prefers a linear reading of the *Aṣṭādhyāyī*, that is, Patañjali believes that in order to decide which rule should apply at any step in a derivation, one need not know the outcomes of previous or following steps. Bronkhorst says, 'It is clear from the above that Patañjali tries both to avoid looking back and looking ahead in explaining grammatical derivations' (2004, 37). He also points out that the *Paribhāṣenduśekhara* teaches the metarule *pūrvaparanityāntaraṅgāpavādānām uttarottaraṁ balīyaḥ* (*paribhāṣā* 38): 'Of [these five kinds of rules,—viz.] a preceding [rule], a subsequent [rule],[29] a *nitya* [rule],[30] an *antaraṅga* [rule],[31]and an *apavāda* [rule],[32]—each following [rule] possesses greater force [than any one of, or all, the rules which in this *paribhāṣā* are mentioned before it]' (Abhyankar 1960, 185). Bronkhurst concludes: '[this][33] clearly shows that, according to the traditional view, decisions concerning the continuation of a grammatical derivation at any particular point are taken on the basis of the situation at hand. More specifically, no information about the earlier or later phases of the derivation is required to make a correct decision at any stage' (2004, 6).[34]

Bronkhorst states that he is unconvinced by Patañjali's evidence suggesting that the *Aṣṭādhyāyī* functions linearly. He thinks that Pāṇini did not intend for the *Aṣṭādhyāyī* to be approached linearly and attempts to establish that, at least for some derivations, the knowledge of the derivation's history and/or its future course is essential to select the right rule at a given step (2004, 6). One of the reasons Bronkhorst thinks looking ahead into the derivation is required is to determine the order in which two rules should apply with respect to each other (2004, 16–17).

Roodbergen has a different opinion on this subject. He recommends some changes to the traditional order in which the following processes occur: the replacement of *lakāra*s 'tense and mood proxies' with *tiṄ* 'verbal endings' and the introduction of *vikaraṇa*s 'affixes placed between verbal roots and *lakāras*/the endings that replace *lakāras*' (1991, 313). This shows that Roodbergen does believe in reading the *Aṣṭādhyāyī* linearly but disagrees to some extent with the tradition's order of rule application. And he thinks that this topic is not related to rule conflict and its resolution: 'this ordering principle has nothing to do with a feeding relation between rules in which the application of one rule is made dependent on the effect of the application of another rule. It has nothing to do either, with the question of conflict of rules. To solve a conflict, other principles apply: *paratva*, *siddha*/*asiddha*[35] and *utsarga*/*apavāda*'.

Scholars working on rule conflict have peripherally addressed the topic of linearity. Cardona says that 'the derivational prehistory of a form is pertinent to the operations which apply to it' (1970, 41). Joshi and Kiparsky think that it is important to look ahead into a derivation. They propose the extended *siddha* principle, which they claim governs Pāṇinian derivations and which 'scans entire candidate derivations' thanks to its 'global [trans-derivational] "look-ahead" condition on derivations' '. . . and chooses the one in which *siddha*-relations [bleeding and feeding][36] are maximized' (2005, 7). So, both Cardona and Joshi and Kiparsky do not support an exclusively linear reading of the *Aṣṭādhyāyī*.

According to Houben, 'a comparison between Pāṇini's grammar and "a machine" may be useful in demonstrating some of the features and procedures it incorporates, but the comparison has now and then been carried too far' (2003, 50). Houben continues:

> [I]n fact, in the practice of Pāṇinīyas through the ages up to the present, no-one can ever have produced a correct form through Pāṇini's system that was not already his starting point, or among his starting options . . . the system is therefore not well characterized as "synthetic", even if synthetic procedures are central and most visible; rather the system is to be called "reconstitutive"—which implies the presence of a user, a preliminary statement, and the application of both analytic and synthetic procedures to the words in it . . . aiming at the best possible, *saṁskṛta* form of his preliminary statement. (2003, 53)

Houben attributes the reception of Pāṇinian grammar as a machine to Bhaṭṭojī Dīkṣita's *Siddhāntakaumudī* and Nāgeśa's *Paribhāṣenduśekhara*: 'in order to provide the desired solid authoritative basis to Sanskrit grammar it was moreover necessary to posit it as a closed system of rules and metarules—something it had never been in a true sense of this term for around two millennia, although Kātyāyana's and Patañjali's investigations on selected *sūtra*s had prepared the ground for such an approach. The culmination in this trend came only a few generations later with Nāgeśa Bhaṭṭa's *Paribhāṣenduśekhara*' (2015, 6).

Let us summarize what we have surveyed so far. Houben is not in favour of perceiving the *Aṣṭādhyāyī* as a derivational machine, thereby also implicitly dismissing both the concept of linearity and consistent conflict-resolution procedures. Roodbergen believes that the *Aṣṭādhyāyī* is a derivational machine and proposes his own version of a linear reading of the *Aṣṭādhyāyī*. Roodbergen also argues that the order of rule application and resolution of rule conflict are not related or associated with each other. Bronkhorst claims that the existence of *paribhāṣā* 38 of the *Paribhāṣenduśekhara*, which creates a hierarchy of conflict-resolution tools (in addition to Patañjali's statements), indicates that the tradition prefers a linear reading of the *Aṣṭādhyāyī*. In doing so, Bronkhorst establishes a correlation between consistent rule conflict-resolution procedures and a linear reading of the *Aṣṭādhyāyī*. Bronkhorst rejects the linear approach. On the other hand, Joshi and Kiparsky and Cardona seem to think that their rejection of a strictly linear reading of the *Aṣṭādhyāyī* does not substantially undermine the mechanistic prowess of the Pāṇinian system and devote much of their scholarly attention to solving rule conflict.

While the functioning of the *Aṣṭādhyāyī* remains the primary focus of this book, we shall also look at its interactions with the structure of the *Aṣṭādhyāyī*. Let me first outline how the *Aṣṭādhyāyī* is structured. The rules of the *Aṣṭādhyāyī* are organized on the basis of their purpose: rules teaching certain *saṁjñās* are grouped together, rules about a certain substitute are placed together, and so on and so forth. In most such groups, the *apavāda sūtras* 'exception rules' are listed immediately after the *utsarga sūtras* 'general rules'.[37] These groups of rules are themselves placed in one of the eight books depending on their role: *saṁjñā sūtras* 'definition rules' and *paribhāṣā sūtras* 'metarules' are generally placed in the first two *adhyāyas*, rules teaching affixation in the following three and rules teaching morphophonological changes in the last three.

The structure and organization of the *Aṣṭādhyāyī*, that is, the general arrangement and serial order of rules in the *Aṣṭādhyāyī*, have an influence on its functioning in different ways. In the opinion of the tradition, 1.4.2 *vipratiṣedhe paraṁ kāryam* teaches that in the case of conflict between two equally powerful rules, the rule that appears later in the *Aṣṭādhyāyī*'s serial order wins, which implies that the serial order of rules in the *Aṣṭādhyāyī* has a direct impact on rule conflict resolution.

Pāṇini has ingeniously composed three *asiddha* sections, headed, respectively, by 6.1.86 *ṣatvatukor asiddhaḥ*,[38] 6.4.22 *asiddhavad atrābhāt*, and 8.2.1 *pūrvatrāsiddham*. 6.4.22 teaches us that two rules treat each other as *asiddhavat* 'as if suspended' when both lie within 6.4.22–129,[39] which helps avoid certain undesirable instances of rule conflict. 8.2.1 teaches us that from there onwards, a preceding rule treats any following rule as *asiddha* 'suspended', which helps facilitate or avoid the application of certain rules. Here too, the position of one rule with respect to other rules has a significant impact on Pāṇinian derivations or the functioning of the *Aṣṭādhyāyī*.

Interestingly, the functioning of the *Aṣṭādhyāyī* may have had an impact on its structure too. Roodbergen argues that 'the word building process proceeds in what is visually a left-to-right direction' (1991, 313). According to Roodbergen, this direction of word building, which underlies the functioning of the *Aṣṭādhyāyī*, impacts its structure, that is, the positioning of rules in different books and chapters of the *Aṣṭādhyāyī*: 'rules dealing with left-side elements are introduced earlier [in earlier sections of the *Aṣṭādhyāyī*][40] than rules dealing with right-side elements' (1991, 313).[41]

We have seen what the existing literature on the subject says about the functioning of the *Aṣṭādhyāyī* and its connection with its structure. In this book, I share my research on rule interaction, and then go on to show how these findings shed light on the functioning of the *Aṣṭādhyāyī*. I conclude that Pāṇini did intend for the *Aṣṭādhyāyī* to be interpreted linearly and as a closed grammatical machine.

1.4 Modern Scholarship on 1.4.2

The tradition thinks that 1.4.2 applies to *tulyabala* conflicts between any two rules of the *Aṣṭādhyāyī*. But many modern scholars, starting with Faddegon (1936), have tried to restrict the scope of 1.4.2 further to include only those rules that lie between 1.4.2 and 2.2.38: they argue that since 1.4.2 lies within the *ekā saṁjñā adhikāra* (cf. 1.4.1 *ā kaḍārād ekā saṁjñā* 'up to 2.2.38 *kaḍārāḥ karmadhāraye*, each item can take only one *saṁjñā*'), the jurisdiction of 1.4.2 too should be suspended at 2.2.38.[42] Kiparsky comes up with his own justification for this interpretation, in which he argues that the alternate version of 1.4.1 mentioned by Patañjali is proof of the fact that 1.4.2 only governs rules between 1.4.2 and 2.2.38. Let us look at Patañjali's commentary first, and then consider Kiparsky's argument based on it. On 1.4.1, Patañjali suggests that Pāṇini has taught two different versions of 1.4.1 to his pupils:

kathaṁ tv etat sūtram paṭhitavyam. kim ā kaḍārād ekā saṁjñeti. āhosvit prāk kaḍārāt paraṁ kāryam iti. kutaḥ punar ayaṁ sandehaḥ. ubhayathā hy ācāryeṇa śiṣyāḥ sūtraṁ pratipāditāḥ. kecid ākaḍārād ekā saṁjñeti. kecit prāk kaḍārāt paraṁ kāryam iti. kaś cātra viśeṣaḥ.

tatraikasaṁjñādhikāre tadvacanaṁ (vt. 2).

tatraikasaṁjñādhikāre tadvaktavyam. kim. ekā saṁjñā bhavatīti. nanu ca yasyāpi paraṁkāryatvaṁ tenāpi paragrahaṇaṁ kartavyam. parārtham mama bhaviṣyati. vipratiṣedhe ca iti. mamāpi tarhy ekagrahaṇam parārthaṁ bhaviṣyati. sarūpāṇām ekaśeṣa ekavibhaktau iti. (Mbh I.296.11–18)

But how should this rule be read? Is it *ā kaḍārād ekā saṁjñā*[43] or *prāk kaḍārāt paraṁ kāryam*?[44] But how [does] this doubt [arise]? Because the students have been taught this rule in both ways by the teacher. Some [have been taught] *ā kaḍārād ekā saṁjñā* [and] some *prāk kaḍārāt paraṁ kāryam*. And what is the difference [between these alternative readings] here?

In that section where one name applies, the statement of that [must be made]. (vt. 2) In that section where one name applies, that should be stated. What [should be stated]? That only one *saṁjñā* applies [per item]. However, one who [believes that] the following rule [prevails] has to include the word *para* too. It will [serve] another [purpose] for me later [that is, by continuation, in] *vipratiṣedhe ca*. For me too then, the mention of *eka* will [serve] another [purpose], in *sarūpāṇām ekaśeṣa ekavibhaktau.*[45]

The two versions of the rule pair 1.4.1–2 are: 1.4.1 *ā kaḍārād ekā saṁjñā*, 1.4.2 *vipratiṣedhe param kāryam*; and 1.4.1 *prāk kaḍārād param kāryam*, 1.4.2 *vipratiṣedhe ca*.[46] The former version is found in the available manuscripts of the *Aṣṭādhyāyī*, while the latter version is first mentioned by Patañjali himself. In the case of the latter, Patañjali only indirectly hints at what I have called 1.4.2, when explaining how he could use *para* from 1.4.1 *prāk kaḍārād paraṁ kāryam* later in the following rule (1.4.2) *vipratiṣedhe ca* through *anuvṛtti*.[47] It logically follows that its coreferent *kāryam* too would be continued into 1.4.2 along with *paraṁ*.

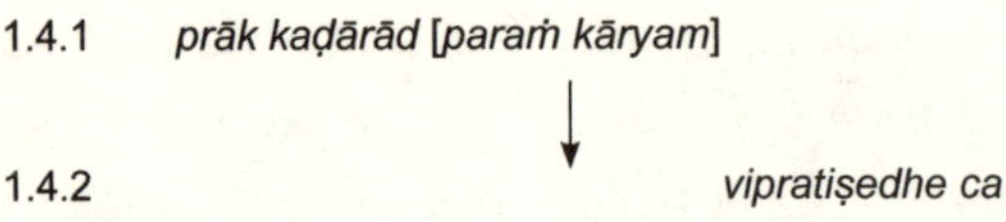

	Original version	Patañjali's alternate version
1.4.1	*ā kaḍārād ekā saṁjñā*	*prāk kaḍārāt paraṁ kāryam*
1.4.2	*vipratiṣedhe paraṁ kāryam*	*vipratiṣedhe ca* (*paraṁ kāryam*)

Note that both versions of 1.4.1 apply only to the section between 1.4.1 and 2.2.38, whereas both versions of 1.4.2 apply to the entire *Aṣṭādhyāyī*. Besides, while the two versions of 1.4.1 say different things (one says *ekā saṁjñā* and the other says *paraṁ kāryam*), the two versions of 1.4.2 essentially say the same thing.

So, what does the alternative version of 1.4.1, that is, *prāk kaḍārāt paraṁ kāryam*, exactly mean? It translates as: 'between 1.4.1 and 2.2.38 the later rule should be applied'. But when? In which context or situation? This version of 1.4.1 is at best ambiguous. Secondly, it seems very unlikely that Pāṇini would teach two different versions of his own rules to his pupils. In the following chapter, I reinterpret the meaning of *para*, which makes it clear that the alternate version of 1.4.1 does not make sense. For all these reasons, I conclusively reject the alternate version.

On the other hand, Kiparsky assumes that the alternate version is the correct one and uses this assumption to argue for restricting the scope of 1.4.2 to the section up to 2.2.38. He says:

> A very suggestive piece of evidence that the domain of 1.4.2 is limited to 1.4-2.2 is that Patañjali actually records a variant reading of Pāṇini's rules in which that *must* be the interpretation. In discussing 1.4.1 Patañjali says, 'How then is this rule to be read: as *ā kaḍārād ekā saṁjñā* "up to *kaḍāra* (2.2.38) (everything gets only) one technical term" or as *prāk kaḍārāt paraṁ kāryam* "up to *kaḍāra* apply the last"?' Why is this an issue? Because the teacher [Pāṇini] had his students recite both ways, some of them *ā kaḍārād ekā saṁjñā*, others *prāk kaḍārāt paraṁ kāryam*. Thus, these were still two versions of the rules in Patañjali's time. Not surprisingly, the version in which the domain of the *para* relation could be extended over the whole grammar eventually won out. But it seems reasonable to

> assume that the version in which the domain obviously *has* to be limited to 1.4 to 2.2 has a greater claim to authenticity. (1982, 114)

In his analysis, Kiparsky does not address the part where Patañjali talks about 1.4.2 *vipratiṣedhe ca* (*param kāryam*). If 1.4.1 is *prāk kaḍārāt paraṁ kāryam*, 1.4.2 would be *vipratiṣedhe ca* (*param kāryam*), as mentioned by Patañjali himself. Thus, the *para* relation would still be applicable to the entire *Aṣṭādhyāyī* even if we accept the alternate version of 1.4.1–2 as being the actual or correct one. So, I conclude that, contrary to Kiparsky's claim, both versions of the pair (1.4.1–2) allow the *para* relation to extend to the entire *Aṣṭādhyāyī*. Thus, his speculation about why the *ekā saṁjñā* version won out does not pass muster, and the argument that *paraṁ kāryam* does not hold beyond 2.2.38 too remains unsubstantiated.

Now going back to the general argument that 1.4.2 does not apply beyond 2.2.38, Faddegon and others reduced the scope of 1.4.2 with the objective of avoiding the application of 1.4.2 to those cases of conflict wherein applying 1.4.2 may give the wrong answer. But we have already seen in the derivation of *ūrṇāyu* that even within 1.4.1–2.2.38, the *pūrva* rule 1.4.16 *siti ca* prevails over the *para* rule 1.4.18 *yaci bham*. In other words, even within 1.4.1-2.2.38, 1.4.2 does not give the right answer.

Besides, those conflicts that we come across in 1.4.2-2.2.38, which are essentially conflicts between *saṁjñā* rules, can be successfully solved by choosing the specific rule (the exception) over the general one, thereby rendering Faddegon's restriction of 1.4.2's scope redundant anyway.[48] For example, 1.4.16 *siti ca*, as we have seen above, is more specific than and therefore an exception of 1.4.18 *yaci bham*. Thus, 1.4.16 wins. Similarly, 1.4.11 *saṁyoge guru* (which teaches that a short vowel is called *guru* 'heavy' when followed by a consonantal conjunct) is more specific than 1.4.10 *hrasvaṁ laghu* (which teaches that a short vowel is called *laghu* 'light'). Thus, 1.4.11 wins.

In the same way, 1.4.100 *taṅānāv ātmanepadam* (which teaches that *taṄ*, *ŚānaC*, and *KānaC*, which replace *la*, take the *ātmanepada saṁjñā*) is more specific than and thus defeats 1.4.99 *laḥ parasmaipadam* (which teaches that the affixes that replace *la* take the *parasmaipada saṁjñā*'). Similarly, 1.4.46 *adhiśīṅsthāsāṁ karma* (which teaches that a *kāraka* that constitutes the locus of the action is called *karma* with the verbs *śīṄ* 'to lie down', *sthā* 'to stand', and *ās* 'to sit' occurring with preverb *adhi*) is more specific than and thus wins against 1.4.45 *ādhāro'dhikaraṇam* (which teaches that a *kāraka* that constitutes the locus of the action is called *adhikaraṇa*).[49] These examples satisfactorily prove that choosing the more specific rule is sufficient to deal with cases of conflict in the section 1.4.1-2.2.38.

Secondly, restricting the scope of 1.4.2 to 1.4.1-2.2.38 implies that Pāṇini has given us no instructions about the conflicts that lie beyond 2.2.38, which I think is a highly unlikely scenario. In any case, the few attempts that have been made to deal with conflicts beyond 2.2.38 by scholars such as Cardona (1970) and Joshi and Kiparsky (1979) address only certain types of rule conflict and fail to paint an overarching picture.[50]

1.5 My View

In my view, firstly, Pāṇini did not expect us to create the categories *tulyabala* and *atulyabala*. Secondly, I think that he taught 1.4.2 as a metarule that, rather than being restricted to a particular section of the *Aṣṭādhyāyī*, is applicable to the entire *Aṣṭādhyāyī*.

I have been asked by multiple colleagues: 'If Pāṇini did not intend for 1.4.2 *vipratiṣedhe paraṁ kāryam* to be applicable only up to 2.2.38 *kaḍārāḥ karmadhāraye*, why did he place it right after 1.4.1 *ā kaḍārād ekā saṁjñā*, that is, in the *ekā saṁjñā* section?' Note that both rules deal with choosing one of multiple options: 1.4.1 teaches us that we must choose one of multiple *saṁjñā*s, and 1.4.2 tells us we must choose the right-hand side (henceforth, RHS) operation of many possible operations at a given step. This is likely why 1.4.1 and 1.4.2 are found next to each other. But in any case, although answers to questions like 'Why did he place this rule here?' can indeed help confirm our findings about the *Aṣṭādhyāyī*, in isolation and without derivation-based evidence, they do not hold any value whatsoever.

I do not agree with both the traditional and the modern perspectives on the scope of 1.4.2 because instead of trying to decipher the actual meaning of 1.4.2 these approaches try to brush 1.4.2 under the carpet, to make it less effective or to weaken its impact. One does it by excluding certain rule pairs from the scope of *vipratiṣedha*, and the other by reducing the jurisdiction of 1.4.2. This approach, which seeks to undervalue Pāṇini's rule interaction mechanism and replaces it with self-invented methods of 'rule conflict resolution', can lead to some success for a limited set or specific type of examples but does not allow us to understand and appreciate the larger picture.

To get instructions about dealing with rule interaction, I try to rely, as much as possible, upon 'internal metarules', that is, those metarules that Pāṇini has taught in his work, setting aside any 'external metarules', that is, those metarules that are not found in the *Aṣṭādhyāyī*, such as *nityatva*, *antaraṅgatva*, post-Pāṇinian *paribhāṣā*s from the *Paribhāṣenduśekhara*, *vārttika*s that discuss rule interaction, and so on. In this book, I have come up with my own interpretation of 1.4.2, and using that, I have reinterpreted Pāṇini's derivational mechanism. I have attempted to show that Pāṇini's grammatical machine is self-sufficient, that is, its own (internal) metarules are able to run it with remarkable perfection, and that no external metarules are able to or required to aid this process.

1.6 Road Map for the Rest of the Book

Chapter 2 presents a broad classification of rule conflict into different types, first through my own lens and subsequently from the traditional perspective. I also explain which categories proposed by me overlap with or are equivalent to those assumed by traditional scholars. While doing so, I explain why my classification is circumspective, optimal, and transparent. My classification includes two categories: Same Operand Interaction (SOI), wherein two or more competing rules are applicable simultaneously to the same item (i.e., operand), and Different Operand Interaction (DOI), wherein two or more competing rules are applicable to different items (i.e., operands), respectively. I argue that Pāṇini has taught 1.4.2 as a solution to DOI. Of the two possible operations, wherein one rule is applicable to the left-hand side (henceforth, LHS) operand and the other to the RHS operand, the RHS rule wins, or put differently, the RHS operation wins. I then provide overwhelming philological evidence, especially surrounding the manner in which Pāṇini has used the term *para* in the entire *Aṣṭādhyāyī*, to justify my interpretation of 1.4.2. I argue that Pāṇini did not feel the need to explicitly teach us the solution to SOI because it is inherent to the *sūtra* style of textual composition, which is also used by authors in numerous genres of Sanskrit literature, like yoga texts, Vedanta, and so on: when two rules are applicable to the same item or thing, the more specific rule constitutes the exception to the more general rule and thus prevails. I then lay out a logical approach that helps identify the more specific rule in a coherent and consistent manner. Giving examples of both SOI and DOI, I demonstrate the success of my method, while also showing how the traditional approach fails to tackle these derivational examples. In this chapter, I focus on examples from nominal inflection because of their simplicity.

In chapter 3, I apply my method of conflict resolution to numerous derivations of compounds and secondary derivatives, that is, nouns derived from other nouns. In chapter 4, I reinterpret certain rules (1.4.13 and 6.4.1) of Pāṇini's grammar and prove that this helps explain the functioning of the Pāṇinian system—by performing derivations of verbs and primary derivatives, which include, most prominently, nouns derived from verbal roots. In chapter 5, I dwell on my methodology, the selection of examples presented in my doctoral thesis, challenges to my interpretation of 1.4.2, why certain topics have not received attention in the first four chapters, how Pāṇini must have come up with 1.4.2, and cases of mutual opposition between pairs of *saṁjñā* or *paribhāṣā* rules. In chapter 6, I reinterpret three key rules dealing with *asiddha*, which involve the treatment of one rule as being suspended or inexistent with respect to another rule. I then discuss how these rules interact with 1.4.2 and show that these interpretations enable the smooth functioning of the Pāṇinian machine. In chapter 7, I present a summary of post-Pāṇinian ideas on 1.4.2. I also adumbrate the evolution of conflict-resolution tools in the early tradition. I undertake this task in the context of my own findings about 1.4.2 presented in this book. In chapter 8, I contextualize my work against the backdrops of the philosophy of Pāṇinian studies, Pāṇinian computational linguistics, computational theory (natural language complexity), and theoretical phonology. I conclude the chapter and the book by reflecting on how my findings will impact the way in which Pāṇini is taught in the future.

CHAPTER TWO

A Novel Approach to Pāṇini's Grammar

In the previous chapter, I have discussed how the tradition has misinterpreted 1.4.2 *vipratiṣedhe paraṁ kāryam*. In this chapter, I lay the conceptual foundation that will help us understand the actual meaning of 1.4.2.

2.1 Two Types of Operational Rule Interaction

Over a period of time, I studied different examples in which two *vidhi sūtra*s 'operational rules' are simultaneously applicable at the same step of a derivation, from both traditional sources and modern literature. Henceforth, we will refer to such interaction between two simultaneously applicable operational rules as Same-Step Rule Interaction, or simply SSRI. I tried to divide these examples into different groups on the basis of the similarities between them.

In my opinion, at any step in a derivation, even though two (or more) rules are applicable, only one rule applies. So, I attempted to determine if, of the two competing rules, a certain kind of rule always prevails over the other rule in all the examples of that group. In other words, I came up with one generalization per group about the result of such competition between rules. The generalization that I made for one particular group of rules immediately caught my attention. In order to highlight the common property that binds together the examples of this group, firstly, I need to explain certain concepts, which I will do in this section. In section 2.2, I will discuss the said group of examples, and how this group of examples led me to discover the actual meaning of 1.4.2.

Consider the two types of SSRI:

We will call Type 1 Same Operand Interaction (SOI) because both rules $R1_A$ and $R2_A$ are applicable to the same operand A at the same step. We will call Type 2 Different Operand Interaction (DOI) because the two rules R_A and R_B are applicable to two different operands A and B, respectively, at the same step.

In their efforts to understand the meaning of 1.4.2, both traditional and modern scholars have failed to make good use of this clear distinction between SOI and DOI.[1] Going further, we will see that this distinction plays a critical role in helping us understand Pāṇini's key rule 1.4.2 and, consequently, the entire derivational system of the *Aṣṭādhyāyī*.

As stated before, in my opinion, at any step in a derivation, even though two (or more) rules are applicable, only one rule applies. So, for both Type 1 and Type 2, we need to determine which of the two rules should be applied at the given step. Please note that the Pāṇinian machine, like any other machine, requires an input and can only give us the correct output if the input is correct. For issues related to this topic, please see section 5.4 of chapter 5.

2.2 Solutions for Type 1 (SOI) and Type 2 (DOI)

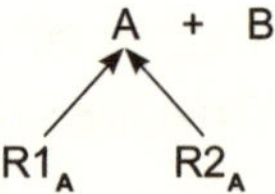

Which one of the two rules $R1_A$ and $R2_A$ should we apply at this step? Pāṇini does not give us any explicit instructions about solving SOI. In my view, if two rules are applicable simultaneously to the same operand, the rule that is more specific, which we may call 'the special or exception rule', wins. Note that this is similar to the traditional notion that an *apavāda* 'exception' rule defeats an *utsarga* 'general' rule.

It is likely that Pāṇini did not deem it necessary to state explicitly that the exception rule defeats the general rule in the case of SOI because the general-exception framework is not a feature of grammar but in fact a feature of the *sūtra* style itself. Freschi and Pontillo (2013, 2) point out that 'the basic framework of Sanskrit *śāstra*s 'systematic treatises' is based on the practical and effective opposition between general and specific rules'.

Note that the traditional approach is different from mine because:

1. The tradition does not draw a clear distinction between SOI and DOI.
2. The tradition often ends up using tools other than *utsarga-apavāda* to resolve SOI.
3. The tradition has not developed a systematic procedure to determine which of the two rules involved in SOI is more specific. I will develop such a procedure later in this chapter.

Now, let us look at DOI.

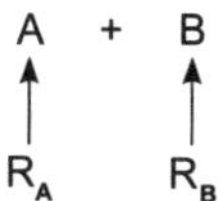

The group of examples referred to in section 2.1 are those that involve DOI. I noticed that in the case of DOI, if we pick the RHS operation, that is, application of rule R_B to its operand B, over the LHS operation, that is, the application of rule R_A to operand A, we always get the correct answer. This led me to realize the meaning of *para* in 1.4.2: *para* stands for the RHS operation. And thus, *vipratiṣedha* 'mutual opposition' in 1.4.2 stands for DOI. I think it is apt to refer to DOI as *vipratiṣedha* because only one of the two operations wins, so in that sense, the two operations oppose each other. In sum, 1.4.2 means: 'in the event of DOI [mutual opposition between the two operations], the RHS operation [wins or must be performed]'.

Note that even though in the previous chapter I frequently used the phrase rule conflict—which has acquired a very specific connotation in modern Pāṇinian scholarship—to discuss the traditional and modern interpretations of 1.4.2, I have tried not to use this phrase in the context of my own interpretation of 1.4.2. I interpret *vipratiṣedha* as DOI and not as rule conflict. DOI and rule conflict are different concepts. I will discuss this topic in detail later in this chapter.

2.3 Evidence for My Interpretation of *Para*

Before going further, let me provide more evidence to support my interpretation of *para*. The meaning of *para* in 1.4.2 can be confirmed by looking at the meaning of *para* in the rest of the *Aṣṭādhyāyī*. The term *para* has been used by Pāṇini on many occasions. Its occurrences can be classified into two groups:

Group A: 1.1.34, 1.4.109, 3.2.39, 3.3.138, 3.4.20, 4.3.5, 5.2.92, 5.3.29, 6.3.8.[2]

Group B: 1.1.47, 1.1.51, 1.1.54, 1.1.57, 1.1.70, 1.2.40, 1.4.2, 1.4.62, 1.4.81, 2.1.2, 2.2.31, 2.4.26, 3.1.2, 6.1.84, 6.1.94, 6.1.112, 6.1.115, 6.1.120, 6.2.199, 6.4.156, 7.3.22, 7.3.27, 7.4.80, 7.4.88, 7.4.93, 8.1.2, 8.1.56, 8.2.92, 8.3.4, 8.3.6, 8.3.26, 8.3.27, 8.3.35, 8.3.87, 8.3.110, 8.3.118, 8.4.28,[3] 8.4.58.[4]

Let us consider an example from Group A. 1.1.34 *pūrvaparāvaradakṣiṇottarāparādharāṇi vyavasthāyām asaṁjñāyām* (*vibhāṣā jasi sarvanāmāni*) teaches that the terms *pūrva*, *para*, and so on are called *sarvanāman* optionally when followed by *Jas*. In 1.1.34 and in the other rules belonging to Group A, *para* is used as an ordinary word of the object language Sanskrit. In these rules, it does not have any special technical connotation with respect to Pāṇini's derivational system. We are not interested in Group A, because 1.4.2 belongs to group B.

Let us consider some examples from Group B. 1.1.47 *mid aco'ntyāt paraḥ* teaches that an item marked with *anubandha M* is placed after, that is, to the right-hand side of, the last vowel of the item to which it is added. 1.1.51 *ur aṇ raparaḥ* teaches that *r* is added after, that is, to the right side of the vowels *a*, *i*, *u* when they are substitutes of *ṛ*. 1.1.54 *ādeḥ parasya* teaches that a substitute taught for the following or right-hand side item replaces its first sound. From these examples, it becomes clear that in the rules I have listed under group B, *para* is used to mean 'right-hand side' in the context of Pāṇinian derivations.

Furthermore, we also see that in the *Aṣṭādhyāyī* the term *pūrva*, the antonym of *para*, when used specifically in the context of Pāṇinian derivations, means LHS. For example, consider the pair of rules 1.1.66 *tasminn iti nirdiṣṭe pūrvasya* and 1.1.67 *tasmād ity uttarasya*. 1.1.66 teaches that when an item is taught (*nirdiṣṭe*) in the locative (*tasminn iti*), it means that the item to its left-hand side (*pūrvasya*) undergoes an operation, and 1.1.67 teaches that when an item is taught in the ablative (*tasmād iti*), it means that the item to its right-hand side (*uttarasya*)[5] undergoes the operation.[6]

Let us confirm this by considering some rules that contain both *pūrva* and *para*. 6.1.84 *ekaḥ pūrvaparayoḥ* teaches that (in the following rules) a single sound replaces both the LHS sound and the RHS sound in the case of *saṁhitā* 'immediate proximity'. Similarly, 1.1.57 *acaḥ parasmin pūrvavidhau* teaches that a substitute for a vowel, if it is conditioned by an RHS context, is treated like its substituendum with respect to an operation on an LHS element.

Besides, the word *kāryam* in 1.4.2 also gives us some crucial information. We know that in the *Aṣṭādhyāyī*, Pāṇini does not generally use finite verbal forms in his rules. For example, in 6.1.77, he does not say *iko yaṇ aci bhavati/kāryam*, but simply *iko yaṇ aci*. So, in the case of 1.4.2 too, we can safely interpret *kāryam* as a noun rather than interpreting it as an optative passive participle meaning 'should be done'. What does the noun *kārya* generally mean? It means 'operation', not 'rule'. If Pāṇini wanted to say what the tradition interprets him as saying, I think he would have simply said *vipratiṣedhe paraṁ sūtram* and not *vipratiṣedhe paraṁ kāryam*. All this corroborates my interpretation of *para* in 1.4.2.

Let me summarize this topic now. In ordinary speech, *para* means 'following, something that lies after'. Accordingly, in 1.4.2, *para* actually means 'that which comes after' in the left-to-right sense in the context of derivations. However, the tradition took it as 'that which comes after' in the top (first)-to-bottom (last) or beginning-to-end sense in the context of the serial order of rules. And so, while *para* in 1.4.2 refers to the operand or operation that lies after, or on the right-hand side relative to another operand or operation, the tradition misunderstood it as the rule that comes after the other rule in the serial order of the *Aṣṭādhyāyī*.

This leads to an important question: if traditional scholars interpreted *para* as 'RHS item/operation' in so many metarules as shown above, why did they interpret it as 'the following rule' in 1.4.2?[7] I think this misunderstanding possibly arose because another metarule, 8.2.1 *pūrvatrāsiddham*, uses *pūrva*, the opposite of *para*, to mean 'preceding rule'. 8.2.1 teaches that from 8.2.1 onwards, a preceding rule treats a following rule as suspended. This may have led Kātyāyana, the first scholar to comment upon Pāṇini's *sūtras*, to think that, in *sūtras* dealing with relationships between rules such as 8.2.1 and 1.4.2, *pūrva* and *para* mean preceding rule and following rule, respectively. However, upon closer examination, one realizes that when Pāṇini wants to indicate that he is referring to the relationship between preceding and following rules rather than operands, he adds the affix *traL*[8] to the base: he says *pūrva-tra* in 8.2.1.[9] This topic deserves our meticulous attention, and we will discuss it in greater detail in chapter 6. Here is the summary of my comprehensive solution:

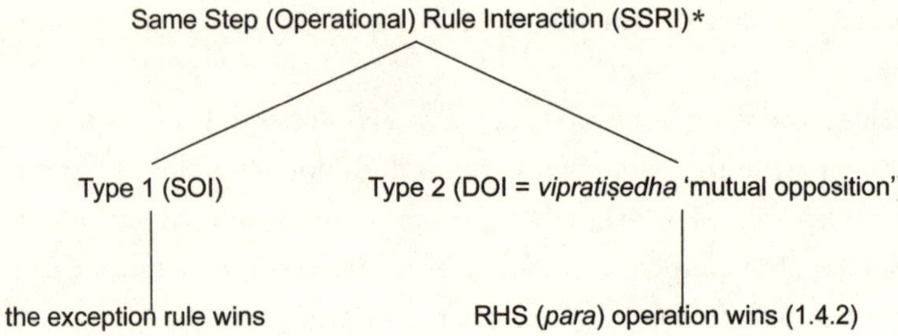

2.4 A Key Difference between SOI and DOI

SOI and DOI have one prominent feature in common: in the case of both SOI and DOI, two (or more) rules are simultaneously applicable at a certain step of the derivation. However, it is important to shed light on a key difference between SOI and DOI. This difference between SOI and DOI pertains to whether or not they involve competition between two operands.

Type 1 (SOI)	Type 2 (DOI)
A + B $R1_A$ → A, $R2_A$ → A	A + B R_A → A, R_B → B

In the case of DOI, we see that the two simultaneously applicable rules R_A and R_B compete for the sole position of the rule that applies at that step. But the two operands A and B too compete for the sole position of the operand that undergoes an operation at that step.

In case of SOI, the two simultaneously applicable rules $R1_A$ and $R2_A$ compete for the sole position of the rule that applies at that step. However, since both are applicable to the same operand A, we do not observe any competition between operands.

Because Pāṇini has not given any instructions about SOI but has taught the metarule 1.4.2 for dealing with DOI, we can say that Pāṇini has given explicit instructions about how we must deal with competition between

*As stated before, by 'rule', here I specifically mean *vidhi sūtra* 'operational rule'.

operands (which we see in DOI but not in SOI) but not about how we must deal with competition between rules (which we see in both DOI and SOI).

Lastly, and very importantly, note that although I often speak of SOI and DOI as two types of SSRI, they are entirely different: while DOI is very much a part of Pāṇini's grammar—perhaps the most important technical constituent of it—SOI is not. SOI, which involves mutual opposition between two (or more) *vidhi sūtra*s 'operational rules' applicable to the same operand, is, much like cases of mutual opposition between two (or more) *saṁjñā sūtra*s 'definition rules' or two (or more) *paribhāṣā sūtra*s 'metarules', a feature of the *sūtra* style itself. All three of them, that is:

1. SOI, which is mutual opposition between two (or more) *vidhi sūtra*s 'operational rules' applicable to the same operand at the same step;
2. mutual opposition between two (or more) *saṁjñā sūtra*s 'definition rules' (applicable to the same item, obviously); and
3. mutual opposition between two (or more) *paribhāṣā sūtra*s 'metarules' (applicable to the same item, obviously)

should be dealt with using the maxim: the more specific rule constitutes an exception to the general rule and thus defeats the latter. I have summarized this in the following diagram:

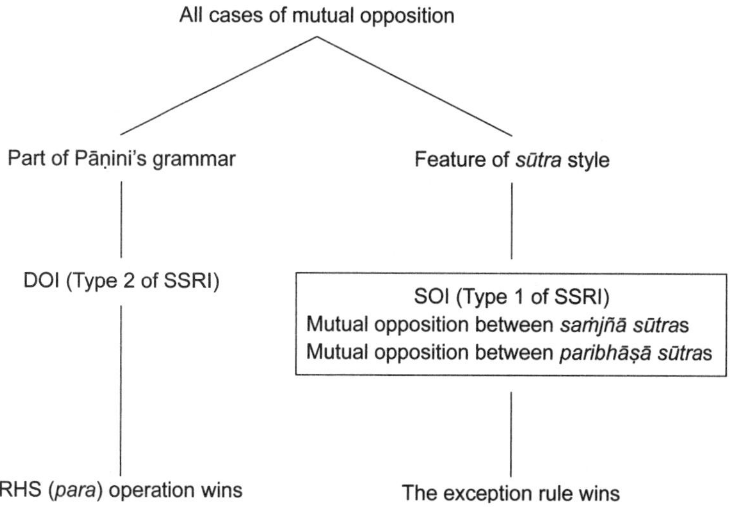

For examples of mutual opposition between pairs of *saṁjñā* and *paribhāṣā sūtras*, see the last section of chapter 5.

2.5 Pāṇinian and Post-Pāṇinian Approaches to Derivations

In order to determine why post-Pāṇinian (both traditional and modern) scholars have misinterpreted Pāṇini's rule 1.4.2, we need to understand that there is a fundamental difference between what I think are Pāṇinian[10] and post-Pāṇinian conceptions of, or perspectives towards, the derivational procedure itself. I will explain exactly what I mean by this statement by means of examining six representative examples of SSRI from both Pāṇinian and post-Pāṇinian perspectives below.

Let us start with the latter. But before we examine these representative examples from the post-Pāṇinian perspective, let me explain certain fundamental concepts that will help us understand this perspective better. Let us divide SSRI into two categories, namely conflict and nonconflict. In order to define conflict and nonconflict, we must first define blocking. Let us say that two rules X and Y are simultaneously applicable at step K. We say that rule X blocks rule Y if Y will not be applicable at the following step (K + 1) after the hypothetical application of X at the present step (K). Conflict is defined as an SSRI that involves some blocking. Nonconflict is defined as an SSRI that does not involve any blocking.

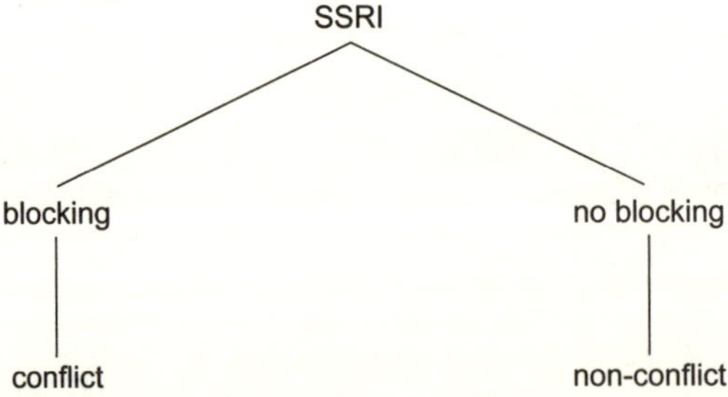

Note that, in my opinion, Pāṇini has not defined or discussed the categories conflict and nonconflict in any way whatsoever, and he does not expect us to know about or use them either. Traditional scholars too have not made an explicit distinction between conflict and nonconflict. In modern Western scholarship, the concept of (rule) conflict has been widely used, but nonconflict has not been used at all.

Then, the question arises: Why have I made this distinction between conflict and nonconflict? I have done this to highlight that, for the most part, post-Pāṇinian scholarship has focused on conflict and has not paid much attention to nonconflict. Why is this the case? To answer this question, let us look closely at nonconflict, wherein the two rules X and Y do not block each other: if X applies at the present step, then Y is applicable at the following step, and if Y applies at the present step, then X is applicable at the following step. Before we go further, note that 'being applicable' is different from 'applying'. Consider the following situation:

$$\text{STEP 1} \quad \underset{X}{\overset{g}{\uparrow}} \;+\; \underset{Y}{\overset{h}{\uparrow}}$$

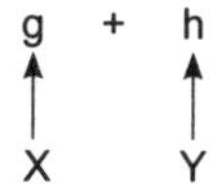

Let us say Y applies at this step, changing h to h* (asterisk here indicating a change). Now, at the following step, not only X but another rule Z too becomes applicable:

$$\text{STEP 2} \quad \underset{X}{\overset{g}{\uparrow}} \;+\; \underset{Z}{\overset{h^*}{\uparrow}}$$

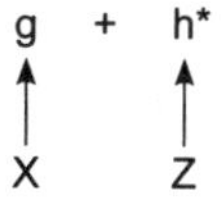

Suppose that Z, and not X, applies at step 2.

Here, we see that if Y applies at step 1, X is applicable at step 2.[11] However, X does not apply at step 2. This is the difference between 'being applicable' and 'applying'.

Now, let us go back to our conversation about why post-Pāṇinian scholarship does not take much interest in nonconflict. In most cases of nonconflict, if X applies at the present step, then Y is not only applicable but also applies at the following step. Similarly, if Y applies at the present step, then X is not only applicable but also applies at the following step. Thus, regardless of the order in which the two rules apply, one gets the correct form at the end of the derivation. This explains why the tradition can afford to overlook such examples of nonconflict, which, as I said, constitute a huge majority of the set of all nonconflict examples.

However, there is a minority of examples of nonconflict wherein if Y applies at the present step, X is applicable at the following step but does not end up applying at the following step. The tradition does take some interest in such examples of nonconflict, which constitute a very tiny minority of the set of all nonconflict examples.

Having defined both blocking and conflict, now let us look at how post-Pāṇinian scholarship views the following representative examples.

1) 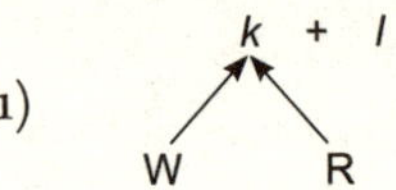

If we apply R at this step, W will be applicable at the following step. R does not block W.

If we apply W at this step, R will not be applicable at the following step. W blocks R.

We call this a case of asymmetrical or unidirectional blocking. Since this interaction involves blocking, this is a case of conflict. Such examples are of interest to post-Pāṇinian scholars.

2) *m* + *n*
S V

If we apply S at this step, V will not be applicable at the following step. S blocks V.

If we apply V at this step, S will not be applicable at the following step. V blocks S.

We call this a case of symmetrical or mutual blocking. Since this interaction involves blocking, this is a case of conflict. Such examples are of interest to post-Pāṇinian scholars.

3) *e* + *f*
P Y

If we apply P at this step, Y will be applicable at the following step. P does not block Y.

If we apply Y at this step, P will not be applicable at the following step. Y blocks P.

We call this a case of asymmetrical or unidirectional blocking. Since this interaction involves blocking, this is a case of conflict. Such examples are of interest to post-Pāṇinian scholars.

4) *g* + *h*
Q X

If we apply Q at this step, X will not be applicable at the following step. Q blocks X.

If we apply X at this step, Q will not be applicable at the following step. X blocks Q.

We call this a case of symmetrical or mutual blocking. Since this interaction involves blocking, this is a case of conflict. Such examples are of interest to post-Pāṇinian scholars.

Post-Pāṇinian scholars are very interested in these four representative examples (REs). But one may ask: what about the remaining two REs? Let us look at them.

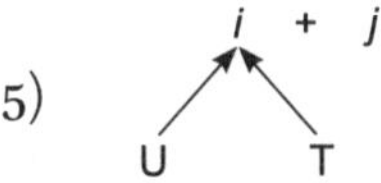

If we apply T at this step, U will be applicable at the following step. T does not block U.

If we apply U at this step, T will be applicable at the following step. U does not block T.

There is no blocking, so this is a case of nonconflict. The tradition does not think about or pay much heed to this kind of situation, for the most part.

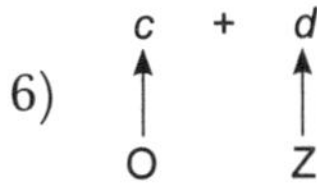

If we apply O at this step, Z will be applicable at the following step. O does not block Z.

If we apply Z at this step, O will be applicable at the following step. Z does not block O.

There is no blocking, so this is a case of nonconflict. The tradition does not think about or pay much heed to this kind of situation, for the most part.

Let us now summarize the relationship between blocking and conflict.

No blocking	Non-Conflict
Unidirectional blocking	Conflict
Mutual blocking	Conflict

Before we continue discussing these six examples from the post-Pāṇinian perspective, let us consider the Pāṇinian perspective on them:

1) 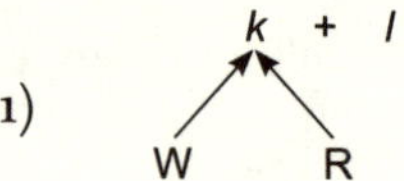

This is a case of SOI. Let us say W is more specific. Thus, W wins.

2) 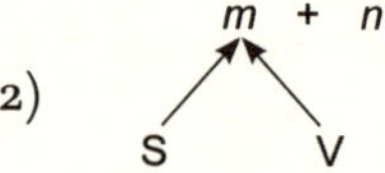

This is a case of SOI. Let us say V is more specific. Thus, V wins.

3) *e* + *f*, P ↑ *e*, Y ↑ *f*

This is a case of DOI. By 1.4.2, the RHS rule Y wins.

4) *g* + *h*, Q ↑ *g*, X ↑ *h*

This is a case of DOI. By 1.4.2, the RHS rule X wins.

5) *i* + *j*, U ↗ *i*, T ↖ *i*

This is a case of SOI. Let us say U is more specific. Thus, U wins.

6) *c* + *d*, O ↑ *c*, Z ↑ *d*

This is a case of DOI. By 1.4.2, the RHS rule Z wins.

Note that in all six representative examples discussed here, Pāṇini does not require us to worry about what happens to the losing rule. For instance, for P, in example 3, we need not be concerned about whether or not P is applicable at the following step, or whether or not P actually applies at the following step. In other words, Pāṇini does not use concepts like blocking and conflict to give instructions about dealing with SOI and DOI.

Even though Pāṇini does not use concepts like conflict to give instructions about SSRI, and even though the tradition makes no explicit distinction between SOI and DOI, let us discuss both Pāṇinian and post-Pāṇinian concepts under one umbrella to understand this topic better. I have included both SOI and DOI examples because Pāṇini deals with them separately and have included examples of both conflict and nonconflict because the post-Pāṇinian approach subconsciously makes this distinction by focusing on conflict alone. Here is a summary of the examples:

RE*	Type	Blocking	Conflict
1	SOI	unidirectional**	Yes
2	SOI	mutual	Yes
3	DOI	unidirectional	Yes
4	DOI	mutual	Yes
5	SOI	none	No
6	DOI	none	No

*RE = Representative Example
**Only a minority of cases of SOI involve unidirectional blocking. Most cases of SOI involve mutual blocking.

Representative examples 1, 2, 3, and 4 are of significant interest to post-Pāṇinian scholarship because they involve some kind of blocking, thereby constituting cases of conflict.

2.6 Traditional Solutions

Now, let us look at how the tradition solves examples of conflict. As stated in the previous chapter, traditional scholars tried to use their interpretation of 1.4.2 (the rule that comes later in the serial order of the *Aṣṭādhyāyī* wins the conflict) to resolve such conflicts. This often gave them the wrong answer, so in order to reduce the challenges posed by their interpretation of 1.4.2, they significantly reduced the scope of applicability of 1.4.2.

They achieved this by restricting the meaning of *vipratiṣedha* to *tulyabalavirodha* 'conflicts between rules of equal strength'. So, 1.4.2 does not apply to pairs of conflicting rules if the two rules are not of equal strength. In the case of such pairs of unequal strength, the rule that is stronger than the other wins. The tradition has come up with certain methods to identify these pairs of unequal strength. While we have already looked at some of them in the previous chapter, I will briefly discuss them below to outline which tool is used to deal with what kind of interaction (SOI or DOI) and what kind of blocking (unidirectional or mutual).[12]

1. *nitya* > *anitya*: in a conflict between two rules A and B, A is called *nitya* with respect to B if A is applicable (both before and) after the application of B. B is called *anitya* with respect to A if B is applicable before but not after the application of A. The *nitya* rule A is stronger than and defeats the *anitya* rule B. In other words, A wins against B if A unidirectionally blocks B.
2. *antaraṅga* > *bahiraṅga*: according to the *Paribhāṣenduśekhara*, '*antaraṅga* is (a rule) the causes (of the application) of which lie within (or before) the sum of the causes of a *bahiraṅga* rule' (Abhyankar 1960, 221–22). Note that this tool is seldom used to solve actual cases of conflict and is mostly only used to solve what I call cases of pseudoconflict. We will delve into this in section 5.6 of chapter 5.
3. *apavāda* > *utsarga*: an exception rule, or a more specific rule, defeats the general rule.
4. *pūrvavipratiṣiddha*: when applying 1.4.2 gives the wrong answer, Kātyāyana comes up with *pūrvavipratiṣiddha vārttikas*. These state that in certain cases, contrary to what is taught by the traditional interpretation of 1.4.2, it is not the *para* rule (the rule that comes after the other rule in the serial order of the *Aṣṭādhyāyī*) but instead the *pūrva* rule (the rule that comes before the other rule in the serial order of the *Aṣṭādhyāyī*) that wins. *Pūrvavipratiṣiddha* too has come to be used like a con-

flict-resolution tool. Here are two well-known examples of such *vārttikas* (vt. 10 and 11, respectively, on 7.1.96 *striyāṁ ca* [Mbh III.275.23–276.12]):

a. vt. 10 *guṇavr̥ddhyauttvatr̥jvadbhāvebhyo num pūrvavipratiṣiddham*: in the case of *vipratiṣedha*, the *pūrva sūtra*, which teaches the insertion of the augment *nUM*, takes precedence over *para sūtras*, which teach (i) *guṇa*,[13] (ii) *vr̥ddhi*,[14] (iii) *auttva*,[15] and (iv) *tr̥jvadbhāva*.[16]

b. vt. 11 *numaciratr̥jvadbhāvebhyo nuṭ* (*pūrvavipratiṣiddham*): in the case of *vipratiṣedha*, the *pūrva sūtra*, which teaches the insertion of the augment *nUṬ*,[17] takes precedence over *para sutras*, which teach (i) *numāgama* 'insertion of augment *nUM*',[18] (ii) replacement with *r* when followed by a vowel (*aC*),[19] and (iii) *tr̥jvadbhāva*.[20]

5. *niravakāśa/anavakāśa* > *sāvakāśa*[21]: In his first *vārttika* on 1.4.2 (Mbh I.304.13), Kātyāyana defines *vipratiṣedha* as a conflict that arises between two *sāvakāśa* rules: *dvau prasaṅgāv anyārthāv ekasmin sa vipratiṣedhaḥ* '[When] two rules [which are] applicable elsewhere (i.e., in other derivations) [become applicable] at the same place, this [situation is called] *vipratiṣedha*'. But when one of the two rules is *niravakāśa*, that is, when it does not have scope to apply elsewhere, such a conflict is not called *vipratiṣedha*. In such cases, the *niravakāśa* rule is thought to be stronger than the *sāvakāśa* rule. The *niravakāśa* rule wins.

As discussed in the previous chapter, the tradition does not apply these tools consistently and, often, applying some of these tools gives the wrong form. Nonetheless, through the table presented below, I try to give a broad and general overview of the tools that are used to deal with different kinds of conflicts:

RE	Type	Blocking	Tools
1	SOI conflict	unidirectional	*nitya* > *anitya*
2	SOI conflict	mutual	*niravakāśa* > *sāvakāśa*, *apavāda* > *utsarga*, *pūrvavipratiṣiddha*
3	DOI conflict	unidirectional	*nitya* > *anitya*
4	DOI conflict	mutual	*niravakāśa* > *sāvakāśa*, *pūrvavipratiṣiddha*

Lastly, alongside these tools, the tradition liberally uses (its interpretation of) 1.4.2 to deal with all kinds of conflict when it is necessary and/or desirable to do so.

2.7 Examples of DOI

In my opinion, 1.4.2 *vipratiṣedhe paraṁ kāryam* means: in the event of DOI, the RHS rule wins. As stated before, I have not used the term *rule conflict* in my interpretation of 1.4.2. This is because I think that Pāṇini does not require us to use such a concept to understand 1.4.2 and, consequently, to perform derivations correctly.

However, as shown above, all post-Pāṇinian discussion pertaining to 1.4.2 has focused on conflict. So, I do need to deal with the topic of conflict to contextualize my findings in the contemporary discourse. In other words, I need to show that my interpretation of 1.4.2 correctly resolves examples of DOI conflict, which I will call Type 2a henceforth. For each example, I will first prove that the example involves conflict, and then discuss my solution to it. In those cases where the traditional solution is known and can shed light on the way in which the tradition approaches the issue at hand, I will discuss it at the end of the derivation.

Even though the tradition is not very interested in nonconflict, I will also show that 1.4.2 helps deal with examples of DOI nonconflict, which I will call Type 2b henceforth.

Before we start looking at examples, here is a diagram that summarizes this topic:

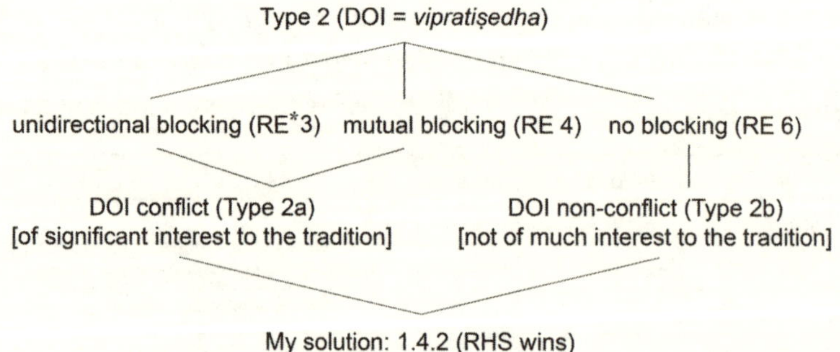

* RE = 'Representative Example'.

Note the difference between *vipratiṣedha,* as interpreted by me, and the concept of conflict, which is popularly discussed in modern post-Pāṇinian literature, in the diagram above.

In this section, I have chosen examples from nominal inflection.[22]

In all derivations performed in this book, I present *only* those steps diagrammatically at which multiple rules are simultaneously applicable. For example, at step a + b, if rules R_1 and R_2 are applicable to a and b, respectively, then I draw the following kind of diagram to illustrate the same:

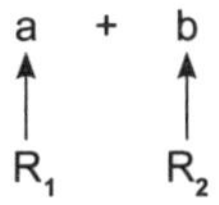

a + b
↑ ↑
R_1 R_2

However, if only one rule K_1 is applicable (to c) at a given step c + d, then I do *not* draw diagrams of the following kind to represent this:

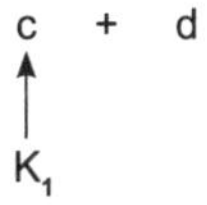

c + d
↑
K_1

Instead, I simply describe this in words or symbolically, as follows: c + d → c* + d (K_1) (asterisk here indicating a change).

Example #1. *deva* + *bhis*—'God' (masculine), instrumental plural

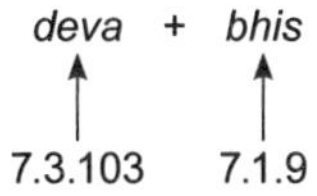

deva + *bhis*
↑ ↑
7.3.103 7.1.9

7.3.103 *bahuvacane jhaly et* (*ataḥ supi*): an *e* replaces the final *a* of a nominal base when a plural declensional affix starting with *jhaL* (a non-nasal stop or a fricative) follows.

7.1.9 *ato bhisa ais*: *ais* replaces *bhis* when *bhis* occurs after an *a*-final base.

If *bhis* is replaced with vowel-initial *ais* by 7.1.9, then 7.3.103, which applies to only those bases that are followed by a *jhaL*-initial affix, will not be applicable at the following step. Similarly, if the *a* of *deva* is replaced with *e* by 7.3.103, then 7.1.9, which applies to affixes that are preceded by *a*-final bases, will not be applicable at the following step.

Therefore, 7.1.9 and 7.3.103 block each other. This is a case of mutual blocking and thus of Type 2a (DOI conflict).

By my interpretation of 1.4.2, the RHS operation 7.1.9 wins, leading to the correct form: *deva* + *ais* → *devais* (6.1.88 *vr̥ddhir eci*) → *devair* (8.2.66 *sasajuṣoḥ ruḥ*) → *devaiḥ* (8.3.15 *kharavasānayor visarjanīyaḥ*).

In his comments on 7.1.9, Patañjali tries to solve this conflict by using *paratva* (the rule that comes later in the serial order of the *Aṣṭādhyāyī* wins), but that gives the wrong answer: **devebhis*. He then asserts that 7.1.9 is *nitya* and thus wins, giving the correct form: *devaiḥ* (Mbh III.244.13–21). His explanation for calling 7.1.9 *nitya* is illogical at best, and we will not delve into it. Suffice it to say that the *nitya* tool, which can only solve cases of unidirectional blocking, cannot be applied to the present case of mutual blocking. *Pradīpa* and *Uddyota*, the two popular commentaries on the *Mahābhāṣya*, suggest that the rule 7.1.9 is *anavakāśa* whereas 7.3.103 is *sāvakāśa*. So, the former wins. The *anavakāśa* tool is simply a technical way of arguing the following:

1. 7.1.9 does not apply anywhere else.
2. Surely, Pāṇini must have composed 7.1.9 because it applies somewhere.

From (1) and (2), the tradition concludes that it has to apply here.

For this and many other examples, instead of following a systematic procedure of rule conflict resolution, the tradition adopts a trial-and-error approach to come up with a justification for the application of the rule, which leads to the correct form.

Example #2. *hari* + *āṄ*—'green' (masculine), instrumental singular

```
hari  +  āṄ*
 ↑        ↑
6.1.77   7.3.120
```

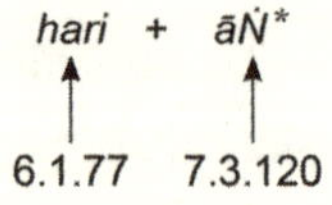

* The instrumental singular affix taught by 4.1.2 *sv-au-jas* . . . is *Ṭā* and not *āṄ*. The use of *āṄ* instead of *Ṭā* "is best understood as reflecting earlier traditions" (Cardona 1997: 51).

6.1.77 *iko yaṇ aci*: *iK* (*i*, *u*, *r̥*, *l̥*) is replaced with *yaṆ* (*y*, *v*, *r*, *l*) when *aC* (any vowel) follows.

7.3.120 *āṅo nāstriyām*: *nā* replaces the affix *āṄ*, when it occurs after a non-feminine base termed *ghi* (a base ending in *i* or *u* except *sakhi*).

If the *i* of *hari* is replaced with *y* by 6.1.77, then 7.3.120, which applies only to bases ending in *i* or *u*, will not be applicable at the following step. And if *āṄ* is replaced with consonant-initial *nā*, then 6.1.77, which could have applied to the *i* of *hari* when it is followed by a vowel, will no longer be applicable. Thus, 7.3.120 and 6.1.77 block each other.

This is a case of mutual blocking and thus of Type 2a (DOI conflict).

By my interpretation of 1.4.2, the RHS operation 7.3.120 wins, leading to the correct form: *hariṇā*.[23]

Example #3. *vāri* + *āṄ*—'water' (neuter), instrumental singular[24]

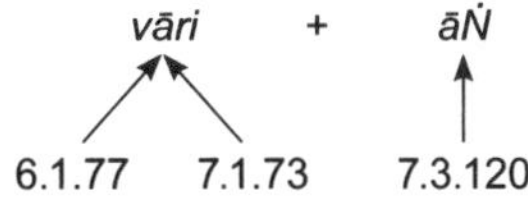

6.1.77 *iko yaṇ aci*: same as above.

7.1.73 *iko'ci vibhaktau* (*num napuṁsakasya*): augment *nUM* is attached to a neuter base ending in *iK* (*i*, *u*, *r̥*, *l̥*) when a vowel-initial declensional affix follows.

7.3.120 *āṅo nāstriyām*: same as above.

We have already seen in the previous example that 6.1.77 and 7.3.120 block each other.

Now, let us look at the DOI interaction between 7.1.73 and 7.3.120. If *vāri* takes the augment *nUM* by 7.1.73, thereby becoming consonant-final *vārin*, then 7.3.120, which applies only to those affixes that are preceded by *ghi* bases ending in *i* or *u*, will not be applicable at the following step. And if consonant-initial *nā* replaces *Ṭā* by 7.3.120, then 7.1.73, which only applies to certain bases followed by vowel-initial affixes, will not be applicable at the following step. Thus, 7.3.120 and 7.1.73 block each other. This is a case of mutual blocking and thus of DOI conflict.

By my interpretation of 1.4.2, we apply the RHS rule 7.3.120[25] and get the correct form: *vāriṇā*.[26]

We have already discussed the traditional position on the conflict between 6.1.77 and 7.3.120 in the previous example. I do not think the tradition discusses the conflict between 6.1.77 and 7.1.73. We can assume that it would use its interpretation of 1.4.2 (the rule that comes later in the serial order of the *Aṣṭādhyāyī* wins) or the *apavāda* tool to solve this conflict. As for the conflict between 7.1.73 and 7.3.120, the *Bālamanoramā* commentary on the *Siddhāntakaumudī* solves it using the traditional interpretation of 1.4.2.

Example #4. *strī* + *ām*—'woman' (feminine), genitive plural

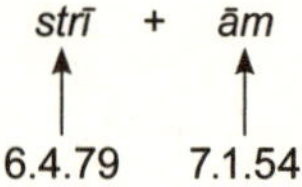

6.4.79 *striyāḥ* (*aci iyaṅ*): the final sound of the base *strī* is replaced with *iyAṄ* when a vowel-initial affix follows.

7.1.54 *hrasvanadyāpo nuṭ* (*āmi*): augment *nUṬ* is introduced to affix *ām* when it occurs after a nominal base that ends in a short vowel, is termed *nadī* (feminine long *ī*- and *ū*-final bases), or has taken the feminine affix *ṬāP*.

If the *ī* of *strī* is replaced with *iyAṄ* by 6.4.79, thereby making it *striy*, then 7.1.54, which applies to *ām* when preceded by *nadī*-final vowels *ī* and *ū*, will not be applicable at the following step.

If the augment *nUṬ* is added to the affix *ām* by 7.1.54, thereby making it consonant-initial *nām*, then 6.4.79, which is only applicable to the base *strī* when it is followed by vowel-initial affixes, will not be applicable at the following step.

This is a case of mutual blocking and thus of Type 2a (DOI conflict). By my interpretation of 1.4.2, the RHS operation, 7.1.54 wins, leading to the correct form: *strīṇām*.[27]

The *Bhaimī* commentary on the *Laghusiddhāntakaumudī* solves the conflict between 6.4.79 and 7.1.54 using the traditional interpretation of 1.4.2 (i.e., the rule that comes later in the serial order of the *Aṣṭādhyāyī* wins).

Example #5. *vāri* + *ām*—'water' (neuter), genitive plural

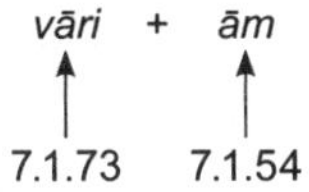

vāri + *ām*
↑ ↑
7.1.73 7.1.54

7.1.73 *iko'ci vibhaktau* (*num napuṁsakasya*): augment *nUM* is attached to a neuter base ending in *iK* (*i, u, r̥, l̥*) when a vowel-initial declensional affix follows.

7.1.54 *hrasvanadyāpo nuṭ* (*āmi*): same as above.

If the augment *nUM* is attached to *vāri* by 7.1.73, thereby making it consonant-final *vārin* (1.1.47 *mid aco'ntyāt paraḥ*), then 7.1.54, which only applies to *ām* when it is preceded by certain vowel-final bases, will not be applicable at the following step.

On the other hand, if the augment *nUṬ* is attached to the affix *ām* by 7.1.54, thereby making it consonant-initial *nām*, then 7.1.73, which is only applicable to certain bases that are followed by vowel-initial affixes, will not be applicable at the following step.

Both 7.1.54 and 7.1.73 block each other. This is a case of mutual blocking and thus of Type 2a (DOI conflict).

By my interpretation of 1.4.2, the RHS operation 7.1.54 wins, leading to the correct form: *vārīṇām*[28] (6.4.3 *nāmi*, 8.4.2 *aṭkupvāṅnumvyavāye'pi*).

The tradition resorts to Kātyāyana's *vārttika* '*numaciratr̥jvadbhāvebhyo nuṭ pūrvavipratiṣiddham*' (vt. 11 [Mbh III.276.6] on 7.1.96 *striyāṁ ca*) to solve this conflict. This *vārttika* teaches that even though the rule teaching the attachment of the augment *nUṬ* (7.1.54) comes before the rule teaching the attachment of the augment of *nUM* (7.1.73) in the serial order of the *Aṣṭādhyāyī*, the former wins. In this and other *pūrvavipratiṣiddha vārttika*s, Kātyāyana simply lists those conflicts that cannot be correctly solved using the traditional interpretation of 1.4.2.

Example #6. *kroṣṭu* + *ām*—'jackal' (masculine), genitive plural

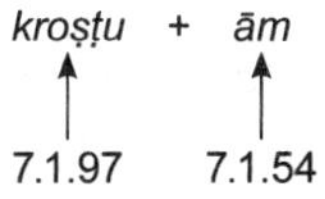

kroṣṭu + *ām*
↑ ↑
7.1.97 7.1.54

7.1.97 *vibhāṣā tr̥tīyādiṣv aci* (*tr̥jvat kroṣṭuḥ*): 'the base *kroṣṭu*, is treated as if ending in affix *tr̥C* optionally, when a vowel-initial ending of the *tr̥tīyā* triplet (instrumental) or any of the following triplets (namely dative, ablative, genitive, or locative) follows.[29]

7.1.54 *hrasvanadyāpo nuṭ* (*āmi*): same as above.

If the *u* of *kroṣṭu* becomes *r̥* by 7.1.97, then 7.1.54, which applies to *ām* when it is preceded by any of the short vowels, will be applicable to *ām* at the following step. But if the augment *nUṬ* is added to *ām* by 7.1.54, thereby making it (consonant-initial) *nām*, then 7.1.97, which applies to *kroṣṭu* only when it is followed by a vowel-initial *tritīyādi* affix, will not be applicable at the following step.

7.1.54 blocks 7.1.97, but 7.1.97 does not block 7.1.54. This is a case of unidirectional blocking, and thus of DOI conflict. By my interpretation of 1.4.2, the RHS operation 7.1.54 wins, leading to the correct form: *kroṣṭūnām* (6.4.3 *nāmi*).

Since this is a case of unidirectional blocking, the tradition could have used the *nitya* tool to solve this conflict. However, it does not do so.[30] Instead, Kātyāyana has written the *vārttika* '*numaciratr̥jvadbhāvebhyo nuṭ pūrvavipratiṣiddham*' (vt. 11 [Mbh III.276.6] on 7.1.96 *striyāṁ ca*) to solve it. This *vārttika* teaches that even though the rule teaching the attachment of the augment *nUṬ* (7.1.54) comes before the rule teaching *tr̥jvadbhāva* (7.1.97) in the serial order of the *Aṣṭādhyāyī*, the former wins.

Example #7. *kartr̥* + *sU*—'doer' (neuter), nominative singular

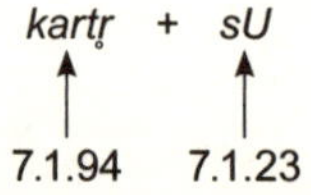

kartr̥ + *sU*
↑ ↑
7.1.94 7.1.23

7.1.94 *r̥duśanaspurudaṁso'nehasāṁ ca* (*asambuddhau anaṅ sau*): the final sound of a base ending in *r̥T* or of the bases *uśanas*, *purudaṁsas*, and *anehas* is substituted with *anAṄ* when followed by nonvocative *sU*.

7.1.23 *svamor napuṁsakāt* (*luk*): affixes *sU* and *am* occurring after a neuter base are substituted with *LUK*.

If we apply 7.1.23, then 7.1.94, which applies only when followed by *sU*, will not be applicable at the following step. If we apply 7.1.94, then 7.1.23, which applies to any neuter base regardless of its final sound, will be applicable at the following step.

This is a case of unidirectional blocking and thus of Type 2a (DOI conflict).

By my interpretation of 1.4.2, the RHS operation 7.1.23 wins, thereby giving the correct form: *kartr̥*.

Example #8. *tad* + *sU*—'that' (neuter), nominative singular

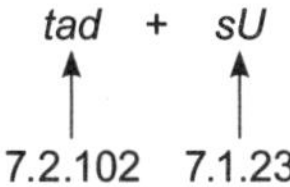

7.2.102 *tyadādīnām aḥ* (*vibhaktau*): the final sound of a base belonging to the group headed by *tyad* 'that' is replaced with *a* when a declensional affix follows.

7.1.23 *svamor napuṁsakāt* (*luk*): same as above.

What kind of interaction occurs between the two rules? The tradition seems to be confused about this. So, let us start by looking at my solution.

This is a case of DOI. By my interpretation of 1.4.2, the RHS rule 7.1.23 wins, giving us the correct answer: *tad*.[31]

In his commentary on 7.1.23 (Mbh III.248.23–249.2), Patañjali first tries to use the traditional interpretation of 1.4.2 (the rule that comes later in the serial order of the *Aṣṭādhyāyī* wins) to determine which of the two rules he must apply. But he gets the wrong answer upon doing so. Then, he tries to use the *nitya* tool.

If we apply 7.1.23 at this step, 7.2.102 will not be applicable at the following step. On the other hand, if we apply 7.2.102 at this step, 7.1.23 will still be applicable at the following step. Thus, this is a case of unidirectional blocking and of Type 2a (DOI conflict). Therefore, the *nitya* tool can be used here.

However, Patañjali then says that 7.1.23 is not *nitya* with respect to 7.2.102. This is because, after the hypothetical application of 7.2.102, 7.1.23 is not the only rule that will be applicable. 7.1.24 *ato 'm*[32] will also be applicable. Since 7.1.24 is an *apavāda* of 7.1.23, the former will win. So 7.1.23 will, despite being applicable, fail to apply, following the application of 7.2.102. For this reason, Patañjali says that 7.1.23 cannot be called *nitya* with respect to 7.2.102. To deal with this problem, Patañjali suggests some changes in the wording of 7.1.23 *svamor napuṁsakāt*. We will not dwell on his argument because it is beyond our scope.

Having looked at examples of DOI conflict (Type 2a), now let us look at examples of DOI nonconflict (Type 2b).

Example #9. *rājan* + *sU*—'king' (masculine), nominative singular

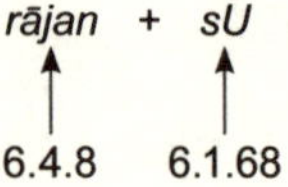

6.4.8 *sarvanāmasthāne cāsambuddhau* (*nopadhāyāḥ dīrghaḥ*): the penultimate sound of a base ending in *n* is replaced with its *dīrgha* 'long' equivalent when a nonvocative *sarvanāmasthāna* affix (*sU*, *au*, *Jas*, *am*, *auṬ* in non-neuter forms or *Śi*) follows.

6.1.68 *halṅyābbhyo dīrghāt sutisyapr̥ktaṁ hal* (*lopaḥ*): there is elision by *LOPA* of the finite verb affixes *ti* and *si* when they consist of a single sound and follow a form that ends in a consonant and of the nominative singular case affix *sU* when it follows a form that ends in a consonant or the long final vowel of feminine affixes *Ṅī* or *āP*.

If 6.4.8 applies at step K, we get *rājān*, which still ends in a consonant. So 6.1.68 will be applicable at step K + 1. If *sU* is replaced with *LOPA* by 6.1.68 at step K, the properties of the affix *sU* still hold (cf. 1.1.62 *pratyayalope pratyayalakṣaṇam*), so 6.4.8 will be applicable at step K + 1.

We see that 6.4.8 and 6.1.68 do not block each other. This is a case of Type 2b (DOI nonconflict). By my interpretation of 1.4.2, the RHS rule 6.1.68 wins and we get *rājan*. Now thanks to 1.1.62 *pratyayalope pratyayalakṣaṇam*, we apply 6.4.8 and get *rājān*. At this juncture, we apply 8.2.7 *nalopaḥ prātipadikāntasya*,[33] which teaches that *n* is replaced with *LOPA* at the end of a nominal stem which is termed *pada* and get the correct form: *rājā*. Note that even if we had applied 6.4.8 (the LHS rule) at the first step, we could have still applied 6.1.68 at the following step. And applying these two rules in this order too would have given us the correct form.

Why then did Pāṇini need to say anything about DOI nonconflict at all? Why did he prescribe that the RHS be applied in such cases (cf. my interpretation of 1.4.2)? We will answer this question while discussing the following examples. The tradition is not interested in such cases of nonconflict.

Example #10. *tri + ām*—'three' (feminine), genitive plural

tri + *ām*
↑ ↑
7.2.99 7.1.54

7.2.99 *tricaturoḥ striyāṁ tisr̥catasr̥*: *tri* and *catur* are replaced with *tisr̥* and *catasr̥*, respectively, in the feminine.

7.1.54 *hrasvanadyāpo nuṭ* (*āmi*): augment *nUṬ* is introduced to affix *ām*[34] when it occurs after a nominal base which ends in a short vowel, or is termed *nadī* (feminine bases ending with *ī* and *ū*), or has taken the feminine affix *ṬāP*.

If we replace *tri* with *tisr̥* at this step, 7.1.54 will still be applicable at the following step because *tisr̥* ends in a short vowel. And if we apply 7.1.54 at this step, 7.2.99 will still be applicable at the following step, because its application does not depend on the affix.

Neither of the two rules blocks the other, and so this is a case of Type 2b (DOI nonconflict). By my interpretation of 1.4.2, we apply the RHS rule 7.1.54 and get *tri + nām*. Thereafter, we apply 7.2.99 *tricaturoḥ striyāṁ tisr̥catasr̥* and get the correct form: *tisr̥ṇām*[35].

In order to understand why Pāṇini has prescribed that we pick the RHS rule in the cases of DOI nonconflict, let us perform this derivation again, this time by picking the LHS rule in the case of DOI nonconflict.

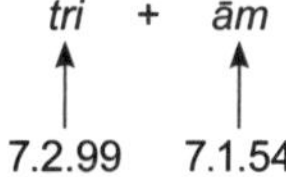

7.2.99 *tricaturoḥ striyāṁ tisr̥catasr̥*: same as above.

7.1.54 *hrasvanadyāpo nuṭ* (*āmi*): same as above.

This is a Type 2b (DOI nonconflict). As stated above, as an experiment, we are going to apply the LHS rule 7.2.99 in this case (of DOI nonconflict). Upon applying 7.2.99, we get *tisr̥ + ām*. Here, two rules are applicable:

tisr̥ + *ām*
↑ ↑
7.2.100 7.1.54

7.2.100 *aci ra r̥taḥ* (*vibhaktau tricaturoḥ tisr̥catasr̥*): a *r* replaces *r̥* of the bases *tisr̥* and *catasr̥*, when a vowel-initial declensional affix follows.

7.1.54 *hrasvanadyāpo nuṭ* (*āmi*): same as above.

If *ṛ* is replaced with consonant *r* by 7.2.100, then 7.1.54, which applies to *ām* when it is preceded by certain vowel-final bases will not be applicable at the following step. And if *ām* takes augment *nUṬ* by 7.1.54, thereby becoming consonant-initial *nām*, then 7.2.100 which applies to *ṛ* when a vowel-initial affix follows will not be applicable at the following step.

Thus, 7.2.100 and 7.1.54 block each other. This is a case of mutual blocking, and thus of Type 2a (DOI conflict).

By my interpretation of 1.4.2, the RHS operation 7.1.54 wins, leading to the correct form: *tisṛṇām.*

We have seen that, regardless of whether we pick the LHS or the RHS rule in the case of Type 2b (DOI nonconflict) here, we get the same answer: *tisṛṇām.* However, the two derivational paths look different from each other. The first path, in which we pick the RHS rule at the first step (as taught by Pāṇini in [my interpretation of] 1.4.2), is significantly shorter than the second path, in which we pick the LHS rule at the first step. In other derivations too, I have noticed that the derivation looks relatively shorter when we pick the RHS rule in the case of type 2b (DOI nonconflict) and relatively longer when we pick the LHS rule.

But is it merely to keep derivations compact that Pāṇini has prescribed the choice of the RHS rule in cases of DOI nonconflict? No. In the next example, we will see that we cannot get the correct answer without picking the RHS rule in the case of DOI nonconflict.

How does the tradition perform this derivation? *Vārttika*s 11 to 14 (Mbh III.276.6–22) on 7.1.96 *striyāṁ ca*, and Patañjali's comments on them, deal with this topic in detail and propose various tools like *pūrvavipratiṣiddha* and *apavāda* to solve this problem. We will not delve into this topic here.

Example #11. *idam* + *Ṅe*—'this' (masculine), dative singular

All cases of DOI in this derivation are of Type 2b (DOI nonconflict). I will not prove this at each step.

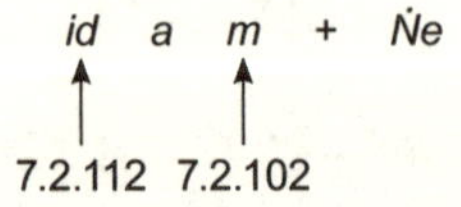

id *a* *m* + *Ṅe*

↑ (*id*) ↑ (*m*)

7.2.112 7.2.102

7.2.112 *an āpy akaḥ* (*vibhaktau idamaḥ idaḥ*): the *id* of *idam* is substituted with *an*, when it does not include a *k*, and when a declensional affix belonging to *āP*, that is, any instrumental, dative, ablative, genitive or locative affix, follows.

7.2.102 *tyadādīnām aḥ* (*vibhaktau*): the final sound of a base belonging to the group headed by *tyad* 'that' is replaced with *a* when a declensional affix follows.

By my interpretation of 1.4.2, the RHS rule 7.2.102 wins, and we get: *ida-a* + *Ṅe*. Here, multiple rules are applicable:

id [*a-a*] + *Ṅe*

7.2.112 6.1.97 7.1.14

7.2.112 *an āpy akaḥ* (*vibhaktau idamaḥ idaḥ*): same as above.

6.1.97 *ato guṇe*: when a short *a*, which is not *pada*-final (word-final) is followed by a *guṇa* vowel, that is, *a*, *e*, or *o*, then both *a* and the following *guṇa* are replaced with the latter.

7.1.14 *sarvanāmnaḥ smai* (*ṅer yaḥ ataḥ*): the affix *Ṅe*, when occurring after a pronominal base ending in *a*, is replaced with *smai*.

By my interpretation of 1.4.2, we apply the right-most rule 7.1.14, and get *ida-a* + *smai*. Here, multiple rules are applicable:

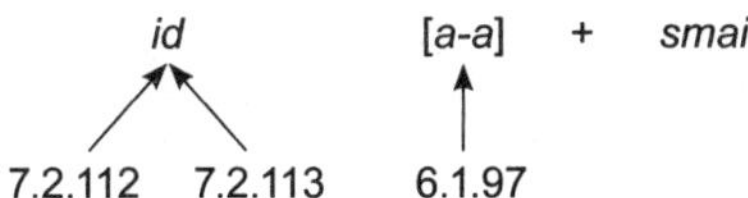

7.2.112 *an āpy akaḥ* (*vibhaktau idamaḥ idaḥ*): the *id* of *idam* is substituted with *an*, when it does not include a *k*, and when a declensional affix belonging to *āP*, that is, any instrumental, dative, ablative, genitive or locative affix, follows.

7.2.113 *hali lopaḥ* (*vibhaktau idamaḥ idaḥ akaḥ*): the *id* of *idam* is replaced with *LOPA*, when it does not include a *k*, and when a **consonant-initial** declensional affix belonging to *āP*, that is, any instrumental, dative, ablative, genitive or locative affix, follows.

6.1.97 *ato guṇe*: same as above.

By my interpretation of 1.4.2, we apply the RHS rule 6.1.97 and get *ida* + *smai*. Here, multiple rules are applicable:

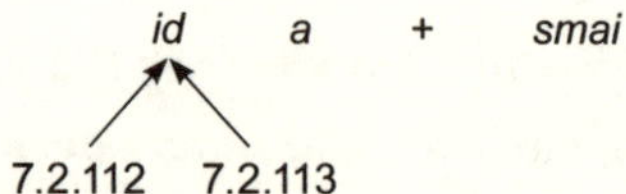

We see that there is a case of SOI between 7.2.112 and 7.2.113. Because 7.2.113 applies only when the base is followed by a consonant initial affix, it is more specific than, and defeats 7.2.112. Thus, we get the correct form: *asmai.*

At the very first step of this derivation, where we see the two rules 7.2.112 and 7.2.102 involved in DOI nonconflict, if we had chosen to apply the LHS rule 7.2.112 instead of the RHS rule 7.2.102, we would have got the wrong form at the end of the derivation: **anasmai*. The same can be said about the second step too: picking 7.2.112 at the second step instead of 7.1.14 too would have given us the wrong form: **anasmai*.

This shows that, even though whether we choose the LHS rule or the RHS rule may not matter in certain cases of DOI nonconflict (see examples 10 and 11 above), in cases of DOI nonconflict like this one, choosing the RHS rule alone gives the correct answer.

Finally, let us look at an example which involves cases of both DOI conflict and DOI nonconflict.

Example #12. *asmad* + *sU*—'I' (any gender), nominative singular

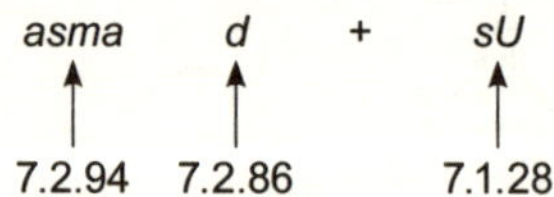

7.2.94 *tvāhau sau* (*yuṣmadasmador maparyantasya vibhaktau*): the parts of *yuṣmad* and *asmad* extending up to *ma*[36] are replaced with *tva* and *aha*, respectively, when followed by the case affix *sU*.

7.2.86 *yuṣmadasmador anādeśe* (*vibhaktau āḥ*): the final sounds of *yuṣmad* and *asmad* are replaced with *ā* when followed by consonant-initial case affixes which have not undergone any substitution.

7.1.28 *ṅeprathamayor am* (*yuṣmadasmadbhyāṁ vibhaktau*): *Ṅe*, and nominative, accusative affixes are replaced with *am* when preceded by *yuṣmad* and *asmad*.

Let us determine the relationship between 7.2.94 and the two other rules.

If we apply 7.2.94 at this step, 7.2.86 will be applicable at the following step.

Similarly, if we apply 7.2.86 at this step, 7.2.94 will be applicable at the following step. There is a Type 2b (DOI nonblocking) relationship between 7.2.94 and 7.2.86.

Similarly, if we apply 7.2.94 at this step, 7.1.28 will be applicable at the following step. If we apply 7.1.28 at this step, 7.2.94 will be applicable at the following step.[37] There is a Type 2b (DOI nonblocking) relationship between 7.2.94 and 7.1.28.

Thus, 7.2.94 has a Type 2b (DOI nonconflict) with the other two rules.

Now, let us determine the relationship between 7.2.86 and 7.1.28. If we apply 7.2.86 at this step, 7.1.28 will still be applicable at the following step. However, if we apply 7.1.28 at this step, then the affix *sU* will undergo *ādeśa* 'substitution' with *am*. 7.2.86 can only apply to *asmad* when followed by a nonsubstituted, consonant-initial affix. Thus, 7.2.86 will not be applicable at the following step. This is a case of unidirectional blocking, and thus of Type 2a (DOI conflict).

By my interpretation of 1.4.2, we apply the right-most rule 7.1.28 and get: *asmad* + *am*. Here again, two rules are applicable:

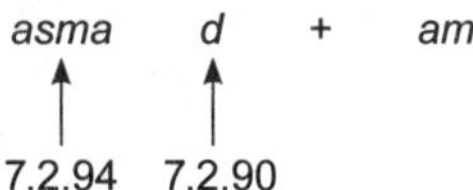

7.2.90 *śeṣe lopaḥ*: the final sounds of *yuṣmad* and *asmad* are replaced with *LOPA* when followed by case affixes not listed in the preceding rules (7.2.86-89).[38]

If we apply 7.2.94 at this step, 7.2.90 will still be applicable at the following step. If we apply 7.2.90 at this step, 7.2.94 will be applicable at the following step. This is a case of no blocking, and thus of Type 2b (DOI nonconflict). By my interpretation of 1.4.2, we apply the RHS rule 7.2.90 and get *asma* + *am*. Lastly, we apply 7.2.94 and get *aha* + *am*, to which we apply 6.1.97 *ato guṇe*.[39] This gives the correct form: *aham*.

As stated in note 36 on 7.2.94, the traditional interpretation of 7.2.94 is different from mine. Thus, its derivational process is different and slightly longer. We will not delve into it here. I will simply say that the tradition would have resolved the DOI conflict in this example using the *nitya* tool.

This brings us to the end of examples of DOI in this chapter. We will, of course, study more examples of DOI conflict in later chapters. Before we go to the next section, here I want to emphasize that I have discussed blocking and conflict in these derivations only because post-Pāṇinian scholarship is interested in these topics. In other words, I have attempted to show that examples of conflict can be solved by my interpretation of 1.4.2. Note that, if we had simply avoided talking about blocking and conflict, we would have completed these derivations almost effortlessly, by simply picking the right-most rule (cf. my interpretation of 1.4.2) in every case of DOI, irrespective of whether or not the rules in question are involved in any kind of conflict.

2.8 Examples of SOI

Having discussed examples of DOI, I will now show, through the following examples, that my solution (i.e., the more specific rule wins) helps deal with cases of SOI. Note that we find very few examples of RE 5 (SOI nonconflict) in Pāṇinian derivations. These cases are neither particularly challenging nor of interest to the tradition. Thus, I will only discuss cases of conflict here. To avoid redundancy, I will refrain from reiterating or proving the existence of conflict in these examples. I will also develop a systematic procedure to decide which rule is more specific. At the end of each example, I will mention the traditional solution.

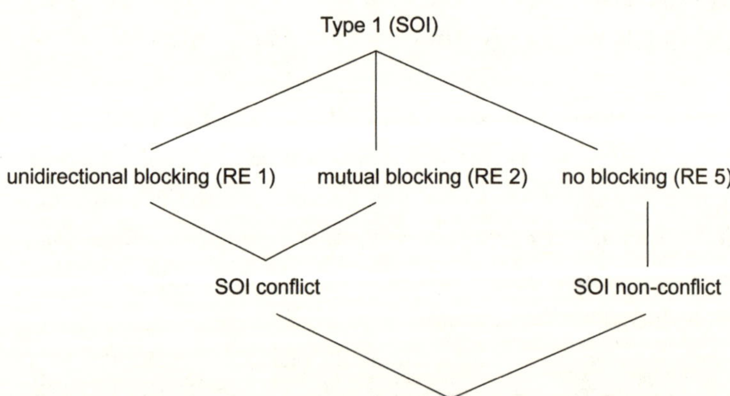

My solution: the rule which is more specific (i.e., the exception rule) wins.

Before we proceed to the examples, it is worth reiterating that SOI is, rather than being a part of Pāṇini's grammar, a feature of the *sūtra* style itself. It is thus that Pāṇini does not give us any instructions about the same in his grammar. In order to deal with SOI, Pāṇini expects us to draw on our logical faculties and consequently to determine which of the two or more operational rules in question is most specific. In Pāṇini's grammar we encounter two kinds of situations when dealing with SOI. One, where it is not possible to describe a certain rule as a subset of the other, competing rule. Such cases bring us to contemplate what a rule actually stands for in Pāṇini's grammar. I will discuss this further when analysing the first example. We will call this SOI-L. On the other hand, in the other situation, one rule can neatly be characterized as a subset of the other—which also brings us to think carefully about Pāṇini's tools and devices. I will dwell on this more when analysing the second example and will call it SOI-M.

Example #1. *rāma + bhyas*—'Rāma' (masculine), dative plural

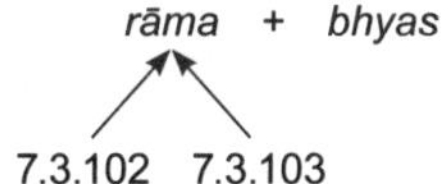

7.3.102 *supi ca* (*ato dīrgho yañi*): the *a* at the end of a nominal base is replaced with its long equivalent when followed by a declensional affix starting with *yaÑ* (i.e., *y, v, r, l, jh, bh* or any nasal).

7.3.103 *bahuvacane jhaly et* (*ataḥ supi*): the *a* at the end of a nominal base is replaced with *e* when followed by a plural declensional affix starting with *jhaL* (any non-nasal stop or fricative).

Note that the sets of operands of both rules are exactly the same, namely the final *a* of a nominal stem.

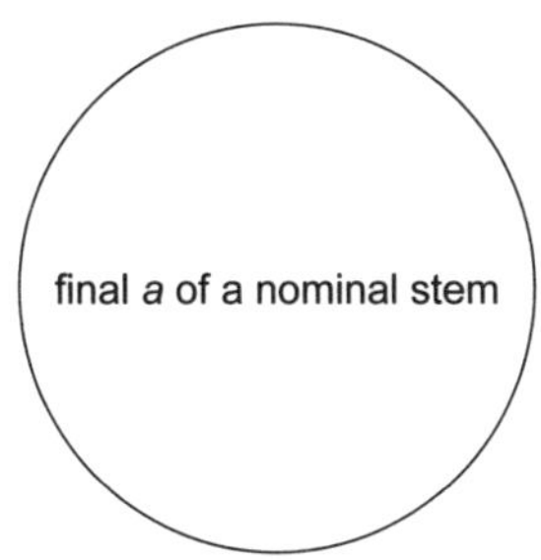

operands of 7.3.102 = operands of 7.3.103

However, the sets of contexts of the two rules are different. Neither set is a subset of the other. Instead, the two sets intersect each other.

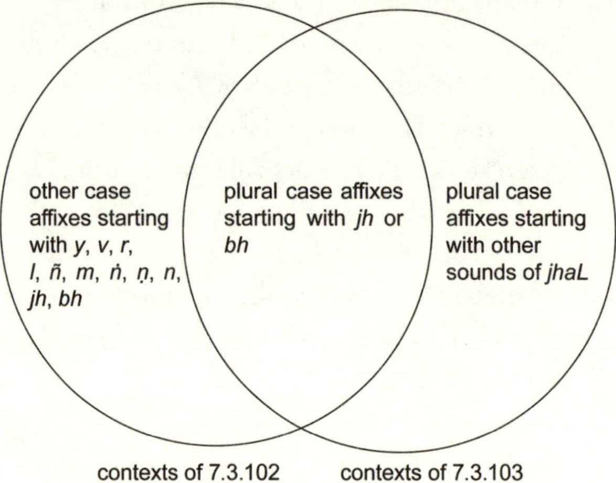

So how do we decide which rule is 'more specific'? Let us develop a procedure that we can use to deal with all examples of SOI.

Each Pāṇinian rule actually represents a collection of one or more subrules. For example, consider 7.3.102, which teaches that

$a^{\&} + ya\tilde{N}^{!} \rightarrow \bar{a}^{\&} + ya\tilde{N}^{!}$

[& = end of nominal stem; ! = beginning of case affix]

7.3.102 represents the following collection of subrules:

1. $a^{\&} + y^{!} \rightarrow \bar{a}^{\&} + y^{!}$
2. $a^{\&} + v^{!} \rightarrow \bar{a}^{\&} + v^{!}$
3. $a^{\&} + r^{!} \rightarrow \bar{a}^{\&} + r^{!}$
4. $a^{\&} + l^{!} \rightarrow \bar{a}^{\&} + l^{!}$
5. $a^{\&} + \tilde{n}^{!} \rightarrow \bar{a}^{\&} + \tilde{n}^{!}$
6. $a^{\&} + m^{!} \rightarrow \bar{a}^{\&} + m^{!}$
7. $a^{\&} + \dot{n}^{!} \rightarrow \bar{a}^{\&} + \dot{n}^{!}$
8. $a^{\&} + ṇ^{!} \rightarrow \bar{a}^{\&} + ṇ^{!}$
9. $a^{\&} + n^{!} \rightarrow \bar{a}^{\&} + n^{!}$
10. $a^{\&} + jh^{!} \rightarrow \bar{a}^{\&} + jh^{!}$
11. $a^{\&} + bh^{!} \rightarrow \bar{a}^{\&} + bh^{!}$

Pāṇini teaches these 11 subrules together in the form of the rule 7.3.102, using his *pratyāhāra* system, purely for the sake of brevity. Similarly, let us deconstruct 7.3.103, which teaches:

$a^{\&} + jhaL^{!\#} \rightarrow e^{\&} + jhaL^{!\#}$

[& = end of nominal stem; ! = beginning of case affix; # = plural]

7.3.103 can be represented by the following collection of subrules:

1. $\underline{a^{\&} + jh^{!\#} \rightarrow e^{\&} + jh^{!\#}}$
2. $\underline{a^{\&} + bh^{!\#} \rightarrow e^{\&} + bh^{!\#}}$
3. $a^{\&} + gh^{!\#} \rightarrow e^{\&} + gh^{!\#}$
4. $a^{\&} + ḍh^{!\#} \rightarrow e^{\&} + ḍh^{!\#}$
5. $a^{\&} + dh^{!\#} \rightarrow e^{\&} + dh^{!\#}$

. . . and so on.

Note that two subrules from the collection represented by 7.3.102 namely 10 and 11, which I have underlined, look similar to their respective underlined counterparts in the collection represented by 7.3.103. The actual SOI takes place between these two pairs of subrules. In fact, when I say that the more specific rule prevails in the case of SOI, I mean, the more specific 'subrule' prevails.

The other (nonunderlined) subrules just happen to be represented by 7.3.102 and 7.3.103, respectively, and are actually completely irrelevant to the SOI at hand.

We know that *jh* is not present at the beginning of any case affix, so we will focus on the subrules which apply to the final *a* of nominal stems when they are followed by *bh*-initial case affixes.

Relevant subrule of 7.3.102	**Relevant subrule of 7.3.103**
11. $a^{\&} + bh^{!} \rightarrow \bar{a}^{\&} + bh^{!}$	2. $a^{\&} + bh^{!\#} \rightarrow e^{\&} + bh^{!\#}$

Note that we find an extra # symbol in the case of subrule 2 under 7.3.103. This # stands for plural. Therefore, we conclude that subrule 2 under 7.3.103 is more specific than subrule 11 under 7.3.102 and thus wins. Henceforth, I shall take the liberty to rephrase this as '7.3.103 is more specific than 7.3.102 and thus wins'.

I will discuss this detailed procedure for the next example too. But after that, to avoid redundancy, I will present this procedure in an abbreviated form for all examples of SOI in this book. I will now present the abbreviated form of the procedure discussed above for the present example.

Let us consider the conditions in which each of the two rules 7.3.102 and 7.3.103 apply. Note that here I draw a distinction between a rule and a condition: a rule can apply in multiple conditions. This clarification is important insofar as the exact conditions in which a rule applies can vary, as I will show below.

7.3.102 applies to:

base ending in *a* + declensional affix starting with *bh*

base ending in *a* + declensional affix starting with any other sound of *yaÑ*

7.3.103 applies to:

base ending in *a* + declensional affix starting with *bh* (plural)

base ending in *a* + declensional affix starting with any other sound of *jhaL* (plural)

Notice that I write sounds, for example, *a, bh, yaÑ, jhaL*, and so on, outside brackets and all their characteristics, such as being a plural affix, being a neuter base, and so on, inside brackets. I treat sounds and their characteristics as two distinct sources of information. Broadly speaking, I will follow this convention for all examples of SOI discussed throughout this book.

In every case of SOI, only one condition per rule is relevant to the conflict. I mark the relevant conditions by writing them in bold fonts, as can be seen above. I will do the same for the rest of the examples. We compare the two and determine which one is more specific.

Here, the rule including the condition 'in the plural' (*bahuvacane*) is more specific than the other rule, which has no restriction based on number. So, the rule teaching the operation reserved for the plural, that is rule 7.3.103, wins, leading to the correct form: *rāmebhyaḥ*.

Now, let me provide a summary of what I have done here. A rule teaches sound change not for individual sounds but for entire clusters represented by *pratyāhāras*. This allows Pāṇini to achieve economy and optimality in his work. But when deciding which of the two rules must be applied, we should only consider those portions of these rules which are relevant to the situation at hand. I have called them subrules here. Upon comparing these subrules, it becomes clear that one has been taught for a more specific group (here, plural constructions). We will call this kind of situation SOI-L. Note that in the case of SOI-L, one rule is not a subset of the other.

The *Mahābhāṣya* on 7.3.103 (Mbh III.340.1–5) and the *Kāśikā* on 1.4.2 state that both 7.3.102 and 7.3.103 are *sāvakāśa*: 7.3.102 applies in derivations of forms like *vṛkṣābhyām* and *plakṣābhyām*, and 7.3.103 applies in derivations of forms like *vṛkṣeṣu* and *plakṣeṣu*. As stated before, Kātyāyana teaches that *vipratiṣedha* takes place between two *sāvakāśa* rules. Thus, by the traditional interpretation of 1.4.2 *vipratiṣedhe paraṁ kāryam*, the rule which comes later in the serial order of the *Aṣṭādhyāyī*, namely 7.3.103, wins.

Example #2

Now, let us consider the *sandhi* between the two words of the compound ***rāmaudārya*** **'Rāma's generosity'**.

We will not look at how this compound is formed, confining ourselves to the relevant step of the derivation:

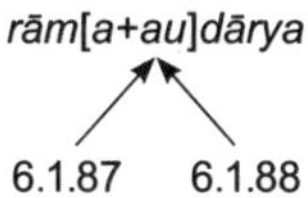

6.1.87 *ād guṇaḥ* (*aci*): *guṇa* (*a, e, o*) replaces both *a* and the vowel immediately following it.

6.1.88 *vṛddhir eci* (*āt*): *vṛddhi* (*ā, ai, au*) replaces both *a* and the *eC* vowel (*e, o, ai, au*) immediately following it.[40]

6.1.87, which teaches that

a + aC → a / e / o

can be rewritten as the following collection of subrules:

a + a → a

a + i → e

a + u → o

a + ṛ → a

a + ḷ → a

a + e → e

a + o → o

a + ai → e

a + au → o

6.1.88, which teaches that

a + eC → ā/ai/au

can be rewritten as the following collection of subrules:

a + e → ai

a + o → au

a + ai → ai

a + au → au

Note that the four underlined subrules under 6.1.87 correspond with the four underlined subrules under 6.1.88, respectively. However, both groups of underlined subrules are applicable in exactly the same four conditions, namely *a* + *e*, *a* + *o*, *a* + *ai*, and *a* + *au*, respectively. In such a case how can we decide which one is more specific? Since we cannot use subrules alone to make this decision, we need to look at the rules themselves. Even though 6.1.87 already deals with these four conditions, among other conditions, Pāṇini composed 6.1.88 exclusively to deal with these four conditions. This tells that Pāṇini wants us to apply 6.1.88, and not 6.1.87 in this example.

In the remaining examples I will present only abbreviated versions of this procedure, as follows:

6.1.87:

a* + *e* / *ai* / *o* / *au

a + any other vowel

6.1.88:

a* + *e* / *o* / *ai* / *au

Unlike example 1, where one condition was slightly different from the other (by virtue of being marked with the grammatical restriction 'plural'), in this example, both conditions highlighted in bold are exactly the same, that is, *a* + *e* / *ai* / *o* / *au*. In such a case, we go a step further and compare the two rules themselves. 6.1.88 applies only to *a* + *e* / *ai* / *o* / *au* whereas 6.1.87 also applies to *a* + any other vowel. Thus, 6.1.88 is more specific and wins the SOI, giving us the correct form: *rāmaudārya.*

Now for a moment, let us stop trying to 'tackle' such examples and actually understand what is going on here. Why do such cases of SOI come up in the first place? Couldn't Pāṇini simply have said: for *a* + *a* / *i* / *u* /*ṛ* / *ḷ*, perform action X, and for *a* + *e* / *o* / *ai* / *au*, perform action Y? Yes, he could have. But we must remember that Pāṇini is working with *pratyāhāras*. In this case, he does not want to use the *pratyāhāra aK*, which stands for *a*, *i*, *u*, *ṛ*, and *ḷ*. Why not? Simply because he wants to be able to use terms from earlier *sūtras* through *anuvṛtti*: the term *aci* is *anuvṛtta* into 6.1.87 *ād guṇaḥ* from 6.1.77 *iko yaṇ aci*. To avoid the undesirable effects of saying *ād guṇaḥ aci*, he says, 6.1.88 *vṛddhir* eci, thereby restricting the actual scope of 6.1.87. We will call such situations SOI-M. Note that in the case of SOI-M, one rule is a subset of the other.

On 6.1.88, the *Kāśikā* says that 6.1.88 is an *apavāda* of, and thus wins against, 6.1.87. Even though the tradition does not explicitly define *apavāda*, I think that the tradition uses the *apavāda* tool in cases of SOI, when, for example, the conditions in which one rule, here 6.1.88, applies (cf. *a* + *e* / *ai* / *o* / *au*), clearly constitute a subset of the conditions in which the other rule, here 6.1.87, applies (cf. *a* + any vowel). In many such cases, the *apavāda* rule is taught in the close vicinity of, and often immediately after, the *utsarga* rule, in the serial order of the *Aṣṭādhyāyī*. For example, the *apavāda sūtra* 6.1.88 is taught right after the *utsarga sūtra* 6.1.87.

Example #3

Let us look at the *sandhi* between two *padas*, that is, words, ***tava*** **'your' and *ātmā*** **'soul'**. Two rules are simultaneously applicable to *a* + *ā*:

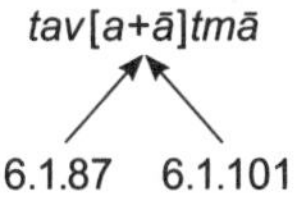

tav[a+ā]tmā

6.1.87 6.1.101

6.1.87 *ād guṇaḥ* (*aci*): *guṇa* (*a, e, o*) replaces both *a* and the vowel immediately following it.

6.1.101 *akaḥ savarṇe dīrghaḥ*: a long vowel replaces both *aK* (*a, i, u, ṛ, ḷ*) and the immediately following *savarṇa* 'homogeneous' vowel.

6.1.101:

a **+ vowel (*savarṇa*)**

i / *u* / *ṛ* / *ḷ* + vowel (*savarṇa*)

6.1.87:

a **+ vowel**

I have written the conditions that are relevant to the conflict in bold. 6.1.101 is applicable only when the following vowel is a *savarṇa*. Thus, it is more specific and wins, thereby leading to the correct form: *tavātmā*.

Example #4

Now, we will derive the genitive plural of the feminine form of ***tri*** **'three'**.

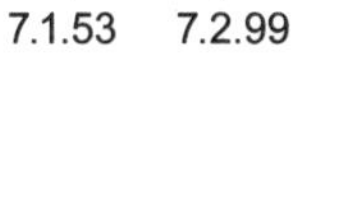

tri + *ām*

7.1.53 7.2.99

7.1.53 *tres trayaḥ* (*āmi*): the base *tri* is replaced with *traya* when *ām* follows.

7.2.99 *tricaturoḥ striyāṁ tisṛcatasṛ* (*vibhaktau*): *tri* and *catur* are replaced with *tisṛ* and *catasṛ*, respectively, in the feminine when a declensional affix follows.

7.1.53:

tri* + *ām

7.2.99:

tri* (feminine) + *ām

tri (feminine) + any other declensional affix

catur (feminine) + any declensional affix

I have written the conditions that are relevant to the conflict in bold. 7.2.99 is applicable only to the feminine *tri* base, whereas 7.1.53 is applicable to the base in all genders. 7.2.99 is more specific and thus wins, thereby giving us the correct form: *tisṛṇām*.

Note that in the four examples above, (1), (3), and (4) are similar to one another and different from (2).

In (1), (3), and (4), the two conditions (in bold) involved in the SOI are not exactly the same. One operation is conditioned by a specification ('plural' in example 1, '*savarṇa*' in example 2, and 'feminine' in example 4), while the other is not. The operation conditioned by the specification wins.

On the other hand, in the case of example (2), the conditions highlighted in bold are exactly the same, and thus we have to go a step further and compare the two rules themselves.

As stated earlier, we will call examples 1, 3, and 4, SOI-L and example 2, SOI-M. SOI-L can be resolved at the first step of comparison: the conditions highlighted in bold are not exactly the same, and so the one that has a specific restriction or marker (e.g., plural) wins. The choice of the winning rule can be made at the first step of comparison itself, that is, by comparing conditions. The other identifying feature of SOI-L is that one rule is not clearly a subset of the other.

On the other hand, SOI-M cases are defined as those where the conditions highlighted in bold are exactly the same, so we cannot decide which one is more specific. We need to go a step further and compare the two rules themselves to determine the winning rule. In case of SOI-M, we find that one rule is clearly a subset of the other.

It is noteworthy that scholars like Pataskar, Cardona, Joshi, and Roodbergen have made important contributions to the topic of conflicts between general and specific rules through various publications. While I do not entirely agree with their approaches and conclusions, I think they were thinking along the same lines as I do in this book and deserve credit for the same.

Example #5

Now, let us look at the *sandhi*-related step of the derivation of the compound ***bhānūdaya* 'sunrise'**:

bhānu + udaya

Here, the following two rules are applicable:

6.1.77 *iko yaṇ aci*: *iK* (*i, u, ṛ, ḷ*) is replaced with *yaṆ* (*y, v, r, l*) when *aC* (any vowel) follows.

6.1.101 *akaḥ savarṇe dīrghaḥ* (*aci*): a long vowel replaces both *aK* (*a, i, u, ṛ, ḷ*) and the following *savarṇa* 'homogeneous' vowel.

However, the problem is that they do not have exactly the same operand. Here, I use round brackets to indicate the operand of 6.1.77 and square brackets to indicate the operand of 6.1.101:

bhān[(*u*) + *u*]*daya*

The operand of 6.1.77 is inside the operand of 6.1.101. How do we solve such an example? I propose that we treat *u* + *u* as the operand of both rules. This means that we have to reanalyse rule 6.1.77: instead of saying that *iK* is replaced with *yaṆ* when *aC* follows, we say that *iK* + *aC* is replaced with *yaṆ* + *aC*.[41]

Now that both rules have the same operand, we can choose the rule that is more specific.

6.1.77:

***u* + vowel**

i / *ṛ* / *ḷ* + vowel

6.1.101

***u* + vowel (*savarṇa*)**

a / *i* / *ṛ* / *ḷ* + vowel (*savarṇa*)

I have written the conditions that are relevant to the conflict in bold. 6.1.101 is applicable only when the following vowel is a *savarṇa*. This is a case of SOI-L. 6.1.101 is more specific and thus wins, leading to the correct form: *bhānūdaya*.

Example #6. ***vana*** **+** ***sU*****—'forest' (neuter), nominative singular**

vana + *sU*

7.1.23 7.1.24

7.1.23 *svamor napuṁsakāt* (*luk*): affixes *sU* and *am* occurring after a neuter base are replaced with *LUK.*

7.1.24 *ato'm* (*svamor napuṁsakāt*): affixes *sU* and *am* occurring after a neuter base **ending in *a*** are replaced with *am.*

7.1.23

a **(neuter) +** ***sU / am***

any other sound (neuter) + *sU / am*

7.1.24

a **(neuter) +** ***sU / am***

The conditions in bold are exactly the same. This is a case of SOI-M. Thus, we now compare the rules. Both rules are meant for *sU* and *am* affixes added to neuter bases, but 7.1.24 is specifically meant for those cases in which *sU* and *am* are preceded by a base ending in *a.* 7.1.24 is more specific and thus wins, leading to the correct form: *vanam.*

On 7.1.24, the *Kāśikā* says that 7.1.24 is an *apavāda* of, and thus wins against, 7.1.23.

Example #7. ***yuṣmad*** **+** ***bhyas*****—'you' (any gender), ablative plural**

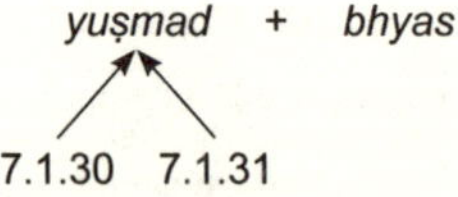

7.1.30 *bhyaso bhyam* (*yuṣmadasmadbhyām*): the affix *bhyas,* which occurs after the bases *yuṣmad* and *asmad* is replaced with *bhyam.*

7.1.31 *pañcamyā at* (*yuṣmadasmadbhyām bhyaso*): the **ablative** affix *bhyas,* which occurs after the bases *yuṣmad* and *asmad* is replaced with *at.*

7.1.30

yuṣmad / asmad **+** ***bhyas***

7.1.31

yuṣmad / asmad **+** ***bhyas*** **(ablative)**

Note that *bhyas* is a plural affix used for both dative and ablative forms. 7.1.31 is specifically about the ablative *bhyas*. This is a case of SOI-L. 7.1.73 is more specific because it mentions the ablative, and thus wins, leading to the correct form: *yuṣmat*.

On 7.1.31, the *Nyāsa* says that 7.1.31 is an *apavāda* of, and thus wins against, 7.1.30.

Example #8. *eka* + *Ṅe*—'one' (masculine), dative singular

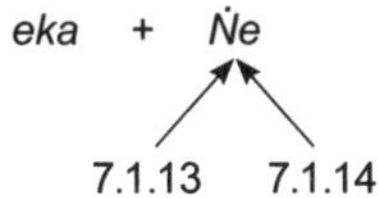

7.1.13 *ṅer yaḥ* (*ataḥ*): the affix *Ṅe*, when occurring after a base ending in *a*, is replaced with *ya*.

7.1.14 *sarvanāmnaḥ smai* (*ṅer yaḥ ataḥ*)[42]: the affix *Ṅe*, when occurring after a **pronominal** base ending in *a*, is replaced with *smai*.

7.1.13

a* + *Ṅe

7.1.14

a* (pronoun) + *Ṅe

This is a case of SOI-L. 7.1.14 concerns only pronominal bases. Thus, it is more specific and wins, leading to the correct form: *ekasmai*.

Example #9. *hari* + *au*—'green' (masculine) nominative dual

hari + *au*

The two rules that are applicable here are:

6.1.77 *iko yaṇ aci*: *iK* (*i*, *u*, *ṛ*, *ḷ*) is replaced with *yaṆ* (*y*, *v*, *r*, *l*) when *aC* (vowel) follows.

6.1.102 *prathamayoḥ pūrvasavarṇaḥ* (*aci akaḥ dīrghaḥ*): *aK* (*a*, *i*, *u*, *ṛ*, *ḷ*) and the following vowel, which constitutes the first sound of nominative and accusative affixes, are both replaced with a long vowel that is homogeneous with the sound on the left-hand side.

Note that, here too, like in example 5 of this section, the operand of one rule is inside the operand of another. We overcome this problem just as we did in example 5.

6.1.77

***i / u / ṛ / ḷ* + any vowel**

6.1.102

a + any vowel (nominative/accusative)

***i / u / ṛ / ḷ* + any vowel (nominative/accusative)**

This is a case of SOI-L. 6.1.102 is more specific and thus wins, leading to the correct form: *harī.*

Example #10. *vāri* + *Ṅi*—'water (neuter)' locative singular

Let us look at the rules that are applicable:

7.3.116 *ṅer ām nadyāmnībhyaḥ*

7.3.117 *idudbhyām*

7.3.118 *aut*

7.3.119 *ac ca gheḥ*

Kielhorn[43] shows that 7.3.117–7.3.119 together originally constituted one *sūtra*: *idudbhyām aud ac ca gheḥ.* Kātyāyana split it into two: *idudbhyām* and *aud ac ca gheh,* and Patañjali further split the latter into two: *aut* and *ac ca gheḥ.* I accept the original version taught by Pāṇini himself: 7.3.117 *idudbhyām aud ac ca gheḥ.*

Now, in *vāri* + *Ṅi,* two rules are applicable:

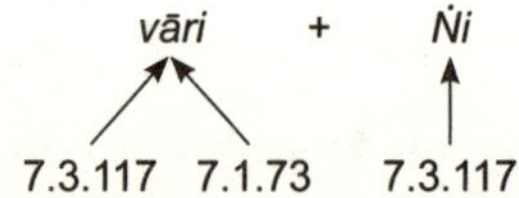

7.1.73 *iko'ci vibhaktau* (*num napuṁsakasya*): augment *nUM* is attached to a neuter *iK*-final (ending in *i, u, ṛ, ḷ*) base when a vowel-initial declensional affix follows.

7.3.117 *idudbhyām aut ac ca gheḥ* (*ṅer*): after *ghi* bases, *Ṅi* is replaced with *au*, and the final sound of the base is replaced with *a.*

Note that 7.3.117 is unusual because it teaches two operations together. We cannot treat this as a case of DOI, so we have to treat this as a case of SOI.

7.1.73 applies to:

i / u* (neuter) + *Ṅi

i / *u* (neuter) + other vowel initial affixes

r̥ / *l̥* (neuter) + vowel initial affixes

7.3.117 applies to:

i/u + ***Ṅi***

This is a case of SOI-L and the condition which is marked 'neuter' is more specific and thus wins, giving us the correct form *vāriṇi*.

The tradition uses the *vārttika*, *guṇavr̥ddhyauttvatr̥jvadbhāvebhyo num pūrvavipratiṣiddham* (vt. 10 on 7.1.96 *striyāṁ ca* [Mbh III.275.23]), to solve this conflict. This *vārttika* teaches that even though the rule teaching the attachment of the augment *nUM* (7.1.73) comes before the rule teaching *auttva* (7.3.117 *idudbhyām aud ac ca gheḥ*) in the serial order of the *Aṣṭādhyāyī*, the former wins.

CHAPTER THREE

Examples of Derived-Base Inflection

In the previous chapter, we have looked at conflicts that arise in the step-by-step derivation of nonderived nominal bases. In this chapter, we will examine another category: conflicts involving the inflection of derived bases such as *taddhita*, *samāsa*, and *kr̥danta*.

3.1 DOI in the Inflection of *Taddhita, Samāsa*, and *Kr̥danta* Nominal Bases

So far, we have looked at cases of DOI in the inflection of simple (i.e., underived) nominal bases (cf. 1.2.45 *arthavad adhātur apratyayaḥ prātipadikam*). Now, let us look at some cases of DOI in the inflection of complex (i.e., derived) nominal bases such as *kr̥t* 'primary derivative', *taddhita* 'secondary derivative', and *samāsa* 'compound' (cf. 1.2.46 *kr̥ttaddhitasamāsāś ca*).

Generally speaking, as compared to the inflection of simple nominal bases, which we have seen in the previous chapter and in this chapter, and verbal inflection and primary derivatives, which we will see in the following chapters, we find a smaller number of examples of conflict in *taddhita* derivations, and even fewer examples in *samāsa* derivations. I will explain why this is the case in the beginning of chapter 5.

We will see that the tradition manages to avoid dealing with conflict in the first four examples. However, it has to rely on certain external (post-Pāṇinian) metarules to correctly derive these four forms. I will show that my solution for DOI (my interpretation of 1.4.2) can help us perform these derivations without relying on such external metarules. In the following four examples, we do find cases of conflict. Here too, I use my solution for DOI (cf. my interpretation of 1.4.2) to get the correct answer and also mention the traditional solution where it is known.

Example #1

Consider the genitive singular form of ***prati-ac***[1] 'turned towards, facing': ***pratīcas***. By 2.2.18 *kugatiprādayaḥ*, *prati-ac* is a *tatpuruṣa* compound made of *prati*, which takes the technical designation *gati* by 1.4.60 *gatiś ca* and *ac*, which is derived as follows: *añcU* + *KvIN* (3.2.59 *ṛtvigdadhṛksragdiguṣṇigañcuyujikruñcāṁ ca*[2]) → *ac* + *v* (6.4.24 *aniditāṁ hala upadhāyāḥ kṅiti*[3]) → *ac* (6.1.67 *ver apṛktasya*[4]).

The *Siddhāntakaumudī* (SK) completes all the operations within the base before adding the genitive singular affix *Ṅas*[5]: *prati-ac* (2.4.71 *supo dhātuprātipadikayoḥ*) → *pratyac* (6.1.77 *iko yaṇ aci*). If the derivation is stopped at the addition of the genitive affix *Ṅas* to *pratyac*, that does not give the correct answer: *pratyac* + *Ṅas* → **pratyacaḥ*.

The tradition has found a way to work around this. In *pratyac* + *Ṅas*, *pratyac* takes the designation *bha* by 1.4.18 because it is followed by a non-*sarvanāmasthāna* affix beginning with a vowel. Then, 6.4.138 *acaḥ* teaches that the *a* of verbal base *ac* (from *añc*), when designated as *bha*, is replaced with *LOPA*: *pratyc* + *Ṅas*. To get the correct form, it takes recourse to the metarule *nimittābhāve naimittikasyāpy abhāvaḥ*,[6] which teaches that when the cause of an operation is lost, the impact or effect of that operation too is lost. In other words, if X causes A to change to B, upon the deletion of X, B becomes A again. Thanks to this *paribhāṣā*, since the cause of the operation 6.1.77 *iko yaṇ aci*, namely *a*, has been deleted, the preceding *y* will go back to its original form *i*. Thus, we get *pratic* + *Ṅas*. At this step the tradition applies 6.3.138 *cau*, which teaches that the final *aṆ* of the preceding *pada* in a compound is replaced with its *dīrgha* equivalent when *c* (from *añc*) follows. This gives the correct form: *pratīcaḥ*.

Another Pāṇinian *paribhāṣā*, which makes this very argument in terms of *antaraṅga* and *bahiraṅga* operations, is cited by the *Siddhāntakaumudī*[7] when discussing this derivation: *akṛtavyūhāḥ pāṇinīyāḥ* 'The Pāṇinīyas do not insist that a rule should take effect if its causes disappear'. Nāgeśa (Pbh 56, *Paribhāṣenduśekhara*), while discussing this *paribhāṣā* in *antaraṅga* and *bahiraṅga* terms, says: *bahiraṅgeṇāntaraṅgasya nimittavināśe paścāt sambhāvite antaraṅgaṁ neti yāvat* 'An *antaraṅga* operation (here, 6.1.77 *iko yaṇ aci*) should not be undertaken if its cause would disappear later due to the *bahiraṅga* operation (here, 6.4.138 *acaḥ*)'.

These two *paribhāṣās* require one to go a step back into the derivation and undo a previous operation. This runs contrary to the idea that derivations should move in one direction, and that each operation should take us one step forward (rather than backward) into the derivation. Besides, if Pāṇini wanted us to use these metarules, he would have taught them explicitly in the *Aṣṭādhyāyī*. For these reasons, I do not accept these two *paribhāṣās*. Now, I will derive this form using my method. Two rules are simultaneously applicable to *prati - ac*:

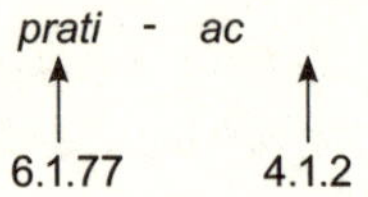

```
prati  -  ac
  ↑        ↑
6.1.77   4.1.2
```

4.1.2 *svaujasamauṭchaṣṭābhyāmbhisṅebhyāmbhyasṅasibhyāmbhyasṅasosāmṅyossup*[8]

6.1.77 *iko yaṇ aci*: *iK* (*i*, *u*, *ṛ*, *ḷ*) is replaced with *yaṆ* (*y*, *v*, *r*, *l*) when *aC* (vowel) follows.

This is a case of DOI. By my interpretation of 1.4.2, we apply the RHS rule 4.1.2 and get *prati - ac* + *Ṅas*. Here, two rules are applicable:

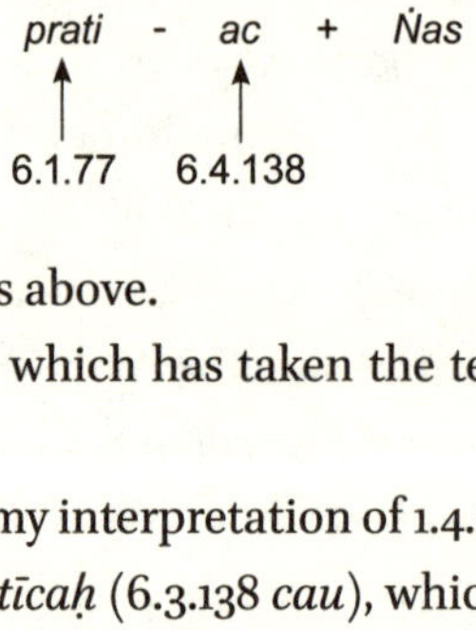

```
prati  -  ac  +  Ṅas
  ↑       ↑
6.1.77  6.4.138
```

6.1.77 *iko yaṇ aci*: same as above.

6.4.138 *acaḥ*: the *a* of *ac* which has taken the technical designation *bha* is replaced with *LOPA*.

This is a case of DOI. By my interpretation of 1.4.2, the RHS rule 6.4.138 wins, and we get: *praticaḥ* → *pratīcaḥ* (6.3.138 *cau*), which is the correct form.

Example #2

Let us derive the genitive singular of the perfect participle of ***sad*** 'to sit', namely ***sad*** + ***vas*** 'one who had sat'. The *Siddhāntakaumudī* attaches the declensional affix *Ṅas* to the base only after the base is fully ready.[9] The base is derived by replacing *LIṬ* with *KvasU*: *sad* + *LIṬ* → *sad* + *KvasU* (3.2.108 *bhāṣāyāṁ sadavasaśruvaḥ*[10]). Now, (i) by 6.1.8 *liṭi dhātor anabhyāsasya*, (which teaches that the unreduplicated root undergoes reduplication when followed by *LIṬ*), (ii) by 6.1.1 *ekāco dve prathamasya* (which teaches that the first syllable of the root undergoes reduplication), and (iii) by 1.1.56 *sthānivad ādeśo'nalvidhau* (which teaches that the substitute should be treated like the substituendum except when an operation relative to the original sound is to be performed), we get *sadsad* + *vas*. By 7.4.60 *halādiḥ śeṣaḥ*, which teaches that all but the first consonant of the *abhyāsa* (first half of *sadsad*) are deleted, we get *sasad* + *vas*. Now, by 6.4.120 *ata ekahalmadhye'nādeśāder liṭi*,[11] we get *sed* + *vas*. At this point, 7.2.67 *vasv ekājādghasām* is applicable, which, according to the tradition,[12] teaches that the augment *iṬ* should be attached to *vasU* when it occurs after a root that, after doubling, consists of a single syllable, or a root ending in *ā*, or *ghas* 'to eat'. By applying this rule, we get the base *sedivas*, but if at the next step we add the genitive singular affix *Ṅas*, we get **sedivasaḥ*, which is the incorrect answer.

Here, again, the tradition uses the two *paribhāṣās* discussed above to circumvent this problem. In *sedivas* + *Ṅas*, *sedivas* takes the designation *bha* because it is followed by a non-*sarvanāmasthāna* affix beginning with a vowel (cf. 1.4.18 *yaci bham*). To this, the tradition applies 6.4.131 *vasoḥ samprasāraṇam*, which teaches that the semivowel of the affix *vasU* in an item termed *bha* is replaced with the corresponding vowel *u*. This gives *sediuas*, and the augment *i* in *sedivas*, which is attached to *vas* by 7.2.67 *vasv ekājādghasām*, is lost because its cause *v* no longer exists (cf. *akr̥tavyūhāḥ pāṇinīyāḥ* and *nimittāpāye naimittikasyāpy apāyaḥ*). Then, the *a* of *seduas* is deleted by 6.1.108 *samprasāraṇāc ca*, which teaches that both the *samprasāraṇa* replacement and the vowel following it are together replaced with the former. This gives us *sedus* + *Ṅas* → *seduṣaḥ*, which is the correct form.

Again, like in the previous example, I reject the use of these two *anitya paribhāṣās*. I perform this derivation as follows. I add the affix *LIṬ* to *sad* by the following rule:

3.2.115 *parokṣe liṭ*: affix *LIṬ* occurs after a verbal root when an unwitnessed (*parokṣa*) action which is not current (*anadyatana*) is denoted in the past (*bhūta*).

Then, the following rules become applicable:

sad + *LIṬ*
↑ ↑
6.1.8 3.2.108

6.1.8 *liṭi dhātor anabhyāsasya*: an unreduplicated root undergoes reduplication when followed by *LIṬ*.[13]

3.2.108 *bhāṣāyāṁ sadavasaśruvaḥ*: the affix *LIṬ* is optionally replaced with *KvasU* in classical Sanskrit after the roots *sadA* 'to sit', *vasA* 'to inhabit' and *śru* 'to listen' when the action has taken place in the past.

This is a case of DOI. By my interpretation of 1.4.2, the RHS rule 3.2.108 wins and we get *sad* + *vas*. Multiple rules are applicable here:

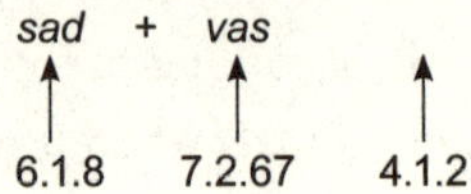

6.1.8 *liṭi dhātor anabhyāsasya*: same as above.

7.2.67 *vasv ekājādghasām*: (my interpretation) augment *iṬ* is introduced to *vasU* when it occurs after a root which either consists of a single syllable, or ends in *a*, or else, is constituted by *ghas* 'to eat'.[14]

4.1.2 *svaujasamauṭchaṣṭābhyāmbhisṅebhyāmbhyasṅasibhyāmbhyasṅaso-sāmṅyossup*[15]

This is a case of DOI. By my interpretation of 1.4.2, the right-most rule 4.1.2 wins and we get *sad* + *vas* + *Ṅas*. Multiple rules are applicable here:

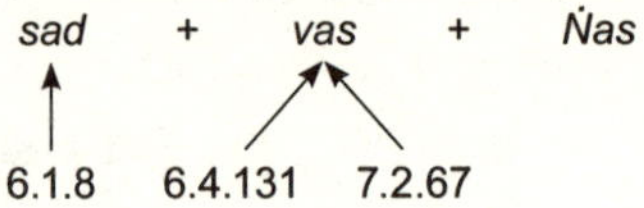

6.1.8 *liṭi dhātor anabhyāsasya*: same as above.

7.2.67 *vasv ekājādghasām*: same as above.

6.4.131 *vasoḥ samprasāraṇam*: *vasU* of an item termed *bha* undergoes *samprasāraṇa.*[16]

There is an SOI between 6.4.131 and 7.2.67. Let us find out which rule is more specific.

6.4.131:

monosyllabic root / *ākārānta* root / *ghas* + *vas* (termed *bha*)

other bases + *vas* (termed *bha*)

7.2.67

monosyllabic root / *ākārānta* root / *ghas* + *vas*

The conditions highlighted in bold are relevant to this SOI. Since 6.4.131 has been taught specifically for a *bha-saṁjñaka vas*, it is more specific and thus wins.

Now, let us consider the DOI relationship between 6.1.8 and 6.4.131. By my interpretation of 1.4.2, the RHS rule 6.4.131 wins and we get: *sad* + *uas* + *Ṅas*. Here, again, two rules are applicable:

6.1.8 *liṭi dhātor anabhyāsasya*: same as above.

6.1.108 *samprasāraṇāc ca*: both the *samprasāraṇa* replacement and the vowel following it are together replaced with the former.

This is a case of DOI. By my interpretation of 1.4.2, the RHS rule 6.1.108 wins and we get *sad* + *us* + *Ṅas*. Thereafter, the derivation proceeds as follows: *sadsad* + *us* + *Ṅas* (6.1.8 *liṭi dhātor anabhyāsasya*) → *seduṣaḥ* (6.4.120 *ata ekahalmadhye'nādeśāder liṭi*), which is the correct form.

Example #3

Let us derive the nominative plural of 'descendant of ***garga***', first through the traditional method and then through mine. The tradition[17] adds the declensional affix only after the base is ready. As per the traditional method, we first add the affix *yaÑ* to *garga* + *Ṅas* by 4.1.105 *gargādibhyo yañ*[18]; then by 2.4.71 *supo dhātuprātipadikayoḥ*[19], *Ṅas* is deleted, which gives us *garga* + *yaÑ*. At this juncture, 7.2.117 *taddhiteṣv acām ādeḥ* prescribes the *vr̥ddhi* substitution of the first vowel of *garga* given that the following affix is marked with *Ñ*. Thus, we get *gārga* + *yaÑ*. The *a* of *gārga* is deleted by 6.4.148 *yasyeti ca*, which teaches that the final *i* or *a* of a *bha* item is deleted when it is followed by *ī* or a *taddhita* affix. Thus, we get our base *gārgya*.

At this point, the tradition prescribes the addition of the affix *Jas* to the base *gārgya*: *gārgya* + *Jas*. This leads to the application of 2.4.64 *yañaños ca*, which teaches that the *gotra* affixes *yaÑ* and *aÑ* are replaced with *LUK* when the following declensional affix denotes plural, except when the base is feminine. Stopping here gives us the incorrect form: *gārgaḥ*.

On 2.4.64, the *Bhaimī* commentary on the *Laghusiddhāntakaumudī* suggests the metarule, *nimittāpāye naimittikasyāpy apāyaḥ*, which we have discussed in the previous two examples, to solve this problem: because *yaÑ* is deleted, the *vr̥ddhi* of the first vowel (cf. 7.2.117) and the deletion of the final *a* (6.4.148), which were caused by *yaÑ*, also must be undone, thereby giving us the correct form: *garga* + *Jas* → *gargāḥ*. However, I do not accept this metarule, as stated above. I perform this derivation as follows. Upon adding the affix *yaÑ* to *garga*, the following rules are applicable:

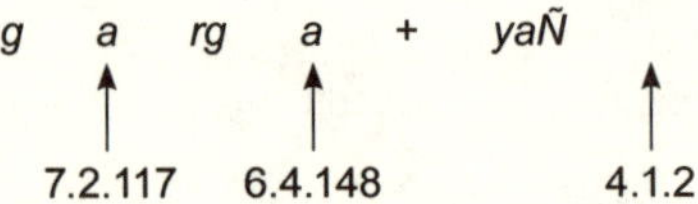

7.2.117 *taddhiteṣv acām ādeḥ*: the first vowel of the base undergoes *vṛddhi* when an affix marked with *Ñ* or *Ṇ* follows in *taddhita* derivations.

6.4.148 *yasyeti ca*: the final *i* or *a* of a *bha* item is deleted when it is followed by *ī* or a *taddhita* affix.

4.1.2 *svaujasamauṭchaṣṭābhyāmbhisṅebhyāmbhyasṅasibhyāmbhyasṅasosāmṅyossup*

This is a case of DOI. By my interpretation of 1.4.2, the right-most rule 4.1.2 applies and we get *gargya* + *yaÑ* + *Jas*. Here, multiple rules are applicable:

[g a rg a + yaÑ] + Jas

7.2.117 6.4.148 2.4.64

7.2.117 *taddhiteṣv acām ādeḥ*: same as above.

6.4.148 *yasyeti ca*: same as above.

2.4.64 *yañañoś ca*: *LUK* replaces the *gotra* affixes *yaÑ* and *aÑ* introduced after a nominal stem when that nominal stem ending in these affixes itself denotes plurality and is not followed by a feminine affix.

This is a case of DOI. By my interpretation of 1.4.2, we apply the right-most rule 2.4.64 and get: *garga* + *Jas* → *gargāḥ* (6.1.102 *prathamayoḥ pūrvasavarṇaḥ*[20]), which is the correct form.

Note that, at this point, 7.2.117 and 6.4.148 no longer have a chance to apply. So, unlike the traditional solution, mine does not require us to go backwards to undo the application of rules like 7.2.117 and 6.4.148. Therefore, my solution is more acceptable than the one provided by the tradition.

Example #4

Now, let us derive the nominative plural of 'a *kṣatriya* descendent of the country of the ***pañcālas***' first through the traditional method, and then through mine.

The tradition first derives the base and then adds the declensional affix at the end. Consider the following rule:

4.1.168 *janapadaśabdāt kṣatriyād añ*: the *taddhita* affix *aÑ* is added to a syntactically related base ending in the genitive which stands for both a *janapada* and its class of *kṣatriyas*, in order to denote the sense of *apatya* 'descendent'.

The tradition[21] starts by adding the affix *aÑ* to *pañcāla* + *ām* by 4.1.168: [*pañcāla* + *ām*] + *aÑ*. *ām* is deleted by 2.4.71 *supo dhātuprātipadikayoḥ*. At this juncture, 7.2.117 *taddhiteṣv acām ādeḥ* teaches that the first vowel of *pañcāla* undergoes *vṛddhi* given that the following affix is marked with *Ñ*. Upon applying this rule, we get: *pāñcāla* + *aÑ*. The *a* of *pāñcāla* is deleted by 6.4.148, which teaches that the final *i* or *a* of a *bha* item is deleted when it is followed by *ī* or a *taddhita* affix. Thus, we get our base *pāñcāla*.

At this point, the tradition prescribes the addition of the affix *Jas* to the base *pāñcāla*: *pāñcāla* + *Jas*. By 4.1.174 *te tadrājāḥ*, the *taddhita* affixes, including *aÑ*, which occur after a syntactically related genitive to indicate a '*kṣatriya* descendent of the *kṣatriyas* of a *janapada*' take the technical designation *tadrāja*. Thus, 2.4.62 *tadrājasya bahuṣu tenaivāstriyām* becomes applicable here: it teaches that *LUK* replaces a *tadrāja* affix introduced after a nominal stem when it denotes plurality if that plurality is expressed by the stem ending in that affix except when followed by a feminine affix.

If the derivation stops here, we get *pāñcāl* + *Jas* → **pāñcālaḥ*, which is not the correct answer. On 2.4.62, the *Bhaimī* commentary on the *Laghusiddhāntakaumudī* suggests the metarule *nimittāpāye naimittikasyāpy apāyaḥ*, which we have discussed above, to solve this problem: because *aÑ* is deleted, the *vṛddhi* of the first vowel (cf. 7.2.117) and the deletion of the final *a* (6.4.148), which were caused by *aÑ*, also must be undone, thereby giving us the correct form: *pañcāla* + *Jas* → *pañcālāḥ*. However, I do not accept this metarule, as stated above. I perform this derivation as follows.

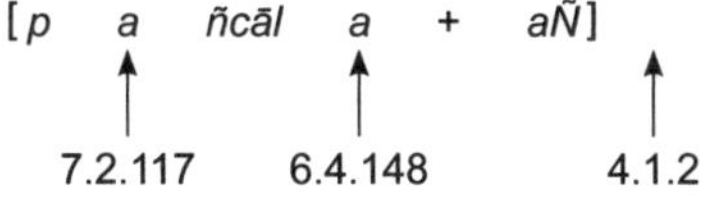

7.2.117 *taddhiteṣv acām ādeḥ*: same as above.

6.4.148 *yasyeti ca*: same as above.

4.1.2 *svaujasamauṭchaṣṭābhyāmbhisṅebhyāmbhyasṅasibhyāmbhyasṅasosāmṅyossup*

This is a case of DOI. By my interpretation of 1.4.2, the right-most rule 4.1.2 applies and we get *pañcāla* + *aÑ* + *Jas*. Here, multiple rules are applicable:

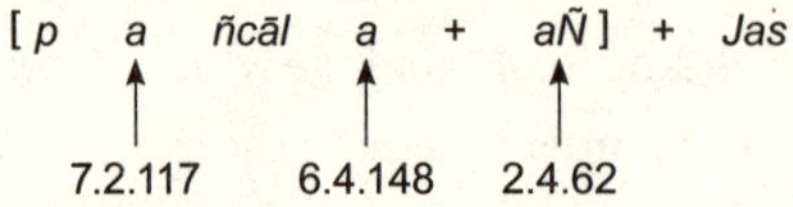

[*p* *a* *ñcāl* *a* + *aÑ*] + *Jas*
↑ 7.2.117 ↑ 6.4.148 ↑ 2.4.62

7.2.117 *taddhiteṣv acām ādeḥ*: same as above.

6.4.148 *yasyeti ca*: same as above.

2.4.62 *tadrājasya bahuṣu tenaivāstriyām*: same as above.

This is a case of DOI. By my interpretation of 1.4.2, the right-most rule 2.4.62 wins and we get: *pañcāla* + *Jas* → *pañcālāḥ* (6.1.102 *prathamayoḥ pūrvasavarṇaḥ*) which is the correct form. As in the previous example, at this point 7.2.117 and 6.4.148 can no longer apply. This shows that my solution is better than the traditional one.

Example #5

Now, let us derive the nominative plural of 'the student of ***gārgya***', or in other words, the 'student of the descendent of ***garga***'. To derive this form, *cha* is added to [*gārgya* + *Ṅas*] by the following rule:

4.2.114 *vṛddhāt chaḥ*: affix *cha* is added to a syntactically related item termed *vṛddha* (cf. 1.1.73 *vṛddhir yasyācām ādis tad vṛddham*) in the remaining senses.

In *gārgya* + *Ṅas* + *cha*, *Ṅas* is deleted by 2.4.71 *supo dhātuprātipadikayoḥ* and we get *gārgya* + *cha*.[22] Let us look at my solution first. I will only highlight the cases of conflict here. The following rules are applicable:

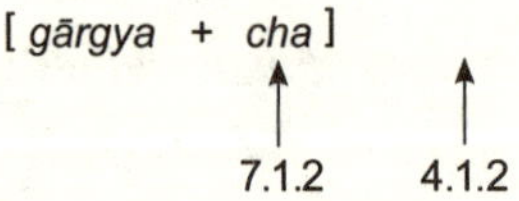

[*gārgya* + *cha*]
↑ 7.1.2 ↑ 4.1.2

7.1.2 *āyaneyīnīyiyaḥ phaḍhakhacchaghāṁ pratyayādīnām*: the sounds *ph, ḍh, kh, ch* and *gh*, when occurring at the beginning of the affix, are replaced with *āyan, ey, īn, īy* and *iy*, respectively.

4.1.2 *svaujasamauṭchaṣṭābhyāmbhisṅebhyāmbhyasṅasibhyāmbhyasṅasosāmṅyossup*

The two rules do not block each other.

By my interpretation of 1.4.2, we apply the RHS rule 4.1.2 and get: *gārgya* + *cha* + *Jas*. Here, multiple rules are applicable:

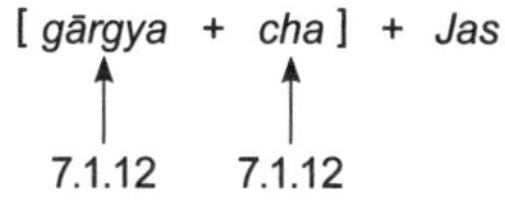

```
[ gārgya  +  cha ]  +  Jas
     ↑          ↑
     |          |
  7.1.12     7.1.12
```

7.1.2 *āyaneyīnīyiyaḥ phaḍhakhacchaghāṁ pratyayādīnām*: same as above.

2.4.64 *yañañoś ca*: *LUK* replaces the *gotra* affixes *yaÑ* and *aÑ* introduced after a nominal stem when that nominal stem ending in these affixes itself denotes plurality and is not followed by a feminine affix.

If we apply 2.4.64 at this step, 7.1.2 will be applicable at the following step. If we apply 7.1.2 at this step, thereby replacing *ch* of *cha* with *īy* (which gives us *gārgya* + *īya*), then 4.1.89 *gotre'lug aci* comes into play:

4.1.89 *gotre'lug aci*: *LUK* does not replace a *taddhita* affix denoting a *gotra* descendant, when the following affix begins with a vowel and is introduced in the *prāgdīvyatīya* section.[23]

Therefore, 2.4.64, which teaches *LUK*, will not be applicable at the following step. 7.1.2 blocks 2.4.64. This is a case of unidirectional blocking, and thus of Type 2a (DOI conflict).

By my interpretation of 1.4.2, the RHS rule 7.1.2 wins, and we get *gārgya* + *īya* + *Jas*. Here by applying 6.4.148 *yasyeti ca*, we get *gārgy* + *īya* + *Jas*. At this stage, 6.4.151 *āpatyasya ca taddhite'nāti* applies: a *y* that occurs after a consonant and is part of a *taddhita affix* signifying an *apatya* 'offspring', which is in turn part of an item termed *bha*, is replaced with *LOPA* when a *taddhita* affix not beginning with *a* follows.

This gives us the correct form: *gārgīyāḥ*.

Even though Patañjali does discuss this derivation in his commentary on vt. 2 (Mbh II.240.14) on 4.1.89 *gotre'lug aci*, he does not discuss this conflict.[24]

Example #6

Let us now derive the nominative singular of ***puṣya*** 'a moon (that is) in conjunction with the constellation ***puṣya***' of the sentence ***adya puṣyaḥ*** 'today the moon is in conjunction with the constellation ***puṣya***'.

We start by adding the affix *aṆ* to *puṣya* + *Ṭā* by 4.2.3:

4.2.3 *nakṣatreṇa yuktaḥ kālaḥ*: the *taddhita* affix *aṆ* is introduced after a nominal form that signifies a particular constellation (*nakṣatra*) and ends in *tr̥tīyā* 'instrumental', to denote the time when the moon is in conjunction with that constellation.

By 2.4.71 *supo dhātuprātipadikayoḥ*, *Ṭā* is deleted, leading to *puṣya* + *aṆ*. Here, the following rules are applicable:

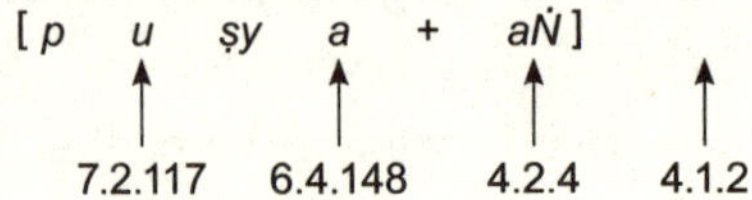

7.2.117 *taddhiteṣv acām ādeḥ*: same as above.

6.4.148 *yasyeti ca*: same as above.

4.2.4 *lub aviśeṣe*: a *taddhita* affix introduced after a nominal stem ending in *tr̥tīyā* and denoting a constellation is replaced with *LUP* when the time of conjunction is not qualified with specifications.[25]

4.1.2 *svaujasamauṭchaṣṭābhyāmbhisṅebhyāmbhyasṅasibhyāmbhyasṅaso-sāmṅyossup*

Let us look at the relationship of 4.2.4 with the two rules 6.4.148 and 7.2.117. If we apply 4.2.4 at this step, thereby deleting the affix that triggers rules 7.2.117 and 6.4.148, neither of these two rules will be applicable at the following step. However, if we apply any of these two rules at this step, 4.2.4 will still be applicable at the following step. So, 4.2.4 unidirectionally blocks 6.4.148 and 7.2.117 and is thus in conflict with both of them.

By my interpretation of 1.4.2, the right-most rule 4.1.2 applies and we get *puṣya* + *aṆ* + *sU*. Here, multiple rules are applicable:

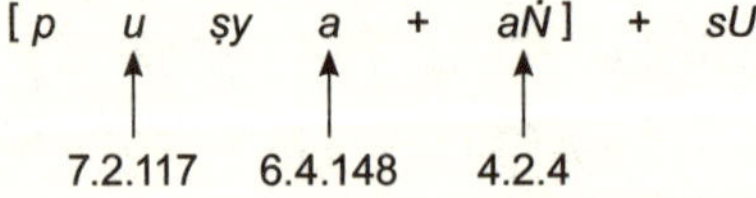

By my interpretation of 1.4.2, the right-most rule 4.2.4 applies, and we get: *puṣya* + *sU* → *puṣyaḥ*, which is the correct form.

The *Bhaimī* commentary on the *Laghusiddhāntakaumudī* does not mention this conflict. However, after applying 4.2.4 at this step, it does say that by 1.1.63 *na lumatāṅgasya*, 7.2.117 and 6.4.148 fail to apply at the following step.

Example #7

Let us now derive the nominative singular form of 'fifth'.

We add *ḌaṬ* to *pañcan* + *Ṅas* by the following rule:

5.2.48 *tasya pūraṇe ḍaṭ*: the *taddhita* affix *ḌaṬ* occurs to denote the sense of *pūraṇa* 'that by which something is brought to completion, ordinal number' after a syntactically related nominal stem that signifies number and ends in *ṣaṣṭhī* 'genitive'.

In *pañcan* + *Ṅas* + *ḌaṬ*, *Ṅas* is deleted by 2.4.71 *supo dhātuprātipadikayoḥ*, so we get *pañcan* + *ḌaṬ*. Thereafter, the following rules become applicable:

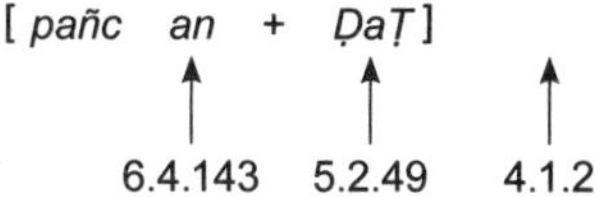

6.4.143 *ṭeḥ*: the *ṭi* (cf. 1.1.64 *aco'ntyādi ṭi*) of an item termed *bha* is replaced with *LOPA* when an affix marked with *Ḍ* follows.

5.2.49 *nāntād asaṁkhyāder maṭ*: the augment *mAṬ* is attached to the *taddhita* affix *ḌaṬ* when used to denote its ordinal, after a *n*-final nominal stem that ends in *ṣaṣṭhī* 'genitive' and does not have a number as its initial constituent.

4.1.2 *svaujasamauṭchaṣṭābhyāmbhisṅebhyāmbhyasṅasibhyāmbhyasṅasosāmṅyossup*

4.1.2 neither blocks nor is blocked by the other two rules.

Now, let us look at the relationship between 5.2.49 and 6.4.143. If we apply 5.2.49 at this step, then *ḌaṬ* will take the augment *mAṬ*. As a result, it will begin with a consonant. This implies that *pañcan* is no longer followed by an affix beginning with a vowel or *y*, and therefore it cannot be called *bha*. Thus, 6.4.143, which applies only to items termed *bha*, will not be applicable to *an* at the following step.

If we apply 6.4.143 at this step, *an* gets deleted, so *ḌaṬ* will no longer be preceded by an item ending in *n*. Therefore, 5.2.49 will not be applicable at the following step.

Both rules block each other. This is a case of mutual blocking and of Type 2a (DOI conflict).

By my interpretation of 1.4.2, we apply the right-most rule 4.1.2 and get *pañcan* + *ḌaṬ* + *sU*. Here, two rules are applicable:

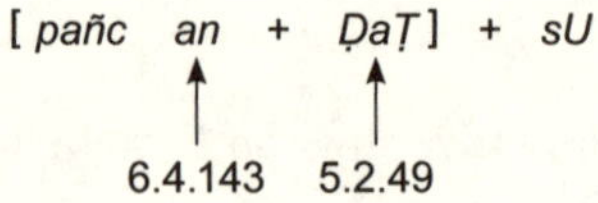

[*pañc* *an* + *ḌaṬ*] + *sU*
6.4.143 5.2.49

6.4.143 *ṭeḥ*: same as above.

5.2.49 *nāntād asaṁkhyāder maṭ*: same as above.

This is a case of DOI. By my interpretation of 1.4.2, we apply the RHS rule 5.2.49 and get: *pañcan* + *ma* + *sU*. By 1.4.17 *svādiṣv asarvanāmasthāne,*[26] *pañcan* takes the technical designation *pada*, and so by 8.2.7 *nalopaḥ prātipadikāntasya*, the *n* of *pañcan* gets deleted. Thus, we get the correct form: *pañcamaḥ*.

On 5.2.49, *Nyāsa* says that 5.2.49 is *antaraṅga* with respect to 6.4.143 and thus wins.

3.2 SOI in *Taddhita* Derivations

The cases of SOI, which we find in *samāsa* derivations, are few and fairly simple. I will not be discussing them in this book. In *taddhita* derivations, we come across examples of SOI between rules teaching affixation. Consider the derivation of *autsa* 'male offspring of *utsa*' (cf. 4.1.92 *tasyāpatyam* 'his offspring'). Three rules teach the addition of three different affixes:

4.1.83 *prāg dīvyato'ṇ*: the *taddhita* affix *aṆ* is added to denote senses taught in rules from here up to 4.4.2 *tena dīvyati khanati jayati jitam*.

4.1.86 *utsādibhyo'ñ*: the *taddhita* affix *aÑ* is added to denote senses taught in rules from here up to 4.4.2 *tena dīvyati khanati jayati jitam* after forms of stem belonging to the list headed by *utsa*.

4.1.95 *ata iñ*: the *taddhita* affix *iÑ* is added to denote 'his offspring' after forms of nominal stems ending in *a*.

Now, let us write down the conditions in which these rules apply. Remember that, as always, we write the sounds outside brackets and their characteristics inside brackets.

4.1.83

-ending in *a*

-ending in any other sound

4.1.86

-ending in *a* (*utsādi* class)

-ending in any other sound (*utsādi* class)

4.1.95
-ending in *a*

Upon comparing the conditions written in bold, we see that 4.1.86 is more specific than the other two rules, on account of the condition '*utsādi* class'. We get the correct form: [*utsa* + *Ṅas*] + *aÑ* → *autsa* 'offspring of *utsa*' (2.4.71 *supo dhātuprātipadikayoḥ*, 7.2.117 *taddhiteṣv acām ādeḥ*, 6.4.148 *yasyeti ca*).

On 4.1.86, the *Kāśikā* says *aṇas tadapavādānāṁ ca bādhakaḥ*, implying that this rule is an exception of both 4.1.83 and exceptions of 4.1.83 such as 4.1.95.

The other examples in the *taddhita* section are quite similar to this one, so we shall not look at them.[27]

This brings us to the end of this chapter and also to the end of our study of examples of conflict from *sandhi, subanta, taddhita*, and *samāsa* derivations. In the following chapter, we shall look at examples from *tiṅanta* and *kṛdanta* derivations.

CHAPTER FOUR

Examples of Finite Verbs and Primary Derivatives

Before I examine examples of rule interaction at the same step in *tiṄ* and *kr̥t* derivations, I will examine rules 6.4.1 *aṅgasya* and 1.4.13 *yasmāt pratyayavidhis tadādi pratyaye'ṅgam*, which play a pivotal role in running Pāṇini's grammatical machine.

4.1 *Aṅgādhikāra*

6.4.1 *aṅgasya* is an *adhikāra* (heading) *sūtra*, the jurisdiction of which continues all the way up to the end of 7.4. Pāṇini defines the term *aṅga* in 1.4.13 *yasmāt pratyayavidhis tadādi pratyaye'ṅgam*. Sharma translates this as follows: 'a form beginning with that after which an affix is introduced is termed *aṅga* when the affix follows'.

I think that the tradition has not correctly understood these rules, as a result of which it faces multiple problems in performing certain derivations. In this section, I will present my interpretations of these rules and show how my interpretations enable us to perform these derivations correctly.

In my opinion, only one item can be called an *aṅga* with respect to a certain *pratyaya* in a derivation. Let me discuss an example from verbal inflection to explain what I mean. Consider the derivation of the present-tense third-person singular form of *cit* 'to think': *cit* + *LAṬ* (3.2.123 *vartamāne laṭ*[1]) → *cit* + *tiP* (3.4.77 *lasya*, 3.4.78 *tiptasjhi . . .*[2]). According to the tradition,[3] *cit* is an *aṅga* with respect to *tiP*. Then, after we add the *vikaraṇa ŚaP* by 3.1.68 *kartari śap*,[4] we get *cit* + *ŚaP* + *tiP*. According to the tradition, *cit* + *ŚaP* too is an *aṅga* with respect to *tiP*. Thereafter, we apply 7.3.86 *pugantalaghūpadhasya ca*[5] to *cit* and get *cet* + *ŚaP* + *tiP*, that is, *ceta* + *tiP*. According to the tradition, *ceta* too can be called an *aṅga* with respect to *tiP.*

So, *cit, cit* + *ŚaP*, and *ceta* can all be called *aṅga* with respect to *tiP*, in the tradition's opinion. I disagree with the traditional perspective: in my opinion, we can have only one *aṅga* per affix per derivation.[6] So, which one of the three options, namely *cit, cit* + *ŚaP*, and *ceta*, should be called an *aṅga* with respect to *tiP*? I think *ceta* alone can be called an *aṅga* with respect to *tiP*.

Let us consider all three possibilities, namely *cit, cit* + *ŚaP*, and *ceta*. Let us first look at *cit*. If Pāṇini wanted us to treat *cit* as an *aṅga* with respect to *tiP*, he could have simply said *yasmāt pratyayavidhis tad pratyaye'ṅgam* 'a form after which an affix is introduced is termed *aṅga* when the affix follows'. Thus, I do not think that we should call *cit* an *aṅga* with respect to *tiP*. This leaves us with two options: *cit* + *ŚaP* and *ceta*. Let us closely consider 1.4.13 in the context of this derivation to decide which of the two should be called an *aṅga* with respect to *tiP*.

yasmāt—to (lit. after) *cit*
pratyayavidhis—(upon the) addition of *tiP*
tadādi—that which begins with *cit*
pratyaye—when *tiP* follows
aṅgam—(is called) *aṅga*.

'Upon the addition of *tiP* to *cit*, that which begins with *cit* is called *aṅga* when *tiP* follows'.

The form that begins with *cit* is an *aṅga* with respect to *tiP*. Can we say that *cit* + *ŚaP* begins with *cit*? I do not think so. I think *cit* + *ŚaP* is still just a string of two separate items, namely the root *cit* and the *vikaraṇa* affix *ŚaP*. Only when they are fused into a single form that begins with *cit*, that form can be called an *aṅga* with respect to *tiP*. When can we fuse *cit* and *ŚaP* into a single form? I think we can do that after applying all possible rules to *cit* and *ŚaP*, except those that are triggered by *tiP*.

So here, we apply 7.3.86 *pugantalaghūpadhasya ca* to *cit* (an operation triggered by *ŚaP*, not by *tiP*) and get *cet* + *ŚaP* + *tiP*. Note that *cet* and *ŚaP* cannot undergo any other operations that are not triggered by *tiP*, so we can fuse *cet* + *ŚaP* into a single form, that is, *ceta*. *Ceta* begins with *cet* and is followed by *tiP*, so it can be called an *aṅga* with respect to *tiP*. I summarize this information in this table:

Step	Question	Traditional opinion	My opinion
cit + *tiP*	Is *cit* an *aṅga* w.r.t.* *tiP*?	Yes	No
cit + *ŚaP* + *tiP*	Is *cit* + *ŚaP* an *aṅga* w.r.t. *tiP*?	Yes	No
ceta + *tiP*	Is *ceta* an *aṅga* w.r.t. *tiP*?	Yes	Yes
*w.r.t. = with respect to.			

In my opinion, through 6.4.1 *aṅgasya*, Pāṇini teaches that for any P + Q, a rule R_P taught in the *aṅgādhikāra* that is triggered by Q is applicable to its intended operand P only if P is an *aṅga* with respect to affix Q. Similarly, a rule R_Q taught in the *aṅgādhikāra* that is triggered by P is applicable to its intended operand Q only if P is an *aṅga* with respect to affix Q. Also, note that I agree with the tradition that *cit* is an *aṅga* with respect to *ŚaP*. So, at the step *cit* + *ŚaP* + *tiP*, 7.3.86 *pugantalaghūpadhasya ca*, which belongs to the *aṅgādhikāra* and which is triggered by *ŚaP*, is applicable to *cit*.[7]

Before we go further, note that we mostly find *vikaraṇas* in *tiṅanta* and *kṛdanta* derivations. So, in the rest of the derivations, it is very easy to determine what we should call an *aṅga* with respect to the affix. For instance, in *deva* + *bhis* (example 1 of section 2.7, chapter 2), *deva* is an *aṅga* with respect to *bhis* simply because the affix *bhis* has been added to *deva*. Similarly, in *sad* + *vas* + *Ṅas* (example 2 of section 3.2, chapter 3), *sad* + *vas* is an *aṅga* with respect to *Ṅas* simply because the affix *Ṅas* has been added to *sad* + *vas*. In derivations involving *vikaraṇas*, because we add affix C to base A and then add another affix B between base A and affix C, the process of identifying the *aṅga* with respect to affix C becomes somewhat complicated, as observed above.

4.2 Examples of Application of 1.4.13 and 6.4.1

Now, I will discuss some examples through which I will show that my interpretation of 1.4.13 and 6.4.1 alone can help us derive the correct final form. But first, let me offer a clarification.

In many of the examples discussed in this chapter, the derivation could well begin with verbal base + *lakāra*. At this stage, there are two possibilities:

1. Only one rule, that is, the rule that teaches the replacement of the *lakāra* is applicable, and this rule applies.

2. Multiple rules, including the rule that teaches the replacement of the *lakāra*, are applicable.

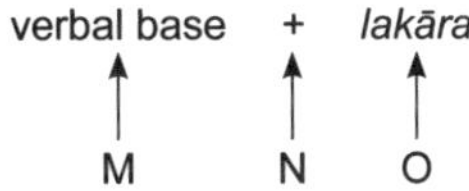

The rule O, which teaches the replacement of the *lakāra*, is the right-most. Thus, by my interpretation of 1.4.2, we apply rule O.

Note that in both cases (1) and (2), the rule that replaces the *lakāra* applies at the first step. So, in order to simplify the presentation, in all the examples where the derivation should start with verbal base + *lakāra*, I simply start it with verbal base + *tiṄ* (one of the eighteen finite replacements of the *lakāras*) instead. For instance, in the first derivation discussed in this section, technically the derivation should proceed as follows: *edh* + *LAṬ* (3.2.123 *vartamāne laṭ*) → *edh* + *jha* (3.4.77 *lasya*, 3.4.78 *tiptasjhi . . .*). However, I start with *edh* + *jha*, purely for the purpose of avoiding redundancy.

Example #1. *edh* + *jha*—'to grow', present third-person plural[8]

As stated in section 4.1 of this chapter, we cannot call *edh* an *aṅga* with respect to *jha*. Consequently, at this step, rules taught in the *aṅgādhikāra* (6.4–7.4), such as 7.1.3 *jho'ntaḥ* (which teaches that a *jh* that is the initial sound of an affix is replaced with *ant*) or 7.1.5 *ātmanepadeṣv anataḥ* (which teaches that a *jh* that is the initial sound of an *ātmanepada* affix preceded by a verbal base that does not end in *a* is replaced with *at*) cannot apply to *jh*.

Here, only two rules are applicable:

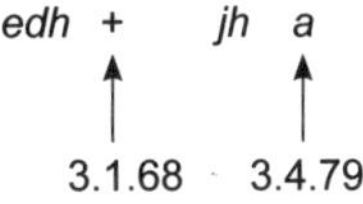

3.1.68 *kartari śap*: same as above.

3.4.79 *ṭita ātmanepadānāṁ ṭer e*: the part that begins with the last vowel (*ṭi*)[9] of an *ātmanepada* replacement of a *lakāra* marked with *Ṭ* is replaced with *e*.

By my interpretation of 1.4.2, we apply the RHS rule 3.4.79 and get: *edh* + *jhe*. At this stage too, we cannot call *edh* an *aṅga* with respect to *jhe*. Thus, 7.1.3 and 7.1.5 are not applicable here. Only one rule, namely 3.1.68, is applicable. Upon applying it, we get *edh* + *ŚaP* + *jhe*. At this step, *edh* and *ŚaP* cannot undergo any further operations that are not triggered by *jhe*, so we can simply write *edh* + *ŚaP* as *edha*. *edha* is an *aṅga* with respect to *jhe*. At this stage, of the two aforementioned rules that belong to the *aṅgādhikāra*, 7.1.3 is applicable but 7.1.5 is not. We apply 7.1.3 and get *edha* + *ante*. By 6.1.97 *ato guṇe*,[10] we get the correct form: *edhante*.

To the best of my knowledge, the tradition does not discuss this example. However, let us consider what would have happened if we had *not* accepted my interpretations of 1.4.13 and 6.4.1, respectively. At the step *edh* + *jha*, four rules would become applicable.

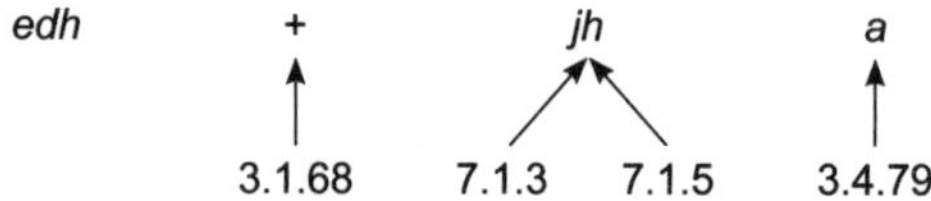

Note that all the DOI relationships here are of Type 2b (DOI nonconflict). As stated before, the tradition is not interested in nonconflict and mostly applies rules in a haphazard order in such cases.

There is an SOI between 7.1.3 *jho'ntaḥ* and 7.1.5 *ātmanepadeṣv anataḥ*. 7.1.5 is more specific and thus wins against 7.1.3 *jho'ntaḥ*. If the tradition applies 7.1.5, which replaces *jh* with *at* first and applies 3.1.68 *kartari śap* at a later step, that gives **edhate*, which is not the correct form.

My interpretations of 1.4.13 *yasmāt pratyayavidhis tadādi pratyaye'ṅgam* and 6.4.1 *aṅgasya*, respectively, ensure that *jh* replacement, which is taught in the *aṅgādhikāra*, takes place only after the application of 3.1.68 *kartari śap*, which is taught outside the *aṅgādhikāra*. After the application of 3.1.68, 7.1.5 *ātmanepadeṣv anataḥ*, which is an exception of 7.1.3 *jho'ntaḥ*, is no longer applicable to *jh*, and thus 7.1.3 *jho'ntaḥ* applies to *jh*. This gives the correct form, *edhante*.

Example #2. *dhā* + *jhi*—'to place', present third-person plural

As stated before, *dhā* cannot be called an *aṅga* with respect to *jhi*. Consequently, rules taught in the *aṅgādhikāra* (6.4–7.4) cannot apply to *dhā* or *jhi*. For example, 7.1.3 *jho'ntaḥ* cannot apply here. The derivation proceeds as follows: *dhā* + *ŚaP* + *jhi* (3.1.68 *kartari śap*) → *dhā* + *ŚLU* + *jhi* (2.4.75 *juhotyādibhyaḥ śluḥ*[11]) → *dhādhā* + *ŚLU* + *jhi* (6.1.10 *ślau*[12]) → *dhadhā* + *ŚLU* + *jhi* (7.4.59

hrasvaḥ[13]). At this point, we notice that *dhadhā* and *ŚLU* cannot undergo any other operations that are not triggered by *jhi*. So, we can write *dhadhā* + *ŚLU* as *dhadhā*. In *dhadhā* + *jhi*, *dhadhā* can be called an *aṅga* with respect to *jhi*. Therefore, the following rules from the *aṅgādhikāra* are applicable here:

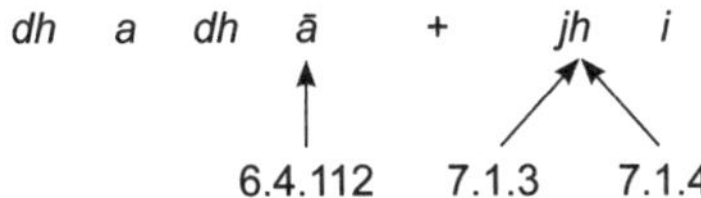

6.4.112 *śnābhyastayor ātaḥ*: the *ā* of the affix *Śnā* or the *ā* at the end of a reduplicated verbal base is replaced with *LOPA* when a *sārvadhātuka* affix marked with *K* or *Ṅ* follows.

7.1.3 *jho'ntaḥ*: a *jh* that is the initial sound of an affix is replaced with *ant*.

7.1.4 *ad abhyastāt*: when preceded by a reduplicated base, a *jh* that is the initial sound of an affix is replaced with *at*.

By my interpretation of 1.4.2, we perform the RHS operation. But there is an SOI between 7.1.3 and 7.1.4, both of which apply to the RHS operand. Because 7.1.4 has been taught for *jh* when it is preceded by a reduplicated base, it is more specific and wins. Thus, we get: *dhadhā* + *ati*. Here, 6.4.112 *śnābhyastayor ātaḥ* applies, and we get *dhadh* + *ati*. Now that all the possible rules from the *sapādasaptādhyāyī* have applied, a rule from the *tripādī* section applies[14]:

8.4.54 *abhyāse car ca*: in an *abhyāsa* (first of two reduplicated syllables), *jhaL* (a non-nasal stop or a fricative) is also replaced with *caR* (*c*, *ṭ*, *t*, *k*, *p*, *ś*, *ṣ*, *s*) or *jaŚ* (*j*, *b*, *g*, *ḍ*, *d*).

Thus, we get *dhadhati* → *dadhati*, which is the correct answer.

Let us now look at how the tradition tackles this problem. Like in the previous example, in this example too, there are no cases of DOI conflict, and so the tradition chooses to apply rules in a random order. But some sequences of rule application can give the wrong answer. For example, *dhā* + *jhi* → *dhā* + *ŚaP* + *jhi* (3.1.68) → *dhā* + *ŚaP* + *anti* (7.1.3) → *dhā* + *ŚLU* + *anti* (2.4.75) → **dadhanti* (6.1.10 *ślau*, etc.). In sum, if *jh* undergoes replacement before the reduplication of *dhā*, we get the wrong answer. To address this issue, the tradition has come up with the following ideas. Consider *paribhāṣās* 62 and 63 of the *Paribhāṣenduśekhara* and their translation by Kielhorn:

> *pūrvaṁ hy apavādā abhiniviśante paścād utsargāḥ* (62).
> *apavādas*, it is certain, are considered first (in order to find out

where they apply); afterwards the general rules (are made to take effect in all cases to which it has thus been ascertained that the *apavāda*s do not apply).

prakalpya vāpavādaviṣayaṁ tata utsargo'bhiniviśate (63).[15]

Or (we may say that) first all (forms) which fall under the *apavāda* are set aside, and that subsequently the general rule is employed (in the formation of the remaining forms).

Let us see what happens if we follow these *paribhāṣā*s at the first step (*dhā* + *jhi*). At this step, 7.1.4 *ad abhyastāt*, which is the *apavāda* of 7.1.3 *jho'ntaḥ*, is not applicable. Since the *apavāda* is not applicable, we go ahead and apply the *utsarga* 7.1.3. But this gives us the wrong form **dadhanti*. Cognizant of this problem, the tradition has come up with the following metarule:

upasaṁjaniṣyamāṇanimitto'py apavāda upasaṁjātanimittam apy utsargaṁ bādhata iti (64).

An *apavāda* supersedes, even though the causes of its (application) are still to present themselves, a general rule the causes (of the application) of which are already present.

In other words, this *paribhāṣā* teaches that even though 7.1.3 is applicable to *jh* from the beginning of the derivation, one must not replace *jh* until the *apavāda* 7.1.4 becomes applicable. This gives the correct answer, *dadhati*.

As stated in the first chapter, the tradition often comes up with a new *paribhāṣā* to address individual problems like this one. *Paribhāṣā* 64 is a good case in point.

My method ensures that the replacement of *jha*, which is taught in the *aṅgādhikāra*, takes place after the reduplication of *dhā*, which is taught outside the *aṅgādhikāra*. Therefore, 7.1.3 *jho'ntaḥ* does not become applicable until 7.1.4 *ad abhyastāt*, its exception, also becomes applicable. 7.1.4 wins, thereby giving the correct form *dadhati*. My method is able to tackle this issue without relying on *paribhāṣā*s like Pbh 64, which require us to look ahead into the derivation.

Before we move on to discussing other examples, note that Pāṇini teaches most substitutions and other operations pertaining to the eighteen finite affixes from 3.4.77 to 3.4.112. For example, 3.4.87 *ser hy apic ca,*[16] 3.4.101 *tasthasthamipāṁ tāṁtaṁtāmaḥ,*[17] and so on. He teaches the substitution of *jhi* from 3.4.108 *jher jus* to 3.4.112 *dviṣaś ca.* However, the three rules teaching the replacement of *jh*, that is, 7.1.3 *jho'ntaḥ*, 7.1.4 *ad abhyastāt*, and 7.1.5 *ātmanepadeṣv anataḥ*, are found in the *aṅgādhikāra* and not in the section 3.4.77–3.4.112. This strongly suggests that Pāṇini wants us to treat 7.1.3–7.1.5 differently, that is, he wants us to apply them only when *jh* is part of an affix that is preceded by what I define as an *aṅga*.

Example #3. *hā* + *tas*—'to abandon', present third-person dual

hā is not an *aṅga* with respect to *tas*. So here, we cannot apply rules from the *aṅgādhikāra*, such as 6.4.116 *jahāteś ca* (see translation below). The derivation proceeds as follows: *hā* + *tas* → *hā* + *ŚaP* + *tas* (3.1.68 *kartari śap*) → *hā* + *ŚLU* + *tas* (2.4.75 *juhotyādibhyaḥ śluḥ*) → *hāhā* + *ŚLU* + *tas* (6.1.10 *ślau*). Here, two rules are applicable, which are from the *aṅgādhikāra* but which are not triggered by *tas*:

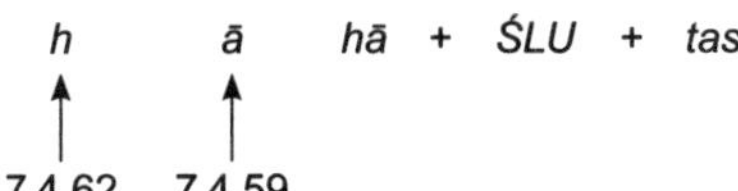

7.4.62 *kuhoś cuḥ*: a consonant of the *k*-series (*kU*), or a *h*, that is part of the *abhyāsa* (first of two reduplicated syllables) is replaced with a consonant of the *c*-series (*cU*).

7.4.59 *hrasvaḥ*: the vowel of the *abhyāsa* (first of two reduplicated syllables) is replaced with its short counterpart.

By my interpretation of 1.4.2, we apply the RHS rule 7.4.59 and get *hahā* + *ŚLU* + *tas*. To this, we apply 7.4.62 and get *jhahā* + *ŚLU* + *tas*. Now, *jhahā* and *ŚLU* cannot undergo any further operations that are not triggered by *tas*, so we can write *jhahā* + *ŚLU* as *jhahā*. Now, *jhahā* is an *aṅga* with respect to *tas*. Thus, the following rules from the *aṅgādhikāra*, which are triggered by *tas*, become applicable:

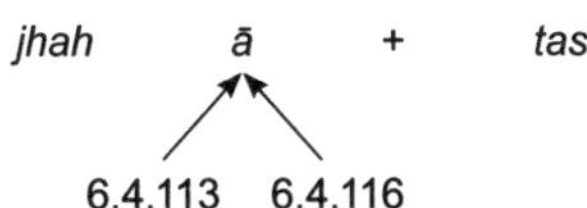

6.4.113 *ī haly aghoḥ*: the final *ā* of a base that ends in *Śnā* or of a reduplicated stem (*abhyasta*), excluding those termed *ghu*, is replaced with *ī* when a *sārvadhātuka* affix beginning with a consonant and marked with *K* or *Ṅ* follows.

6.4.116 *jahāteś ca*: the final *ā* of *hā* 'to abandon', is optionally replaced with *i*, when a *sārvadhātuka* affix beginning with a consonant and marked with *K* or *Ṅ* follows.

There is an SOI relationship between 6.4.113 and 6.4.116. Since 6.4.116 has been taught specifically for *hā*, it wins, as a result of which we get *jhahitas*. Finally, since all rules from the *sapādasaptādhyāyī* have been applied, we apply 8.4.54 *abhyāse car ca* from the *tripādī* and get *jhahitaḥ* → *jahitaḥ*, which is the correct answer.

Note that 6.4.116 *jahāteś ca* is an optional rule. If we do not implement[18] it, 6.4.113 *ī haly aghoḥ* applies, giving us *jahītaḥ*, which is also correct.

To the best of my knowledge, the tradition has not discussed this problem. But since this derivation does not involve any DOI conflicts, the tradition would have applied rules in any haphazard order. Let us look at one of the possible paths this derivation would have taken if we had not accepted my interpretations of 1.4.13 and 6.4.1, respectively: *hā* + *tas* → *hā* + *ŚaP* + *tas* (3.1.68 *kartari śap*) → *hā* + *ŚLU* + *tas* (2.4.75 *juhotyādibhyaḥ śluḥ*) → *hi* + *ŚLU* + *tas* (6.4.116 *jahāteś ca*) → **jihitaḥ* (6.1.10 *ślau*, etc).

The possibility of getting such a wrong answer is completely eliminated by following my interpretations of 1.4.13 and 6.4.1, respectively. This is because my method ensures that 6.4.116, which is taught in the *aṅgādhikāra* and replaces *ā* of *hā* with *i*, applies only after the reduplication of root *hā* by 6.1.10 *ślau*, which is taught outside the *aṅgādhikāra*.

Example #4. *vap* + *ta*—'to sow', imperfect passive third-person singular

Note that *vap* is not an *aṅga* with respect to *ta*, so rules like 6.4.71 *luṅlaṅlṛṅkṣv aḍ udāttaḥ* (see translation below), which are part of the *aṅgādhikāra*, cannot apply at this step. The following rules are applicable to *vap* + *ta*:

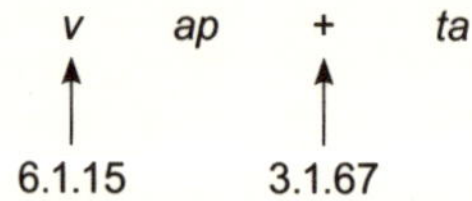

6.1.15 *vacisvapiyajādīnām ca*: roots *vac* 'to speak', *svap* 'to sleep', and those headed by *yaj* 'to perform sacrifice' undergo *samprasāraṇa* when an affix marked with *K* follows.[19]

3.1.67 *sārvadhātuke yak*: affix *yaK* occurs after a verbal root when a *sārvadhātuka* affix that denotes *bhāva* or *karman* follows.

By my interpretation of 1.4.2, the RHS rule 3.1.67 applies, and we get: *vap* + *yaK* + *ta*. Thereafter, the derivation proceeds as follows: *vap* + *yaK* + *ta* → *uap* + *yaK* + *ta* (6.1.15) → *up* + *yaK* + *ta* (6.1.108 *samprasāraṇāc ca*[20]). Since *up* and *yaK* cannot undergo any other operations that are not triggered by *ta*, we can write *up* + *yaK* as *upya*. In *upya* + *ta*, *upya* is an *aṅga* with respect to *ta*. Thus, the following rules from the *aṅgādhikāra*, which are triggered by *ta*, become applicable:

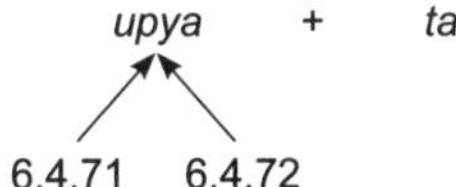

6.4.71 *luṅlaṅl̥ṅṣv aḍ udāttaḥ*: the *udātta* 'high-pitched' augment *aṬ* is attached to a verbal base when affixes *LUṄ*, *LAṄ*, and *L̥RṄ* follow.

6.4.72 *āḍ ajādīnām*: the *udāttaḥ* 'high-pitched' augment *āṬ* is attached to a verbal base that begins with a vowel (*aC*) when affixes *LUṄ*, *LAṄ*, and *L̥RṄ* follow.

This is a case of SOI. 6.4.72 has been taught specifically for bases that begin with a vowel and thus wins, thereby giving us the correct form *ā-upya* + *ta* → *aupyata* (6.1.90 *āṭaś ca*[21]).

Let us now consider how the tradition deals with this example. Like in the previous examples, here too, we do not find any instances of DOI conflict. Therefore, the tradition applies rules in a random order. If the attachment of the augment had been undertaken before *samprasāraṇa*, we would have gotten the incorrect form: *a-vapyata* (6.4.71 *luṅlaṅl̥ṅṣv aḍ udāttaḥ*) → *a-uapyata* (6.1.15 *vacisvapiyajādīnām ca*) → **opyata* (6.1.108 *samprasāraṇāc ca*, 6.1.87 *ād guṇaḥ*). To overcome this problem, the *Kāśikā*, on 6.4.72 *āḍ ajādīnām*, suggests that there is a conflict between augment addition and processes such as replacement of *LAṄ* and introduction of the *vikaraṇa yaK*, and by *nityatva* and *antaraṅgatva*, respectively, these two processes defeat the addition of the augment *aṬ*.[22]

We may conclude that the tradition comes up with a tailored solution to this problem. In contrast with this, my method eliminates the need to rely on post-Pāṇinian tools and *paribhāṣā*s. My respective interpretations of 1.4.13 and 6.4.1 ensure that the addition of the augment, which is taught in the *aṅgādhikāra*, takes place only after *samprasāraṇa*, which is taught outside the *aṅgādhikāra*. As a result of this, 6.4.71 *luṅlaṅlr̥ṅṣv aḍ udāttaḥ* does not become applicable until 6.4.72 *āḍ ajādīnām*, which is its exception, also becomes applicable. 6.4.72 wins, thereby giving the correct form *aupyata*.

In sum, these four examples prove that my interpretations of 1.4.13 and 6.4.1, respectively, are correct. In all four derivations, the tradition applies rules in a haphazard order, as a result of which it often gets the wrong form at the end of the derivation. It is forced to come up with individual solutions for each of these problems.

It is also noteworthy that in cases of the type 'base + affix (1) + affix (2)', Pāṇini teaches those processes that contribute towards the construction of the *aṅga* with respect to affix (2) before 6.4.1, in the *Aṣṭādhyāyī*'s serial order. For example, he teaches the addition of *vikaraṇa*s in *pāda* 3.1 and vowel *sandhi*, reduplication, and *samprasāraṇa* in *pāda* 6.1.

4.3 Examples of DOI

Now, I will discuss examples of DOI conflict, which are of interest to the tradition, and show how my interpretation of 1.4.2 is able to solve these cases. I will also consistently apply my interpretations of 1.4.13 and 6.4.1, respectively, in all these examples.

In each example, I will prove the existence of DOI conflict and apply my interpretation of 1.4.2 to solve it. As stated in chapter 2, generally speaking, to deal with examples of DOI conflict, the tradition uses *nityatva* (for cases of unidirectional blocking), *niravakāśatva*, or its interpretation of 1.4.2, as per convenience. To avoid repetition, I will not mention the traditional solution for each example below. Note that almost all cases of DOI conflict in derivations of finite verbs and primary derivatives involve unidirectional and not mutual blocking. We will investigate this further in the next chapter.

Lastly, also note that *kr̥danta* forms are *prātipadika*s by 1.2.46 *kr̥ttaddhitasamāsāś ca*, and thus they can take *suP* affixes by 4.1.1 *ṅyāpprātipadikāt*.

However, in the examples I have discussed in this section, I have not added *suP* affixes to *kr̥danta* forms. This is purely to avoid repetition and redundancy. This does not affect the derivations discussed in this chapter.[23] For example, the first derivation *śvi* + *Ktvā* should actually begin in the following manner: *śvi* + *Ktvā* → *śvi* + *Ktvā* + *sU* (4.1.2 *su-au-jas*...)→ *śvi* + *Ktvā* (1.1.40 *ktvātosunkasunaḥ*, 2.4.82 *avyayād āpsupaḥ*). Here onwards, the derivation proceeds as follows:

Example #1. *śvi* + *Ktvā*—'to swell', absolutive

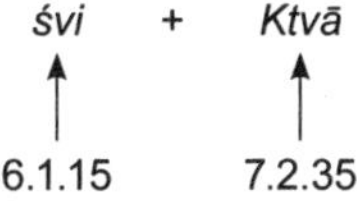

6.1.15 *vacisvapiyajādīnām kiti*: roots *vac* 'to speak', *svap* 'to sleep', and those headed by *yaj* 'to perform sacrifice' undergo *samprasāraṇa* when an affix marked with *K* follows.

7.2.35 *ārdhadhātukasyeḍ valādeḥ*: augment *iṬ* is attached to an *ārdhadhātuka* affix beginning with *vaL* (any consonant except *y*).

If *iṬ* is attached to *Ktvā* by 7.2.35, then according to 1.2.18 *na ktvā seṭ* (which teaches that a *Ktvā* that has taken the augment *iṬ* is not treated as marked with *K*), *itvā* will no longer be treated as marked with *K*. And so, 6.1.15, which applies to certain roots that are followed by a *K*-marked affix, will not be applicable at the following step. So, 7.2.35 blocks 6.1.15. On the other hand, 7.2.35 will still be applicable after the application of 6.1.15. So, 6.1.15 does not block 7.2.35. This is a case of unidirectional blocking and thus of DOI conflict.

By my interpretation of 1.4.2, the RHS rule 7.2.35 wins, and we get: *śvi* + *itvā*. Since *itvā* can no longer be treated as marked with *K*, 7.3.84 *sārvadhātukārdhadhātukayoḥ*[24] causes *guṇa* of *i*, thereby giving us *śve* + *itvā*. By 6.1.78 *eco'yavāyāvaḥ*, we get the correct form: *śvayitvā*.

Example #2. *han* + *Kta*—'to kill', past passive participle

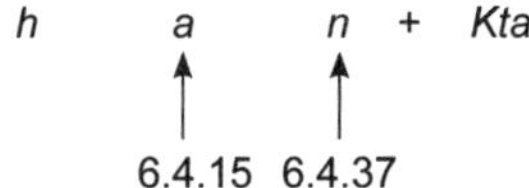

6.4.15 *anunāsikasya kvijhaloḥ kṅiti*: the penultimate vowel of a base that ends in a nasal (*anunāsika*) is replaced with its long counterpart when affix *KvI* or an affix beginning with *jhaL* (a non-nasal stop or a fricative) and marked with *K* or *Ṅ* follows.

6.4.37 *anudāttopadeśavanatitanotyādīnām anunāsikalopo jhali kṅiti*: the final nasal of a base marked with *anudātta* when taught in the *Dhātupāṭha*, as well as of *vanA* 'to like' and the roots headed by *tanU* 'to extend', is replaced with *LOPA* when an affix beginning with *jhaL* (a non-nasal stop or a fricative) and marked with *K* or *Ṅ* follows.

If *n* of *han* is replaced with *LOPA* by 6.4.37, 6.4.15 will not be applicable at the following step. But if the vowel of *han* is lengthened by 6.4.15, 6.4.37 will still be applicable at the following step. This is a case of unidirectional blocking and thus of DOI conflict.

By my interpretation of 1.4.2, we apply the RHS rule 6.4.37 and get the correct form *hata*.

Example #3. *han* + *jhi*—'to kill', present third-person plural

As per my interpretation of 1.4.13, *han* cannot be called an *aṅga* with respect to *jhi*. Thus, rules from the *aṅgādhikāra* are not applicable at this step. I will not repeat this clarification henceforth and will assume that the reader is by now familiar with it.

han + *jhi* → *han* + *ŚaP* + *jhi* (3.1.68 *kartari śap*[25]) → *han* + *LUK* + *jhi* (2.4.72 *adiprabhṛtibhyaḥ śapaḥ*[26]). Now *han* and *LUK* cannot undergo any other operations that are not triggered by *jhi*, so *han* + *LUK* can be written as *han*, which is an *aṅga* with respect to *jhi*. Here, the following rules from the *aṅgādhikāra* (6.4 to 7.4) are applicable:

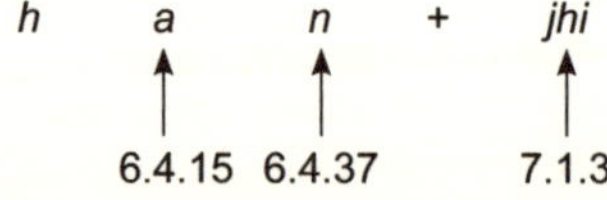

6.4.15 *anunāsikasya kvijhaloḥ kṅiti*: same as above.

6.4.37 *anudāttopadeśavanatitanotyādīnām anunāsikalopo jhali kṅiti*: same as above.

7.1.3 *jho'ntaḥ*: a *jh* that constitutes the initial sound of an affix is replaced with *ant*.

We already know from the previous example that there is a Type 2a (DOI conflict) between 6.4.15 and 6.4.37 and that 6.4.37 wins. So now let us consider the relationship between 6.4.37 and 7.1.3.

If we apply 6.4.37 at this step, 7.1.3 will be applicable at the following step. But if we apply 7.1.3 at this step, the affix will no longer begin with a *jhaL* sound, and therefore 6.4.37 will not be applicable at the following step. This is a case of unidirectional blocking and thus of DOI conflict. By my interpretation of 1.4.2, the RHS rule 7.1.3 wins, and we get *han* + *anti* → *hn* + *anti* (6.4.98 *gamahanajanakhanaghasāṁ lopaḥ kṅity anaṅi*[27]) → *ghnanti* (7.3.54 *ho hanter ñṇinneṣu*[28]), which is the correct form.

Example #4. *kramU* + *Ktvā*—'to stride', absolutive

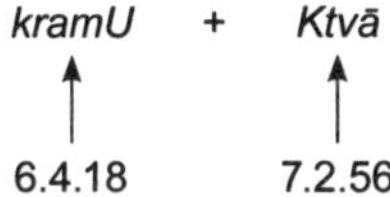

6.4.18 *kramaś ca ktvi*: the penultimate vowel of *kramU* 'stride' is optionally replaced with its long counterpart when affix *Ktvā*, beginning with *jhaL* (a non-nasal stop or a fricative), follows.

7.2.56 *udito vā*: augment *iṬ* is, optionally, attached to affix *Ktvā* when it follows a verbal root marked with *U*.

If, by 7.2.56, the *iṬ* augment is attached to *Ktvā*, then 6.4.18, which requires the affix to begin a specific kind of consonant, will not be applicable at the following step. But if we apply 6.4.18, 7.2.56 will still be applicable at the following step. This is a case of unidirectional blocking and thus of DOI conflict.

By my interpretation of 1.4.2, we apply the RHS rule 7.2.56 and get the correct form: *kramitvā*. Note that both 6.4.18 and 7.2.56 are optional rules. So, for each of these rules we have a choice. We can either implement the rule or not do so. Let us consider what happens in different scenarios:

If we do not implement the optional rule 7.2.56, we get:

(i) *krantvā*, if we do not implement the optional rule 6.4.18; and
(ii) *krāntvā*, if we do implement the optional rule 6.4.18.

If we implement 7.2.56 but not 6.4.18, we get, again, *krāntvā*.

All three forms, *krantvā*, *krāntvā*, and *kramitvā* are correct.

Example #5. *atikram* + *Ktvā*—'to surpass', absolutive

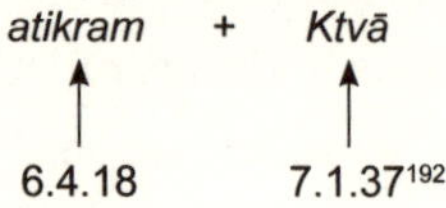

6.4.18 *kramaś ca ktvi*: same as above.

7.1.37 *samāse'nañpūrve ktvo lyap*: in a compound, the first member of which is not *naÑ*, the affix *Ktvā* in the second member of the compound is replaced with *LyaP*.

If we apply 7.1.37, *LyaP* replaces *Ktvā*, and so 6.4.18 will not be applicable at the following step. But if we apply 6.4.18, 7.1.37 will still be applicable at the following step. This is a case of unidirectional blocking and thus of DOI conflict.

By my interpretation of 1.4.2, we apply the RHS rule 7.1.37 and get the correct form: *atikramya*.

It is important to point out an anomaly here. Pāṇini's rule 2.2.18 *kugatiprādayaḥ* teaches that the particle *ku*, items termed *gati* (including *ati*), and items belonging to the group headed by *pra* (which also includes *ati*) combine with syntactically related *padas* to form *tatpuruṣa* compounds. We know, thanks to 2.1.4 *saha supā*, that a compound is composed of forms ending in *suP*. Since the three forms *krantvā, krāntvā,* and *kramitvā* (see example 4 of this section) end in *suP* (which is replaced with *LUK* by 2.4.82 *avyayād āpsupaḥ*), *ati* can combine with any of these forms to construct a *tatpuruṣa* compound. Let us consider each of the three scenarios:

a. Compound between *ati* and *krantvā*.

   By 7.1.37 *samāse'nañpūrve ktvo lyap*, we replace *Ktvā* with *LyaP* and get **atikranya*, which is not the correct form.

b. Compound between *ati* and *krāntvā*.

   By 7.1.37, we replace *Ktvā* with *LyaP* and get **atikrānya*, which is also not the correct form.

c. Compound between *ati* and *kramitvā*.

By 7.1.37 *samāse'nañpūrve ktvo lyap*, we replace *Ktvā* with *LyaP* and get *atikramiya* → **atikramitya* (6.1.71 *hrasvasya piti kṛti tuk*), which is not the correct form. To derive the correct form, we have to start the derivation by adding the verbal root *kram* to *ati* which constitutes the *pūrvapada*. To that, we add affix *Ktvā*: *atikram* + *Ktvā*. This alone gives us the correct answer.[29]

We see the same phenomenon in examples 6–8 below. But this runs contrary to how we generally construct compounds—by combining two or more *subanta* forms.

Thus, the following question arises: if it is difficult to derive *atikramya* correctly as a compound, why does Pāṇini want us to view *atikramya* as a compound in the first place? This likely has to do with accentuation, which is not the focus of this book. The distinction between *atikramya* and *atikrāmati* (where *ati* is only a morpho-syntactically bound particle cf. 1.4.8 *te prāg dhātoḥ*), the status of particles like *ati* in Vedic and the relationship between *Ktvā* and *LyaP* in Vedic can all shed more light on this matter, but we cannot delve into these topics here.

Example #6. *prasthā* + *Ktvā*—'to depart', absolutive

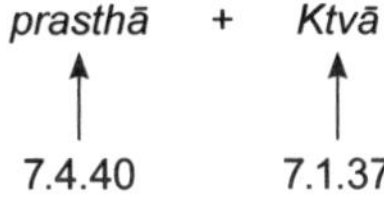

7.4.40 *dyatisyatimāsthām it ti kiti*: a short *i* replaces the final sound of *do* 'to cut', *ṣo* 'to end, terminate', *mā* 'to measure', and *sthā* 'to stay', when a *t*-initial affix marked with *K* follows.

7.1.37 *samāse'nañpūrve ktvo lyap*: same as above.

If we replace *Ktvā* with *LyaP* by 7.1.37, the affix no longer begins with *t* and thus 7.4.40 will not be applicable at the following step. On the other hand, if we apply 7.4.40, 7.1.37 will still be applicable at the following step. This is a case of unidirectional blocking and thus of DOI conflict. By my interpretation of 1.4.2, we apply the RHS rule 7.1.37, which gives the correct form: *prasthāya*.

Example #7. *āgam* + *Ktvā*—'to come', absolutive

āgam + *Ktvā*

6.4.37 7.1.37

6.4.37 *anudāttopadeśavanatitanotyādīnām anunāsikalopo jhali kṅiti*: the final nasal of a base marked with *anudātta* when taught in the *Dhātupāṭha*, as well as of *vanA* 'to like' and the roots headed by *tanU* 'to extend', is replaced with *LOPA* when an affix beginning with *jhaL* (a non-nasal stop or a fricative) and marked with *K* or *Ṅ* follows.

7.1.37 *samāse'nañpūrve ktvo lyap*: same as above.

If we replace *Ktvā* with *LyaP* by 7.1.37, the affix no longer begins with *jhaL*, and thus 6.4.37 will not be applicable at the following step. On the other hand, if we apply 6.4.37, 7.1.37 will still be applicable at the following step. This is a case of unidirectional blocking and thus of DOI conflict. By my interpretation of 1.4.2, we apply the RHS rule 7.1.37 and get: *āgam* + *tvā* → *āgam* + *ya* (7.1.37) → *āga* + *ya* (6.4.38 *vā lyapi*[30]) → *āgatya* (6.1.71 *hrasvasya piti kṛti tuk*[31]), which is the correct form. Note that the application of 6.4.38 is optional. If we do not implement this rule, we get *āgamya*, which is also correct.

Example #8. *śās* + *siP*—'to instruct', imperative second-person singular

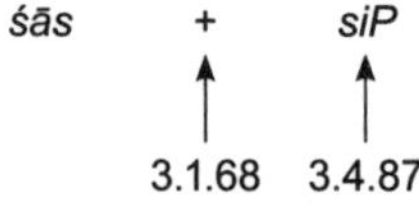

3.1.68 *kartari śap*: affix *ŚaP* occurs after a verbal root when a *sārvadhātuka* affix that denotes *kartṛ* 'agent' follows.

3.4.87 *ser hy apic ca*: a *siP* replacement of *LOṬ* is replaced with *hi* and is treated as if not marked with *P*.

These two rules do not block each other. This is not a case of conflict.

By my interpretation of 1.4.2, we apply the RHS rule 3.4.87 and get *śās* + *hi* → *śās* + *ŚaP* + *hi* (3.1.68) → *śās* + *hi* (2.4.72 *adiprabhr̥tibhyaḥ śapaḥ*[32]). *śās* can now be called an *aṅga* with respect to *hi* (cf. my interpretation of 1.4.13). Thus, the following rules from the *aṅgādhikāra* become applicable:

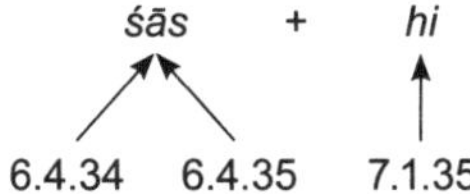

6.4.34 *śāsa id aṅhaloḥ*: the penultimate sound of *śās* is replaced with short *i* when followed by *aṄ*, or an affix that begins with a consonant and is marked with *K* or *Ṅ*.[33]

6.4.35 *śā hau*: *śās* is replaced with *śā* when affix *hi* follows.

7.1.35 *tuhyos tātaṅ āśiṣy anyatarasyām*: affixes *tu* and *hi* are optionally replaced with *tātAṄ*, provided benediction (*āśiḥ*) is denoted.[34]

Here, we see that there is an SOI interaction between 6.4.34 and 6.4.35[35] and a DOI interaction between them and 7.1.35. Let's first deal with the SOI between 6.4.34 and 6.4.35. 6.4.35 is more specific because it pertains to the *hi* affix alone and thus wins.[36] So now let us discuss the relationship between 6.4.35 and 7.1.35.

If we apply 6.4.35, 7.1.35 will still be applicable at the following step. But if we apply 7.1.35, *hi* will be replaced with *tātAṄ*, and thus 6.4.35 will not be applicable at the following step. This is a case of unidirectional blocking and thus of DOI conflict. By my interpretation of 1.4.2, we apply the RHS rule 7.1.35 and get: *śās* + *tāt* → *śis* + *tāt* (6.4.34 *śāsa idaṅhaloḥ*) → *śiṣṭāt* (8.3.60 *śāsivasighasīnāṁ ca*, 8.4.41 *ṣṭunā ṣṭuḥ*), which is the correct form.

Example #9. *han* + *siP*—'to hurt', imperative second-person singular

3.1.68 *kartari śap*: same as above.

3.4.87 *ser hy apic ca*: same as above.

Neither of the two rules blocks the other. This is a case of DOI nonconflict.

By my interpretation of 1.4.2, we apply the RHS rule 3.4.87 and get *han* + *hi* → *han* + *ŚaP* + *hi* (3.1.68) → *han* + *hi* (2.4.72 *adiprabhṛtibhyaḥ śapaḥ*). *han* can now be called an *aṅga* with respect to *hi* (cf. my interpretation of 1.4.13). Thus, the following rules from the *aṅgādhikāra* become applicable:

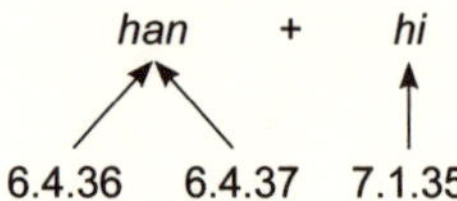

6.4.36 *hanter jaḥ*: the root *han* is replaced with *ja* when the affix *hi* follows.

6.4.37 *anudāttopadeśavanatitanotyādīnām anunāsikalopo jhali kṅiti*: the final nasal of a base marked with *anudātta* when taught in the *Dhātupāṭha*, as well as of *vanA* 'to like' and the roots headed by *tanU* 'to extend', is replaced with *LOPA* when an affix beginning with *jhaL* (a non-nasal stop or a fricative) and marked with *K* or *Ṅ* follows.[37]

7.1.35 *tuhyos tātaṅ āśiṣy anyatarasyām*: same as above.

There is an SOI relationship between 6.4.36 and 6.4.37. 6.4.36 is specifically taught for *han* + *hi*, and so it is clearly more specific than 6.4.37. So, we put 6.4.37 aside. Now let us consider the relationship between 6.4.36 and 7.1.35.

If we apply 6.4.36 at this step, 7.1.35 will still be applicable at the following step. However, if we replace *hi* with *tātAṄ* by 7.1.35 at this step, then 6.4.36, which applies only when *han* is followed by *hi*, will not be applicable at the following step. This is a case of unidirectional blocking and thus of DOI conflict. By my interpretation of 1.4.2, we apply the RHS rule 7.1.35 and get *han* + *tātAṄ* → *hatāt* (6.4.37 *anudāttopadeśavanatitanotyādīnām anunāsikalopo jhali kṅiti*), which is the correct form. (For more such examples, please see Appendix C.)

4.4 Examples of SOI

We have already looked at several examples of SOI while discussing examples of DOI conflict. Here, I will present a few more examples. As I have done earlier, I will spell out and examine the conditions in which the rules apply and then determine which of the two rules is more specific.

Example #1. *cal* + *tiP*—'to walk', simple future third-person singular

3.1.33 *syatāsī l̥rluṭoḥ*: affixes *sya* and *tāsI*, respectively, occur after verbal roots when *LR̥* and *LUṬ* follow.

3.1.68 *kartari śap*: affix *ŚaP* occurs after a verbal root when a *sārvadhātuka* affix that denotes *kartr̥* 'agent' follows.

3.1.33

when (affixes that replace) *LR̥* and *LUṬ* follow—all of which happen to be *sārvadhātuka*

3.1.68

when *sārvadhātuka* affixes that replace *LR̥* and *LUṬ* follow

when *sārvadhātuka* affixes that replace other *lakāras* follow

The conditions highlighted in bold are exactly the same. This is a case of SOI-M. Thus, we compare the two rules themselves. 3.1.33 has been taught specifically for *LR̥* and *LUṬ*. So, it is more specific and thus wins. We get *cal* + *sya* + *ti* → *caliṣyati* (7.2.35 *ārdhadhātukasyeḍ valādeḥ*), which is the correct form.

Example #2. *vad* + *miP*—'to speak', imperative first-person singular

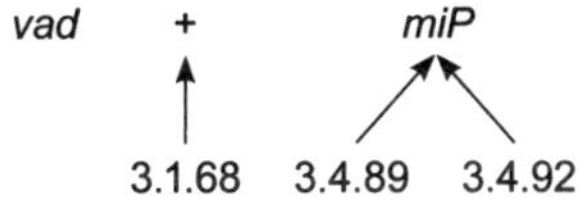

3.1.68 *kartari śap*: same as above.

3.4.89 *mer niḥ*: a *miP* substitute of *LOṬ* is replaced with *ni*.

3.4.92 *āḍ uttamasya pic ca*: a first-person substitute of *LOṬ* receives the initial augment *āṬ*, which is treated as marked with *P*.

3.1.68 is not in conflict with 3.4.89 or 3.4.92. By my interpretation of 1.4.2, we should perform the RHS operation. But which one of the two RHS rules, namely 3.4.89 and 3.4.92, should we apply? Let us examine the SOI between 3.4.89 and 3.4.92.

3.4.89

***miP* (replacement of *LOṬ*)**

3.4.92

***miP* (replacement of *LOṬ*)**

other first-person affixes (replacements of *LOṬ*)

The conditions highlighted in bold are exactly the same. This is a case of SOI-M. Thus, we compare the two rules themselves. 3.4.89 has been taught specifically for *miP.* So, it is more specific and thus wins. Thus, we get *vad* + *ni.* Thereafter, the derivation proceeds as follows: *vad* + *ni* → *vad* + *āni* (3.4.92 *āḍ uttamasya pic ca*) → *vad* + *ŚaP* + *āni* (3.1.68 *kartari śap*) → *vadāni* (6.1.97 *ato guṇe*), which is the correct form.

Example #3. *tṝ* + *tiP*—'to cross', present third-person singular

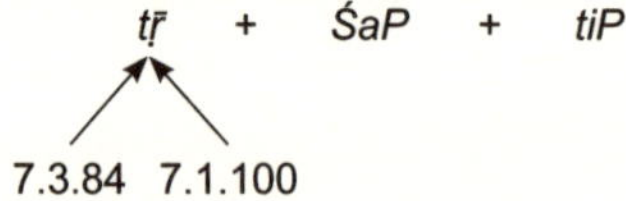

7.3.84 *sārvadhātukārdhadhātukayoḥ*: *guṇa* replaces the final sound *iK* (*i, u, r̥, l̥*) of a verbal base when a *sārvadhātuka* or *ārdhadhātuka* affix follows.

7.1.100 *r̥̄ta id dhātoḥ*: *r̥̄*, which occurs at the end of a verbal base, is replaced with *i.*

Note that we have to take into account rules like 1.1.5 *kṅiti ca* (which prohibits *guṇa* and *vr̥ddhi* of the *iK* [*i, u, r̥, l̥*] of a verbal base when the following affix is marked with *K, G* or *Ṅ*) when determining the exact conditions in which the aforementioned rules are applicable. Because of 1.1.5, 7.3.84 is applicable only when the affix is not marked with *K, G*, or *Ṅ.*

7.3.84

***r̥̄* + affix (*sārvadhātuka* or *ārdhadhātuka*) (not marked with *K, G, Ṅ*)**

other *iK* sounds + affix (*sārvadhātuka* or *ārdhadhātuka*) (not marked with *K, G, Ṅ*)

7.1.100

***r̥̄* + affix (*sārvadhātuka* or *ārdhadhātuka*)**

The conditions highlighted in bold are not the same. Thus, this is a case of SOI-L. 7.3.84 is more specific because it is applicable only if the affix is not marked with *K, G*, or *Ṅ*, whereas 7.1.100 is applicable regardless of whether the affix is marked with *K, G*, or *Ṅ*. Thus, 7.3.84 wins, giving the correct form *tarati* (cf. 1.1.51 *ur aṇ raparaḥ*).

Let us now consider Cardona's method of deriving this form. He uses a principle that he calls 'limited blocking' to deal with this aforementioned SOI. He explains it as follows: 'though a rule R_2 as a whole does not state an *apavāda* of an R_1, as a whole, it can do so for some operands or environments common to both'. Further, he says:

> [Consider] rules: 7.3.84 *sārvadhātukārdhadhātukayoḥ* and 7.1.100 *ṝta id dhātoḥ*. By the latter, the *ṝ* of an *aṅga* which is a verb root is replaced with *i*. The rules are not related as *utsarga* and *apavāda* in their entirety: the operands of 7.3.84 are *i, u, ṛ* while that of 7.1.100 is *ṝ*. Nor are the contexts identical. Although 7.1.100 operates when the root is followed by any affix introduced after it and *sārvadhātuka* and *ārdhadhātuka* affixes, the contexts for 7.3.84, include all post-radical affixes, the context of 7.3.84 is restricted by 1.1.5 (*kṅiti ca*). In the case of the single shared operand (*ṝ*), then, 7.1.100 will counter 7.3.84 [sic],[38] since all the contexts of the former are included in those of the latter. Thus, given the root *stṝ* followed by the affix *ana*, one obtains the desired form *staraṇa-* 'spreading' without recourse to *paratva*. (1970, 57–58)

Kiparsky criticizes this solution, saying that using such arguments, one could have arrived at exactly the opposite conclusion. He says: 'So [Cardona's statement] is compatible with two different procedures yielding opposite results':

> If the environments of R_2 are properly included in the environments of R_1, and the operands of R_1, are properly included in the operands of R_2, then
>
> a. R_2 blocks R_1, (for the environments of R_2 are properly included in the environments of R_1, in the shared operand domain).
>
> b. R_1 blocks R_2 (for the operands of R_1 are properly included in the operands of R_2 in the shared environment domain).
>
> In case (a) of Cardona 1970 (p. 57) the two rules are: 7.3.84 *sārvadhātukārdhadhātukayoḥ* (*guṇaḥ*) and 7.1.100 *ṝta id dhātoḥ*. So,

> Cardona applies procedure a: 'in the case of the single shared operand (ṝ) then, 7.1.100 will counter 7.3.84 [sic—this is evidently a slip and he must have meant to say '7.3.84 will counter 7.1.100'], since all the contexts of the former are included in those of the later'. If the facts were the other way round (i.e., if the outcome was **stiraṇa*), he would have said 'in the case of the single shared context (non-*kit* suffixes), 7.1.100 will counter 7.3.84, since all the operands of the former are included in those of the latter (procedure b)'. (1991, 350–51)

I think that Cardona's limited blocking principle is similar to my method of dealing with SOI. However, Kiparsky correctly points out that the explanation offered by Cardona is ambiguous. On the other hand, my solution overcomes such ambiguity by following the clearly defined procedure that I have developed and used to tackle all examples of SOI in this book.

This brings us to the end of our survey of SOI and DOI examples from derivations of finite verbs and primary derivatives.

CHAPTER FIVE

Situating Examples Within and Outside 1.4.2's Ambit

In chapters 2, 3, and 4, I presented examples of both SOI conflict and DOI conflict. Instead of focusing on only those steps that involve conflict, I performed entire derivations, right from the first step to the last one—drawing diagrams for each step where two or more rules are simultaneously applicable. In this chapter, I first discuss how and why I selected these examples and dwell on the examples that pose a challenge to my interpretation of 1.4.2. Having discussed examples that lie within the ambit of 1.4.2, I then discuss examples that lie outside it (e.g., accentuation rules and so-called *antaraṅga-bahiraṅga* 'conflicts'). While on the subject of *antaraṅga* and *bahiraṅga*, I also discuss a related topic, namely Joshi and Kiparsky's *siddha* principle, in the light of my findings. And finally, I dwell on the pivotal question surrounding Different Operand Interaction: how and why did Pāṇini come up with 1.4.2? Having discussed interactions among operational rules, I then shift my focus towards the question of choosing one of two *saṁjñā* or *paribhāṣā* rules. I reiterate my position that this decision does not lie within the ambit of 1.4.2 and discuss important examples—including some that involve the reinterpretation of key Pāṇinian metarules.

5.1 Selection of Examples

In this section, I discuss the process through which I conducted my searches for examples, the rationale behind the choice of these examples, and also the distributional patterns I noticed in this process.

I performed numerous derivations from the *Laghusiddhāntakaumudī* and chose those that involve examples of conflict. Having studied the various *prakaraṇa*s 'chapters' of this text, namely those on *sandhi, subanta, taddhitānta, samāsa, tiṅanta*, and *kṛdanta*, I have selected a diverse and representative set of examples to the best of my abilities. To avoid redundancy, I have excluded those examples that are only superficially different from those included in this book.

To show that my method can tackle all kinds of conflicts in various derivational contexts, I have tried to strike a balance:

1. between short derivations that involve only two or three steps and fewer cases of same-step interaction and long ones that involve many steps and several cases of same-step interaction;
2. between simple examples that help the reader gain conceptual clarity and complex ones that demonstrate the potency of my solution; and
3. between examples that have been extensively discussed in traditional literature and examples that I have newly spotted during my research.

To underscore the far-reaching impact of my research:

1. I have given precedence to derivations that involve popular, broad, general, and widely applicable rules, whilst also ensuring the inclusion of derivations that involve rarely applicable and highly specific rules.
2. I have prioritized the exposition of those examples that highlight the contrast between my method and the traditional method.
3. I have paid special attention to certain challenging examples discussed in the *Mahābhāṣya*, the *Kāśikā*, Cardona (1970), Kiparsky (1982), Pataskar (1985), Bronkhorst (2004), Joshi and Kiparsky (2005), and so on, with the aim of showing that my method is singlehandedly able to overcome a wide variety of problems associated with this topic. In Appendix A, I provide more information on the examples that are present in some of these sources and have also been discussed by me.

5.2 Distribution of Examples

Now, let us examine the distribution of examples of conflict across various kinds of derivations (e.g., *subanta, kṛdanta*, etc.). Since Pāṇini uses the general-exception framework throughout the *Aṣṭādhyāyī*, we find cases of SOI conflict in all kinds of derivations. And while we might find more examples of SOI conflict in some kinds of derivations than others, we do not come across any unique or peculiar patterns that merit discussion here.

So, I will focus on the distribution of DOI conflicts in Pāṇinian derivations in this section. Let us inquire why, on the whole, DOI conflicts, and especially certain kinds of DOI conflicts (e.g., mutual blocking), are found more frequently in certain kinds of derivations than others. I request the reader to bear in mind that I will be making some broad generalizations here in order to paint an overarching picture. Therefore, my statements will not be entirely accurate. Since we are talking about DOI conflict here, I will not touch upon those instances of DOI that do not involve conflict.

To start with, let us consider *subanta* derivations.

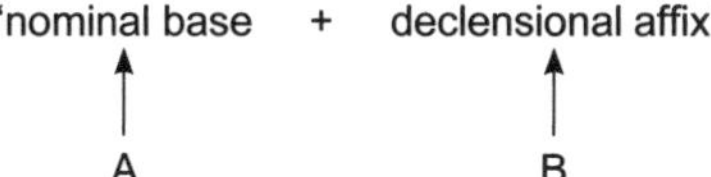

We will focus on cases where the application of A to the base is triggered by the first sound of the affix, and the application of B to the affix is triggered by the last sound of the base. If the first sound of the affix changes, A is not applicable to the base anymore, and if the last sound of the base changes, B is not applicable to the affix anymore. Therefore, when two such rules are simultaneously applicable in *subanta* derivations, A to the base and B to the affix, both rules block each other, leading to a situation of DOI conflict.

In other cases, we find that the application of B to the affix is triggered simply by the grammatical gender, word category (e.g., pronoun), and so on of the base. In such a case, even if the base undergoes phonological change, B will still be applicable at the following step. On the contrary, we observe that the application of A to the base is triggered by the first sound or the mere presence of an affix. So, if the affix is deleted, for example, by *LUK*, or if its first sound changes, then A will no longer be applicable at the following step. These are cases of unidirectional blocking.

Thus, we see both kinds of examples of DOI conflict, namely those of mutual blocking and those of unidirectional blocking, in *subanta* derivations. Note that I have overlooked, for the sake of simplicity, examples of DOI conflict where both rules apply to two different parts of the base or to two different parts of the affix, respectively.

Let us contrast this with *tiṅanta* derivations. One of the early steps of these derivations looks like this:

Vikaraṇas on the whole do not undergo many changes. Even when they do, the application of D (which may teach replacement with *LUK* or other substitutes, augmentation, etc.) is not triggered by the last sound of the verbal root. So even if the verbal root undergoes some changes, D will still be applicable to the *vikaraṇa* at the following step. On the other hand, the application of C (which may entail *guṇa*, *samprasāraṇa*, augmentation, lengthening of the penultimate vowel, deletion of nasal, etc.) is dependent on the existence of the *vikaraṇa*, its being marked with *K* or *Ṅ*, and so on. So, if the *vikaraṇa* undergoes certain changes, such as replacement with *LUK* or attachment of certain augments like *iṬ*, which annul the effect of *K*/*Ṅ* (cf. 1.2.18 *na ktvā seṭ*), C will not be applicable to the base at the following step. These are cases of unidirectional blocking.

Most rules (E) that are applicable to finite endings at this stage are triggered by the type of *lakāra* that the ending has replaced, whether that *lakāra* is marked with *Ṭ* or *Ṅ*, the number and person of the ending, whether the ending is *parasmaipada* or *ātmanepada*, and so on. They do not block and are not blocked by other rules (for example, see rules 3.4.77–3.4.112 of the *Aṣṭādhyāyī*). Therefore, we will not focus on them here.

Once the *aṅga* is ready, we get:

The application of F (such as *guṇa*, *vṛddhi*, *samprasāraṇa*, etc.) is triggered by the existence of the affix, the first sound of the affix, whether or not it is marked with *K* or *Ṅ*, and so on. Thus, if the affix undergoes certain changes, F is not applicable at the following step. But G is not triggered by the last sound of the *aṅga*. Thus, even if the *aṅga* undergoes certain changes, G is still applicable at the following step. This is a case of unidirectional blocking.

Let us now look at *kṛdanta* derivations.

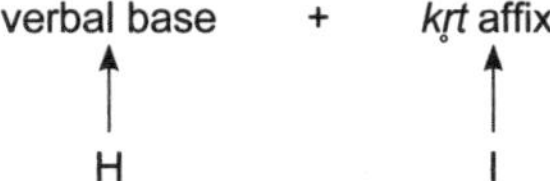

The application of H (such as *guṇa*, *samprasāraṇa*, etc.) is triggered by or depends on the first sound of the affix, whether it has taken the augment *iṬ*, whether it is marked with *K* or *Ṅ*, and so on. Thus, if the affix undergoes certain changes, H is not applicable at the following step. Let us call H the dependent rule. On the other hand, I is triggered by the first sound of the affix itself (e.g., 7.2.35 *ārdhadhātukasyeḍ valādeḥ*) and other factors. Essentially, the application of I is not dependent on the final sound of the base. So even if the base changes, I is still applicable at the following step. Let us call I the independent rule. This is a case of unidirectional blocking, where the independent rule blocks the dependent rule.

Before we proceed further, notice that, in almost all cases of unidirectional blocking in DOI discussed in this book, it is the RHS rule that unidirectionally blocks the LHS rule and not vice versa. This is because it is the RHS rule that is independent, and it is the LHS rule that is dependent. In other words, in almost all cases of unidirectional blocking, the applicability of the RHS rule does not depend on whether the penultimate or last sound of the base changes, but the applicability of the LHS rule does depend on whether the affix is marked with *K* or *Ṅ*, whether it starts with a vowel, whether it has taken the augment *iṬ*, and so on. In traditional terms, this is exactly why the traditional *nitya* tool, which teaches that the *nitya* rule defeats the *anitya* rule, always correctly resolves cases of DOI conflict involving unidirectional blocking: the *nitya* rule is applicable to the RHS operand, and the *anitya* rule to the LHS operand. By (my interpretation of) 1.4.2, the RHS rule (which is also the *nitya* rule) defeats the LHS rule (which is the *anitya* rule).

Coming back to the larger theme of this section, we see that almost all cases of DOI conflict in both *tiṅanta* and *kṛdanta* derivations involve only unidirectional blocking. This can be observed in the examples discussed in section 4.3 and Appendix C.

To sum up my observations, we find examples of both mutual and unidirectional blocking in *subanta* derivations, but of unidirectional blocking alone in *tiṅanta* and *kr̥danta* derivations.

As seen in this book, we find relatively fewer examples of DOI conflict in *taddhitānta* and *samāsa* derivations than we do in *subanta*, *tiṅanta*, and *kr̥danta* sections. How can we explain this phenomenon?

Let us first answer this question in the context of *samāsa* derivations. The *samāsa* template is '[(base$_1$ *suP*$_1$) (base$_2$ *suP*$_2$)] + *suP*$_3$'. *suP*$_1$ and *suP*$_2$ are replaced with *LUK* by 2.4.71 *supo dhātuprātipadikayoḥ*. Thus, we are left with 'base$_1$ base$_2$ + *suP*$_3$'. Given that the only remaining affix, that is, *suP*$_3$, is also a *suP* affix, there is almost no scope for any other conflicts to arise apart from those that can potentially arise in *subanta* derivations. The only exceptions to this are those cases wherein the *uttarapada* can potentially trigger changes in the *pūrvapada* (see example 1 of section 3.1, chapter 3). This explains why we find very few examples of DOI conflict that are exclusive to *samāsa* derivations, that is, that are not already found in *subanta* derivations.

In *taddhitānta* derivations too, we find very few examples of DOI conflict. These examples too are quite similar to one another (see examples 3–7 of section 3.1, chapter 3) and arise because of the nominal inflection of *taddhitānta* forms. Why is this the case? The majority of *taddhita* rules actually teach addition of *taddhita* affixes and not any substitutions or modifications. The *taddhita* template is '(nominal base + *suP*) + *taddhita* affix'. *suP* is replaced with *LUK* by 2.4.71 *supo dhātuprātipadikayoḥ*. Thus, we are left with 'nominal base + *taddhita* affix'.

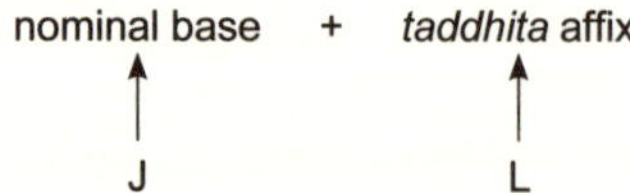

Taddhita affixes undergo very few generic changes by rules (L), such as 7.1.2 *āyaneyīnīyiyaḥ phaḍhakhacchaghāṁ pratyayādīnām*, which are independent of the final sound of the nominal base. So, any change in the base by rule J cannot block these operations (L) on *taddhita* affixes.

The nominal bases preceding *taddhita* affixes can also undergo certain general changes by rules (J), such as 7.2.117 *taddhiteṣv acām ādeḥ*, 7.2.118 *kiti ca*, and so on, which do not depend on the first sound of the *taddhita* affix for their application and thus are not blocked by L in the case of DOI. And even those operations (J), such as 6.4.146 *or guṇaḥ* and 6.4.148 *yasyeti ca*, which are triggered by the first sound of the following *taddhita* affix, are seldom blocked, simply because the following *taddhita* affixes themselves undergo very few changes. So, barring replacement with *LUK* (see examples 3–7 of section 3.1, chapter 3), most changes in the *taddhita* affix cannot block these operations (J) on the nominal base. Since there is little scope for DOI blocking between J and L, we come across very few examples of DOI conflict in *taddhita* derivations.

5.3 Challenges to My Interpretation of 1.4.2[1]

Let us now look at examples of DOI that pose a challenge to my interpretation of 1.4.2. In these cases, it can be argued that the *Aṣṭādhyāyī*'s derivational machine does not follow its own algorithm. I have consulted with several scholars, colleagues, and enthusiasts to ensure that I have included all valid counterexamples here. These are the only counterexamples known to us.

Like I have done so far, I will first prove that the example involves conflict, given the interest of the post-Pāṇinian discourse in the subject of conflict, and then discuss both my solution and the traditional solution to the same.

Example #1. *tri* + *ām*—'three' (masculine), genitive plural

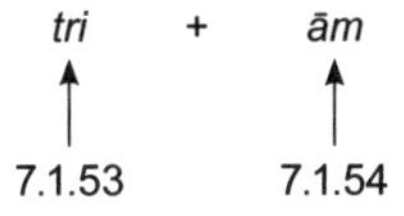

tri + *ām*
↑ 7.1.53 ↑ 7.1.54

7.1.53 *tres trayaḥ*: *tri* is replaced with *traya* when *ām* follows.

7.1.54 *hrasvanadyāpo nuṭ*: augment *nUṬ* is introduced to affix *ām* when it occurs after a base that ends in a short vowel (*hrasvānta*), or in a form that is termed *nadī* (*nadyanta*), or else ends in the feminine affix *āP* (*ābanta*).

If we apply 7.1.53 at this step, we get *traya* + *ām*, to which 7.1.54 will be applicable. If we apply 7.1.54 at this step, we get *tri* + *nām*, to which 7.1.53 will not be applicable. This is because 7.1.53 is applicable to *tri* if it is followed by *ām*, not *nām*.

This is a case of unidirectional blocking and thus of Type 2a (DOI conflict).

By my interpretation of 1.4.2, the RHS rule 7.1.54 wins, and we get: *tri* + *nām* (7.1.54) → *trīnām* (6.4.3 *nāmi*) → **trīṇām* (8.4.2 *aṭkupvāṅnumvyavāye'pi*), which is not the correct form.

To get the correct answer, we must apply 7.1.53 here: *traya* + *ām* (7.1.53) → *traya* + *nām* (7.1.54) → *trayānām* (6.4.3 *nāmi*) → *trayāṇām* (8.4.2 *aṭk-upvāṅnumvyavāye'pi*).

To the best of my knowledge, the tradition does not say anything on this matter.

We know that Pāṇini was familiar with the form *trayāṇām* because he uses it in his rule 7.4.75 *nijāṁ trayāṇāṁ guṇaḥ ślau* 'a *guṇa* vowel replaces the *abhyāsa* of a base constituted by the list of three roots beginning with *nijIR* "to cleanse, nourish" when *ŚLU* follows'. However, he may also have been familiar with the form *trīṇām*: even though *trīṇām* is not to be found in classical Sanskrit, it is in fact used in Vedic Sanskrit: *trīṇām api samudrāṇām* 'also of the three oceans'.[2] It is possible that when Pāṇini composed the *Aṣṭādhyāyī*, or at least its first layer of rules, both *trīṇām* and *trayāṇām* were acceptable as the genitive plural form of *tri* (masculine) in *bhāṣā* 'everyday Sanskrit'. So, even though he uses the form (*trayāṇām*) in his *sūtra*, perhaps he wanted to teach the derivation of the other acceptable form (*trīṇām*).

In the course of time, as the language underwent further change, *trīṇām* got fully replaced with *trayāṇām*.[3] And to accommodate this change, it is possible that a later scholar added the *sūtra* 7.1.53 *tres trayaḥ* to the *Aṣṭādhyāyī*. This scholar may not have known the actual meaning of 1.4.2 *vipratiṣedhe paraṁ kāryam*, which is perhaps why he did not realize that this would create a problem.

In fact, we do find a very similar and related example of language change reflected in Pāṇini's own rules. Consider the genitive plural of *tri* (feminine): *tri* + *ām*. As shown in example 2 of section 2.3, after performing some operations, we get *tisr̥* + *nām*. Here, 6.4.3 *nāmi*, which teaches the elongation of *r̥*, is not applicable, thanks to 6.4.4 *na tisr̥catasr̥*, which forbids us from applying 6.4.3 vis-à-vis *tisr̥* and *catasr̥*. However, the next rule 6.4.5 *chandasy ubhayathā* teaches that, when constructing the Vedic form, one can optionally elongate *ṛ* in the genitive plural of *tri* (feminine). This gives us two acceptable Vedic forms: *tisṛṇām* and *tisṝṇām*. It is likely that when Pāṇini composed the *Aṣṭādhyāyī*, the older version *tisṝṇām* was becoming obsolete and simultaneously making way for the newer version *tisṛṇām*.

Similarly, it seems plausible that, in order to register the change from *trīṇām* to *trayāṇām* in the *Aṣṭādhyāyī*, or put differently, to update the *Aṣṭādhyāyī*, someone added the *sūtra* 7.1.53 *tres trayaḥ* to it. 7.1.53 *tres trayaḥ* must have been placed after 7.1.52 *āmi sarvanāmnaḥ suṭ* to continue *āmi* into 7.1.53 by *anuvṛtti*. But observe how oddly located it is—a substitution rule in the midst of augment insertion rules.

Number	Content	Topic
7.1.50	*āj jaser asuk*	*asug-āgama*
7.1.51	*āśvakṣīravṛṣalavaṇānām ātmaprītau kyaci*	*asug-āgama*
7.1.52	*āmi sarvanāmnaḥ suṭ*	*suḍ-āgama*
7.1.53	*tres trayaḥ*	*tri* → *traya*
7.1.54	*hrasvanadyāpo nuṭ*	*nuḍ-āgama*
7.1.55	*ṣāṭcaturbhyaś ca*	*nuḍ-āgama*
7.1.56	*śrīgrāmaṇyoś chandasi*	*nuḍ-āgama*
7.1.57	*goḥ pādānte*	*nuḍ-āgama*

We also have another reason to believe that 7.1.53 might be an interpolation. Consider Pāṇini's rule 6.4.3 *nāmi* (*dīrghaḥ*). If he had said *āmi dīrghaḥ* instead of *nāmi dīrghaḥ*, then in *deva* + *ām*, two rules would have been simultaneously applicable:

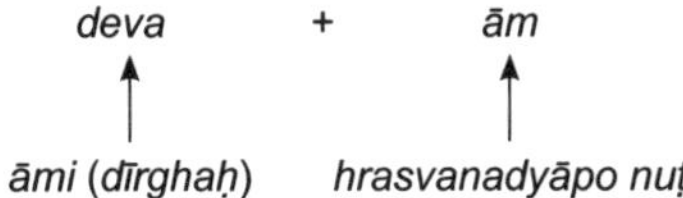

Both rules would block each other. This is a Type 2a interaction (DOI conflict). By my interpretation of 1.4.2, the RHS rule would win leading to *rāmanām* → **rāmaṇām* (8.4.2 *aṭkupvāṅnumvyavāye'pi*), which is not the correct form. It is for this reason that Pāṇini said *nāmi* and not *āmi*, thereby requiring us to add the *nUṬ* augment first and to lengthen the vowel after doing so. Since Pāṇini was careful enough about this derivation, he would also have been careful about the derivation of *trayāṇām*—that is, if he had wanted to derive this form—which also deals with *ām* and *nuḍāgama*.

If Pāṇini had wanted to derive the word *trayāṇām*, I think he would have come up with a rule similar in style to 6.4.3 *nāmi* (*dīrghaḥ*): *tres trayaḥ nāmi*. The derivation would have proceeded as follows: *tri* + *ām* → *tri* + *nām* (7.1.54 *hrasvanadyāpo nuṭ*). At this juncture there would arise an SOI conflict between 6.4.3 *nāmi* and *tres trayaḥ nāmi*. The latter would win by virtue of being more specific, and we would get the correct form: *trayāṇām* (8.4.2 *aṭkupvāṅnumvyavāye'pi*). This suggests that Pāṇini may not be the composer of 7.1.53 *tres trayaḥ*.

To conclude, as stated before, it is possible that when Pāṇini composed the *Aṣṭādhyāyī*, or at least its first layer of rules, both *trīṇām* and *trayāṇām* were acceptable as the genitive plural form of *tri* (masculine) in *bhāṣā* 'everyday Sanskrit'. It is possible that Pāṇini, despite using the form *trayāṇām* in his rule, taught us the derivation of *trīṇām*, while a later scholar added the rule 7.1.53 *tres trayaḥ* to the *Aṣṭādhyāyī* to facilitate the derivation of *trayāṇām*.

Example #2. *tad* + *sU*—'He', nominative singular

7.2.106 *tadoḥ saḥ sāv anantyayoḥ*: the nonfinal *t* and *d* of a base belonging to the group headed by *tyad* 'that' is replaced with *s* when *sU* follows.

7.2.102 *tyadādīnām aḥ*: the final sound of a base belonging to the group headed by *tyad* 'that' is replaced with *a* when a declensional affix follows.

6.1.68 *halṅyābbhyo dīrghāt sutisy apṛktaṁ hal*: there is elision by *LOPA* of the finite verb affixes *ti* and *si* when they consist of a single sound and follow a form that ends in a consonant and of the nominative singular case affix *sU* when it follows a form that ends in a consonant or the long final vowel of feminine affixes *Ṅī* or *āP*.

For now, let us not think about 7.2.106.

If we apply 6.1.68 at this step, *sU* will get replaced by *LOPA*, after which 7.2.102 will not be applicable. On the other hand, if we apply 7.2.102 at this step, 6.1.68 will not be applicable at the following step.

This is a case of mutual blocking and thus of Type 2a (DOI conflict).

By my interpretation of 1.4.2, the RHS rule 6.1.68 wins, and we get: **tad*, which is not the correct form.

In order to get the correct form *saḥ*, we ought to apply 7.2.102, after the application of which, 6.1.68 will no longer be applicable.

The correct derivation proceeds as follows: *tad* + *sU* → *taa* + *sU* (7.2.102 *tyadādīnām aḥ*) → *ta* + *sU* (6.1.97 *ato guṇe*[4]) → *sa* + *sU* (7.2.106 *tadoḥ saḥ sāv anantyayoḥ*) → *saḥ*.

Before I discuss the solution to this problem, note that similar derivational problems arise when we try to derive certain second- and third-person singular imperfect (*LAṄ*) forms, such as *alikhat, apaṭhat*, and so on or vocative singular forms of stems ending in *o*, for example, *gauḥ*.

What all these have in common is that, by my interpretation of 1.4.2, the rule 6.1.68 *halṅyābbhyo dīrghāt sutisy apr̥ktaṁ hal* (or the rule that immediately follows it, i.e., 6.1.69 *eṅhrasvāt saṁbuddheḥ*[5]), is applicable to the right-most element (*sU, ti*, or *si*) and applies at the very beginning of the derivation, as seen above. However, for us to get the correct answer, 6.1.68 or 6.1.69 should not apply at all in any of these derivations. How should this problem be overcome?

As stated before, all three examples of this group involve one of the following two rules: 6.1.68 *halṅyābbhyo dīrghāt sutisyaprktaṁ hal* and 6.1.69 *eṅhrasvāt sambuddheḥ*.

Notice the placement of these rules in the *Aṣṭādhyāyī*:

6.1.66 *lopo vyor vali*[6]

6.1.67 *ver apr̥ktasya*[7]

6.1.68 *halṅyābbhyo dīrghāt sutisy apr̥ktaṁ hal*

6.1.69 *eṅhrasvāt sambuddheḥ*

Notice that:

a. The item undergoing *LOPA* should be in the genitive, as it is in 6.1.66 (cf. *vyor*), 6.1.67 (cf. *ver apr̥ktasya*), and 6.1.69 (cf. *sambuddheḥ*). But *sutisi apr̥ktam* in 6.1.68 is in the nominative. This is odd.

b. The presence of the term *apr̥kta* in 6.1.68 is quite telling too. *apr̥ktasya* from 6.1.67 should have become *anuvr̥tta* 'continued'

> into 6.1.68. There was no need for *apr̥kta* to be mentioned again in 6.1.68.

This tells us two things: one, that someone has possibly edited 6.1.68 and two, that they may have tried to move 6.1.68 from its original position to its current position, perhaps in an attempt to put the two *sūtras* teaching *apr̥kta LOPA* together (but they forgot to delete *apr̥kta* from 6.1.68). In his *bhāṣya* on 6.1.68, Patañjali discusses 6.1.68 in the context of some rules from the *asiddha* section—such as 8.2.7 *nalopaḥ prātipadikāntasya* and 8.2.23 *saṁyogāntasya lopaḥ*, which also deal with deletion of word final consonants. It is likely that the original position of 6.1.68 and 6.1.69 was also somewhere in the *asiddha* section and likely right after 8.2.2 *nalopa supsvaratugvidhiṣu* (so *LOPA* could become *anuvr̥tta* from 8.2.2 into these two rules). Putting these two rules in this position in the *asiddha* section (which starts with 8.2.1 *pūrvatrāsiddham*) allows us to correctly derive all three kinds of examples mentioned above (because there is no longer any scope for simultaneous applicability of these rules with rules that lie outside the *asiddha* section).

I am not suggesting that we should change the order of the rules of the *Aṣṭādhyāyī* for my convenience. I am not arguing for any such reordering at all. I am simply saying that clearly someone has fiddled with both the contents and the position of 6.1.68, 6.1.69, and also 6.1.70 in the *Aṣṭādhyāyī*, so it is not surprising that their current position is creating the derivational problems discussed above.

5.4 Some Clarifications about SSRI

After my doctoral thesis received media attention, I was asked to address certain interesting questions about my understanding of Pāṇinian derivations. I will mention some here to offer clarity on SSRI and related issues.

First, as stated at the end of section 2.1 (chapter 2), it is important for each derivation to begin with the correct input for us to get the correct output using the Pāṇinian machine. Let us try to derive the potential passive participle of *as* 'to be' without establishing any minimal-input requirement (e.g., a base and an affix). Here, two rules are potentially applicable:

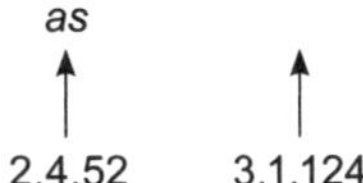

2.4.52 *aster bhūḥ*: when an *ārddhadhātuka* affix is to be added, *as* is replaced with *bhū*.

3.1.124 *r̥halor ṇyat*: the affix *ṆyaT* is added to verbal bases ending in *r̥* or a consonant.

By my interpretation of 1.4.2, if we choose the RHS rule, we get *as* + *ṆyaT*, which would give us the incorrect form. This is because *as* is not the correct verbal base and *ṆyaT* is not the correct affix.

Like any machine, Pāṇini's machine needs to be fed an input, namely the initial string, so that it might be able to produce an output. The input has to be both correct and semantically sufficient, failing which the machine will not be able to produce the grammatically correct output. What do I mean by 'correct'? You cannot give the machine the wrong affix (e.g., *ṆyaT* instead of *yaT*) and then expect it to give you the grammatically correct output. And what do I mean by 'semantically sufficient'? I mean that each meaning-bearing part of the word being derived must find representation in the initial string being fed as the input to Pāṇini's machine. So, for example, you cannot just give the machine the root *bhū* and expect it to derive *bhavya* or *bhavanti* or any such form for us. To derive *bhavanti*, we need to give the machine both the root *bhū*, which means 'to be', and the suffix *tiP*, which indicates that we are deriving a third-person singular form. Similarly, to derive the potential passive participle *bhavya*, we need to give the machine a root that means 'to be' and also a *kr̥tya* affix that can make it a potential passive participle. The derivation of the word begins only after the correct and semantically sufficient input is provided to the machine. So, in this case, before we have *bhū* + *yaT*, the derivation cannot begin. And before the derivation begins, DOI cannot arise, and 1.4.2, as I interpret it, cannot be applied either. It is for this reason that I did not include such derivations as examples of DOI in my doctoral thesis. In sum, this is not a valid counterexample of my interpretation of 1.4.2.

But the question remains: How then do we derive the correct form *bhavya* if we wish to derive this using the root *as*, since Pāṇini does permit this? Firstly, we have to work towards getting our input for the Pāṇinian machine ready. To do this, we must go to the *Dhātupāṭha* to pick our root. We pick *as*.

We must also have before us all the affixes that can potentially be added to any root to construct a potential passive participle, as we have to pick one of them. To get our root ready, we must check the *Aṣṭādhyāyī* for applicable rules. We know that irrespective of which suffix we choose from amongst those available for constructing the potential passive participle of *as*, it is going to be an *ārdhadhātuka* suffix. So, we must write: *as* + <*ārddhadhātuka* affix>. We must then apply 2.4.52 *aster bhūḥ* (*ārdhadhātuke*). With the base ready, we pick the correct affix *yaT* (cf. 3.1.97 *aco yat*). Now that we have the correct initial string *bhū* + *yat*, we can use it as the input. Once we enter this input into the Pāṇinian machine, it performs the derivation and gives us the correct output *bhavya*.

If fact, we must also consider the following possibility: What if we said that not only the base and one affix but, along with the base, all possible affixes must be assembled before the derivation can begin? For example, in chapter 4, I start the first derivation under section 4.1 with *cit* + *tiP*. What if we said that the starting point of the derivation should be not *cit* + *tiP* but instead *cit* + *ŚaP* + *tiP*? This would take a step out of the Pāṇinian derivational machine, namely *cit* + *tiP* → *cit* + *ŚaP* + *tiP*. Our goal is to keep as many steps inside the Pāṇinian derivational machine as possible, so this is not ideal. However, it has its own advantage: in our present example, if the derivation begins with *cit* + *ŚaP* + *tiP*, then we do not need to insist that 'only one item can be called an *aṅga* with respect to a certain *pratyaya* in a derivation', as I have done in chapter 4. This is because we do not have to worry about eliminating the possibility of calling *cit* an *aṅga* with respect to *tiP* at the very beginning of the derivation (*cit* + *tiP*) and can get the same, correct derivational outcomes, nevertheless. This time, without insisting on the only-one-*aṇga*-per-affix-per-derivation assumption, let us consider 1.4.13 again:

yasmāt—to (lit. after) *cit*
pratyayavidhis—(upon the) addition of *tiP*
tadādi—that which begins with *cit*
pratyaye—when *tiP* follows
aṅgam—(is called) *aṅga*.

The input of the derivation is: *cit* + *ŚaP* + *tiP*. The form that begins with *cit* is an *aṅga* with respect to *tiP*. Can we say that *cit* + *ŚaP* begins with *cit*? I do not think so. I think *cit* + *ŚaP* is still just a string of two separate items, namely the root *cit* and the *vikaraṇa* affix *ŚaP*. Only when they are fused into a single form that begins with *cit*, that form can be called an *aṅga* with respect to *tiP*. When can we fuse *cit* and *ŚaP* into a single form? I think we can do that after applying all possible rules to *cit* and *ŚaP*, except those that are triggered by *tiP*.

So here, we apply 7.3.86 *pugantalaghūpadhasya ca* to *cit* (an operation triggered by *ŚaP*, not by *tiP*) and get *cet* + *ŚaP* + *tiP*. Note that *cet* and *ŚaP* cannot undergo any other operations that are not triggered by *tiP*, so we can fuse *cet* + *ŚaP* into a single form, that is, *ceta*. *Ceta* begins with *cet* and is followed by *tiP*, so it can be called an *aṅga* with respect to *tiP*. We can summarize this information in this table:

Step	**Question**	**Traditional opinion**	**My opinion**
cit + *ŚaP* + *tiP*	Is *cit* + *ŚaP* an *aṅga* w.r.t. *tiP*?	Yes	No
ceta + *tiP*	Is *ceta* an *aṅga* w.r.t. *tiP*?	Yes	Yes

This approach allows us to produce the same results and overcome the same challenges as the approach I have taken in chapter 4 does. By insisting that the input of the machine should include the base and all affixes, that is, by starting the derivation with *cit* + *ŚaP* + *tiP*, we can dispense with the only-one-*aṇga*-per-affix-per-derivation assumption that I work with in chapter 4. I think this needs to be discussed further, so I do not want to pronounce my final opinion on this matter just yet. Since this question has to do with the nature of the input that we feed into the Pāṇinian machine, it also has implications for how we teach Pāṇini's grammar to the computer. For more on this, see chapter 8, section 8.2.

One may ask: Is it also true then that SOI too cannot occur before the correct input has been assembled? As stated in section 2.4 (chapter 2), while DOI is a part of Pāṇini's grammar, SOI is not and is simply a feature of the *sūtra* style instead. Thus, while DOI cannot exist until the correct input has been assembled and entered into the Pāṇinian machine, SOI certainly can exist at any stage. Thus, for example, when we have to choose one affix of three possible affixes, we can call it a case of SOI—so long as we have already chosen the correct base to ensure that the affix chosen is the correct one. For an example of this, see section 3.2, chapter 3. Let me diagrammatically summarize this difference between DOI and SOI here:

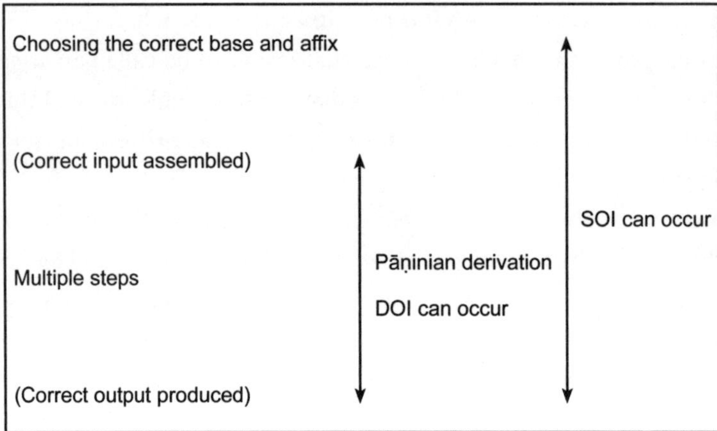

Second, I was asked if the interaction between the rules 7.2.117 *taddhiteṣv acām ādeḥ* and 7.2.116 *ata upadhāyāḥ* is a case of DOI, and if not, what it is and how it should be tackled. At first glance, it is possible to mistake this for DOI in the following manner:

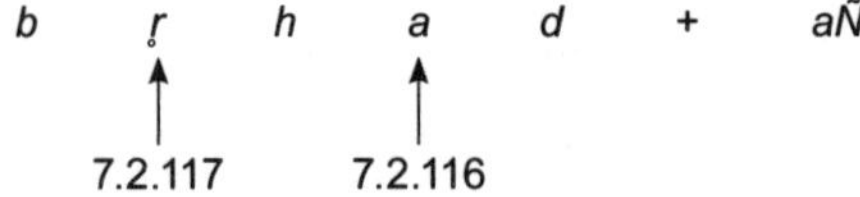

7.2.117 *taddhiteṣv acām ādeḥ*: the first vowel of the base undergoes *vr̥ddhi* when an affix marked with *Ñ* or *Ṇ* follows in *taddhita* derivations.

7.2.116 *ata upadhāyāḥ*: the penultimate sound *a* of a verbal base undergoes *vr̥ddhi* when an affix marked with *Ñ* or *Ṇ* follows.

If we are to treat this as an instance of DOI, then by my interpretation of 1.4.2, we apply the RHS rule and get *br̥hāda*. Thereafter, 7.2.117 is still applicable and applies, giving us the incorrect form: **bārhāda*. The correct form requires us to apply only 7.2.117.

In the *Aṣṭādhyāyī*, most *vidhi sūtra*s 'operational rules' are governed by *paribhāṣā sūtras* 'metarules', and there can also be conflicts between *paribhāṣā sūtras*. For example, the operational rule 7.2.101 *jarāyā jaras anyatarasyām*[8] can be governed by two metarules potentially, namely 1.1.52 *alo'ntyasya* and 1.1.55 *anekālśit sarvasya*. We choose the latter because it is specifically taught for substitutes made up of more than one sound or marked with *Ś*.[9]

However, there are also some rules that themselves play the role of both *vidhi sūtra* and the *paribhāṣā sūtra*—for want of a better word. Or put differently, they do not need a separate *paribhāṣā sūtra* to govern them. 7.2.116 and 7.2.117 are such rules. I say this because, in these rules, both the operation, that is, *vr̥ddhi*, and the exact sound(s) undergoing the operation, that is, first vowel or penultimate sound (which in the case of 7.2.101 has to be clarified by the *paribhāṣā sūtra* 1.1.55), have been mentioned. The operation in both 7.2.116 and 7.2.117 is exactly the same: *vr̥ddhi*. So, we need only decide which sound of the base undergoes this operation. The real conflict is between the '*paribhāṣā*' components (for want of a better word) and not the '*vidhi*' components. Or put differently, all that needs to be decided now is which vowel will undergo the operation and not what the operation should be.

Here, I list the conditions under which each of these rules are applicable and then compare the two relevant conditions, which are highlighted in bold.

7.2.116

an *a*, when followed by an item marked with *Ṇ* or *Ñ*

7.2.117

an *a*, when followed by an item marked with *Ṇ* or *Ñ* (in *taddhita*)

any other vowel, when followed by an item marked with *Ṇ* or *Ñ* (in *taddhita*)

7.2.117 is more specific because it is relevant for *taddhita* constructions alone. It wins, so the first vowel undergoes *vr̥ddhi*, and we get the correct form. Note that not only in the case of SOI but also in cases of mutual opposition between two *paribhāṣā* rules or two *saṁjñā* rules, we choose the more specific rule. As I have stated in chapter 2, this is an inherent feature of the *sūtra* style and is not exclusively related to Pāṇini's grammar.

5.5 Vedic and Accentuation Rules

As observant readers may have noticed, I have not included in the chapters of this book any special commentary on what may be called 'Vedic' and 'accentuation' rules.

Unfortunately, in the field of Pāṇinian studies, these two subjects have not been scrutinized thoroughly. In relatively modern treatises teaching Pāṇinian derivations such as the *Kaumudī*, Vedic rules do not receive as much attention as do rules that are applicable to both classical and Vedic forms. Similarly, in Pāṇinian derivations, accents are generally left unmarked, and therefore, accentuation rules are not taken into account at all.

Since the completion of my PhD, I have studied the derivation of various Vedic forms using Pāṇinian rules, that is, Pāṇinian rules that apply exclusively to Vedic language. One must remember that Pāṇini does not derive all Vedic forms but only some of them.[10] With respect to those that I assume he wants to derive, I can say that I have not found any such Vedic derivations that contradict my findings about 1.4.2. For this reason, I have decided not to discuss Vedic derivations separately here: there is nothing more to be said on the subject of rule conflict in the derivations of Vedic words than has already been said about rule conflict in the derivations of words found in both Vedic and classical Sanskrit.

On the other hand, one ought to comment on accentuation in the context of rule conflict. It is worth noting here that Pāṇini teaches us accents for not only Vedic language but also for ordinary language or what we now call 'classical Sanskrit'. Based on my study of accents, which I conducted post the completion of my PhD, I have come to the following conclusions.

At each step of the derivation, only after a rule has been applied does the question of accent become relevant. Note that, we apply a rule only after dealing with SSRI (or colloquially, 'rule conflict'). In sum, accent does not influence the process of rule conflict resolution at all.

Pāṇini has taught an important rule that enables us to derive accented words correctly: 6.1.158 *anudāttaṁ padam ekavarjam*, which teaches that a *pada* is entirely low pitched (*anudātta*) with the exception of one syllable. However, there are many cases where both the base and the suffix have been taught as high pitched (*udātta*) by Pāṇini. If both were to be allowed to retain their *udātta* accent, that would violate 6.1.158. To avoid this, we have to choose one of the two as the *udātta*. How should we make this choice? One might be tempted to argue that we must use my interpretation of 1.4.2 *vipratiṣedhe paraṁ kāryam* (i.e., RHS operation wins) to make this choice. However, this would be an unwarranted application of 1.4.2 because 1.4.2 is meant for the selection of one *kārya* (i.e., operation) of multiple possible *kārya*s and not for the selection of one *udātta* of multiple possible *udātta*s. Only after the *kārya* has been chosen, that is, only after the winning (RHS) rule has been applied, can the question of accent become relevant. Thus, as stated above, accent does not influence rule conflict resolution at all; nor can we use 1.4.2 to choose one of two or more possible *udāttas*.

Having studied Sanskrit accent using both Pāṇini's grammar and Macdonell's Vedic grammar, I have concluded that in Pāṇini's grammar, the *udātta* accent of the morpheme that is introduced most recently to the derivation, irrespective of whether it is a suffix or augment or something else, should be retained and all others should be made *anudātta* by 6.1.158 *anudāttaṁ padam ekavarjam.*

This is also what Kātyāyana teaches in vt. 9 on 6.1.158: *satiśiṣṭasvarabalīyastvaṁ ca* 'The accent [of the item] that is taught [i.e., introduced] relatively later [i.e., most recently to the derivation] is stronger [and thus prevails]'. Patañjali says, while commenting on vt. 11 under the same *sūtra*: *. . . satiśiṣṭo'pi vikaraṇasvaro lasārvadhātukasvaraṁ na bādhata iti* '. . . even though taught later, the accent of the *vikaraṇa* does not defeat the accent of the *sārvadhātuka lakāra*'. This version caught on in later traditional texts. The *Nyāsa* on 1.4.60 *gatiś ca* reads: *satiśiṣṭasvarasya balīyastvam anyatra vikaraṇasvarebhya iti* 'The accent [of the item] that is taught [i.e., introduced] relatively later [i.e., most recently to the derivation] is stronger [and thus prevails] except in the case of the accent of the *vikaraṇa*'. This went on to become a famous maxim among later Pāṇinīyas.

It is noteworthy that this topic is discussed in the *Mahābhāṣya* under 6.1.158 in the context of rule conflict.[11] However, as I have concluded above, accent does not interact with or influence rule conflict at all. As regards the maxim *satiśiṣṭasvarasya balīyastvam anyatra vikaraṇasvarebhya iti*, I disagree with the tradition in that I think a special waiver for the *vikaraṇas* need not be mentioned. With the help of examples, I will show why. In conclusion, I think the general principle followed by Pāṇinian accentuation is as follows: the *udātta* or *svarita* accent of the item introduced most recently to the derivation is retained and the rest are turned into *anudātta* by 6.1.158 *anudāttaṁ padam ekavarjam.* To make this process convenient, systematic, and transparent, we can implement the teaching of 6.1.158 at each step of the derivation. Note that this is not strictly correct because we do not have a *pada* at each step of the derivation; we are doing it purely for the sake of convenience.

To exemplify what I have stated above, I will derive two forms of the root *jñā* 'to know'. We will first derive the present third-person singular. By virtue of being a verbal root, the *ā* of *jñā* is *udātta* by 6.1.162 *dhātoḥ*, which teaches that the final vowel of a root takes the *udātta* 'high-pitch' accent. In the derivations presented below, I will mark *udātta*s the Western way (like Greek acutes) and will not use any Indian diacritics for accents. Because of technical issues, the acute will appear immediately after (*a*´) rather than above the letter.

jñā´

To this root now we add the third-person singular suffix *tiP*, which is *udātta* by 3.1.3 *ādyudāttaś ca* 'the first vowel of the suffix takes the *udātta* accent'.

jñā´ + *ti*´

Note that by 6.1.158 *anudāttaṁ padam ekavarjam* only one vowel per word can be *udātta* or *svarita*. Whichever item has been introduced most recently to the derivation (here, *tiP*) gets to keep its *udātta* and the remaining vowels lose it.

jñā + *ti*´

Now by 3.1.81 *kryādibhyaḥ śnā*[12] we get:

jñā + *Śnā* + *ti*´

Since *Śnā* is also a suffix, by 3.1.3 *ādyudāttaś ca*, it is *udātta*.

jñā + *Śnā*´ + *ti*´

But since only one of them can be *udātta* (cf 6.1.158), the one introduced last (here, *Śnā*) retains its *udātta* and *ti* loses it.

jñā + *Śnā*´ + *ti*

By 7.3.79 *jñājanor jā*,[13] we get:

jānā´*ti*

By 8.4.66 *udāttād anudāttasya svaritaḥ*, which teaches that an *anudātta* following an *udātta* becomes a *svarita*, the *i* of *ti* becomes *svarita*. This can be shown using the Indian convention as follows: जा॒ना॑ति॑.

Let us now derive the present third-person dual. The initial steps of this derivation are similar to those of the previous one:

jñā´	(6.1.162 *dhātoḥ*)
jñā + *ta*´*s*	(3.1.3 *ādyudāttaś ca*, 6.1.158 *anudāttaṁ padam ekavarjam*)
jñā + *Śnā*´ + *tas*	(3.1.81 *kryādibhyaḥ śnā*, 3.1.3 *ādyudāttaś ca*, 6.1.158 *anu* . . .)
jā + *Śnā*´ + *tas*	(7.3.79 *jñājanor jā*)
jānā´ + *tas*	

Now that *jānā* is an *aṅga* with respect to *tas*, the following rule from the *aṅgādhikāra* becomes applicable here:

6.4.113 *ī haly aghoḥ*: the final *ā* of a base that ends in *Śnā*, or of a reduplicated stem (*abhyasta*) excluding those termed *ghu*, is replaced with *ī* when a *sārvadhātuka* affix beginning with a consonant and marked with *K* or *Ṅ* follows.[14]

Note that the *ī*, which replaces *ā*, does not have an inherent accent. It cannot accept the accent of the item it replaces either because this operation is an *al-vidhi*, and thus, 1.1.56 *sthānivad ādeśo'nalvidhau*[15] is not applicable here. Consequently, we do not mark its accent at all.

jānītas

Now, with the loss of the *udātta ā*, there is no *udātta* accent in this form, and thus, we can permit the item that was introduced latest to the derivation to retain its *udātta* accent. Here, it is *tas*. By 6.1.158 *anudāttaṁ padam ekavarjam*, the rest of the *pada* becomes *anudātta*, and thus, *ā*, which did not have an accent so far, also takes the *anudātta* accent thanks to 6.1.158. Thus, we get: *jānīta´s* (जा॒नी॒तस्).

Note that the traditional maxim *satiśiṣṭasvarasya balīyastvam anyatra vikaraṇasvarebhya iti* suffers from the following weakness: we are dealing with *vikaraṇas* in both derivations, yet the accent is on different syllables in these two forms. Thus, contrary to the traditional position, there is no need to treat *vikaraṇas* as exceptions. If one follows Pāṇini meticulously in such derivations, one does not face problems vis-à-vis accentuation.

In conclusion, accentuation does not influence rule conflict at all. The principle of allowing the most recently introduced item to retain its *udātta* or *svarita* accent while making the remaining vowels *anudātta* by 6.1.158 *anudāttaṁ padam ekavarjam* allows us to perform derivations correctly.

5.6 'Conflicts' between *Antaraṅga* and *Bahiraṅga* Rules

So far, traditional examples of *antaraṅga-bahiraṅga* conflict have not received much attention in my work. Through this section, I seek to explain why such is the case by discussing some such examples. Before we begin, let us revise the basic definition of *antaraṅga*. According to the *Paribhāṣenduśekhara*,[16] '*antaraṅga* is [a rule] the causes [of the application] of which lie within [or before] the sum of the causes of a *bahiraṅga* rule'.[17] An *antaraṅga* rule is stronger than and thus defeats a *bahiraṅga* rule.[18]

However, note that Kātyāyana and Patañjali, despite talking about *antaraṅga* and *bahiraṅga*, do not define these terms and consequently do not explain why a certain rule is to be regarded as *antaraṅga*. In vt. 8 on 1.4.2 *vipratiṣedhe paraṁ kāryam*, Kātyāyana says: *antaraṅgam ca*. On this *vārttika*, Patañjali elaborates: *antaraṅgam ca balīyo bhavatīti vaktavyam* 'It should also be said that [an] *antaraṅga* [rule] is stronger [than a *bahiraṅga* rule]'. Let us examine some examples discussed by Patañjali (Mbh I.304.10 onwards) while commenting on various *vārttikas* on 1.4.2.

Example #1.

Let us follow Patañjali's method to derive ***syona*** 'a stitched item, that is, a sack'. First, we add *na* to *siv* 'to stitch' by 3.3.1 *uṇādayo bahulam*.[19] By 6.4.19 *chvoḥ śūḍ anunāsike ca* (which teaches that *ch* and *v* are replaced with *ś* and *ūṬH*, respectively, when an affix beginning with a nasal, or affix *KvI*, or one beginning with *jhaL* [a non-nasal stop or a fricative] and marked with *K* or *Ṅ*, follows), we get *siū* + *na*. According to Patañjali, two rules are simultaneously applicable to *siū* + *na*:

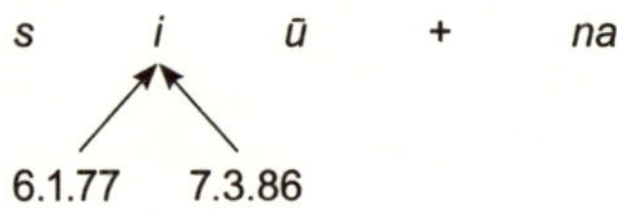

6.1.77 *iko yaṇ aci*: *iK* (*i, u, ṛ, ḷ*) is replaced with *yaṆ* (*y, v, r, l*) when *aC* (any vowel) follows.

7.3.86 *pugantalaghūpadhasya ca*: *guṇa* replaces *iK* of a verbal base that ends in the augment *pUK* or that has a *laghu* 'light' vowel as its penultimate sound when a *sārvadhātuka* or *ārdhadhātuka* affix follows.

According to Patañjali, the rule teaching substitution with *yaṆ* (6.1.77) is *antaraṅga* with respect to the rule teaching *guṇa* (7.3.86). This is corroborated by the definition of *antaraṅga* given by the commentary on Pbh 50 of the *Paribhāṣenduśekhara*: the cause of application of 6.1.77 (i.e., *ū*) lies before, that is, to the left of the cause of application of 7.3.86 (i.e., *na*). Let us use this example to speculate about how Kātyāyana might have defined *antaraṅga* and *bahiraṅga*. Note that the cause of application of 6.1.77 lies *antar* 'inside' the *aṅga siū*, while the cause of application of 7.3.86 lies *bahir* 'outside' it. Thus, the term *antaraṅga* could stand for *aṅgasya antaḥ*, and the term *bahiraṅga* for *aṅgād bahiḥ*.

The *antaraṅga* rule 6.1.77 wins, and thus the derivation proceeds as follows: *siū + na* → *syū + na* (6.1.77) → *syona* (7.3.84 *sārvadhātukārdhadhātukayoḥ*).

Now, let me present my opinion about this example. There is no evidence that Pāṇini has composed the *Uṇādi sūtras*. Therefore, this derivation, which requires us to add *na* to *siv* as per an *Uṇādisūtra* (289) is not Pāṇinian at all.

Example #2.

Let us use Patañjali's method to derive the form ***dyaukāmi*** 'male offspring of ***dyukāma***'. We start by adding the *taddhita* affix *iÑ* to the *bahuvrīhi* compound made up of *div* and *kāma* by 4.1.95 *ata iÑ* (which teaches that the *taddhita* affix *iÑ* occurs to denote an offspring after a syntactically related nominal stem that ends in *a*). After deleting the inflectional affixes inside the compound by 2.4.71 *supo dhātuprātipadikayoḥ*, we get *div + kāma + iÑ*. Here, by 6.1.131 *diva ut* (which teaches that the final sound of the *pada div* is replaced with *uT*), we get *diu + kāma + iÑ*. At this stage, according to Patañjali, two rules are simultaneously applicable:

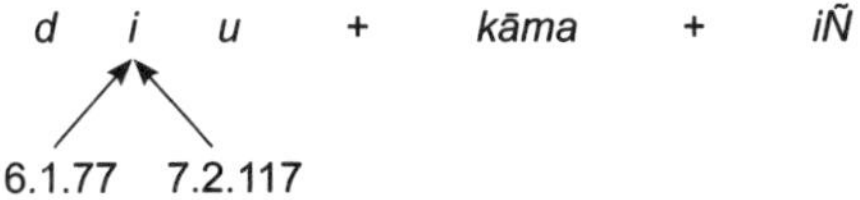

6.1.77 *iko yaṇ aci*: same as above.

7.2.117 *taddhiteṣv acām ādeḥ*: the first vowel of the base undergoes *vṛddhi* when an affix marked with *Ñ* or *Ṇ* follows in *taddhita* derivations.

This example is similar to the previous one: the cause of application of 6.1.77 (i.e., *u*) lies before, namely to the left of the cause of application of 7.2.117 (i.e., *iÑ*). Here too, Patañjali says that 6.1.77 is *antaraṅga* and thus wins. The derivation proceeds as follows: *diu + kāma + iÑ* → *dyu + kāma + iÑ* (6.1.77) → *dyau + kāma + iÑ* (7.2.117) → *dyaukāmi* (6.4.148 *yasyeti ca*[20]).

In my opinion, no such conflict arises in the first place. We want to derive a word that means: *dyukāmasya apatyam pumān* 'male offspring of *dyukāma*'. Since we are talking about *dyukāma*'s offspring and not (*div + kāma*)'s offspring, the derivation should start with *dyukāma* and not with *div + kāma*. Thus, we have: *dyukāma* + *Ṅas* + *iÑ*. *Ṅas* is deleted by 2.4.71 *supo dhātuprātipadikayoḥ* and we get *dyukāma* + *iÑ*. Here, two rules are simultaneously applicable:

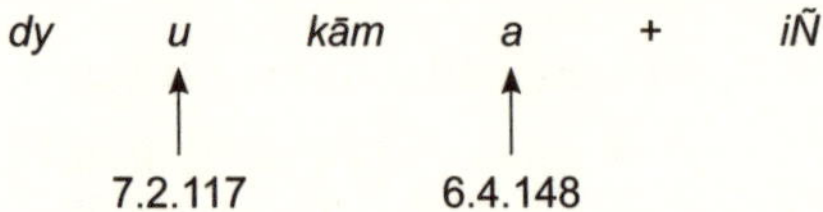

7.2.117 *taddhiteṣv acām ādeḥ*: same as above.

6.4.148 *yasyeti ca*: same as above.

This is a case of DOI. By my interpretation of 1.4.2, we apply the RHS rule 6.4.148 and get *dyukām* + *iÑ*. Then we apply 7.2.117 and get *dyaukāmi*, which is the correct form. [21]

Several other examples discussed by Patañjali in his comments on different *vārttikas* on 1.4.2, such as *sautthatiḥ, kādraveyaḥ, stairṇiḥ, khaṭvīyati, kāmaṇḍaleya, cauḍi*, and so on are similar to this example. For instance, in the derivation of the nominal base *sautthati*, Patañjali starts with *su* + *utthita*, whereas one should actually start with *sūtthita*.

Example #3.

Let us follow Patañjali's method to derive the form ***dudyūṣati*** 'desires to shine'. We start by adding the desiderative affix *saN* to the root *div* 'to shine' by 3.1.7 *dhātoḥ karmaṇaḥ samānakartr̥kād icchāyāṁ vā* (which teaches that the affix *saN* is optionally introduced after a verbal stem, the action denoted by which is the object of a verbal stem expressing desire and both actions have the same agent). Thereafter, by 6.4.19 *chvoḥ śūḍ anunāsike ca* (see translation in example 1), we get *diū* + *saN*. Here, according to Patañjali, two rules are simultaneously applicable:

{*d* [*i*]} *ū* + *saN*

6.1.77 *iko yaṇ aci* is applicable to *i* while 6.1.9 *sanyaṅoḥ*[22] is applicable to *di*. Notice that the cause of application of 6.1.77 (i.e., *ū*) lies to the left of the cause of application of 6.1.9 (i.e., *saN*). Patañjali says that 6.1.77 is *antaraṅga* and thus wins, thereby giving *dyū* + *saN*. Thereafter, 6.1.9 applies, and we get *dyūdyū* + *saN*. After applying other rules, we get the correct form *dudyūṣati*.

In my opinion, such a conflict does not arise in the first place. I interpret *sanyaṅoḥ* as a genitive form, not as a locative form.[23] So, in my view, 6.1.9 *sanyaṅoḥ* teaches that a verbal base ending in *saN* or *yaṄ*, which has not undergone reduplication, is reduplicated.[24] Note that *diū* + *saN* is not a verbal base ending in *saN*, but instead two separate items, namely *diū* and *saN*. So, 6.1.9 is not applicable here. However, 6.1.77 is applicable here, and on applying it, we get *dyū* + *saN*. Now, since no other rules can be applied here, we can fuse the two items *dyū* and *saN* into a single item *dyūṣa*, which we can call a verbal base ending in *saN*. Therefore, 6.1.9 applies here, and we get *dyūdyūṣa*. After applying other rules, we get the correct verbal base *dudyūṣa* (and the correct final form *dudyūṣati*).

The examples *jujñaudanīyiṣati* and *ātestīryate* discussed by Patañjali are similar to this one.

Example #4.

Patañjali says that in the string ***ayaja* + *i* + *indram*** 'I worshipped Indra', two rules are simultaneously applicable:

6.1.87 *ād guṇaḥ* is applicable to *a* + *i*, and 6.1.101 *akaḥ savarṇe dīrghaḥ* is applicable to *i* + *i*. He adds that 6.1.87 is *antaraṅga* and thus wins, thereby giving the correct form: *ayaje indram*.

I do not think that such a conflict arises at all. I think that in the Pāṇinian system all possible rules that can be applied while constructing a word ought to be applied before the word is considered within the context of the sentence. In other words, these rules, which contribute towards the construction of a word, cannot be applied after the word enters the sentence. Here, the rule 6.1.87 applies to *ayaja* + *i*, giving the form *ayaje*. Now that the word is ready, it enters the sentence: *ayaje indram*.[25]

Other examples of this nature discussed by Patañjali include *agnir indraḥ*, *pacatv atra*.

Example #5.

Let us derive the form ***vānīya*** 'should be weaved' using Patañjali's method. We add the affix *anīyaR* to *veÑ* 'to weave' by 3.1.96 *tavyattavyānīyaraḥ*. Here, according to Patañjali, two rules are simultaneously applicable:

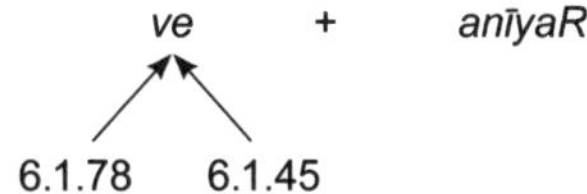

6.1.78 *eco'yavāyāvaḥ*: the sounds represented by *eC* (*e*, *o*, *ai*, and *au*) are replaced with *ay*, *av*, *āy*, and *āv*, respectively, when a vowel follows.

6.1.45 *ād eca upadeśe'śiti*: the final sound of a verbal root that ends in *eC* (*e*, *o*, *ai*, and *au*) in the *Dhātupāṭha* is replaced with *ā*, when an affix that is not marked with *Ś* follows.

Patañjali says that 6.1.45 is *antaraṅga* with respect to 6.1.78 and thus wins. Note that this contradicts what the commentary on Pbh 50 tells us. We would expect the cause of application of the *antaraṅga* rule to be within or before that of the *bahiraṅga* rule. But here, the cause of application of the *bahiraṅga* rule 6.1.78 (i.e., *a* at the beginning of *anīyaR*) lies inside the cause of the *antaraṅga* rule 6.1.45 (i.e., *anīyaR*). This exemplifies the fact that the *antaraṅga* tool is poorly defined and not always useful.

According to me, this is a case of SOI, and we do not need the *antaraṅga* tool to deal with cases of SOI. In case of SOI, the more specific rule wins. Let us compare the two rules:

6.1.78

***e* / *o* / *ai* / *au* + vowel**

6.1.45

***e* / *o* / *ai* / *au* (end of verbal root) + vowel (beginning of affix not marked with *Ś*)**

e / *o* / *ai* / *au* (end of verbal root) + nonvowel (beginning of affix not marked with *Ś*)

6.1.45 is more specific because it applies only when the affix is not marked with *Ś*. Thus, it wins, giving us the correct form *vā* + *anīya* → *vānīya* (6.1.101 *akaḥ savarṇe dīrghaḥ*).

Other examples discussed by Patañjali such as *glācchatram*, *agnicid idam* are similar to this one.

Finally, Patañjali does not simply say that *antaraṅga* rules defeat *bahiraṅga* rules in the case of conflict. He goes a step further to claim: *asiddhaṁ bahiraṅgam antaraṅge* 'a *bahiraṅga* rule is *asiddha* with respect to an *antaraṅga* rule'. Thus, he implies that an *antaraṅga* rule cannot see a *bahiraṅga* rule and therefore cannot see the outcome of the application of the *bahiraṅga* rule either. This is true not only for cases of Same Step Rule Interaction (including conflict) but also for any pair of *antaraṅga-bahiraṅga* rules that are not simultaneously applicable. Consider the following example.

Example #6.
Consider ***pacāva*** + ***idam***. By 6.1.87 *ād guṇaḥ*, we get ***pacāvedam***. Here, Patañjali claims that by 3.4.93 *eta ai* (which teaches that *eT*, which is a substitute of the first-person replacement of *LOṬ*, is replaced with *ai*), the *e* in *pacāvedam* could get replaced with *ai*, thereby giving the incorrect phrase **pacāvaidam*. He says that this is prevented by the fact that the rule 6.1.87 is *bahiraṅga* and thus *asiddha* with respect to the *antaraṅga* rule 3.4.93. Thus, 3.4.93 cannot apply to *e*, which is the outcome of the application of 6.1.87. This ensures that we get the correct phrase: *pacāvedam*.

I do not agree with Patañjali. As stated before, according to me, in the Pāṇinian system all possible rules that can be applied while constructing a word ought to be applied before the word is considered within the context of the sentence. In other words, these rules, which contribute towards the construction of a word, cannot be applied to the word after it enters the sentence. Note that 3.4.93 *eta ai* is a rule that helps the construction of a word (e.g., *edhāvahai*), and therefore, it is not applicable at sentence level.

In conclusion, I think that the *antaraṅga* tool is completely unnecessary in both SSRI and non-SSRI contexts. Most examples (like 1, 2, 3, 4, and 6), which it allegedly solves, are not problematic in the first place. Some examples (like 5) it deals with are actually ordinary cases of SOI, which can be solved by choosing the more specific rule.

5.7 Some Thoughts on the *Siddha* Principle

Joshi and Kiparsky too have rejected the *antaraṅga* principle in multiple publications (1979, 1982) and have proposed the *siddha* principle. I will first highlight their views on the subject of *antaraṅga-bahiraṅga*. Thereafter, I will share my opinion about their *siddha* principle.

About the *antaraṅga* principle, Kiparsky (1982, 87–88) writes: 'When the force of the *siddha* principle is correctly appreciated, the *antaraṅga-paribhāṣā* can be seen to play no role whatever with the word. The ordering of rules in the derivation of a word is regulated exclusively by the *siddha*-principle (as well as, of course, the *utsarga/apavāda* principle) and so-called *bahiraṅga* rules may very well be *siddha* w.r.t. so-called *antaraṅga* rules, contrary to Pbh.

50 *asiddhaṁ bahiraṅgam antaraṅge*, provided only that the *siddha* principle requires it'.

Let us now consider the fundamental justification given by Joshi and Kiparsky (1979) for their *siddha* principle. In the paper titled 'The Ordering of Rules in Pāṇini's Grammar', Kiparsky (1982) gives a detailed explanation of the *siddha* principle. I will quote from this paper here.

Kiparsky proposes the *siddha* principle on the basis of a *vārttika* on 6.1.86 *ṣatvatukor asiddhaḥ* 'a single replacement in place of the preceding and the following sound segments is suspended[26] with respect to any potential replacement with *ṣ* or insertion of augment *tUK*'. Kiparsky explains: 'Kātyāyana says that making a rule *asiddha* has two functions: [*ṣatvatukor*][27] *asiddhavacanam ādeśalakṣaṇapratiṣedhārtham utsargalakṣaṇabhāvārthaṁ ca* (6.1.86, vt. 1). *Utsarga* here means *sthānin*, the element which undergoes substitution in a rule' (1982, p. 77).

I translate this *vārttika* as follows: 'the statement that *ṣ* [replacing *s*] and [the insertion of the augment] *tUK* are *asiddha* [has been made] for the purpose of preventing the operations that are due for application to the substitute, and facilitating the operations that are due for application to the substituendum [original item]'.

Kiparsky then says: 'to use terms common in linguistics, *asiddhatva* blocks bleeding and feeding between rules'. Before going further, let us understand what he means by feeding and bleeding: A feeds B if the application of A facilitates the application of B, and P bleeds Q if the application of P obstructs the application of Q.

Kiparsky concludes:

> [I]t can be said that *asiddha* and the other devices are restrictions (*niyamas*) on a general *paribhāṣā* that determines how rules interact when no special statement about their ordering is made in the grammar. This *paribhāṣā* is not stated in the grammar itself but it is presupposed by the correct operation of rules in it and implied by the various restrictions on it that *are* stated in the grammar. It is to be formulated as "*sarvatra siddham*" and we refer to it as the *siddha* principle. . . . [W]hat the *siddha* principle says is that in the general case we have *ādeśalakṣaṇabhāva* and *utsargal-*

> *akṣaṇapratiṣedha* . . . in short, the *siddha* relations of bleeding and feeding are given free by the underlying theory of the *Aṣṭādhyāyī* and if we must *not* have them in some particular case, *then* only something must be said in the grammar itself. . . . As far as feeding is concerned, this really goes without saying. In almost any derivation, the application of one rule creates scope for another rule to apply, that rule applies creating scope for a third rule and so on. That all rules in such a chain of rules are to be applied is taken for granted in the tradition. (1982, 79)

Kiparsky adds: 'By this point anyone familiar with the topic will already have recognized that the principle of bleeding order is simply equivalent to the *nitya*-principle in the traditional inventory of the *paribhāṣās*' (1982:84–85).

Thus, we can say feeding and bleeding together are simply equivalent to *nityatva* in the Pāṇinian tradition. And the *siddha* principle, which means the maximization of feeding and bleeding, is tantamount to the maximization, wherever possible, of the use of *nityatva* for rule conflict resolution, that is, in all cases involving unidirectional blocking.

Now, using diagrams, I will explain why I think Joshi and Kiparsky have made a logical error in interpreting the aforementioned *vārttika*. I will focus on bleeding and not on feeding, because as Kiparsky himself says, what he calls 'feeding' is built into the Pāṇinian system, and there is no controversy about it.

What Kātyāyana's *vārttika* implies:

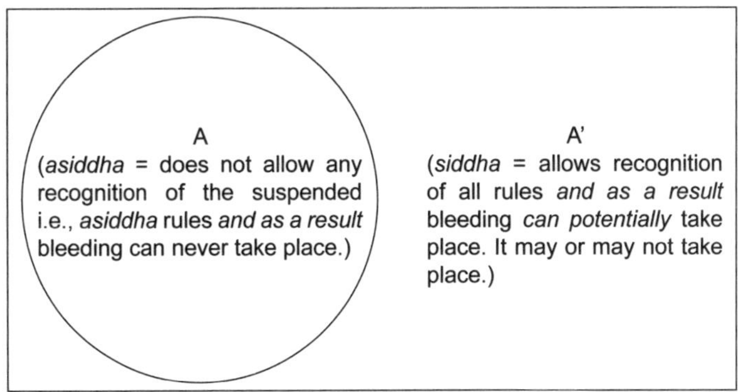

Kiparsky takes the liberty to interpret this as:

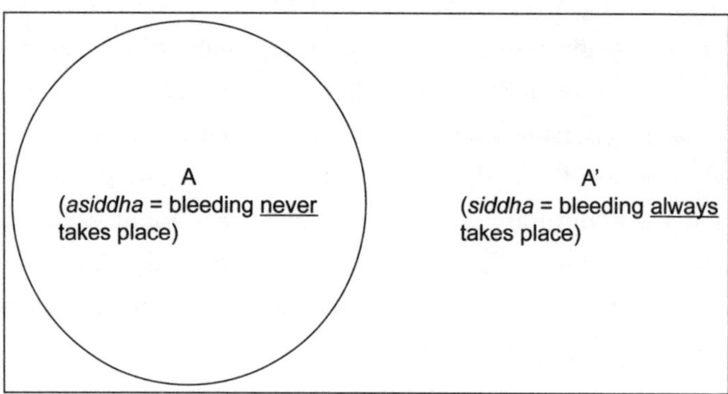

Let us use an analogy to understand this, just like Patañjali often does. Imagine that a young boy, who is obedient to his parents, can be given one of two possible instructions by his parents about going near the fire:

Parental instruction	What this instruction actually entails	What Kiparsky assumes it entails
You are not allowed to go near the fire. (These rules are *asiddha.*)	The child will never burn his hand. (Bleeding will never take place).	The child will never burn his hand. (Bleeding will never take place).
You are allowed to go near the fire. (These rules are *siddha.*)	The child can potentially burn his hand. He may or may not burn his hand. (Bleeding can potentially take place. It may or may not take place.)	The child will always burn his hand. (Bleeding will always take place).

I conclude that it is not logically possible to infer the *siddha* principle from vt. 1 on 6.1.86.

Regardless of that, let me briefly comment on the following question: How useful is the *siddha* principle in dealing with cases of SSRI? The *siddha* principle rejects the *antaraṅga* tool and essentially resorts to the *nitya* tool to solve not only those cases that the tradition solves using *nityatva*, but also those that it solves using *antaraṅgatva*. Of course, this means that the *siddha* principle is able to tackle cases of unidirectional blocking but not of mutual blocking—which is one of its drawbacks. Another drawback of the *siddha* principle is that it pays little attention to and offers no solutions for those cases of SSRI that do not involve any blocking at all ('nonconflict').

How useful is the *siddha* principle in dealing with cases of unidirectional blocking? Since the *siddha* principle is no different from the *nitya* principle, albeit with a wider scope of application than the traditional one, the answer to this question is the same as my answer to the question about the potency of the *nitya* principle: "This is exactly why the traditional *nitya* tool which teaches that the *nitya* rule defeats the *anitya* rule, always correctly resolves cases of DOI involving unidirectional blocking: the *nitya* rule is applicable to the RHS operand and the *anitya* rule to the LHS operand. By (my interpretation of) 1.4.2, the RHS rule (which is also the *nitya* rule) defeats the LHS rule (which is the *anitya* rule)." However, I do not know if the *nitya/siddha* principle is always correctly able to solve cases of SOI involving unidirectional blocking. A majority of the examples discussed in Kiparsky (1982) involve DOI and not SOI.

A major shortcoming of the *nitya* and, therefore, the *siddha* principle is its propensity to look ahead into the derivation: one needs to know what will happen at the next step *if*, hypothetically speaking, a certain rule is applied at the present step. I think this very much qualifies as 'looking ahead', even though it involves considering merely the potential—and not the actual—future course of the derivation. Joshi and Kiparsky take this a step further by proposing the extended *siddha* principle, which 'scans entire candidate derivations' thanks to its 'global (trans-derivational) "lookahead" condition on derivations' 'and chooses the one in which *siddha*-relations (i.e., bleeding and feeding) are maximized' (2005, 7). In simple words, they ask us to choose, from amongst all possible derivational paths, that derivational path in which the *nitya* tool has been applied the highest number of times.

Why does the derivational path in which *siddha* relations are maximized lead to the correct answer though? It is easy to explain this with respect to DOI. In case of DOI, Pāṇini teaches us (according to my interpretation of 1.4.2) that we must pick the RHS rule. But as stated above, it is the RHS rule that is also the *nitya* rule in cases of DOI involving unidirectional blocking. So, it is natural that, of all the possible derivational paths, the correct one has the highest number of instances in which the *nitya* (RHS rule) defeats the *anitya* (LHS) rule—in cases of DOI involving unidirectional blocking. It is difficult to verify if Joshi's and Kiparsky's extended *siddha* principle holds true with respect to SOI.

Now let us ask: How useful is the extended *siddha* principle in resolving cases of SSRI? If one has to chart out all possible derivational paths to make a decision, how is choosing the derivational path in which *siddha* relations are maximized any better than simply choosing the derivational path that gives the correct grammatical form—which we know thanks to our knowledge of Sanskrit? And in the latter case, why perform derivations at all if we have to rely on the correct final form to choose the correct derivational path?

Joshi and Kiparsky have discussed several examples in the aforementioned papers, a number of which I have solved using my method in this book. Please see Appendix A for relevant tables of concordance. While it is not within the scope of this book to discuss in detail Joshi and Kiparsky's solutions for individual examples, we ought to study the work produced by them in greater depth in the future to gain new insights into the functioning of Pāṇini's grammar.

5.8 How and Why Pāṇini Composed 1.4.2

Before we discuss how and why Pāṇini composed 1.4.2, I think we might benefit from thinking about why he composed the *Aṣṭādhyāyī* or, put differently, what his motivation might have been behind composing such a unique grammar. Unlike modern, descriptive grammars of English, Hindi, and so on, which aim to provide structural information about the target language to the learner, Pāṇini's grammar assumes that its user already knows the language, which makes one wonder what purpose it serves. If Pāṇini merely wanted to help us decide whether a certain form is grammatically correct or not, he could simply have given us a descriptive grammar with lots of instructions and paradigms. I think Pāṇini's main aim was to achieve what he knew was an extraordinary intellectual feat, namely that of conceptualizing the Sanskrit language as a well-oiled and closed machine—a feat that, much to his credit, remains unrivalled in the history of theoretical linguistics.

And 1.4.2 plays a major role in it, which is precisely why later grammars that mimicked Pāṇini's grammar, and whose authors did not know the correct meaning of 1.4.2, failed to produce grammatical machines. These later grammars might look like Pāṇini's at first glance because they too contain *sūtra*s and are derivational in nature, but they simply don't have a mechanism in place to successfully tackle rule conflict.

By discovering the correct meaning of 1.4.2, my research not only helps establish that Pāṇini's grammar functions like a machine but also helps find an acceptable and plausible answer to the question of why Pāṇini composed his grammar in the first place. He did it because, as I said earlier, he wanted to conceptualize human language as a closed, autonomous machine!

I will now try to reconstruct how Pāṇini must have designed his system and, more pertinently, how he must have come up with what is arguably one of his most important rules—1.4.2 *vipratiṣedhe paraṁ kāryam.* It must be borne in mind that this is a purely speculative endeavour. Nonetheless, since it stands on the foundation of the evidence provided in this book and since it helps one gain a better understanding of the functioning of the *Aṣṭādhyāyī*, I think it is worthwhile to engage in such speculation.

Let us use nominal inflection as our example here and the form *devaiḥ* ('God' masculine, instrumental plural) as our pivot for this discussion. We know that Pāṇini wanted to derive not only *devaiḥ*, but also other forms such as *devāt* (ablative singular), *deveṣu* (locative plural), and so on.

	Singular	**Dual**	**Plural**
Nominative (Vocative)	*devaḥ* (*deva*)	*devau* (*devau*)	*devāḥ* (*devāḥ*)
Accusative	*devam*	*devau*	*devān*
Instrumental	*devena*	*devābhyām*	*devaiḥ*
Dative	*devāya*	*devābhyām*	*devebhyaḥ*
Ablative	*devāt*	*devābhyām*	*devebhyaḥ*
Genitive	*devasya*	*devayoḥ*	*devānām*
Locative	*deve*	*devayoḥ*	*deveṣu*

To derive the aforementioned forms, Pāṇini came up with one common base to which he could add different affixes. As traditional grammarians have correctly pointed out, Pāṇini attributed great value to *lāghava* 'brevity', and thus he wanted to create the base in such a way that he would have to make the least number of changes to it. In other words, he wanted to write as few rules as possible. From the paradigm presented above, we can see that the candidates for the position of the common base were *dev, deva, deve, devai, devā, devay,* and so on. After taking into account several other inflected forms, Pāṇini concluded that it would be convenient and optimal to choose *deva* as the base and then to convert it, where required, to *deve, devai, devā, devāy,* and so on, using *guṇa*, vowel *sandhi*, substitution, and so on. Thus, he chose *deva* as the common base for deriving forms like *devasya, devāya, devayoḥ,* and *deve.*

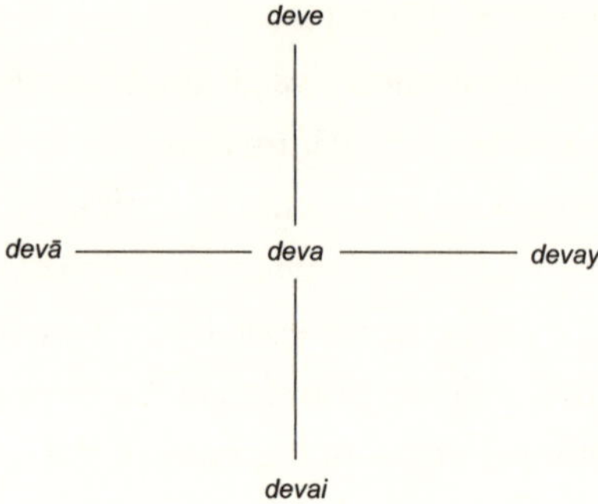

Secondly, Pāṇini wanted to derive not only *devaiḥ* but also instrumental plural forms of bases ending in other sounds and/or of other genders, such as *mālābhiḥ* ('garland' feminine, ending in *ā*, instrumental plural) and *vāribhiḥ* ('water' neuter, ending in *i*, instrumental plural).

kavibhiḥ	*mālābhiḥ*	*marudbhiḥ*	*vanaiḥ*
nadībhiḥ	*bhānubhiḥ*	*vāribhiḥ*	*devaiḥ*

He wanted to come up with one common affix each for every case-number combination (e.g., one affix for nominative plural, one for dative dual, etc.). Given his goal of conciseness, he wanted to create these affixes in such a way that he would need to compose as few rules as possible to bring about changes in these affixes. So, when he was trying to decide what the instrumental plural affix should be, he examined all possible instrumental plural forms like *kavibhiḥ, mālābhiḥ, marudbhiḥ, nadībhiḥ, bhānubhiḥ, vāribhiḥ, vanaiḥ, devaiḥ,* and so on. He realized he had two options: he could have chosen either *bhis* or *ais* as the instrumental plural affix. He noticed that most of these forms end in *bhis*, and a minority of them end in *ais*. Because he wanted to compose as few rules as possible, he chose *bhis* as the instrumental plural affix. Consequently, he had to compose only one rule, namely 7.1.9 *ato bhisa ais*, to deal with the affixation process for instrumental plurals. 7.1.9 teaches the substitution of *bhis* with *ais* when *bhis* is preceded by a nominal base ending in *a*.

Using the two processes mentioned above, Pāṇini came up with different classes of nominal bases, on the basis of the final sound and grammatical gender of the base, and with declensional affixes, which he has listed in 4.1.2 *sv-au-jas-am-auṭ-chaṣ-ṭā-bhyām-bhis-ṅe-bhyām-bhyas-ṅasi-bhyām-bhyas-ṅas-os-ām-ṅy-os-sup*.

	Singular	Dual	Plural
Nominative	*sU*	*au*	*Jas*
Accusative	*am*	*auṬ*	*Śas*
Instrumental	*Ṭā*	*bhyām*	*bhis*
Dative	*Ṅe*	*bhyām*	*bhyas*
Ablative	*ṄasI*	*bhyām*	*bhyas*
Genitive	*Ṅas*	*os*	*ām*
Locative	*Ṅi*	*os*	*suP*

Then, he composed certain rules teaching that the affix should be placed to the right-hand side of the base (cf. 3.1.1 *pratyayaḥ*, 3.1.2 *paraś ca*). But simply juxtaposing the affix with the base could not always give the correct form. So, what did Pāṇini do to deal with this problem? Naturally, he wrote rules to prescribe the requisite changes.

Firstly, Pāṇini wrote rules to substitute certain affixes with other equivalent items (see 7.1.9 discussed above). For example, in *deva* + *Ṅe* (dative singular), *Ṅe* had to be replaced with *ya* (cf. 7.1.13 *ṅer yaḥ*[28]). But **devaya* is not the correct form. So, thereafter, Pāṇini had to modify the nominal base, that is, replace *a* of *deva* with its *dīrgha* counterpart *ā* (cf. 7.3.102 *supi ca*[29]) to get the correct form *devāya*. Pāṇini decided to follow this order for the whole *Aṣṭādhyāyī*: first, he substituted the affix if required, and second, he modified the base (or both base and affix together, in the case of *ekādeśa*) if required.

Sometimes, only affix substitution was required, and base modification was not required. For example, consider *deva* + *Ṅas* (genitive singular). Here, Pāṇini simply had to replace *Ṅas* with *sya* (cf. 7.1.12 *ṭāṅasiṅasām inātsyāḥ*[30]) to get the correct form *devasya*. On the other hand, in some other cases, only base modification was required, and affix substitution was not required. For example, consider *deva* + *bhyām* (instrumental-dative-ablative dual). Here, Pāṇini simply had to replace *a* of *deva* with its long counterpart (cf. 7.3.102 *supi ca*[31]) to get the correct form *devābhyām*. Similarly, consider *deva* + *bhyas* (dative-ablative plural). Here, Pāṇini simply had to replace *a* of *deva* with *e* (cf. 7.3.103 *bahuvacane jhaly et*[32]) to get the correct form *devebhyaḥ*. But regardless of the situation, Pāṇini always followed the same order: first, he substituted the affix if required, and then he modified the base (or both base and affix together, in the case of *ekādeśa*) if required.

Now, consider *deva* + *bhis* (instrumental plural). Here too, first Pāṇini substituted the affix *bhis* with *ais* (cf. 7.1.9 *ato bhisa ais*) and then, in *deva* + *ais*, modified both base and affix by performing an *ekādeśa* operation, that is, by replacing *a* + *ai* with *ai* (cf. 6.1.88 *vr̥ddhir eci*[33]). This led to the correct form *devaiḥ*. However, he realized that students using his grammar might encounter a hurdle when deriving the form *devaiḥ*. He noticed that at the step *deva* + *bhis*, 7.1.9 *ato bhisa ais* is not the only rule applicable: 7.3.102 *supi ca* and 7.3.103 *bahuvacane jhaly et*, which he had composed to derive the forms *devābhyām* and *devebhyaḥ*, respectively, are also applicable.

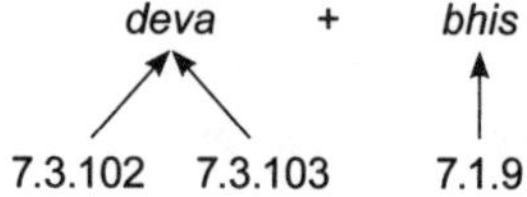

When multiple rules became simultaneously applicable, he decided to call the competition between the rule(s) applicable to the LHS operand and the rule(s) applicable to the RHS operand *vipratiṣedha* 'mutual opposition'. As we have seen above, Pāṇini's goal was to replace the affix first, where required, and only then to modify the base (or modify both base and affix together, in the case of *ekādeśa*) where required. So, despite the applicability of the LHS rules 7.3.102 and 7.3.103 at this step, Pāṇini wanted the RHS rule 7.1.9, and not any of these two LHS rules, to apply at this step. Thus, he stated 1.4.2 *vipratiṣedhe paraṁ kāryam* 'in the event of *vipratiṣedha* "mutual opposition" [i.e., DOI], the *para kārya* "RHS operation" takes place'. Upon applying 7.1.9, we get *deva* + *ais*, and rules like 7.3.102 *supi ca* and 7.3.103 *bahuvacane jhaly et* are no longer applicable. Here, the rule 6.1.88 *vr̥ddhir eci* applies, giving the correct form, *devaiḥ*.

One pertinent question that merits our attention here is: While making changes, why does Pāṇini start from the right-hand side (i.e., the affix) and then move leftwards (i.e., towards the interface between the affix and the base)? Notice that, in the forms *devaiḥ*, *devasya*, *devānām*, *deveṣu*, and so on, *dev*, which we can call the 'LHS part', is common to all the forms. So, the LHS part does not need to undergo any modification whatsoever. But one may ask, why not first make changes in the middle, that is, at the interface between base and affix, and then move rightwards to make changes in the affix? This would be counterproductive because the changes at the base-affix interface depend on the phonological composition of the affix. For these reasons, when making modifications, it is optimal for Pāṇini to start from the right end and move leftwards.

Pāṇini used this SSRI resolution mechanism not only for nominal inflection, but also for other kinds of derivations too—such as verbal inflection, primary and secondary derivatives, compounds, and so on. While in the examples of DOI discussed above, the two rules are applicable to two different items, that is, one to the base and the other to the affix, Pāṇini built his system in such a way that he could extend the application of 1.4.2 to those cases of DOI wherein both rules are applicable to two different parts of the same item.

Where required, he also composed other rules to deal with DOI. For example, he composed rules 1.4.13 *yasmāt pratyayavidhis tadādi pratyaye'ṅgam* and 6.4.1 *aṅgasya* to correctly derive forms like *edhante*, *dadhati*, and so on. I have discussed this in detail in chapter 4. He also composed rules like 6.4.22 *asiddhavad atrābhāt* and 8.2.1 *pūrvatrāsiddham* to counter the impact of 1.4.2 on DOI. I have discussed this in detail in chapter 6. Lastly, note that Pāṇini did not compose any rules to deal with SOI because, unlike DOI, SOI is not a part of his grammar but instead a feature of the *sūtra* style. In such cases, we must choose the more specific rule, as I have shown in detail in chapter 2.

5.9 'Conflicts' between Pairs of *saṁjñā* or *paribhāṣā* Rules

In this book, I have focused on *vidhi sūtra*s 'operational rules' and, to be precise, on how we choose one rule from amongst the two or more operational rules that are simultaneously applicable in a derivation. While operational rules play an important, perhaps central role in Pāṇinian derivations, they cannot be correctly interpreted or applied without the help of two other categories of rules, namely *saṁjñā sūtra*s 'definition rules' and *paribhāṣā sūtra*s 'metarules'. That said, as I have explained in chapter 2, unlike DOI, which is an integral part of Pāṇini's grammar, SOI and conflicts between two *saṁjñā* rules or two *paribhāṣā* rules are not a part of Pāṇini's derivational mechanism but instead a feature of the *sūtra* style itself. The more specific rule prevails in such cases. Here, I first reproduce some examples of mutual opposition between *saṁjñā* rules from chapter 1 to drive home my argument.

1.4.11 *saṁyoge guru* (which teaches that a short vowel is called *guru* 'heavy' when followed by a consonantal conjunct) is more specific than 1.4.10 *hrasvaṁ laghu* (which teaches that a short vowel is called *laghu* 'light'). Thus, 1.4.11 wins. In the same way, 1.4.100 *taṅānāv ātmanepadam* (which teaches that *taṄ*,

ŚānaC and *KānaC*, which replace *la*, take the *ātmanepada saṁjñā*) is more specific than and thus defeats 1.4.99 *laḥ parasmaipadam* (which teaches that the affixes that replace *la* take the *parasmaipada saṁjñā*'). Similarly, 1.4.46 *adhiśīṅsthāsāṁ karma* (which teaches that a *kāraka* that constitutes the locus of the action is called *karma* with the verbs *śīṄ* 'to lie down', *sthā* 'to stand', and *ās* 'to sit' occurring with preverb *adhi*) is more specific than and thus wins against 1.4.45 *ādhāro'dhikaraṇam* (which teaches that a *kāraka* that constitutes the locus of the action is called *adhikaraṇa*).

Besides, there are some cases that may appear to be conflicts between rules teaching *kāraka saṁjñās* but that, according to me, are not conflicts at all. For example, whether one says *geham praviśati* (cf. 1.4.49 *kartur īpsitatamaṁ karma* → 2.3.2 *karmaṇi dvitīyā*) or *gehe praviśati* (cf. 1.4.45 *ādhāro'dhikaraṇam* → 2.3.36 *saptamy adhikaraṇe ca*) depends entirely on the nonlinguistic feature that the speaker wishes to express—that is, whether he or she wants to express *kartur īpsitatama* or *ādhāra*. So, this choice lies outside the domain of Pāṇini's *Aṣṭādhyāyī*. So, in my opinion, rule conflict does not arise between 1.4.45 and 1.4.49.

In conclusion, choosing the more specific rule is sufficient to deal with cases of conflict in section 1.4.1–2.2.38. But if such is the case, one might ask, as many have: If Pāṇini did not intend for 1.4.2 *vipratiṣēdhe paraṁ kāryam* to be applicable only up to 2.2.38 *kaḍārāḥ karmadhāraye*, why did he place it right after 1.4.1 *ā kaḍārād ekā saṁjñā*, that is, in the *ekā saṁjñā* section? Note that both rules deal with choosing one of multiple options: 1.4.1 teaches us that we must choose one of multiple *saṁjñās*, and 1.4.2 tells us we must choose the RHS operation of many possible operations at a given step. This is likely why 1.4.1 and 1.4.2 are found next to each other. But in any case, although answers to questions like 'Why did he place this rule here?' can indeed help confirm our findings about the *Aṣṭādhyāyī*, in isolation and without derivation-based evidence, they do not hold any value whatsoever.

Now, we will look at some cases of competition between *paribhāṣā* rules that the tradition has failed to solve satisfactorily. In keeping with the general-exception template that pervades the entire *Aṣṭādhyāyī*, I think that the more specific rule emerges victorious in cases of competition between *paribhāṣā* rules. Let us first examine competition between *paribhāṣā* rules 1.1.52–1.1.55. To do so, let us derive the imperative third-person singular form of the root *likh* 'to write'. I will not discuss DOI and SOI here since our focus is on metarules. Nonetheless, I will perform the derivation bearing in mind my method of solving SOI and DOI: *likh* + *LOṬ* (3.3.162 *loṭ ca*) → *likh* + *tiP* (3.4.77 *lasya*, 3.4.78 *tip-tas-jhi . . .*[34]) → *likh* + *tu* (3.4.86 *er uḥ*) → *likh* + *ŚaP* + *tu* (3.1.68 *kartari śap*). Since *likh* + *ŚaP* cannot undergo any other operations that are not triggered by *tu*, we can write *likh* + *ŚaP* as *likha*. *likha* is an *aṅga* with respect to *tu*. Thus, we can apply 7.1.35 *tuhyostātaṅ āśiṣy anyatarasyām* here. This rule teaches that *tu* and *hi* should be replaced with *tātAṄ* in a benedictive form. If this rule is applied, which part of *tu* does *tātAṄ* replace? To get the correct answer, *likhatāt*, *tātAṄ* needs to replace *tu* entirely. But what do the relevant metarules have to say in this regard? Do they help us derive the correct answer, *likhatāt*? Let us look at them:

1.1.52 *alo'ntyasya*: a substitute replaces the final sound of the item for which it is taught.
1.1.53 *ṅic ca* (*alaḥ antyasya*): a *Ṅ*-marked substitute replaces the final sound of the item for which it is taught.
1.1.54 *ādeḥ parasya* (*alaḥ*): a substitute taught for the following item replaces its first sound.
1.1.55 *anekālśit sarvasya*: a multisound substitute or a substitute marked with *Ś* replaces the entirety of the item for which it is taught.

Before we go further, I should clarify the traditional interpretation of 1.1.54 *ādeḥ parasya*. According to the tradition, the metarule 1.1.54 governs only those rules that follow the following template: the substitute B_1 is taught for B when B is preceded by A (where A is mentioned in the ablative). The *Kāśikā* says: *parasya kāryaṁ śiṣyamāṇam āder alaḥ pratyetavyam. kva ca parasya kāryaṁ śiṣyate. yatra pañcamīnirdeśaḥ.* 'An operation taught for the following item will apply to the first sound [of the following item]. And where [i.e., in which cases] is the operation taught for the following sound? Where [an item has been] mentioned in the ablative'. It also gives an example: 6.3.97 *dvyantarupasargebhyo 'pa īt* 'the substitute *īT* is taught for [the nominal base] *ap* 'water' when *ap* is preceded by *dvi*, *antar*, or an *upasarga* 'preverb'. Since *dvyantarupasargebhyo* is taught in the ablative, 1.1.54 mandates that *īT* replace the first sound of *ap*, that is, *a*. In sum, the *Kāśikā* implies that 1.1.54 does not govern rules in which the preceding term is not mentioned in the ablative.

The *Siddhāntakaumudī* (SK) mentions the following relationships between these metarules:

(i) 1.1.54 *ādeḥ parasya* is an exception of 1.1.52 *alo'ntyasya*. Thus, 1.1.54 wins against 1.1.52.[35]
(ii) 1.1.55 *anekālśit sarvasya* is an exception of 1.1.52 *alo'ntyasya*. Thus, 1.1.55 wins against 1.1.52.[36]
(iii) 1.1.53 *ṅic ca* is an exception of 1.1.55 *anekālśit sarvasya*. Thus, 1.1.53 wins against 1.1.55.[37]
(iv) 1.1.55 *anekālśit sarvasya* comes after 1.1.54 *ādeḥ parasya* in the serial order of the *Aṣṭādhyāyī*. Thus, by the traditional interpretation of 1.4.2, 1.1.55 wins against 1.1.54.[38]

Below, I have represented this information in the form of a diagram. The arrows point towards the winning rules.

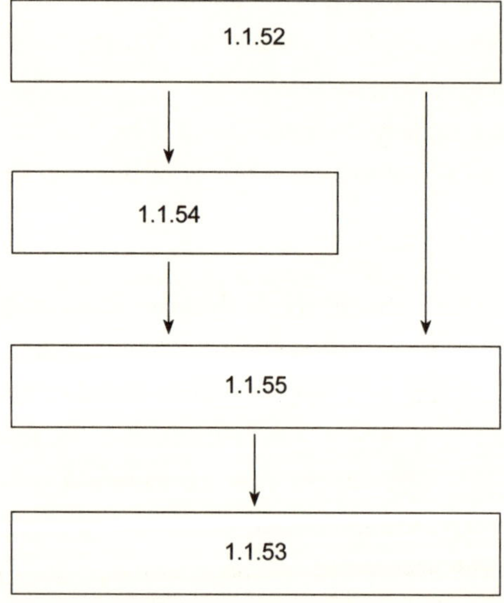

Let us go back to the rule 7.1.35 *tuhyos tātaṅ āśiṣy anyatarasyām*. It teaches the substitute *tātAṄ* for *tu*. The metarules eligible to govern the application of 7.1.35 are 1.1.52, 1.1.53, and 1.1.55. 1.1.55 is an exception of 1.1.52, and 1.1.53 is an exception of 1.1.55. Thus, 1.1.53 should govern the application of 7.1.35, which leads to *tātAṄ* replacing only the final sound of *tu*. However, this gives the incorrect form **likhattāt*. In his only *vārttika* on 1.1.53,[39] Kātyāyana recognizes this problem and says that the operation concerning *tātAṄ* should not be governed by 1.1.53 *ṅic ca* because here the only purpose of *anubandha Ṅ* is to block any potential *guṇa* or *vr̥ddhi* substitution in the preceding base (cf. 1.1.5 *kṅiti ca*), rather than facilitate the substitution of the last sound (cf. 1.1.53). However, we know that, in Pāṇini's grammar, if a certain item is marked with *Ṅ*, then it automatically possesses all the properties associated with *Ṅ*-marking, unless Pāṇini has said something to the opposite effect. One cannot arbitrarily choose which function of *Ṅ* is relevant to a particular rule and which function is not. Thus, Kātyāyana's explanation is not acceptable.

Is there a way to derive the correct form *likhatāt* without flouting Pāṇini's metarules? To answer this question, let me discuss this problem from my perspective. To begin with, let me present my interpretation of 1.1.54 *ādeḥ parasya*, which is different from that of the tradition. I think that there is no evidence in the wording of 1.1.54 or elsewhere to suggest that the presence of an ablative form in an operational rule constitutes a necessary condition for the application of 1.1.54. So, according to me, 1.1.54 governs any *para* or right-hand side (RHS) operation.

Let us look at the implications of these two interpretations of 1.1.54. According to the traditional interpretation, since an ablative form is not present in 7.1.35 *tuhyos tātaṅ āśiṣy anyatarasyām*, 1.1.54 would not be able to govern it. However, according to my interpretation, 1.1.54 is eligible to govern 7.1.35 simply because the operand *tu* is *para*, that is, placed to the right-hand side of *likha*.

I also disagree with the tradition with respect to the scope of 1.1.52 *alo'ntyasya* and 1.1.53 *ṅic ca*. According to the tradition, 1.1.53 is applicable to any substitute marked with *Ṅ*. However, I think that, since Pāṇini has specifically taught 1.1.54 for RHS substitutions, he has likely taught both 1.1.52 and 1.1.53 only for LHS substitutions. I agree with the tradition on the scope of 1.1.55: I think that Pāṇini has taught 1.1.55 for both LHS and RHS substitutions. Let us now establish general-exception relationships separately for LHS and RHS substitutions.

First, let us consider LHS substitutions, which can potentially be governed by 1.1.52, 1.1.53, and 1.1.55.

1. While 1.1.55 *anekālśit sarvasya* can govern only those substitutes that contain multiple sound segments or are marked with

Ś, 1.1.52 *alo'ntyasya* can govern any substitute. Thus, 1.1.55 is an exception of 1.1.52.

2. In case of substitutes that are made up of multiple sounds and marked with Ṅ, there arises competition between 1.1.53 *ṅic ca* and 1.1.55 *anekālśit sarvasya*. I think the only reason behind teaching a rule (i.e., 1.1.53) specially dealing with Ṅ-marked substitutes is to suggest that Ṅ-marked substitutes, despite containing multiple sounds, replace only the final sound of the operand and not the entirety of it. Thus, I think 1.1.53 is an exception of 1.1.55.

Now, let us consider RHS substitutions, which can potentially be governed by 1.1.54 and 1.1.55. Since 1.1.55 has been specifically taught for substitutes made up of multiple sounds, it is an exception of 1.1.54.

This information can be diagrammatically represented as follows. The arrows point towards the exception or specific rule:

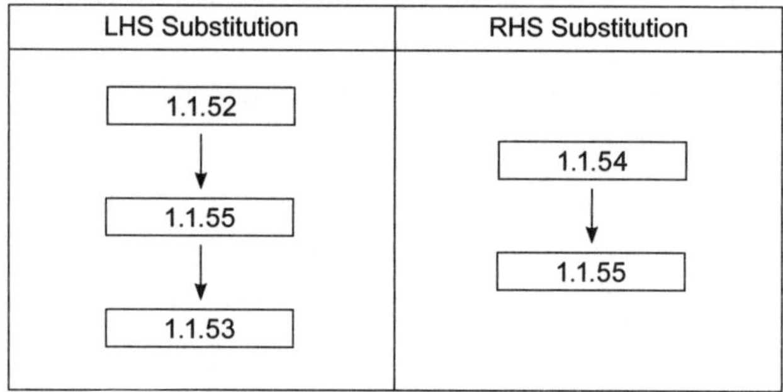

Thus, we can conclude that 7.1.35, which deals with an RHS substitute, that is, *tātAṄ*, cannot be governed by 1.1.52 and 1.1.53, which have been taught only for LHS substitutions. The only rules that can potentially govern 7.1.35 are 1.1.54 and 1.1.55. Since 1.1.55 has been specifically taught for substitutes made up of multiple sounds, it is more specific than 1.1.54. Therefore, by 1.1.55, *tu* is entirely replaced with *tātAṄ*, giving the correct form *likhatāt*.

Let us now examine the interaction between metarules 1.1.66 *tasminn iti nirdiṣṭe pūrvasya* and 1.1.67 *tasmād ity uttarasya* in the context of augmentation. To do this, let us look at the operational rule 7.1.52 *āmi sarvanāmnaḥ suṭ* (*āt*), which the tradition interprets, based on the two *paribhāṣās* mentioned above, as follows: the augment *sUṬ* is introduced to affix *ām* when it occurs after a *sarvanāman* 'pronominal base' ending in *a*. Even though I think this is indeed the correct interpretation, I disagree with the tradition on the process through which it arrives at this interpretation. Let us first consider the individual parts of this *sūtra*:

āmi = locative singular form of *ām*
sarvanāmnaḥ (*āt*) = ablative singular forms of *sarvanāman* and *a*, respectively
sUṬ = nominative singular form of *sUṬ*

Since Pāṇini has used the locative singular form *āmi*, 7.1.52 could potentially be governed by the metarule 1.1.66 *tasminn iti nirdiṣṭe pūrvasya*, which the tradition interprets as follows: if an item is mentioned in the operational rule in the locative, then the item to its left undergoes the operation.[40] Similarly, since Pāṇini has used the ablative forms *sarvanāmnaḥ* and *āt*, 7.1.52 could potentially be governed by the metarule 1.1.67 *tasmād ity uttarasya*, which the tradition interprets as follows: if an item is mentioned in the operational rule in the ablative, then the item to its right undergoes the operation.[41]

In sum, according to the tradition, in x + y, if rule K is applicable, then if:

(i) y is mentioned in the locative, then, by 1.1.66, x undergoes the operation taught by K, and
(ii) x is mentioned in the ablative, then by 1.1.67, y undergoes the operation taught by K.

Consider the derivation of the genitive plural of the pronominal stem *sarva* 'everything'[42]: *sarva* + *ām*. Here, the pronominal stem *sarva* ends in *a* and is followed by *ām*. So, 7.1.52 *āmi sarvanāmnaḥ suṭ* (*āt*) is applicable. By 1.1.66, the augment *sUṬ* should be attached to *sarva*, but by 1.1.67, the augment *sUṬ* should be attached to *ām*. Which of the two metarules should be chosen to govern 7.1.52?

Through his *vārttika*s on 1.1.67, Kātyāyana offers a solution to this problem. He says that when both locative and ablative forms have been used in a rule like 7.1.52, the ablative prevails (vt. 3: *ubhayanirdeśe vipratiṣedhāt pañcamīnirdeśaḥ* [Mbh I.173.1]) and the locative should be reinterpreted as a genitive (vt. 14: *yathārthaṁ vā ṣaṣṭhīnirdeśaḥ* [Mbh I.174.6]). Therefore, according to Kātyāyana, 7.1.52 *āmi sarvanāmnaḥ suṭ* (*āt*) means *āmaḥ sarvanāmnaḥ suṭ* (*āt*): the augment *sUṬ* is introduced to affix *ām* when it occurs after a *sarvanāman* 'pronominal base' ending in *a*.

By 1.1.46 *ādyantau ṭakitau* (which, according to the tradition, teaches that items marked with *Ṭ* and items marked with *K* should be attached to the beginning and end, respectively, of items taught in the genitive[43]), the augment *sUṬ* is attached at the beginning of *ām*. The derivation proceeds as follows: *sarva* + *ām* → *sarva* + *sām* (7.1.52 *āmi sarvanāmnaḥ suṭ*) → *sarve* + *sām* (6.1.97 *bahuvacane jhaly et*) → *sarveṣām* (8.3.59 *ādeśapratyayoḥ*).

But does Kātyāyana's solution enable us to correctly interpret all of Pāṇini's operational rules that teach augments? No, it fails to help us correctly interpret rules that teach the insertion of augments marked with *K* and contain ablative and/or locative forms, for example, 6.1.75 *dīrghāt* (*che tuk*), 6.1.76 *padāntād vā* (*dīrghāt che tuk*), 7.2.82 *āne muk* (*ataḥ*), and 8.3.31 *śi tuk* (*naś ca*). Let us discuss the rule 6.1.76 *padāntād vā* (*dīrghāt che tuk*). In order to correctly interpret this rule, let us first analyse its parts: *che* is a locative form, and *dīrghāt* and *padāntāt* are both ablative forms. Since Pāṇini has used the locative form *che*, 6.1.76 could potentially be governed by the metarule 1.1.66 *tasminn iti nirdiṣṭe pūrvasya*, but since Pāṇini has used the ablative forms *dīrghāt* and *padāntāt*, 6.1.76 could also be governed by the metarule 1.1.67 *tasmād ity uttarasya*.

Consider the compound *kuṭīcchāyā* 'shade of a hut'. When deriving this form at step *kuṭī* + *chāyā*, since *kuṭī* ends in a long vowel and since *chāyā* begins with a *ch*, 6.1.76 is applicable. By 1.1.66, the augment *tUK* should be attached to *kuṭī*, but by 1.1.67, the augment *tUK* should be attached to *chāyā*. Which of the two metarules should be chosen to govern 6.1.76? By *vārttika*s 3 and 14, when there is a competition between the ablative and the locative, the ablative prevails and the locative is reinterpreted as a genitive. Thus, according to the aforementioned *vārttika*s, 6.1.76 *padāntād vā* (*dīrghāt che tuk*) means: *padāntād vā dīrghāt chaḥ tuk* 'the augment *tUK* is optionally introduced to the item beginning with *cha* when it is preceded by a *pada* ending in a long vowel'. By 1.1.46 *ādyantau ṭakitau*, the augment *tUK* is attached at the end of *chāyā*. However, this gives the incorrect form: **kuṭīchāyāt*. To get the correct form, we need to attach the augment *tUK* at the end of *kuṭī*: *kuṭī-t-chāyā* → *kuṭīcchāyā* (8.4.40 *stoś ścunā ścuḥ*). This shows that Kātyāyana's *vārttika*s cannot help us correctly interpret augment-insertion rules like 6.1.76.

Let me now expound on how I tackle this problem. In my opinion, Kātyāyana's interpretation of the metarules 1.1.66 and 1.1.67 is not correct.

Kātyāyana interprets *pūrvasya* and *uttarasya* in 1.1.66 and 1.1.67 as 'in the place of the LHS item' and 'in the place of the RHS item', respectively. In my opinion, this is not warranted. I think that that we can infer 'in the place of X' only when X has been mentioned (or continued by *anuvr̥tti*) in the genitive in the operational rule (cf. 1.1.49 *ṣaṣṭhī sthāneyogā*, which teaches that a genitive ending, which is not otherwise interpretable in its context, signifies the relation 'in the place of'). Let me explain what I mean by this through examples. In 6.1.77 *iko yaṇ aci*, *iK* is mentioned in the genitive and *aC* in the locative. Thus, by 1.1.49 *ṣaṣṭhī sthāneyogā* and 1.1.66 *tasminn iti nirdiṣṭe pūrvasya*, respectively, we can interpret 6.1.77 as:

However, notice that in 6.1.76 *padāntād vā* (*dīrghāt che tuk*), Pāṇini has not used a genitive form, so we cannot interpret it as:

padānta dīrgha + *cha*
↑
6.1.76

I interpret *pūrvasya* in 1.1.66 merely as an indication of the left-hand side and similarly *uttarasya* in 1.1.67 merely as an indication of the right-hand side. The best way to offer clarity on this is to summarize the difference between the traditional interpretation and my interpretation of 1.1.66 and 1.1.67 with diagrams. In the table below, I have stated the case in which the word is mentioned in the operational rule in parentheses:

	Traditional Interpretation	My Interpretation
1.1.66 *tasminn iti nirdiṣṭe pūrvasya*	x y (locative) ↑ (under x) K	x y (locative) ↑ (between x and y) K
1.1.67 *tasmād ity uttarasya*	x (ablative) y ↑ (under y) K	x (ablative) y ↑ (between x and y) K

Let me now explain how I interpret the operational rules 7.1.52 *āmi sarvanāmnaḥ suṭ* (*āt*) and 6.1.76 *padāntād vā* (*dīrghāt che tuk*), based on my interpretations of 1.1.66 and 1.1.67, respectively. Let us start with 7.1.52.

According to me, there is no competition between metarules 1.1.66 and 1.1.67. In fact, I think that both 1.1.66 and 1.1.67 are required to interpret 7.1.52:

a. 1.1.66 tells us that the augment *sUṬ* should be placed to the left of affix *ām*.

sUṬ *ām*

b. 1.1.67 tells us that the augment *sUṬ* should be placed to the right of *sarvanāman* 'the pronominal base'.

sarva *sUṬ*

Now, if we put together the teachings of metarules 1.1.66 and 1.1.67, we get:

sarva *sUṬ* *ām*

Before we continue, note that there is a difference between *Kāśikā*'s and my interpretation of 1.1.46 *ādyantau ṭakitau*. *Kāśikā*'s interpretation is: *ādiḥ ṭit bhavati antaḥ kit bhavati ṣaṣṭhīnirdiṣṭasya* 'items marked with *Ṭ* and items marked with *K* should be attached to the beginning and end, respectively, of items taught in the genitive'. I do not think that we should take the liberty to read *ṣaṣṭhīnirdiṣṭasya* 'taught in the genitive' into this rule. I think 1.1.46 simply means 'items marked with *Ṭ* and items marked with *K* should be attached to the beginning and end, respectively'. Coming back to 7.1.52, we have:

sarva *sUṬ* *ām*

sUṬ lies between the end of *sarva* and the beginning of *ām*. By my interpretation of 1.1.46 *ādyantau ṭakitau, sUṬ* should be attached to the beginning of an item. Thus, it is attached to (the beginning of) *ām*. We get: *sarva* + *sām*, which, as seen above, leads to the correct form *sarveṣām*.

Now, let us interpret 6.1.76 *padāntād vā* (*dīrghāt che tuk*) using my interpretation of 1.1.66 and 1.1.67. As stated above, I do not think that there is any competition between 1.1.66 and 1.1.67. In fact, I think that both 1.1.66 and 1.1.67 are required to interpret 6.1.76.

a. 1.1.66 tells us that the augment *tUK* should be placed to the left of *ch.*

tUK *chāyā*

b. 1.1.67 tells us that the augment *tUK* should be placed to the right of the long vowel.

kuṭī *tUK*

Now, if we put together the teachings of metarules 1.1.66 and 1.1.67, we get:

kuṭī *tUK* *chāyā*

tUK lies between the end of *kuṭī* and the beginning of *chāyā*. By my interpretation of 1.1.46 *ādyantau ṭakitau*, *tUK* should be attached to the end of an item. Thus, it is attached to (the end of) *kuṭī*. We get *kuṭīt* + *chāyā*, which, as seen above, leads to the correct form *kuṭīcchāyā*.

I have shown that, using my interpretation of 1.1.46, 1.1.66, and 1.1.67, we can correctly interpret Pāṇini's operational rules, which teach the insertion of augments marked with *Ṭ* or *K* using ablative and locative forms. Kātyāyana's *vārttikas*, on the other hand, are not able to accomplish the same.

CHAPTER SIX

Asiddha(vat) and 1.4.2

In the previous chapters, I have shed light on how I think Pāṇini perceives the interactions between simultaneously applicable rules and, more specifically, how he resolves cases of SOI and DOI. In this process, I have also discussed my interpretation of 1.4.2 *vipratiṣedhe paraṁ kāryam*. In this chapter, I will dwell on three very important rules of the *Aṣṭādhyāyī*, which deal with the concepts of *asiddha* and *asiddhavat*. 6.1.86 *ṣatvatukor asiddhaḥ* and 8.2.1 *pūrvatrāsiddham* teach the former, and 6.4.22 *asiddhavad atrā bhāt* the latter. I will discuss both the traditional interpretation of these rules and my own interpretation of them. I will also demonstrate how these rules impact SOI and DOI, if at all they do, and how they interact with (my interpretation of) 1.4.2.

6.1 Traditional Views on *Asiddha* and *Asiddhavat*

Let me start by presenting the English translation of these three rules as per the traditional interpretations. To highlight the differences of opinion within the tradition, I will make relevant comments on what texts like *Mahābhāṣya*, *Kāśikā*, *Siddhāntakaumudī*, and *Nyāsa* say about these rules.

6.1.86 *ṣatvatukor asiddhaḥ* (*ekaḥ pūrvaparayoḥ saṁhitāyām*): a single replacement (*ekaḥ*) in place of the preceding and the following sound segments (*pūrvaparayoḥ*) in continuous utterance (*saṁhitāyām*) is suspended[1] (*asiddhaḥ*) with respect to any potential replacement with *ṣ* or insertion of augment *tUK* (*ṣatva-tuk-or*). Here, should the *kārya* (i.e., 'operation', or more aptly, 'outcome of application of the rule') be suspended or the *śāstra* (i.e., the rule) itself? In traditional literature, if the *kārya* is suspended, this is called *kāryāsiddhi*, whereas if the *śāstra* is suspended, this is called *śāstrāsiddhi*.

According to the *Kāśikā*, *asiddha* implies *kāryāsiddhi*,[2] but according to the *Siddhāntakaumudī*, *asiddha* stands for *śāstrāsiddhi*.[3,4]

8.2.1 *pūrvatrāsiddham*: that which is taught from here onwards is *asiddham* 'suspended' with respect to *pūrvatra* 'what precedes it'.

As per the tradition's interpretation, 8.2.1 can be rewritten as follows:

Q is suspended with respect to P if:

(i) Q is taught after P in the serial order of the *Aṣṭādhyāyī*, and
(ii) Q is taught after 8.2.1 in the serial order of the *Aṣṭādhyāyī*.

Here, again, the *Kāśikā* favours the *kāryāsiddhi* interpretation, whereas the *Siddhāntakaumudī* prefers the *śāstrāsiddhi* interpretation. There is some discussion in *Nyāsa* on 8.2.1 about whether *asiddha* stands for *kāryāsiddhi* or for *śāstrāsiddhi*.

6.4.22 *asiddhavad atrā bhāt*: that which is taught in the section starting here and extending up to *bh* (*ā bhāt*)[5] is *asiddhavat* 'suspended',[6] if both rules have a *samānāśraya* 'common substratum' (*atra*).

According to the *Kāśikā* on 6.4.22, we must infer *samānāśrayatva* from the presence of word *atra*.[7] The *Nyāsa* glosses *āśraya* as *nimitta* 'cause'. If this is the case, *samānāśraya* would mean 'common cause'. However, I do not think this is the correct interpretation. I will explain my understanding of the meaning of *samānāśraya* later in this chapter, when discussing a germane example.

On 6.4.22, Kātyāyana presents two different views on the meaning of the word *atra*. One view is that it stands for *samānāśrayatva*.[8] The other opinion is that *atra* has been used to indicate that it is with respect to the rules taught *atra* 'here' (in the section headed by 6.4.22) that the rules of this section (i.e., those rules headed by 6.4.22) are *asiddhavat*.[9] In other words, if *atra* had not been mentioned, the rules taught in this section would have become *asiddhavat* even with respect to rules lying outside this section, such as 7.2.116 *ata upadhāyāḥ*,[10] which is not desirable,[11] hence the need to state '*atra*'. We can say that *atra*, according to this view, stands for 'with respect to the rules taught here (i.e., in the section headed by 6.4.22)'.

Both the *Kāśikā* and the *Siddhāntakaumudī* interpret *ā bhāt* not as 'up to 6.4.129 *bhasya*' but instead as 'up to the end of the section headed by 6.4.129 *bhasya*'. The jurisdiction of 6.4.129 continues up to 6.4.175, which is the end of

6.4. Thus, according to the *Kāśikā*, *ā bhāt* implies 'up to the end of 6.4'.[12] On the other hand, Kātyāyana and Patañjali discuss both possibilities (Mbh III.192.10–193.19): one, that the jurisdiction of 6.4.22 ends at 6.4.129, and the other, that it continues up to the end of 6.4. We will study this later in this chapter.

From what both the *Kāśikā* and the *Siddhāntakaumudī* say about 6.4.22, the traditional interpretation of this rule can be rewritten as follows:

A is suspended with respect to B if:

(i) both A and B are taught in 6.4.22–6.4.175, and
(ii) both A and B have a *samānāśraya*

Note that the tradition does not make any actual distinction between *asiddha* and *asiddhavat*, which is why I have translated both terms as 'suspended'.

6.2 My Interpretation of These Three Rules

In this section, I will present my interpretation of the three rules and support the same with evidence and examples. I will also show how SOI and DOI function in these sections.

Let us first examine 6.1.86 *ṣatvatukor asiddhaḥ* and 8.2.1 *pūrvatrāsiddham*, respectively. I think that *asiddha* in these two rules denotes *śāstrāsiddhi*: rule X is *asiddha* with respect to rule Y. However, when rule X (*śāstra*) is *asiddha* with respect to rule Y, the outcome of the application of rule X (*kārya*) too will automatically be *asiddha* with respect to rule Y. In other words, I think that *śāstrāsiddhi* always entails *kāryāsiddhi*. Thus, we conclude that 6.1.86 and 8.2.1 teach *śāstrāsiddhi* and, therefore, also teach *kāryāsiddhi*.[13]

What impact does the fact that one rule is *asiddha* with respect to the other rule have on 1.4.2? We cannot use 1.4.2 to resolve a case of DOI unless both rules involved in the DOI acknowledge each other's existence. How do we resolve cases of DOI where one rule does not acknowledge the existence of the other? In such cases of DOI, the rule that does not acknowledge the existence of the other rule prevails. This will become clearer through the examples discussed later in this chapter. Consider the following examples:

Example #1. *adhī* + *Ktvā*—'to study', absolutive

Note that *adhī* is formed by applying rule 6.1.101 *akaḥ savarṇe dīrghaḥ* (which teaches that a long vowel replaces both *aK* '*a*, *i*, *u*, *r̥*, or *l̥*' and the immediately following *savarṇa* 'homogeneous' vowel) to *adhi* + *i*. I have explained why we need to begin the derivation with *adhī* + *Ktvā* when discussing example 5 of section 4.3, chapter 4.

To *adhī* + *Ktvā*, we apply the rule 7.1.37 *samāse'nañpūrve ktvo lyap*, which teaches that in a compound, the first member of which is not *naÑ*, the affix *Ktvā* in the second part of the compound is replaced with *LyaP*. Thus, we get *adhīya*. 6.1.86 teaches that a rule prescribing a single replacement in place of the preceding and the following sound segments is *asiddha* with respect to rules teaching replacement with *ṣ* or attachment of augment *tUK*. Thus, we deem both 6.1.101 *akaḥ savarṇe dīrghaḥ* and the outcome of its application (because remember, *śāstrāsiddhi* always entails *kāryāsiddhi*) to be suspended with respect to the rule 6.1.71 *hrasvasya piti kr̥ti tuk*, which teaches that augment *tUK* is attached to a verbal base ending in a short vowel when a *kr̥t* affix marked with *P* follows. Therefore, we consider *adhīya* to be *adhi-i-ya*, apply 6.1.71 to it, and get the correct form *adhītya*.

If Pāṇini had not taught 6.1.86, 6.1.71 would not have applied here, leading to the incorrect form **adhīya*.[14]

Example #2. *kas* + *asiñcat* 'Who sprinkled?'

The derivation proceeds as follows: *kas* + *asiñcat* → *kar* + *asiñcat* (8.2.66 *sasajuṣoḥ ruḥ*[15]) → *ka-u* + *asiñcat* (6.1.113 *ato ror aplutād aplute*[16]) → *ko asiñcat* (6.1.87 *ād guṇaḥ*) → *ko'siñcat* (6.1.109 *eṅaḥ padāntād ati*), which is the correct phrase.

We have derived *ko'siñcat* by applying 6.1.109 *eṅaḥ padāntād ati*, which teaches *pūrvarūpa ekādeśa*, that is, the replacement of *o* + *a* in *ko* + *asiñcat* with the LHS sound *o*. By 6.1.86 *ṣatvatukor asiddhaḥ*, 6.1.109 and the outcome of its application (*o*) are *asiddha* with respect to the following rule teaching *ṣatva*:

8.3.59 *ādeśapratyayoḥ*: *ṣ* replaces non-*pada*-final *s* of a substitute or of an affix occurring after *iṆ* (any vowel except *a*; *h*, *y*, *v*, *r*, and *l*) or a velar stop, even when there is intervention of *nUM*, *visarjanīya*, or *śaR* (*ś*, *ṣ*, *s*).

Thus, 8.3.59 is not able to apply to *ko'siñcat*. If Pāṇini had not composed 6.1.86, then 8.3.59 would have applied to *ko'siñcat*, giving us the incorrect form: **ko'ṣiñcat.*

However, there is a problematic aspect of this derivation that merits discussion: we know that 8.2.66 *sasajuṣoḥ ruḥ* is *asiddha* with respect to 6.1.113 *ato ror aplutād aplute* by 8.2.1 *pūrvatrāsiddham*. Therefore, 6.1.113 cannot acknowledge 8.2.66 and the outcome of its application and consequently cannot apply there. But this contradicts what we observe in the derivation of *ko'siñcat* where, in order to get the correct final form, we ought to apply 6.1.113 to *kar* + *asiñcat*, which is the direct outcome of the application of 8.2.66.

Nyāsa on 6.1.113 acknowledges this problem but is unable to solve it. It says: the only *rU* that we find in the *Aṣṭādhyāyī* results from the application of 8.2.66. So Pāṇini would not have composed 6.1.113, which applies to *rU*, if he intended for the outcome of the application of 8.2.66 (i.e., *rU*) to be *asiddha* with respect to 6.1.113.[17] Buiskool (1939, 101) thinks that Pāṇini has placed 6.1.113 in 6.1 only because of its similarity with the rules that precede and follow it.

Here is a possible solution to this problem: I think that in the Pāṇinian system all possible rules that can be applied while constructing a word ought to be applied before the word enters a sentence. Let us call them word-level rules. Let us call those rules that apply after the word enters the sentence sentence-level rules. I think Pāṇini does not consider word-level rules to be *asiddha* with respect to sentence-level rules. 8.2.66 is a word-level rule simply because it can be applied before the word enters the sentence and thus is not *asiddha* with respect to 6.1.113, which by virtue of applying at the boundary between two words is a sentence-level rule.[18]

We do not find any examples of SOI or DOI involving 6.1.86 *ṣatvatukor asiddhaḥ*. Let us now look at some derivations involving 8.2.1 *pūrvatrāsiddham* and also how this rule interacts with SOI and DOI.

Example #3. *rājan* + *bhis*—'king', instrumental plural

Here, we apply 8.2.7 *nalopaḥ prātipadikāntasya* (which teaches that the final *n* of a nominal stem termed *pada* is replaced with *LOPA*) and get *rāja* + *bhis*. By 8.2.1 *pūrvatrāsiddham*,[19] rules like 7.1.9 *ato bhisa ais*,[20] 7.3.102 *supi ca*,[21] and 7.3.103 *bahuvacane jhaly et*,[22] which are applicable when deriving the instrumental plural of *a*-final stems, do not acknowledge the existence of 8.2.7. Consequently, they cannot acknowledge the outcome of its application either. Therefore, they are not applicable here. The correct form is *rājabhiḥ*.

If Pāṇini had not taught 8.2.1, we would have got the incorrect form **rājaiḥ* (cf. 7.1.9 *ato bhisa ais*).

Example #4. *asmai* + *uddhara* 'lift (it) for him'

The derivation proceeds as follows: *asmai* + *uddhara* → *asmāy* + *uddhara* (6.1.78 *eco'yavāyāvaḥ*[23]) → *asmā* + *uddhara* (8.3.19 *lopaḥ śākalyasya*[24]). By 8.2.1, 8.3.19 is *asiddha* with respect to 6.1.87 *ād guṇaḥ*, which teaches that *guṇa* (*a, e, o*) replaces both *a* and the vowel immediately following it. Thus, the outcome of the application of 8.3.19 (i.e., *asmā* + *uddhara*) too is *asiddha* with respect to 6.1.87. Therefore, 6.1.87 is not applicable here. The correct phrase is *asmā uddhara*.

If Pāṇini had not taught 8.2.1, we would have got the incorrect phrase **asmoddhara* (cf. 6.1.87 *ād guṇaḥ*).

Derivations 3 and 4 involve 8.2.1 but do not involve any cases of DOI or SOI. Now let us look at examples 5 and 6, which, alongside 8.2.1, also involve cases of DOI and SOI, respectively.

Example #5. *bhujO* + *Kta*—'to bend', past passive participle

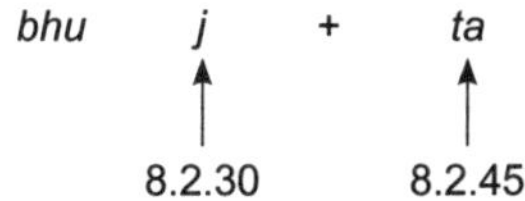

8.2.30 *coḥ kuḥ*: a sound denoted by *cU* (palatals) is replaced with a corresponding sound denoted by *kU* (velars) when *cU* occurs at the end of a *pada* or is followed by *jhaL* (a non-nasal stop or a fricative).

8.2.45 *oditaś ca*: the *t* of a *niṣṭhā* affix,[25] which occurs after a verbal root marked with *O* is replaced with *n*.

This is a case of DOI. Both rules lie in the *tripādī*. Thus, 8.2.30 does not acknowledge the existence of 8.2.45. As stated before, I think that 1.4.2 comes into play only if the two rules can acknowledge each other's existence. Thus, 1.4.2 cannot address this case of DOI.

Therefore, the rule that cannot see the other rule applies here, and we get: *bhug* + *ta* (8.2.30). Now, 8.2.45 applies, and we get the correct form *bhugna*.

In order to understand the crucial role played by 8.2.1 *pūrvatrāsiddham* in this derivation, let us analyse how this derivation would have proceeded in its absence:

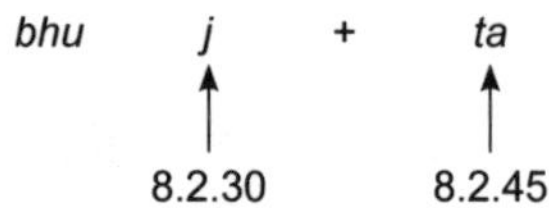

8.2.30 *coḥ kuḥ*: same as above.

8.2.45 *oditaś ca*: same as above.

This is a case of DOI. But before we look at the outcome (as per my interpretation of 1.4.2), let us understand the relationship between 8.2.30 and 8.2.45. If we apply 8.2.30 at this step, 8.2.45 will be applicable at the following step (as seen in the derivation of *bhugna* above). But if we apply 8.2.45 at this step, then *t* will be replaced with *n*, which does not belong to *jhaL*. Thus, 8.2.30 will not be applicable at the following step. In other words, the RHS rule 8.2.45 blocks the LHS rule 8.2.30, but the LHS rule 8.2.30 does not block the RHS rule 8.2.45. This is a case of unidirectional blocking.

By my interpretation of 1.4.2, the RHS rule 8.2.45 applies and we get *bhuj* + *na*. As stated above, 8.2.45 blocks 8.2.30. Thus, 8.2.30 is unable to apply to *bhuj* + *na*, and we get the incorrect form *bhujna* → **bhujña* (8.4.40 *stoś ścunā ścuḥ*). To get the correct form, one needs to apply both rules, 8.2.30 and 8.2.45, in two consecutive steps. Since 8.2.45 unidirectionally blocks 8.2.30, the only way to apply both rules is to apply them in the following order: first, 8.2.30, and then, 8.2.45. For this, one needs to devise a way to neutralize the impact of 1.4.2. Pāṇini has achieved this with the help of 8.2.1. He has placed 8.2.45 (the RHS rule) after 8.2.1 *pūrvatrāsiddham* and also after the LHS rule 8.2.30 in the serial order of the *Aṣṭādhyāyī*. This enables 8.2.30 to ignore 8.2.45 and, consequently, to apply before the application of 8.2.45.

Let me state in general terms how Pāṇini uses 8.2.1 to impact certain cases of DOI. In those cases of DOI wherein the RHS rule unidirectionally blocks the LHS rule and where Pāṇini wants both the RHS and LHS rules to apply, he places the RHS rule after 8.2.1 and after the LHS rule in the serial order of the *Aṣṭādhyāyī*. In simple words, when required, Pāṇini uses 8.2.1 *pūrvatrāsid-*

dham to neutralize the impact of 1.4.2 on those cases of DOI that involve unidirectional blocking, where it is desirable for him to do so.[26]

Example #6. *dah* + *tumUN*—'to burn', infinitive

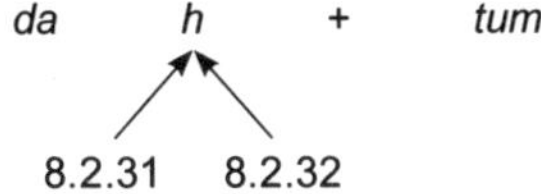

8.2.31 *ho ḍhaḥ*: *h* is replaced with *ḍh* when *h* occurs at the end of a *pada* or is followed by *jhaL* (a non-nasal stop or a fricative).

8.2.32 *dāder dhātor ghaḥ*: *gh* replaces the final *h* of a verbal root beginning with *d* when it occurs at the end of a *pada* or is followed by *jhaL* (a non-nasal stop or a fricative).

Because 8.2.32 is in the section governed by 8.2.1 and follows 8.2.31 in the serial order of the *Aṣṭādhyāyī*, it is *asiddha* with respect to 8.2.31. According to the tradition, since 8.2.32 is *asiddha* with respect to 8.2.31, 8.2.31 should apply here. This, however, gives *daḍh* + *tum*, which leads to the wrong form **dāḍhum*.[27]

Kātyāyana acknowledges the fact that, to get the correct answer, we need to apply 8.2.32, which is the exception, and not 8.2.31, which is the general rule. However, he assumes that the exception rule cannot win if it is *asiddha* with respect to the general rule. To tackle this problem, in vt. 2 (Mbh III.385.19–21), on 8.2.1, he says: *apavādo vacanaprāmāṇyāt* 'the exception [wins] on the authority of the statement [of rule 8.2.32]'. Thus, for the tradition, the exception rule 8.2.32 is not *asiddha* with respect to the general rule 8.2.31, thanks to Kātyāyana's *vārttika*. Therefore, the former wins, leading to the correct form: *dah* + *tum* → *dagh* + *tum* (8.2.32 *dāder dhātor ghaḥ*) → *dagh* + *dhum* (8.2.40 *jhaṣas tathor dho'dhaḥ*) → *dagdhum* (8.4.53 *jhalāṁ jaś jhaśi*).

I disagree with the tradition. I think that, in the case of SOI, the more specific rule wins even if it is *asiddha* with respect to the general rule. Let me explain why. We know that Pāṇini has instructed us on how to tackle DOI through his rule 1.4.2, but he has not given any instructions about dealing with SOI. This is because, as I have stated before, SOI is not a part of Pāṇini's grammar but a feature of the *sūtra* style itself. Similarly, I think that, in teaching 8.2.1 *pūrvatrāsiddham* and 6.4.22 *asiddhavad atrā bhāt*, Pāṇini has given instructions vis-à-vis DOI but not vis-à-vis SOI. In other words, 8.2.1 and 6.4.22 have no impact on SOI. Consider the following situation:

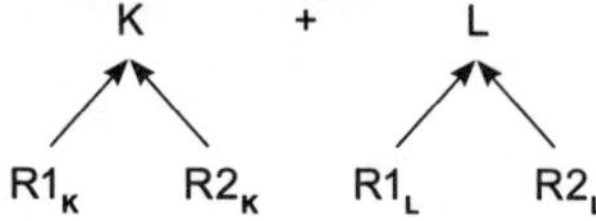

We know that there is an SOI between $R1_K$ and $R2_K$, and an SOI between $R1_L$ and $R2_L$. Before 1.4.2, 8.2.1, and 6.4.22 can potentially exert their influence, we ought to resolve both these SOIs. Let us assume that $R1_K$ is more specific that $R2_K$, thus $R1_K$ wins. Similarly, let us assume that $R1_L$ is more specific than $R2_L$, thus $R1_L$ wins. The above diagram can be redrawn as follows, by omitting to mention the losing rules:

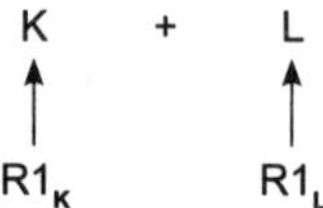

Now, 1.4.2, 8.2.1, and 6.4.22 can potentially come into play. If neither of the two rules are governed by 8.2.1 or 6.4.22, then by my interpretation of 1.4.2, the RHS rule $R1_L$ applies at this step. If 8.2.1 governs one of the two rules, that is, for example, if $R1_L$ is *asiddha* with respect to $R1_K$, then 1.4.2, which I think comes into the picture only when both rules acknowledge each other's existence, cannot resolve this DOI. By 8.2.1, $R1_K$ applies at this step. I hope this disambiguates my proposition that 1.4.2, 8.2.1, and so on are relevant in regard with DOI but not in regard with SOI.

Coming back to the present example, I think the fact that 8.2.32 is *asiddha* with respect to 8.2.31 has no bearing on our method of resolving SOI, which requires us to pick the more specific rule. The more specific rule 8.2.32 wins despite being *asiddha* with respect to the general rule 8.2.31.

Now, let us examine 6.4.22 *asiddhavad atrā bhāt*. As stated in section 6.1 of this chapter, according to the *Kāśikā*, 6.4.22 means:

A is *asiddhavat* with respect to B if:

(i) both A and B are taught in 6.4.22–6.4.175 (*ā bhāt*), and
(ii) both A and B have a *samānāśraya* 'common substratum' (*atra*).

I disagree with *Kāśikā*'s interpretation of all three parts of this rule, namely *asiddhavat*, *ā bhāt*, and *atra*. Let us begin by looking at *asiddhavat*. As stated in section 6.1, the tradition does not differentiate between *asiddha* and *asiddhavat*. It interprets both of them as 'suspended'. However, I do not think that Pāṇini would have added *-vat* to *asiddha* if he wanted to convey a meaning that can be conveyed by *asiddha* itself.

In fact, *asiddhavat* is derived by adding the *taddhita* affix *vatI* to *asiddha* + *Ṭā* (cf. 5.1.115 *tena tulyaṁ kriyā cedvatiḥ*[28]). *Ṭā* is later deleted by 2.4.71 *supo dhātuprātipadikayoḥ*, thereby leading to the form *asiddhavat*, which means 'like *asiddha*'. So, *asiddhavat* is different from yet similar to *asiddha*. We know that *asiddha* implies *śāstrāsiddhi* ('Rule X is suspended with respect to rule Y') which in turn always entails *kāryāsiddhi* ('The outcome of the application of rule X is suspended with respect to rule Y'). Because *asiddha* and *asiddhavat* have different meanings, the only possible interpretation of *asiddhavat* is *kāryāsiddhi*: 'the outcome of the application of rule X is suspended with respect to rule Y'.[29] I will support this conclusion with more evidence later in this chapter. The meanings of *asiddha* and *asiddhavat* can be summarized as follows:

Type	*śāstrāsiddhi*	*kāryāsiddhi*
asiddha	Yes	Yes
asiddhavat	No	Yes

So, how does 6.4.22, which teaches *asiddhavat*, interact with 1.4.2?

1. In case of DOI between two rules, if these two rules are *asiddhavat* with respect to each other, they acknowledge each other's existence (because there is no *śāstrāsiddhi*). This allows the resolution of the DOI by 1.4.2.
2. Each of these two rules involved in DOI does not acknowledge the outcome of the application of the other (because there is *kāryāsiddhi*). This ensures that, after the RHS rule has applied (by my interpretation of 1.4.2), the LHS rule *always* applies at the following step because it does not acknowledge the outcome of the application of the RHS rule.

This will become clearer in the examples below. Now let us attempt to decipher the meaning of *ā bhāt* in 6.4.22 *asiddhavad atrā bhāt*. As stated in section

6.1 of this chapter, Kātyāyana and Patañjali discuss both possibilities: one, that the jurisdiction of 6.4.22 ends at 6.4.129, and the other, that it continues up to the end of 6.4.

I think that the *adhikāra* of 6.4.22 ends at 6.4.129. Let me explain why this is the case. We know how Pāṇini indicates the boundary of *adhikāra sūtras*: he uses either *ā* or *prāk* in conjunction with a term from the *sūtra*, which constitutes the boundary, in the ablative. For example, consider 1.4.1 *ā kaḍārād ekā saṁjñā*, the jurisdiction of which ends at 2.2.38 *kaḍārāḥ karmadhāraye*, and 4.1.83 *prāg dīvyato'ṇ*, the jurisdiction of which ends at 4.4.2 *tena dīvyati khanati jayati jitam*. So, if Pāṇini wanted to state that the *adhikāra* of 6.4.22 continues up to 6.4.175 *ṛtvyavāstvyavāstvamādhvīhiraṇyayāni cchandasi*, then he would have said, in 6.4.22, *asiddhavad atra ā ṛtvyāt* (which, after *sandhi*, becomes *asiddhavad atrārtvyāt*). But since he has said *asiddhavad atrābhāt*, the jurisdiction of 6.4.22 continues only up to 6.4.129 *bhasya*. The examples discussed below will buttress my position.

Now, let us examine the word *atra* in 6.4.22. As stated in section 6.1 of this chapter, Kātyāyana discusses two possible interpretations of the word *atra*. One is *samānāśrayatva* 'common substratum' and the other 'with respect to the rules taught here'. Only one of the two interpretations can be correct, and I think that it is the latter, for reasons that I will now explain.

Firstly, notice that in 8.2.1 we find another term, which like *a-tra*, ends in the affix *traL*, namely *pūrva-tra*. There, *pūrva-tra* means 'with respect to the rules taught before (in the *Aṣṭādhyāyī*'s serial order)'. This strongly suggests that in 6.4.22, *atra*, which also ends in *tra*, means 'with respect to the rules taught here (in the section governed by 6.4.22)'.

Secondly, consider *Kāśikā*'s interpretation of 6.4.22: that which is taught in the section starting here and extending up to the end of 6.4 (*ā bhāt*) is suspended (*asiddhavat*), if both rules have a *samānāśraya* 'common substratum' (*atra*). It infers *samānāśrayatva* from the word *atra*. But if we assume that *atra* implies *samānāśrayatva*, then it follows that Pāṇini has not said anything about the rules with respect to which the rules in the section headed by 6.4.22 are *asiddhavat*. As I have stated earlier, in such a case, rules in the *ābhīya* section become *asiddhavat* with respect to, for example, rules from *adhyāya* seven, which is not desirable. This too indicates that *atra* means 'with respect to the rules taught here (i.e., in the section 6.4.22–6.4.129)'. I will discuss this further when dealing with specific examples below.

Now that I have discussed my opinion about all three parts of 6.4.22, namely *asiddhavat, atra,* and *ā bhāt,* here is my interpretation of 6.4.22:

6.4.22 *asiddhavad atrā bhāt*: the outcome of the application of a rule taught in the section 6.4.22–6.4.129, is not acknowledged by any other rule taught here (*atra*), that is, in the section 6.4.22–6.4.129.

For the sake of clarity, I reproduce the table dealing with the difference between *asiddha* and *asiddhavat* below:

Type	*śāstrāsiddhi*	*kāryāsiddhi*
asiddha	Yes	Yes
asiddhavat	No	Yes

Before we look at derivations involving 6.4.22, here is a summary of my interpretation of all three rules:

A	B	C
Rule	Rules which are *asiddha* (under 6.1.86 and 8.2.1) / *asiddhavat* (under 6.4.22)	Rules with respect to which rules in column B are *asiddha* (under 6.1.86 and 8.2.1) / *asiddhavat* (under 6.4.22)
6.1.86 *ṣatvatukor asiddhaḥ* (*ekaḥ pūrvaparayoḥ*)	Any rule teaching *ekādeśa* (6.1.84-6.1.108)	Any rule teaching introduction of augment *tUK* (e.g., 6.1.71 *hrasvasya piti kṛti tuk*) or replacement of *s* with *ṣ* (e.g., 8.3.59 *ādeśapratyayoḥ*)
8.2.1 *pūrvatrāsiddham*	Any rule G that comes after 8.2.1 in the serial order of the *Aṣṭādhyāyī*	Any rule F which comes before rule G (see column B) in the serial order of the *Aṣṭādhyāyī*
6.4.22 *asiddhavad atrā bhāt*	Any rule taught in 6.4.22-6.4.129	Any rule taught in 6.4.22-6.4.129

Let us now look at derivations which involve both SOI and 6.4.22.

Example #7. *han + siP*—'to hurt', imperative second-person singular[30]

3.1.68 *kartari śap*: affix *ŚaP* occurs after a verbal root when a *sārvadhātuka* affix that denotes *kartṛ* 'agent' follows.

3.4.87 *ser hy apic ca*: a *siP* replacement of *LOṬ* is replaced with *hi* and is treated as if not marked with *P*.

This is a case of DOI. By my interpretation of 1.4.2, we apply the RHS rule 3.4.87 and get *han* + *hi*. Thereafter, the derivation proceeds as follows: *han* + *hi* → *han* + *ŚaP* + *hi* (3.1.68) → *han* + *hi* (2.4.72 *adiprabhr̥tibhyaḥ śapaḥ*). Now, *han* can be called an *aṅga* with respect to *hi* (cf. my interpretation of 1.4.13). Thus, the following rules from the *aṅgādhikāra* become applicable:

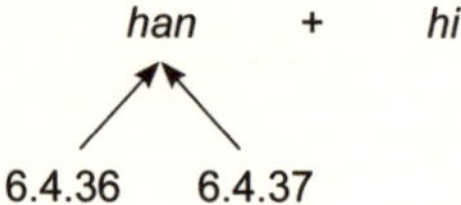

6.4.36 *hanter jaḥ*: the root *han* is replaced with *ja* when the affix *hi* follows.

6.4.37 *anudāttopadeśavanatitanotyādīnām anunāsikalopo jhali kṅiti*: the final nasal of a base marked with *anudātta* when taught in the *Dhātupāṭha*, as well as of *vanA* 'to like' and the roots headed by *tanU* 'to extend', is replaced with *LOPA* when an affix beginning with *jhaL* (a non-nasal stop or a fricative) and marked with *K* or *Ṅ* follows.[31]

There is an SOI relationship between 6.4.36 and 6.4.37. 6.4.36 is specifically taught for *han* + *hi*, so it is more specific than 6.4.37.

Note that the two rules 6.4.36 and 6.4.37 have been taught in the *asiddhavat* section. However, as argued above (see example 6), Pāṇini's rules 8.2.1 and 6.4.22 deal with DOI, but not with SOI. Like 8.2.1, 6.4.22 too has no impact on SOI. Here, the more specific rule 6.4.36 wins, and we get *jahi*, which is the correct form.

Now let us imagine what would have happened in the absence of 6.4.22. The following rule would have become applicable to *ja* + *hi*:

6.4.105 *ato heḥ*: a *hi*, which comes after a base ending in *a*, is replaced with *LUK*.

This would have given the incorrect form **ja*. 6.4.22 helps us avoid deriving this incorrect form: as taught by 6.4.22, 6.4.36 is *asiddhavat* with respect to 6.4.105. So even though 6.4.105 can acknowledge the existence of 6.4.36, it cannot acknowledge the outcome of the application of 6.4.36. As a result, 6.4.105 is not applicable to *jahi*.

Example #8. *bhū* + *tas*—'to be', perfect third-person dual

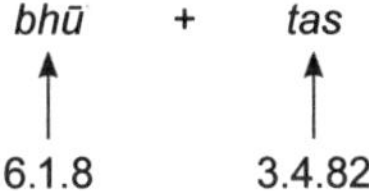

6.1.8 *liṭi dhātor anabhyāsasya*: a verbal base that has not undergone reduplication undergoes reduplication when followed by *LIṬ*.[32]

3.4.82 *parasmaipadānāṁ ṇalatususthalathusaṇalvamāḥ*: *ṆaL*, *atus*, *us*, *thaL*, *athus*, *a*, *ṆaL*, *va*, and *ma*, respectively, come in place of the nine *parasmaipada* replacements of *LIṬ*, namely *tiP*, *tas*, *jhi*, *siP*, *thas*, *tha*, *miP*, *vas*, and *mas*.

By my interpretation of 1.4.2, we apply the RHS rule 3.4.82 and get: *bhū* + *atus*. Here, three rules are applicable:

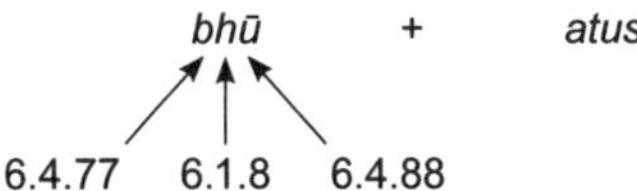

6.1.8 *liṭi dhātor anabhyāsasya*: same as above.

6.4.77 *aci śnudhātubhruvāṁ yvor iyaṅuvaṅau*: the final *i* and *u* of *Śnu*, and of any verbal base, and of *bhrū* 'brow' are replaced with *iyAṄ* and *uvAṄ*, respectively, when an affix beginning with a vowel follows.

6.4.88 *bhuvo vug luṅliṭoḥ*: augment *vUK* is attached to *bhū* when a *LUṄ* or *LIṬ* affix beginning with a vowel follows.

This is a case of SOI. Note that 6.4.77 and 6.4.88 both belong to the section headed by 6.4.22. However, as stated above, 6.4.22 does not impact SOI. Let us find out which of the three rules is the most specific.

6.4.77 *aci śnudhātubhruvāṁ yvor iyaṅuvaṅau*

bhū* + affix beginning with *aC

other conditions

6.1.8 *liṭi dhātor anabhyāsasya*

***bhū* + affix beginning with *aC* (*LIṬ*)**

other conditions

6.4.88 *bhuvo vug luṅliṭoḥ*

***bhū* + affix beginning with *aC* (*LIṬ*)**

bhū + affix beginning with *aC* (*LUṄ*)
other conditions

6.4.88 and 6.1.8 are both more specific than 6.4.77 because 6.4.77 has not been taught specifically for *LIṬ*. Between 6.4.88 and 6.1.8, 6.1.8 is more specific because it has been taught exclusively for *LIṬ*, whereas 6.4.88 has been taught for both *LUṄ* and *LIṬ*.

Thus, 6.1.8 emerges as the most specific rule. Upon applying it, we get: *bhūbhū* + *atus*. Here, the following rules are applicable:

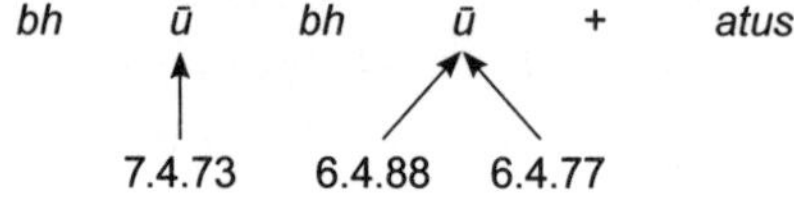

7.4.73 *bhavater aḥ*: *a* replaces the last sound of the *abhyāsa* of *bhū* 'to be' when *LIṬ* follows.

6.4.88 *bhuvo vug luṅliṭoḥ*: same as above.

6.4.77 *aci śnudhātubhruvāṁ yvor iyaṅuvaṅau*: same as above.

By my interpretation of 1.4.2, we perform the RHS operation. But which of the two RHS rules should we apply? As stated above, there is an SOI between 6.4.88 and 6.4.77, and the more specific rule 6.4.88 wins. Thus, we get: *bhūbhūv* + *atus*. At this step, 7.4.43 applies, giving us *bhabhūv* + *atus*. Now that all rules from the *sapādasaptādhyāyī* have applied, the rule 8.4.54 *abhyāse car ca* applies, thereby giving the correct form: *babhūvatuḥ*.

In vt. 14 on 6.4.22 (Mbh III.191.15), Kātyāyana alludes to the interaction between *vUK* (6.4.88) and *uvAṄ* (6.4.77). He says: *vugyuṭāv uvaṅyaṇoḥ* 'rules teaching augments *vUK* and *yUṬ* [should be *siddha* and not *asiddhavat*] with respect to rules teaching *uvAṄ* and *yaṆ*'. This *vārttika* is premised on the assumption that if 6.4.88 *bhuvo vug luṅliṭoḥ* is *asiddhavat* (which, according to the tradition, has the same meaning as *asiddha*) with respect to 6.4.77 *aci śnudhātubhruvāṁ yvor iyaṅuvaṅau*, then 6.4.77 will apply, giving the wrong answer *babhuvatuḥ. However, as I have shown in the derivation above, there is an SOI between 6.4.77 and 6.4.88, and 6.4.22 has no impact on SOI. Thus, Pāṇini's system correctly derives this form, and this *vārttika* is not required to assist in the process.

Now let us consider an example that demonstrates the impact of 6.4.22 on DOI.

Example #9. *śās* + *siP*—**'to teach', imperative second-person singular**[33]

3.1.68 *kartari śap*: affix *ŚaP* occurs after a verbal root when a *sārvadhātuka* affix that denotes *kartr̥* 'agent' follows.

3.4.87 *ser hy apic ca*: a *siP* replacement of *LOṬ* is replaced with *hi* and is treated as if not marked with *P*.

This is a case of DOI. By my interpretation of 1.4.2, we apply the RHS rule 3.4.87 and get *śās* + *hi*. Thereafter, the derivation proceeds as follows: *śās* + *hi* → *śās* + *ŚaP* + *hi* (3.1.68) → *śās* + *hi* (2.4.72 *adiprabhr̥tibhyaḥ śapaḥ*[34]). *śās* can now be called an *aṅga* with respect to *hi* (cf. my interpretation of 1.4.13). Thus, the following rules from the *aṅgādhikāra* become applicable:

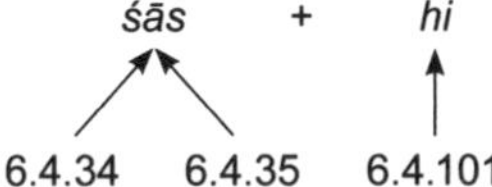

6.4.34 *śāsa id aṅhaloḥ*: the penultimate sound of *śās*, is replaced with short *i* when followed by *aṄ*, or an affix that begins with a consonant and is marked with *K* or *Ṅ*.[35]

6.4.35 *śā hau*: *śās* is replaced with *śā* when affix *hi* follows.

6.4.101 *hujhalbhyo her dhiḥ*: *hi* is replaced with *dhi* when it occurs after root *hu* or after a form ending in *jhaL* (a non-nasal stop or a fricative). There is an SOI between 6.4.34 and 6.4.35. As stated before, 6.4.22 does not impact SOI. 6.4.35 is more specific because it pertains to *hi* alone and thus wins.

Now, we shall focus on the interaction between 6.4.35 and 6.4.101. Note that both these rules fall under the heading rule 6.4.22 *asiddhavad atrābhāt*. Thus, 6.4.35 can acknowledge the existence of 6.4.101 but cannot acknowledge the outcome of the application of 6.4.101. Similarly, 6.4.101 can acknowledge the existence of 6.4.35 but not the outcome of the application of 6.4.35.

Since 6.4.35 and 6.4.101 acknowledge each other's existence, we can use 1.4.2 to deal with this case of DOI. By my interpretation of 1.4.2, we apply the RHS rule 6.4.101 and get *śās* + *dhi*. Since 6.4.101 is *asiddhavat* with respect to 6.4.35, 6.4.35 does not acknowledge the outcome of the application of 6.4.101. Thus, 6.4.35 applies, and we get the correct form: *śādhi*.

In order to understand the crucial role played by 6.4.22 in this derivation, let us analyse how this derivation would have proceeded in its absence. We will directly look at the relevant step:

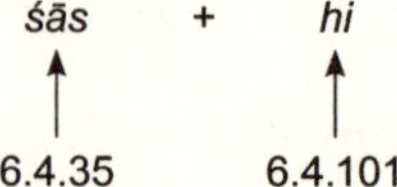

Let us examine the relationship between 6.4.35 and 6.4.101. If, by 6.4.35, we replace *śās* with *śā* at this step, then 6.4.101, which applies to *hi* when *hi* is preceded by *jhaL*, will not be applicable at the following step. If, by 6.4.101, we replace *hi* with *dhi* at this step, then 6.4.35, which applies to *śās* when it is followed by *hi*, will not be applicable at the following step. This is a case of mutual blocking in DOI.

By my interpretation of 1.4.2, we apply the RHS rule 6.4.101 and get *śās* + *dhi*. As stated above, 6.4.35 is not applicable after the application of 6.4.101. Thus, the final form is **śāsdhi*, which is incorrect. To get the correct form *śādhi*, we need to apply both 6.4.35 and 6.4.101. However, since both rules block each other, only one can apply in this derivation. To overcome this problem, Pāṇini has put them both in the section headed by 6.4.22.

6.4.22 teaches that the two rules within 6.4.22–6.4.129 are *asiddhavat* with respect to each other. At the risk of repetition, let me state that this ensures two things:

1. Both rules acknowledge each other's existence. This allows the resolution of the DOI by (my interpretation of) 1.4.2.
2. Each of the two rules does not acknowledge the outcome of the application of the other. This ensures that, after the RHS rule has applied (by my interpretation of 1.4.2), the LHS rule applies at the following step because it does not acknowledge the outcome of the application of the RHS rule.

Let me state in general terms what we have seen in this derivation. In those cases of DOI wherein two rules block each other, and where Pāṇini wants both rules to apply, he places them in the section 6.4.22–6.4.129. In simple words, when required, Pāṇini uses 6.4.22 *asiddhavad atrā bhāt* to neutralize the impact of 1.4.2 (as interpreted by me) on those cases of DOI that involve mutual blocking, where it is desirable for him to do so. Contrast this with 8.2.1, which, as I have stated earlier, is leveraged by Pāṇini to neutralize the impact of 1.4.2 on those cases of DOI that involve unidirectional blocking.

Note that if Pāṇini had taught 6.4.22 as *asiddham atrā bhāt* instead of *asiddhavad atrā bhāt*, then both rules, namely 6.4.35 and 6.4.101, would not be able to acknowledge each other. Thus, both would try to apply to their respective operands. Since only one rule can apply at any given step, the machine would have come to a halt.

Now, through the following derivation, I will provide evidence to support my claim that the jurisdiction of 6.4.22 ends at 6.4.129.

Example #10.

Let us derive the accusative plural of the Vedic perfect participle of ***pā*** 'to drink': ***pā*** + ***LIṬ*** 'he who had drunk'.[36]

pā + *LIṬ*

↑ ↑

6.1.8 3.2.107

6.1.8 *liṭi dhātor anabhyāsasya*: an unreduplicated verbal base undergoes reduplication when followed by *LIṬ*.[37]

3.2.107 *kvasuś ca*: *KvasU* optionally replaces *LIṬ* in Vedic when the action is denoted in the past.

By my interpretation of 1.4.2, we apply the RHS rule 3.2.107 and get *pā* + *KvasU*. Here, the following rules are applicable:

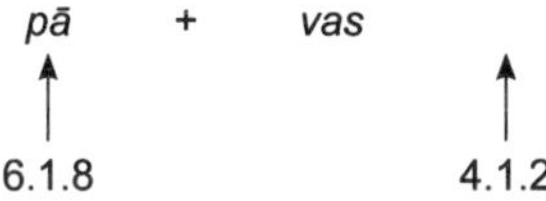

6.1.8 *liṭi dhātor anabhyāsasya*: same as above.

4.1.2 *svaujasamauṭchaṣṭābhyāmbhisṅebhyāmbhyasṅasibhyāmbhyasṅasosāmṅyossup*[38]

By my interpretation of 1.4.2, we apply the RHS rule 4.1.2 and get: *pā* + *vas* + *Śas*. Here, the following rules are applicable:

6.1.8 *liṭi dhātor anabhyāsasya*: same as above.

6.4.131 *vasoḥ samprasāraṇam*: the semivowel of the affix *vasU* in an item termed *bha* is replaced with the corresponding vowel *u*.

By my interpretation of 1.4.2, we apply the RHS rule 6.4.131 and get *pā* + *uas* + *Śas*. Here, the following rules are applicable:

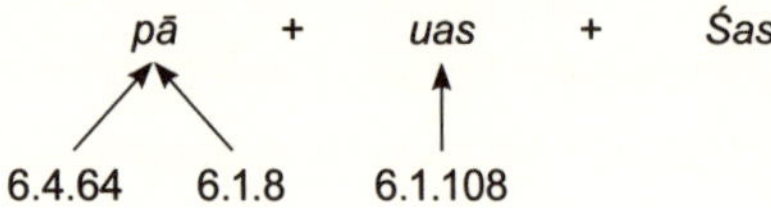

6.4.64 *āto lopa iṭi ca*: the final *ā* of a base is replaced with *LOPA* when followed by augment *iṬ* or an *ārdhadhātuka* affix that begins with a vowel and is marked with *K* or *Ṅ*.

6.1.8 *liṭi dhātor anabhyāsasya*: same as above.

6.1.108 *samprasāraṇāc ca*: a *samprasāraṇa* vowel and the following vowel are together replaced with the former.

By my interpretation of 1.4.2, we apply the RHS 6.1.108 rule and get *pā* + *us* + *Śas*. Here, two rules are applicable:

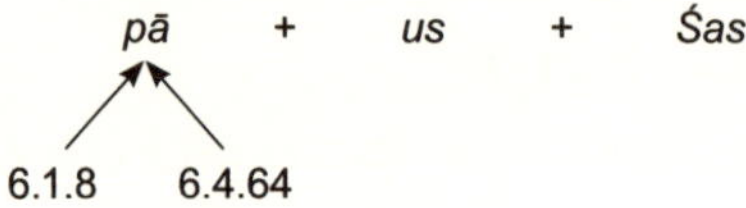

6.4.64 *āto lopa iṭi ca*: same as above.

6.1.8 *liṭi dhātor anabhyāsasya*: same as above.

This is a case of SOI. Let us compare the two rules to determine which one is more specific:

6.4.64

***ā* + affix beginning with vowel (*ārdhadhātuka*) (marked with *K* or *Ṅ*)**

other conditions

6.1.8

***ā* + affix beginning with vowel (*LIṬ*)**

other conditions

We cannot say that one rule is more specific than the other in this scenario.

So, which of the two rules should we apply here? Let us understand the relationship between the two rules.

In *pā* + *us* + *Śas*, if we apply 6.1.8 *liṭi dhātor anabhyāsasya*, we get *pāpā* + *us* + *Śas*. 6.4.64 *āto lopa iṭi ca* is still applicable here.

But in *pā* + *us* + *Śas*, if we apply 6.4.64 (which teaches the substitution of *ā* with ø, i.e., *LOPA*), we get *pø* + *us* + *Śas*. Here, is 6.1.8 applicable?

Pāṇini has taught the rule 1.1.59 *dvirvacane'ci*, which, according to the *Kāśikā*,[39] teaches that the substitute of a vowel is treated like its substituendum (i.e., the said vowel)—for the purpose of reduplication alone—when it is followed by a vowel-initial affix, which conditions reduplication of the verbal base. So, in *pø* + *us* + *Śas*, by 1.1.59, we can treat *LOPA* (ø), which is the substitute of vowel *ā*, as the substituendum *ā* because it is followed by the vowel-initial affix *us*, which causes reduplication. Therefore, 6.1.8 *liṭi dhātor anabhyāsasya* is applicable here.

We have seen that the two rules do not block each other, and we can apply them in any order. I think Pāṇini composed 1.1.59 to ensure that if we apply 6.4.64 to *pā* + *us* + *Śas*, 6.1.8 can still be applied at the following step.

After applying both 6.4.64 and 6.1.8, we get *pāp* + *us* + *Śas*. To this we apply 7.4.59 *hrasvaḥ*[40] and get the correct form: *papuṣaḥ*.[41] As stated before, according to my interpretation of 6.4.22 *asiddhavad atrā bhāt*, the jurisdiction of 6.4.22 ends at 6.4.129.

However, in the opinion of the *Kāśikā*, this jurisdiction continues up to the end of 6.4 (i.e., 6.4.175), and therefore, it creates a difficulty in the derivation of *papuṣaḥ*. As seen above, 6.4.131 *vasoḥ samprasāraṇam* changes *vas* to *uas*. Since *uas* begins with a vowel, 6.4.64 *āto lopa iṭi ca* becomes applicable to the *ā* of *pā*. However, both 6.4.64 and 6.4.131 lie within 6.4.22–6.4.175, which is the jurisdiction of 6.4.22 according to the *Kāśikā*. Thus, the *Kāśikā* deems them *asiddhavat* with respect to each other. Consequently, 6.4.64 does not acknowledge the outcome of the application of 6.4.131. In other words, it does not acknowledge the change from *vas* to *uas* and cannot apply. This gives the incorrect form: *papā* + *usas* → **paposas* (6.1.87 *ād guṇaḥ*).

I think the tradition interprets *atra* as *samānāśraya* for the sole purpose of overcoming this problem. According to the *Kāśikā*, two rules can be called *asiddhavat* by 6.4.22 only if they have a *samānāśraya* 'common substratum'.

Without explaining exactly what this means, the *Kāśikā* gives the following example: 6.4.131 and 6.4.64 do not have a *samānāśraya*, and thus they are not *asiddhavat* with respect to each other.[42] Consequently, 6.4.64 acknowledges 6.4.131 and applies to *papā* + *uṣaḥ* (which has been derived by applying 6.4.131). In this way, we get the correct form *papuṣaḥ*.

But what exactly does *samānāśraya* stand for? The *Nyāsa* glosses *āśraya* as *nimitta* 'cause'. So according to the *Nyāsa*, a rule is *asiddhavat* with respect to another only if the two rules have a *samānāśraya* 'common cause'. However, I do not think that here *āśraya* means *nimitta*. Let me explain why, by looking at another derivation: at the step *śās* + *hi* (see derivation 9 of this section), 6.4.35 *śā hau*, which applies to *śās*, is caused by *hi*, while 6.4.101 *hujhalbhyo her dhiḥ*, which applies to *hi*, is caused by *śās*. Even though the two rules do not have the same cause, the tradition deems them *asiddhavat* with respect to each other. So, when Kātyāyana uses the word *samānāśraya* in vt. 12 *samānāśrayavacanāt siddham*, he does not imply 'common cause'. What then does he mean?

It is not possible to answer this question with certainty. But one can speculate that when Kātyāyana says two rules are *samānāśraya*, he likely means that they pertain to the same set of items. Both rules 6.4.101 and 6.4.35 pertain to *śās* + *hi*, thus they are *samānāśraya* and *asiddhavat* with respect to each other. However, in our present example, 6.4.131 pertains to *vas* + *Śas*, whereas 6.4.64 *āto lopa iṭi ca* pertains to *papā* + *uas*. The two rules have different *āśraya*s 'substrata', and thus, according to the tradition, they are not *asiddhavat* with respect to each other.

Kātyāyana also offers another solution, which basically amounts to stating that this set of examples should be exempt from following 6.4.22. In vt. 9 on 6.4.22 (Mbh III.190.11), he teaches: *siddhaṁ vasusamprasāraṇam ajvidhau* 'the *samprasāraṇa* of *vasU* should be *siddha* (rather than *asiddhavat*) with regard to an operation concerning vowels'.

It is evident that the tradition struggles to resolve this problem and comes up with not one, but two alternative ways of dealing with it. Not only does Kātyāyana write a *vārttika* contradicting 6.4.22, but he also concocts the concept of *samānāśrayatva* to address this difficulty.

On the contrary, notice that, according to my interpretation of 6.4.22, 6.4.131 does not lie in the *ābhīya* section (6.4.22–6.4.129). Thus, in my opinion, 6.4.131 is not *asiddhavat* with respect to 6.4.64. Therefore, if we accept that the jurisdiction of 6.4.22 stops at 6.4.129, the challenges faced by the tradition in deriving this form do not rise. My interpretation of *atra* (with respect to the rules taught here, i.e., in the section headed by 6.4.22) and *ā bhāt* (up to 6.4.129) allows us to correctly derive *papuṣaḥ* without flouting 6.4.22.

Kātyāyana also discusses other examples of this nature, wherein he has had to write ad hoc *vārttika*s claiming that certain rules taught in the section 6.4.129–6.4.175, which, according to him, constitute a part of the *ābhīya* section (6.4.22–6.4.175), are not *asiddhavat*, contrary to his own interpretation of 6.4.22 (generally adopted by the later tradition). For example, the problem faced by the tradition in deriving *paśuṣaḥ* (accusative plural of *paśu* + *saN* 'bestowing cattle') is the same as the one faced in deriving *papuṣaḥ*. To avoid redundancy, I will derive it by my method here without showing the DOI and SOI that might arise at different steps: *paśusaN* + *vIṬ* (3.2.67 *janasanakhanakramagamo viṭ*) → *paśusan* + *vIṬ* + *Śas* (4.1.2 *svaujas . . .*) → *paśusan* + ø + *Śas* (6.1.67 *ver apr̥ktasya*) → *paśusaā* + ø + *Śas* (6.4.41 *viḍvanor anunāsikasyāt*, 1.1.62 *pratyayalope pratyayalakṣaṇam*) → *paśusa* + *Śas* (6.4.140 *āto dhātoḥ*) → *paśusas* (6.1.97 *ato guṇe*) → *paśuṣaḥ* (8.3.108 *sanoter anaḥ*).

As seen in this derivation, in order to correctly derive *paśuṣaḥ*, one needs to first apply 6.4.41 *viḍvanor anunāsikasyāt* and then 6.4.140 *āto dhātoḥ*. However, according to the tradition, since the jurisdiction of 6.4.22 continues up to 6.4.175, 6.4.41 is *asiddhavat* with respect to 6.4.140. Consequently, 6.4.140 cannot apply after the application of 6.4.41. This creates an obstacle in correctly deriving *paśuṣaḥ*. To deal with this problem, Kātyāyana has composed vt. 11 on 6.4.22, effectively negating 6.4.22 (Mbh III.190.17): *āttvaṁ yalopāllopayoḥ paśuṣo na vājān*[43] *cākhāyitā cākhāyitum* '*āttva* (here, taught by 6.4.41) should be *siddha* when *y*-deletion and *ā*-deletion (here, taught by 6.4.140) [can potentially take place, e.g.,] *paśuṣo na vājān, cākhāyitā* [and] *cākhāyitum*'. But if one thinks, as I do, that the jurisdiction of 6.4.22 ends at 6.4.129, then this problem simply does not arise. This is because 6.4.140 lies beyond 6.4.129, and therefore, in my view, 6.4.41 is not *asiddhavat* with respect to 6.4.140.[44]

Now, I will derive a certain form, then highlight the problem faced by the tradition in this derivation vis-à-vis 6.4.22, and will show how, by following my method, we do not encounter this problem at all.

Example #11. *praśam* + *ṆiC*[45]—'to be pacified', causative absolutive

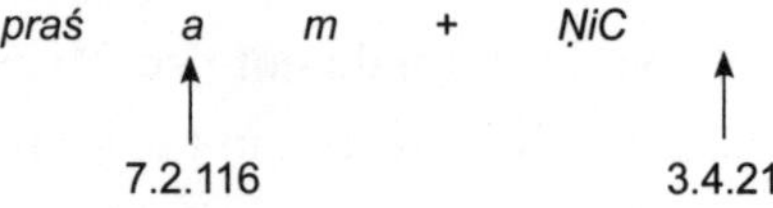

7.2.116 *ata upadhāyāḥ*: *vr̥ddhi* replaces the penultimate sound *a* of a base when an affix marked with *Ṇ* or *Ñ* follows.

3.4.21 *samānakartr̥kayoḥ pūrvakāle*: affix *Ktvā* occurs after a verbal root that denotes a prior action relative to some subsequent action provided both actions share the same agent.

By my interpretation of 1.4.2, we apply the RHS rule 3.4.21 and get: *praśam* + *ṆiC* + *Ktvā*. Here, the following rules are applicable:

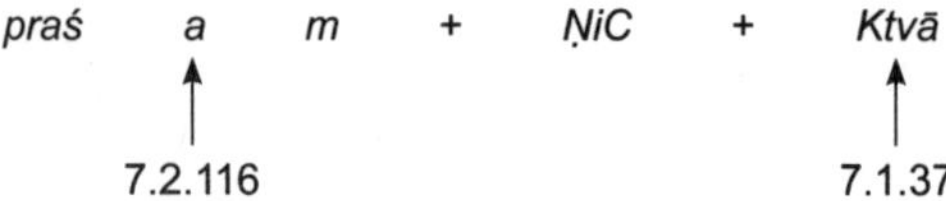

7.2.116 *ata upadhāyāḥ*: same as above.

7.1.37 *samāse'nañpūrve ktvo lyap*: in a compound, the first member of which is not *naÑ*, the affix *Ktvā* in the second member of the compound is replaced with *LyaP*.

By my interpretation of 1.4.2, we apply the RHS rule 7.1.37 and get: *praśam* + *ṆiC* + *LyaP*. Here, the following rules are applicable:

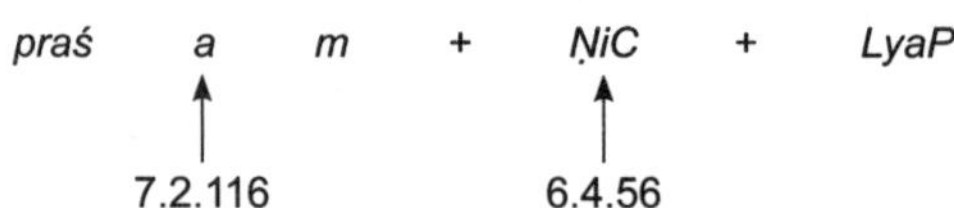

7.2.116 *ata upadhāyāḥ*: same as above.

6.4.56 *lyapi laghupūrvāt*[46]: *Ṇi*, when occurring after a sound segment which is preceded by a *laghu* 'light' vowel, is replaced with *ay*, provided the *ārdhadhātuka* affix *LyaP* follows.

By my interpretation of 1.4.2, we apply the RHS rule 6.4.56 and get *praśam* + *ay* + *LyaP*. Here, 7.2.116 *ata upadhāyāḥ* applies, and we get *praśām* + *ay* + *LyaP*. At this stage, 6.4.92 *mitām hrasvaḥ* applies, which teaches that the penultimate vowel of a base marked with *M* (in the *Dhātupāṭha*) is replaced with its short counterpart when affix *Ṇi* follows. But here, *praśām* is not followed by

ṆiC but instead by *ay*. Then how can 6.4.92 apply? 6.4.92 considers 6.4.56 to be *asiddhavat* and thus cannot see the outcome of the latter's application: it sees *praśām* + *ay* + *LyaP* as *praśām* + *ṆiC* + *LyaP* and thus applies, giving us the correct form, *praśamayya*.

Owing to a relevant *vārttika* (vt. 13 on 6.4.22), which we will discuss soon, it becomes clear that Kātyāyana, when trying to derive *praśamayya*, applies some of these rules in a different order: first, 7.2.116 *ata upadhāyāḥ*, second, 6.4.92 *mitāṁ hrasvaḥ*, and third 6.4.56 *lyapi laghupūrvāt*. Let us apply these three rules as per Kātyāyana's order to understand the problem faced by him: *praśam* + *ṆiC* + *LyaP* → *praśām* + *ṆiC* + *LyaP* (7.2.116 *ata upadhāyāḥ*) → *praśam* + *ṆiC* + *LyaP* (6.4.92 *mitāṁ hrasvaḥ*) → *praśamayya* (6.4.56 *lyapi laghupūrvāt*).

But applying rules in this order is against what Pāṇini has taught in 6.4.22. Let me explain how. 6.4.56 is applicable to *ṆiC* when it is preceded by a sound (*m* of *praśam*), which is in turn preceded by a light vowel (the penultimate sound *a* of *praśam*). But the light vowel *a* is the outcome of the application of 6.4.92, which, as per 6.4.22, should be considered *asiddhavat* with respect to 6.4.56. So, in this derivation, if we are to follow 6.4.22, 6.4.56 should not apply after the application of 6.4.92.

To ensure that the correct form *praśamayya* is derived, Kātyāyana formulates vt. 13 (Mbh III.191.9), which basically goes against 6.4.22: *hrasvayalopāllopaś cāyādeśe lyapi* 'a short vowel (here, taught by 6.4.92), *y*-deletion and *ā*-deletion [should not be suspended] when *ay*-substitution before *LyaP* (here, taught by 6.4.56) [can take place]'. On the contrary, by following my interpretation of 1.4.2, we get the correct answer without violating 6.4.22. This provides further proof that my interpretation of 1.4.2 is indeed correct.

In this chapter, I have discussed my opinion about the exact meanings of the three suspension rules, the difference between *asiddha* and *asiddhavat*, how these suspension rules impact SOI and DOI, how they interact with 1.4.2, and how my interpretations enable us to perform various kinds of derivations without having to rely on Kātyāyana's *vārttikas*. I do not claim to have solved every problem associated with the three suspension rules, nor do I claim to have discussed each kind of example associated with these three rules. To the extent possible, I have attempted to display the diversity of derivational examples impacted by the suspension rules.

Modern scholars, such as Bronkhorst (1980), Joshi (1982), Joshi and Roodbergen (1987), and Yagi (1992) have published papers on the three suspension rules. Some of their opinions are similar to mine, and others considerably different. However, in the interest of clarity, I have restricted the discussions in this chapter to a limited set of traditional opinions and my own opinion on this topic, without examining the opinions of modern scholars.

CHAPTER SEVEN

The Evolution of Conflict Resolution Tools in the Pāṇinian Tradition

In this chapter, I will present a summary of post-Pāṇinian ideas on 1.4.2. I will also adumbrate the evolution of conflict-resolution tools in the early tradition. I will undertake this task in the context of my own findings about 1.4.2 presented in this book.[1]

7.1 Kātyāyana on 1.4.2

Since Kātyāyana is the first scholar to have commented on the *Aṣṭādhyāyī*, we cannot study the evolution of conflict-resolution tools without examining some of his *vārttikas*. To begin with, we know that Kātyāyana interprets the term *para* in 1.4.2 as 'the rule which comes later in the *Aṣṭādhyāyī*'s serial order'.

For example, consider 3.1.67 *sārvadhātuke yak*, which teaches that affix *yaK* occurs after a verbal root when a *sārvadhātuka* affix that denotes *bhāva* or *karman* follows. Consider vt. 4 (Mbh II.59.1) on this rule: *vipratiṣedhād dhi śapo balīyastvam* 'Given the *vipratiṣedha* [between *yaK* (cf. 3.1.67 *sārvadhātuke yak*) and *ŚaP* (cf. 3.1.68 *kartari śap*)], *ŚaP* is more powerful [and wins, because it is *para*, i.e., taught later in the serial order of the *Aṣṭādhyāyī*]'.[2]

While this interpretation of *para* taught by Kātyāyana has been fully endorsed and internalized by the later tradition, most traditional and modern scholars have almost entirely overlooked a very important idea about *paratva* that we find in a *vārttika* on 6.1.158 *anudāttaṁ padam ekavarjam*. 6.1.158 teaches that a *pada* is entirely low pitched (*anudātta*) with the exception of one syllable. But how should we decide which syllable is not low pitched? Is it a syllable of the *prakr̥ti* 'base' or a syllable of the *pratyaya* 'affix'? After discussing this topic in multiple *vārttika*s on this rule, Kātyāyana says, in vt. 12 (Mbh III.100.12): *śāstraparavipratiṣedhāniyamād vā śabdaparavipratiṣedhāt siddham* '[in the event of *vipratiṣedha* between two operations] because it has not been [explicitly] mandated that *paratva* of rules [alone should be used to resolve] *vipratiṣedha*, alternatively *paratva* of sounds [may also be used to] accomplish [the task of resolving] *vipratiṣedha*'.[3] In other words, here, Kātyāyana suggests that alongside inferring that the rule that is *para* (i.e., comes later in the serial order of the *Aṣṭādhyāyī*) wins, we may also infer that the operation that is applicable to the *para* (i.e., RHS sound or group of sounds) wins.[4]

This shows that Kātyāyana was either exposed to or himself thought about the possibility that *para* in 1.4.2 could stand for the RHS operation. If he had chosen to further develop this line of thought, this idea could potentially have reached its logical conclusion, namely the correct interpretation of *para* in 1.4.2. One could argue that by choosing to focus on and subsequently by accepting the wrong interpretation from amongst the two possible interpretations of *para* discussed in the aforementioned *vārttika*, Kātyāyana completely changed the developmental trajectory of the Pāṇinian tradition. Kātyāyana's successors too failed to recognize the sheer potential of this *vārttika*, and thus the key to the *Aṣṭādhyāyī*'s algorithm remained before everyone's eyes and yet hidden from everyone's mind.

One key repercussion of Kātyāyana's belief that *para* in 1.4.2 stands for 'the rule that comes later in the *Aṣṭādhyāyī*'s serial order' must have been that he likely got numerous incorrect forms at the end of derivations where he solved conflicts using his interpretation of 1.4.2. Perhaps it is to avoid these undesirable outcomes, wherever possible, that he decided to reduce the jurisdiction of 1.4.2. For example, in vt. 1 on 1.4.2, he defines *vipratiṣedha* in a way that allows him to exclude *anavakāśa-sāvakāśa* pairs[5] from the jurisdiction of 1.4.2: *dvau prasaṅgāv anyārthāv ekasmin sa vipratiṣedhaḥ* (Mbh I.304.10–305) (1) '[When] two rules [which are] applicable elsewhere [become applicable] to the same place, this [is called] *vipratiṣedha*'. Thus, a conflict between two *sāvakāśa* rules (i.e., rules that are applicable elsewhere) is called *vipratiṣedha*.

In vt. 2 on 1.4.2, he says: *ekasmin yugapat asaṁbhavāt pūrvaparaprāpter ubhayaprasaṅgaḥ* '[Given the] impossibility [of] coapplication at one [i.e., the same step, there arises] the undesirable scenario of both *pūrva* and *para* being applicable'. In vt. 5, Kātyāyana says: *apratipattir vobhayos tulyabalatvāt* 'Or [maybe this results in] the failure of both [rules] to apply because of [their] equal strength'. In vt. 6 he says: *tatra pratipattyartham etad vacanam* 'So, this [*sūtra*] has been formulated in order to instruct us about this [i.e., the decision regarding which rule should apply]'. From vts. 1, 2, 5, and 6 on 1.4.2, we can conclude that, according to Kātyāyana, the conflict between two *sāvakāśa* rules is called *vipratiṣedha*, and that these two rules are treated as *tulyabala* 'of equal strength'. Note that this is the only occasion on which Kātyāyana uses the term *tulyabala*. Patañjali too uses the word *tulyabala* only once—when commenting on vt. 5 on 1.4.2.[6]

Before proceeding, it is noteworthy that Kātyāyana considers *anavakāśa* rules to be *apavāda*s 'exceptions' to *sāvakāśa* rules, which he treats as *utsarga*s 'general rules'. This becomes clear from the following *vārttika* on 4.3.156 *krītavat parimāṇāt* (which teaches the addition of the *taddhita* affix *aÑ* to different syntactically related nominal stems): vt. 5 *vānavakāśatvād apavādo mayaṭ* 'Or, by virtue of not applying elsewhere, *mayaṬ* is an exception (and thus wins)'. So, we can safely conclude that he excludes *anavakāśa-sāvakāśa* and, therefore, *apavāda-utsarga* pairs from the ambit of *vipratiṣedha*. In the same vein, it would not be wrong to say that *anavakāśatva* and *apavādatva* are conflict-resolution tools explicitly used by Kātyāyana. As stated before, Kātyāyana excludes these pairs from the jurisdiction of *vipratiṣedha* in order to reduce the scope of application of 1.4.2 and therefore to reduce the likelihood of (his interpretation of) 1.4.2 giving us incorrect outcomes.

7.2 Kātyāyana on *nitya*

The role of Kātyāyana in the evolution of the Pāṇinian tradition is paramount: Patañjali weaves his commentary around Kātyāyana's *vārttika*s, not Pāṇini's *sūtra*s. And the rest of the tradition looks to Patañjali for topics to discuss, opinions on various issues, and, generally speaking, intellectual inspiration and guidance. So, if it had not been for Kātyāyana's *vārttika*s, perhaps a broad spectrum of ideas that are now central to traditional literature would not have occurred to Patañjali, his successors, and, for that matter, us. The tradition would have proceeded on an altogether different trajectory, for better or worse. Yet, for someone who has made such a valuable contribution, Kātyāyana today receives little recognition: the largest share of praise is apportioned to Patañjali, who is accredited with everything from shedding light on *sūtra* syntax (topics like *anuvṛtti* 'continuation' and *yogavibhāga* 'splitting of Pāṇinian *sūtras* into two') to demonstrating the workings of Pāṇini's derivational mechanism. Patañjali's work dominates the discourse to the extent that his interpretations of, and comments on, Kātyāyana's *vārttikas* are assumed to be tantamount to, and even allowed to eclipse, the actual meaning and import of those *vārttikas*.

To avoid making unjustified assumptions, when studying the evolution of the *nitya* tool, we must attempt to look at each occurrence of the term *nitya* in Kātyāyana's *vārttikas* without allowing Patañjali's comments to influence this inquiry. The term *nitya* features many times in Kātyāyana's *vārttikas*,[7] and so do words formed using it, such as *nityagrahaṇānarthakya*, *nityatva*, *nityanimittatva*, *nityapūrvārtha*, *nityapratyayatva*, *nityapravṛtta*, *nityavacana*, *nityaśabdatva*, *nityasaṁbandha*, *nityasamāsa*, *nityasamāsavacana*, *nityasamāsārtha*, *nityādiṣṭatva*, and *nityārtha*. Of these, *nityasamāsa*, *nityasamāsavacana*, and *nityasamāsārtha* deal with a type of compound that has nothing to do with *nitya* as a conflict-resolution tool. We shall look at the rest to ascertain the contexts in which *nitya* is used.

Most occurrences of *nitya* in the *vārttikas*, both as a stand-alone stem and as a member of compounds, are those meant to indicate that something is not *vaikalpika* 'optional', but *nitya* 'always takes place'. On many of these occasions, *nitya* is used to prescribe the suspension of optionality, that is, to block the *anuvṛtti* 'continuation' of terms like *vā*, *vibhāṣā*, and *anyatarasyām*—which instruct us to follow the given instruction optionally—into the present *vārttika*. Let us look at Kātyāyana's first two *vārttikas* on 3.1.11:

3.1.11 *kartuḥ kyaṅ salopaś ca* (*vā supaḥ upamānād ācāre*)

'Affix *KyaṄ* optionally occurs to denote *ācāra* after a *pada* which ends in a *sUP* and denotes an agent serving as an *upamāna*; in addition, the final *-s* of the nominal stem (*prātipadika*) is replaced with *LOPA*'.

Vt. 1 *salopo vā*

'The replacement of *-s* with *LOPA* is optional [in the said situation]'.

Vt. 2 *ojo'psarasor nityam.*

'[But when *-s* is at the end of stems] *ojas* and *apsaras* [then the replacement of *-s* with *LOPA*] always [takes place]'.

Here, the word *nitya* is used to disallow the optionality associated with *-s* deletion in the given situation for words *ojas* and *apsaras*. On most other occasions, in either philosophical or ordinary grammatical discussion, Kātyāyana simply uses *nitya* as it is used in common speech—as a noun, adjective, or adverb—that is, to mean 'constant, permanent, permanently existent, always, everywhere, eternally, etc.' And Patañjali too uses the word *nitya* in the same sense in his commentary on these *vārttika*s. Note that the meaning of *nitya* in all the cases mentioned so far is roughly the same, regardless of whether it is used to perform a specific technical function in the *Aṣṭādhyāyī* (i.e., suspend optionality) or as a word from everyday Sanskrit.

Now let us turn to the two specific instances of the use of the word *nitya* by Kātyāyana on which Patañjali glosses *nitya* as: *kṛte'pi prāpnoty akṛte'pi prāpnoti*[8] '[Even when the other rule] has been applied, [this rule] is applicable, [and even when the other rule] has not been applied, [this rule] is applicable'. This is what is conventionally called the *nitya* tool for rule conflict resolution by Patañjali and his successors in the tradition. Put differently, when two rules A and B are in conflict with each other, if A remains applicable at that place both before and after the application of B, but B is not applicable after the application of A, then A is called *nitya* and B *anitya*, and the *nitya* rule A defeats the *anitya* rule B. In modern theoretical linguistics, we call this unidirectional blocking. Since Patañjali interprets the word *nitya* used in these two *vārttika*s as a conflict-resolution tool, we must study them.

Let us first look at vt. 4 on 1.3.60 *śadeḥ śitaḥ*[9] in which Kātyāyana uses the term *nitya* and where Patañjali interprets this word *nitya* as a conflict-resolution tool. Before we go to vt. 4, let us first look at vt. 3 to get some context. Vt. 3 does not discuss 1.3.60 but instead talks about another rule (1.3.17 *ner viśaḥ*), which also deals with *ātmanepada* suffixes:

Vt. 3 *upasargapūrvaniyame'ḍvyavāya upasaṁkhyānam*

'It should be added that if it is taught [that a root takes *ātmanepada* suffixes] when it is preceded by a preverb (1.3.17 *ner viśaḥ*), [this holds true also when the augment] *aṬ* is interposed [between *ni* and *viś*] (6.4.71 *luṅlaṅlṛṅṣv aḍ udāttaḥ*).'[10]

The rule that this *vārttika* refers to is:

1.3.17 *ner viśaḥ*

'An *ātmanepada* affix occurs after *viś* 'to enter' when it is preceded by the preverb *ni*'.

An example of what 1.3.17 teaches is *niviśate* (*LAṬ*, third-person singular). An example of what vt. 3 teaches is *nyaviśata* (*LAṄ*, third-person singular).

Now, in vt. 4, Kātyāyana suggests that the derivation may not proceed as desired if vt. 3 is not stated:

Vt. 4 *nityatvāl lādeśasya ātmanepade'ḍāgama iti cedaṭo'pi nityanimittatvād ātmanepadābhāvaḥ.*

'If [one argues that] the augment *aṬ* can be [introduced] when *ātmanepada* endings occur [after the *dhātu*] because the substitution of *la* suffixes is *nitya* [i.e., it always takes place], [one can object to this saying that] *ātmanepada* endings cannot occur because the augment *aṬ* also has a *nityanimitta* "permanent cause"'.

On this *vārttika*, Patañjali remarks:

nityattvāl lādeśasyātmanepada evāḍāgama iti cedevamucyate. aḍapi nityanimittaḥ. kṛte'pi lādeśe prāpnoty akṛte'pi prāpnoti. aṭo nityanimittatvād ātmanepadasyābhāvaḥ.

'If it is said in this way that the augment *aṬ* can be [introduced] when *ātmanepada* endings occur [after the *dhātu*] because the substitution of *la* suffixes is *nitya*, [it is objected that] the augment *aṬ* also has a *nitya* cause. [The augment *aṬ*] is [introduced] anyway, whether the substitution of *la* occurs or does not occur. Since the cause of *aṬ* is *nitya*, *ātmanepada* endings will not occur'.

Vt. 5 *tatra upasaṁkhyānam*

'And so that addition (vt. 3) must be made'.

Kātyāyana, in vt. 5, concludes that vt. 3 must be formulated to deal with the issue raised in vt. 4. Note that, in his comments on vt. 4, Patañjali simply paraphrases everything Kātyāyana says, except he interprets *nitya* as a conflict-resolution tool: *aḍ api nitynimittaḥ. kṛte'pi lādeśe prāpnoty akṛte'pi prāpnoti.*

Kātyāyana is aware that in *nir* + *viś* + *LAṄ* the presence of *LAṄ* to the right of *viś* will always trigger the application of the rule 6.4.71 *luṅlaṅlṛṅṣv aḍ udāttaḥ*, thereby introducing the augment *aṬ*. Thus, he calls the augment *nityanimitta* 'having a regularly occurring cause', that is, *LAṄ*. Kātyāyana uses the word *aḍvyavāya* 'the interposition *aṬ*' in vt. 3. This implies that Kātyāyana seems to assume that augment *aṬ* does not become an integral part of root *viś* but instead occurs as an independent morpheme or a separate item between *nir* and *viś*.

In *nir* + *aṬ* + *viś* + *LAṄ*, *viś* is never immediately preceded by *nir*, and so 1.3.17 *nerviśaḥ*, which mandates the substitution of *lakāra*s with *ātmanepada* endings when *viś* is preceded by *nir*, is unable to apply. Thus, Kātyāyana has composed vt. 3 allowing *nir* + *viś* to take *ātmanepada* endings even when *aṬ* intervenes between *nir* and *viś*. And my contention is that when Kātyāyana states that *aṬ* is *nityanimitta*, he simply means that whenever the cause of *aṬ*, namely *LAṄ*, is present, the augment *aṬ* will also be present, but he does not use *nitya* here as a conflict-resolution tool. This is simply because there is no evidence to be found in the aforementioned *vārttika*s to warrant Patañjali's interpretation of *nitya* as a conflict-resolution tool.

Now let us consider the other *vārttika* wherein Kātyāyana uses the word *nitya* and while commenting on which Patañjali interprets this word as a conflict-resolution tool, namely vt. 1 on 1.2.6:

1.2.6 *indhibhavatibhyāṁ ca* (*liṭ kit*)

'A *LIṬ* affix that occurs after verbal roots *indh* 'to kindle' and *bhū* 'to be, become' also is treated as though marked with *K*'.

On this *sūtra*, Patañjali says:

kimartham idam ucyate. indheḥ saṁyogārthaṁ vacanam bhavateḥ pidartham. ayaṁ yogaḥ śakyo avaktum. katham.

'Why has this been said? [This] statement [has been made] because of the conjunct of *indh* [and those suffixes placed after] *bhu* that are marked by *P*. [This] may be left unsaid. How?'

Then he introduces Kātyāyana's *vārttika*:

Vt. 1 *indheś chandoviṣayatvād bhuvo vuko nityatvāt tābhyām kidvacanānarthakyam.*

'Because *indh* [belongs to] the domain of *Veda* [and because the augment] *vUK* added to *bhū* is *nitya*, [the statement that the suffix] after them [should be treated as if] marked with *K* is redundant'.

On this Patañjali says:

indheś chandoviṣayo liṭ. na hy antareṇa cchanda indher anantaro liḍ labhyaḥ. āmā bhāṣāyām bhavitavyam. bhuvo vuko nityatvāt. bhavater api nityo vuk. kṛte'pi prāpnoty akṛte'pi. tābhyām kidvacanānarthakyam. tābhyām indhibhavatibhyāṁ kidvacanānarthakyam.

'*LIṬ* 'perfect affixes' [occur after the root] *indh* only in the *Veda*s. For, outside the *Veda*, we do not find *LIṬ* placed immediately after *indh*. In ordinary speech, *ām* should be affixed [to *indh*] (3.1.36 *ijādeś ca gurumatonṛcchaḥ*). Because of the *nitya* nature of *vUK* (6.4.88 *bhuvo vuk luṅ liṭoḥ*) after *bhū*, the augment *vUK* added after *bhū* is *nitya*. It occurs if [*guṇa*] (7.3.84 *sārvadhātukārdhadhātukayoḥ*)/[*vṛddhi*] (7.2.115 *aco ñṇiti*) is performed [and] also if [*guṇa* or *vṛddhi*] is not performed. [Thus,] prescribing *kitva* [of the suffix] after them is redundant. Prescribing *kitva* [of the suffix] after *indh/bhū* is redundant'. *indh* 'to kindle' is a seventh-class *ātmanepada* root. If one wishes to derive, for example, the third-person singular Vedic *LIṬ* form of *indh*, *LIṬ* would be replaced by *ta*. Before introducing Kātyāyana's *vārttika*, Patañjali says *indheḥ saṁyogārthaṁ vacanam*. He means that in *indh* + *ta*, given the *saṁyoga* 'conjunct' at the end of *indh*, the rule 1.2.5 cannot be used to make the suffix *ta*, *kidvad* 'behaving as if it were marked with *K*':

1.2.5 *asaṁyogāl liṭ kit* (*apit*)

'A *LIṬ* affix not originally marked with *P* is treated as marked with *K* when it occurs after roots which do not terminate in a conjunct'.

Hence, the need for the *sūtra* 1.2.6. This *kitvadbhāva* 'state of behaving as if marked with *K*' is required for the replacement of the penultimate *n* of *indh* with *LOPA* by 6.4.24:

6.4.24 *aniditām hala upadhāyāḥ kṅiti* (*nalopaḥ*).

'The penultimate *n* of an *aṅga* which ends in a consonant and does not contain *I* as a marker is replaced with *LOPA* when an affix marked with *K* or *Ṅ* follows'.

This justifies the need for the presence of the verb *indh* in 1.2.6 *indhibhavatibhyāṁ ca*. In his *vārttika*, Kātyāyana also says that, since the reduplicated perfect of *indh* is only found in the *Veda*, the *sūtra* enjoining of *kidvadbhāva* for *LIṬ* substitutes after *indh* is futile.[11] In the case of the *laukika* 'colloquial' form *ām*, prevailing over other operations (derivational details not discussed here), is introduced between *indh* and *LIṬ* from an early stage in the derivation, thereby disallowing the trigger of any operation on *indh* that could be caused by *LIṬ*:

3.1.36 *ijādeś ca guromatonṛcchaḥ*. (*ām amantre liṭi*)

'Affix *ām* occurs after a verbal root which begins with *iC* "any vowel except *a*", and contains a *guru* vowel (1.4.11 *saṁyoge guru*, 1.4.12 *dīrghaṁ ca*), except *ṛcch* "to go", provided *LIṬ* follows, and the usage is not from the *mantra* part of the Vedic'.

***bhū* – *LIṬ* forms**	**Singular**	**Dual**	**Plural**
3rd	*babhūva*	*babhūvatuḥ*	*babhūvuḥ*
2nd	*babhūvitha*	*babhūvathuḥ*	*babhūva*
1st	*babhūva*	*babhūviva*	*babhūvima*

Now, let us look at what Kātyāyana and Patañjali say about *bhū*. Patañjali, before quoting the *vārttika*, says: *bhavater pidartham vacanam*. He means that while the *LIṬ* suffixes that are not marked with *P* (i.e., dual and plural suffixes added to *bhū* 'to be') can be treated as marked with *K* thanks to 1.2.5 (see above), 1.2.5 is not applicable to suffixes marked with *P* (i.e., singular suffixes), and this rule has been composed so that suffixes marked with *P* can be treated as suffixes marked with *K*. This *kitva* is required to block the *vṛddhi* (7.2.115 *aco ñṇiti*) or *guṇa* (7.3.84 *sārvadhātukārdhadhātukayoḥ*) of the root vowel of *bhū* in all its perfect forms by 1.1.5 *kṅiti ca* (*na iko guṇavṛddhi*).

On the other hand, in his first *vārttika* on 1.2.6, Kātyāyana says that treating the *LIṬ* suffixes after *bhū* as marked with *K*, which is done to block *guṇa* or *vṛddhi*, is also redundant, because there arises no occasion to perform *guṇa* or *vṛddhi*, thanks to the *nityatva* of *vUK*. The rule that teaches the addition of augment *vUK* is: 6.4.88 *bhuvo vuk luṅliṭoḥ* (*aṅgasya aci*) 'Augment *vUK* is introduced to an *aṅga*, namely *bhū*, when a *LUṄ* or *LIṬ* affix beginning with a vowel follows'.

Here, Patañjali comments: *bhavater api nityo vuk. kṛte'pi prāpnoty akṛte'pi.* He means that since *vUK* can be attached both before and after *guṇa or vṛddhi*, and since the reverse is not true, *vUK* is *nitya* and *guṇa/vṛddhi, anitya*. He interprets the word *nitya* as a tool for resolving conflict between the addition of augment *vUK* (6.4.88) and *guṇa/vṛddhi*. But is this conclusion warranted? Consider all nine forms (three persons and three numbers) of *bhū* + *LIṬ*. In each of them, we notice the presence of *vUK* taught by 6.4.88 *bhuvo vuk luṅ liṭoh* (*aci*).

As I have shown above (cf. Kātyāyana's use of the term *aḍvyavāya*), Kātyāyana thinks that augments are separate from the item to which they are added. Thus, he does not see *vUK* as a part of *bhū*. According to Kātyāyana, the step at which *vUK* is added looks like this: *bhū* + *vUK* (treated as a distinct morpheme) + *LIṬ*. To cause the *guṇa/vṛddhi* of the *ū* of *bhū, LIṬ* needs to be immediately after *bhū*. But *vUK*, which is an item unto itself, acts as an obstruction, thereby obstructing *LIṬ* from causing the *guṇa/vṛddhi* of *bhū*. Since *vUK* appears in each of the nine *LIṬ* forms of *bhū*—as can be corroborated by looking at the paradigm above—Kātyāyana says that *vUK* is *nitya* 'always present', and so it never allows *LIṬ* to cause the *guṇa/vṛddhi* of *bhū*. Therefore, he concludes that trying to block the *guṇa/vṛddhi* of *bhū* by treating *LIṬ* as marked with *K* (cf. 1.1.5 *kṅiti ca*) in 1.2.6 is unnecessary because there never arises an occasion for such *guṇa/vṛddhi* to occur in the first place. It is in this sense that he says: *bhuvo vuko nityatvāt kidvacanānarthakyam.* Having studied these two crucial *vārttikas*, I have inferred that, contrary to Patañjali's interpretation, Kātyāyana does not use *nitya* in the sense of a rule conflict-resolution tool but simply as a word of day-to-day language, to mean 'always, always existent, permanent' and so on. This leads us to the conclusion that the *nitya* tool for conflict resolution is effectively Patañjali's inadvertent invention resulting from a misinterpretation of Kātyāyana's words.

Before moving forward, let me discuss a *vārttika* that corroborates my conclusion. Consider vt. 11 on 7.1.96 *striyāṁ ca,*[12] which reads: *numaciratṛjvadbhāvebhyo nuṭ (pūrvavipratiṣiddham)*: '[in cases of conflict] the attachment of the augment *nUṬ*[13] [which is taught by a preceding rule in the serial order of the *Aṣṭādhyāyī*] takes precedence over [the following processes, which are taught by rules that come later in the *Aṣṭādhyāyī*'s serial order]: (1) attachment of augment *nUM,*[14] (2) replacement with *r* when followed by a vowel,[15] or (3) *tṛC*-like treatment'.[16]

Let us derive the genitive plural of the masculine stem *kroṣṭu* 'jackal' by adding suffix *ām* to it. Here, two competing rules become applicable to two different operands, respectively, at once:

7.1.97 *vibhāṣā tṛtīyādiṣv aci*

'The *aṅga, kroṣṭu,* is treated as if ending in affix *tṛC,* only optionally, when a vowel initial nominal ending of *tṛtīyā* triplet "instrumental" or any of the following triplets namely dative, ablative, genitive, or locative follows'.

7.1.54 *hrasvanadyāpo nuṭ*

'Augment *nUṬ* is introduced to affix *ām* when it occurs after an *aṅga* which ends in a short vowel (*hrasvānta*), or in a form which is termed *nadī* (*nadyanta*), or else ends in the feminine affix *āP* (*ābanta*)'.

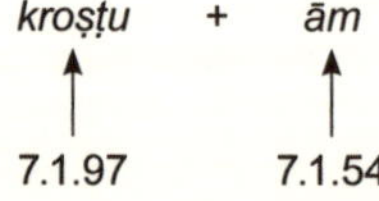

Following the traditional interpretation of 1.4.2 *vipratiṣedhe paraṁ kāryam,* if we chose 7.1.97, which comes later in the serial order of the *Aṣṭādhyāyī,* we get the wrong answer **kroṣṭṝṇām.*[17] Thus, Kātyāyana has composed the above *vārttika,* which states that 7.1.54, despite being the *pūrva sūtra,* ought to win the conflict so as to give the correct answer *kroṣṭūṇām* (6.4.3 *nāmi*).

There is no evidence to support the claim that *pūrvavipratiṣiddha* is a tool for rule conflict resolution. Instead, it seems to simply be a label given to all those cases of *vipratiṣedha* where the application of the Pāṇinian rule 1.4.2—as understood by Kātyāyana—gives the wrong answer.

Note that 7.1.97 does not block 7.1.54, but 7.1.54 does block 7.1.97. Since this is a case of unidirectional blocking, this is the classic opportunity to use Patañjali's conflict-resolution tool, *nityatva*. The *nitya* rule, that is, the rule that unidirectionally blocks the other rule, wins. This means that 7.1.54 applies, and we get the correct answer *kroṣṭūnām*.

Now the question arises: If Kātyāyana had regarded *nityatva* as a conflict-resolution tool, why would he include this example, which can be solved using the *nityatva* tool, in the *pūrvavipratiṣiddham vārttika* mentioned above? This only goes on to show yet again that Kātyāyana has uniformly and consistently used the term *nitya* just as it is used in ordinary speech, that is, to mean 'always, permanent, constantly occurring' and so on, and not as a conflict-resolution tool.

On this *vārttika*, Kaiyaṭa, in his commentary on the *Mahābhāṣya* titled *Pradīpa*, tries to argue that 7.1.54 is not *nitya*,[18] thanks to the *sannipātaparibhāṣā*, which is Pbh 85 of the *Paribhāṣenduśekhara*: *sannipātalakṣaṇo vidhir animittaṁ tadvighātasya*. Kielhorn translates it as follows: '(That which is taught in) a rule (the application of) which is occasioned by the combination (of two things), does not become the cause of the destruction of that (combination)'. Thus, according to this *paribhāṣā*, because *nUṬ* addition is occasioned by the combination of the *aṅga* ending in *ṛ* and the affix beginning in a vowel, *nUṬ* addition cannot be allowed to disrupt this combination, so it cannot be treated as *nitya* and does not take place. But by this logic, the tradition should never use the *nitya* tool in the first place because it always disrupts such combinations. Hence, I think the *sannipāta* argument is unacceptable.

Therefore, our conclusion that Kātyāyana did not intend for *nitya* to be used as a conflict-resolution tool still holds true, notwithstanding the so-called *sannipāta* argument of Kaiyaṭa. Note that what we looked at was only one of multiple *pūrvavipratiṣiddha vārttika*s written by Kātyāyana on different Pāṇinian rules. Patañjali's comments on all these *vārttika*s are mostly the same. Before moving forward, it would be instructive for us to inspect them. Consider what he says, for example about vt. 10 (which we need not discuss here) on the same rule, that is, 7.1.96: *na vaktavyaḥ. iṣṭavācī paraśabdaḥ. vipratiṣedhe paraṁ yad-*

iṣṭaṁ tadbhavati '[This] should not be said. The word *para* means desirable. In [the event of] *vipratiṣedha*, the *para*, that is, desirable [rule] applies'. He implies that we should apply whichever rule we like as long as it helps us get the grammatically correct form at the end of the derivation. He makes similar comments on 1.4.2 as well, which I will not repeat here, to avoid being redundant.

On the one hand, by interpreting *para* as desirable, Patañjali implies that there is no need to worry about which rule should apply where, as long as we find a way to apply a certain permutation of 'desirable' rules that can help us derive the correct form. On the other hand, in complete contradiction with this suggestion, he invents new conflict-resolution tools like *nitya*. What Patañjali wants to actually achieve, only he knows. But are we being too harsh to Patañjali when we criticize him for these reasons? Yes, we are. This is because it is likely that, throughout the *Mahābhāṣya*, Patañjali is in dialogue with his pupils; so, some of these statements might have been produced by one speaker and certain others by another. Nevertheless, one cannot deny that the *Mahābhāṣya* does frequently confuse its reader, especially one looking for consistency in the logic employed to defend certain positions it takes.

7.3 Kātyāyana on *Antaraṅga-bahiraṅga*

Having examined how Kātyāyana uses the term *nitya*, now let us consider what he has to say about *antaraṅga* and/or *bahiraṅga*. Kātyāyana uses *antaraṅga* thrice as a stand-alone stem, twice as a part of the compound *antaraṅgabalīyastva*, and thrice as a part of the compound *antaraṅgalakṣaṇatva*. Its antonym *bahiraṅga* too is used on many occasions by Kātyāyana. However, he does not define the terms *antaraṅga* and *bahiraṅga*.

Let us look at vt. 7 on 6.1.135 *suṭ kāt pūrvaḥ* [19]:

Vt. 7 *avipratiṣedho hi bahiraṅgalakṣaṇatvāt*

'This cannot be a case of *vipratiṣedha*, because of the *bahraṅga* nature (of *sUṬ*)'.

We do not need to look into the derivational context in which this has been stated. But this *vārttika* shows that Kātyāyana thinks that *vipratiṣedha*, whatever it means, cannot exist between an *antaraṅga* rule and a *bahiraṅga* rule, whatever the two terms mean. In principle, there are two possibilities. One, that the tradition is correct, and that by teaching such a *vārttika*, Kātyāyana is simply suggesting that *antaraṅga-bahiraṅga* pairs are not of equal strength and thus are excluded from the domain of *vipratiṣedha* 'conflict between rule pairs of equal strength'. But the other possibility is that he simply means that there is no *vipratiṣedha* 'conflict' between *antaraṅga* and *bahiraṅga* rule pairs. We will explore this second possibility further below. For now, suffice it to say that of the two reasons the second one is more plausible. One, because Occam's razor or the principle of parsimony favors the simpler one. And two, because Kātyāyana does not say anything about *antaraṅga* and *bahiraṅga* not being *tulyabala* 'of equal strength' in his *vārttika*s.

Now, let us look at a *vārttika* where Kātyāyana uses the term *antaraṅga* to get some clarity on what he means by *antaraṅga* and *bahiraṅga* and what, according to him, the relationship of these terms is, if any, with 1.4.2. On 1.4.2 *vipratiṣedhe paraṁ kāryam*, Kātyāyana's vt. 8 says '*antaraṅgam ca*'. This *vārttika* does not seem to be directly related to any of the preceding *vārttika*s on 1.4.2, so we shall simply treat it as an independent *vārttika* on 1.4.2. Patañjali does not say anything new on it and simply paraphrases it as follows: *antaraṅgaṁ ca balīyo bhavatīti vaktavyam.* Kātyāyana then illustrates the usefulness of stating *vārttika* 8 in the following *vārttika*:

Vt. 9 *prayojanaṁ yaṇekādeśettvottvāni guṇavṛddhidvirvacanāllopasvarebhyaḥ.*

Note that Kātyāyana uses the ablative plural form for one set of operations, whereas he uses the nominative plural form for the other set. This is how he consistently suggests that one set (in the nominative) takes precedence over the other (in the ablative) in all his *vārttika*s. So, he means that those mentioned in the nominative are *antaraṅga*, and they take precedence over the *bahiraṅga* ones mentioned in the ablative. We can translate the *vārttika* as follows: 'The purpose [of the previous *vārttika* is]: [the *antaraṅga* operations] *yaṆ*, *ekādeśa*, *ittva* and *uttva* [prevail] over [each of the *bahiraṅga* operations] *guṇa*, *vṛddhi*, *dvirvacana*, *allopa* and *svara*'.

Let us consider some of Patañjali's arguments on vt. 9 on 1.4.2:

guṇād yaṇādeśaḥ. syonaḥ syonā. guṇaś ca prāpnoti yaṇādeśaś ca. paratvād guṇaḥ syāt. yaṇādeśo bhavaty antaraṅgataḥ.

'The substitution [of vowels *iK*] with consonants *yaṆ* (*yaṇādeśa*) prevails over *guṇa*, [e.g.] *syonaḥ*, *syonā*. [The rule teaching] *guṇa* is applicable, and [the rule teaching] substitution [of *iK*] with *yaṆ* is also applicable. Because of the *para* [tool, that is, by applying 1.4.2], *guṇa* would prevail, but due to the *antaraṅga* [tool], *yaṇādeśa* occurs'.

The sentence *guṇaś ca prāpnoti yaṇādeśaś ca* and the mention of the *para* tool here indicate that Patañjali does indeed treat the interaction between *antaraṅga* and *bahiraṅga* as a conflict and also uses *antaraṅga* as a tool to resolve such conflict. Consider another excerpt from Patañjali's comments on vt. 9:

dvirvacanād yaṇādeśaḥ. dudyūṣati susyūṣati. dvirvacanaṁ ca prāpnoti yaṇādeśaś ca. nityatvāt dvirvacana syāt. yaṇādeśo bhavaty antaraṅgataḥ.

'The substitution [of vowels *iK*] with consonants *yaṆ* (*yaṇādeśa*) prevails over reduplication, [e.g.] *dudyūṣati, susyūṣati.* [The rule teaching] reduplication is applicable, and [the rule teaching] substitution [of *iK*] with *yaṆ* is also applicable. Because of the *nitya* [tool], reduplication would prevail, but due to the *antaraṅga* [tool], *yaṇādeśa* occurs'.

Here too, the sentence *dvirvacanaṁ ca prāpnoti yaṇādeśaś ca* and the mention of the *nitya* tool show that Patañjali uses *antaraṅga* as a tool to solve rule conflict. In both these examples, Patañjali compares the outcomes from using *para, nitya,* and *antaraṅga* as tools for rule conflict resolution, in order to demonstrate the superiority of *antaraṅga* as a conflict-resolution tool.

But is Patañjali's interpretation of vts. 8 and 9 on 1.4.2, correct? Let us discuss some of the derivations mentioned above to answer this question. Let us first follow Patañjali's method to derive the form *dudyūṣati* 'desires to shine'. We start by adding the desiderative affix *saN* to the root *div* 'to shine' by 3.1.7 *dhātoḥ karmaṇaḥ samānakartṛkād icchāyāṁ vā.*[20] Thereafter, by 6.4.19 *chvoḥ śūḍ anunāsike ca,*[21] we get *diū* + *saN*. Here, according to Patañjali, two rules are simultaneously applicable:

{*d* [*i*] *ū* + *saN*

6.1.77 *iko yaṇ aci*[22] is applicable to *i* while 6.1.9 *sanyaṅoḥ*[23] is applicable to *di.* Notice that the cause of application of 6.1.77 (i.e., *ū*) lies to the left of the cause of application of 6.1.9 (i.e., *saN*). Patañjali says that 6.1.77 is *antaraṅga* and thus wins, thereby giving: *dyū* + *saN*. Thereafter, 6.1.9 applies, and we get *dyūdyū* + *saN.* After applying other rules, we get the correct form *dudyūṣati.*

Before going forward, let us use this example to speculate about how Kātyāyana might have defined *antaraṅga* and *bahiraṅga*. Note that the cause of application of 6.1.77, namely *ū*, lies *antar* 'inside' the *aṅga diū,* while the cause of application of 6.1.9, namely *saN*, lies *bahir* 'outside' it. Thus, the term *antaraṅga* could stand for *aṅgasya antaḥ* and the term *bahiraṅga* for *aṅgād bahiḥ*.

Now, here is what I think Kātyāyana actually meant. 6.1.9 *sanyaṅoḥ*[24] teaches that a verbal base ending in *saN* or *yaṄ*, which has not undergone reduplication, is reduplicated.[25] Note that *diū* + *saN* is not a verbal base ending in *saN* but instead two separate items, namely *diū* and *saN*. So 6.1.9, the so-called *bahiraṅga* rule, is not yet applicable here. However, 6.1.77 is applicable here, and on applying it, we get *dyū* + *saN*. Now, since no other rules can be applied here, we can fuse the two items *dyū* and *saN* into a single item *dyūṣa*, which we can call a verbal base ending in *saN*. Therefore, 6.1.9 applies here, and we get *dyūdyūṣa*. After applying other rules, we get the correct verbal base *dudyūṣa* (and the correct final form *dudyūṣati*). In sum, I think Kātyāyana simply means that the *bahiraṅga* rule is not applicable and thus cannot be applied before the *antaraṅga* rule is applied. In effect, he prescribes a certain order of rule application at best. Consider another example. Let us use Patañjali's method to derive the form *dyaukāmi* 'male offspring of *dyukāma*'. We start by adding the *taddhita* affix *iÑ* to the *bahuvrīhi* compound made up of *div* and *kāma* by 4.1.95 *ata iÑ* (which teaches that the *taddhita* affix *iÑ* occurs to denote an offspring after a syntactically related nominal stem that ends in *a*). After replacing the inflectional affixes inside the compound with *LUK* by 2.4.71 *supo dhātuprātipadikayoḥ*,[26] we get *div* + *kāma* + *iÑ*. Here, by 6.1.131 *diva ut* (which teaches that the final sound of the *pada div* is replaced with *uT*), we get *diu* + *kāma* + *iÑ*. At this stage, according to Patañjali, two rules are simultaneously applicable:

6.1.77 *iko yaṇ aci*: same as above.

7.2.117 *taddhiteṣv acām ādeḥ*: the first vowel of the base undergoes *vṛddhi* when an affix marked with *Ñ* or *Ṇ* follows in *taddhita* derivations.

Patañjali says that 6.1.77 is *antaraṅga* and thus wins. The derivation proceeds as follows: *diu* + *kāma* + *iÑ* → *dyu* + *kāma* + *iÑ* (6.1.77) → *dyau* + *kāma* + *iÑ* (7.2.117) → *dyaukāmi* (6.4.148 *yasyeti ca*[27]).

But I think Kātyāyana views this derivation differently. His goal is to derive a word that means: *dyukāmasya apatyam pumān* 'male offspring of *dyukāma*'.

Since we are talking about *dyukāma*'s offspring, and not (*div* + *kāma*)'s offspring, the derivation should start with *dyukāma* and not with *div* + *kāma*. Thus, we have: *dyukāma* + *Ṅas* + *iÑ*. *Ṅas* is replaced with *LUK* by 2.4.71 *supo dhātuprātipadikayoḥ* and we get *dyukāma* + *iÑ*. After applying other rules, we get the correct answer, *dyaukāmi*. In sum, Kātyāyana is simply telling us: 7.2.117 is not applicable before 6.1.77 has applied. But this is not a case of conflict.

To conclude, when Kātyāyana says *antaraṅgaṁ ca* in vt. 8 on 1.4.2, he simply means *antaraṅgaṁ ca kāryam*. Thereafter, in the following *vārttika*s, he lists the cases where *antaraṅga* rules need to be applied for their *bahiraṅga* counterparts to become applicable. I think that because he did not see the relationship between *antaraṅga* and *bahiraṅga* rules as one involving conflict, he did not see *antaraṅga* as a conflict-resolution tool.

7.4 Style and Attitude

Kātyāyana's *vārttika*s are often a medium for him to share all kinds of thoughts with fellow grammarians—not just the 'correct' ones. Very often, we find him use *na vā* 'or rather not' and *ca* 'and' in a series of consecutive *vārttika*s to discuss alternative or even contradicting possibilities and explanations. Let me give an example relevant to the topic of rule conflict. Consider vts. 3, 4, and 5 on 7.1.6 *śīṅo ruṭ*[28] (Mbh III.243.12–21).

Vt. 3 *jhādeśād āḍ leṭi*

'[It must be stated that, contrary to 1.4.2, the introduction of] *āṬ*, [which is taught by the *pūrva* rule 3.4.94 *leṭo'ḍāṭau*[29] wins against] the substitution of *jh* [which is taught by the *para* rule 7.1.5 *ātmanepadeṣv anataḥ*[30]]'.

Vt. 4 *na vā nityatvād āṭaḥ*

'Or rather [this does] not [need to be stated] because [the rule teaching] *āṬ* is *nitya* [and thus defeats the other rule, which is *anitya*]'.

Vt. 5 *antaraṅgalakṣaṇatvāc ca*

'And [also], because [the rule teaching] *āṬ* is *antaraṅga* [and thus defeats the other rule, which is *bahiraṅga*]'.

This style of discussing multiple possibilities without striving to always be correct is very much akin to Patañjali's style, which also involves a discussion about the pros and cons of various perspectives. In both Kātyāyana's and Patañjali's work, we find no rigidity or urgency to establish the truth. Instead, their work is characterized by curiosity and a willingness to critically examine a motley of ideas.

On many occasions, solving conflicts using 1.4.2 led to an incorrect answer at the end of the derivation. Thus, Kātyāyana wrote the '*pūrvavipratiṣiddha*' *vārttikas*. As stated above, by using the expression '*pūrvavipratiṣiddha*', Kātyāyana points out that instead of the *para sūtra*, which should win as per his interpretation of 1.4.2 *vipratiṣedhe paraṁ kāryam*, it is the *pūrva sūtra* that emerges victorious. We have already looked at some such *vārttikas*, so I will simply mention one of them here. On 7.1.96 *striyāṁ ca*, vt. 10 (Mbh III.275.23) reads: *guṇavr̥ddhyauttvatr̥jvadbhāvebhyo num pūrvavipratiṣiddham* 'In case of *vipratiṣedha*, the *pūrva sūtra*, which teaches that the insertion of the augment *nUM* takes precedence over *para sūtras*, which teach (i) *guṇa*, (ii) *vr̥ddhi*, (iii) *auttva*, and (iv) *tr̥jvadbhāva*'. By writing this and other *pūrvavipratiṣiddha vārttikas*, Kātyāyana draws attention to the perceived failures of, loopholes in, or exceptions to the rule 1.4.2.

Commenting on most *pūrvavipratiṣiddha vārttikas*, Patañjali says that they are not required at all. He gives various reasons for this, of which the following one is used by him on multiple occasions. On vt. 10 on 7.1.96 stated above, he says: *na vaktavyaḥ. iṣṭavācī paraśabdaḥ. vipratiṣedhe paraṁ yad iṣṭaṁ tad bhavati* '[This] should not be said. The word *para* means desirable. In [the event of] *vipratiṣedha*, the *para*, i.e., desirable, [rule] applies'. It is evident that in this context Patañjali tries to defend 1.4.2 against Kātyāyana's criticism. In fact, this is anything but an isolated instance: scholars like Goldstücker (1861, 119–21) and Weber (1872, 297–98) were amongst the earliest modern scholars to argue that Kātyāyana was severely critical of Pāṇini's *sūtras* and that Patañjali invested significant effort in countering such negative remarks. While many scholars, starting with Kielhorn, have presented rebuttals to this, even Kielhorn (1876, 50) cannot deny 'that Patañjali has refuted some of the [i.e., Kātyāyana's][31] objections, that he has rejected some of the additional rules of Kātyāyana'.

Coming back to vt. 10 on 7.1.96, I would argue that by hurrying to dismiss Kātyāyana's *pūrvavipratiṣiddha vārttikas*, using a rather feeble argument, namely that *para* means *iṣṭa*, Patañjali missed the opportunity to discover the truth of 1.4.2. Instead, if he had accepted Kātyāyana's statement as valid and had pondered over the cause of this phenomenon, he could possibly have realized that Kātyāyana's interpretation of *para* itself was incorrect and that it was this misinterpretation that had led him to write the *pūrvavipratiṣiddha vārttikas*. This would certainly have been a far superior defence of Pāṇini's rule 1.4.2 against Kātyāyana's criticism than the one mounted by Patañjali.

7.5 Summary of Traditional Developments

Having studied Kātyāyana's *vārttikas* dealing with a number of terms that are now used as conflict-resolution tools, let us summarize our findings. As stated earlier, while Kātyāyana does use *tulyabala* 'equal strength' in the context of *vipratiṣedha*, and while he excludes *anavakāśa-sāvakāśa* pairs from the ambit of *vipratiṣedha* and thereby from the jurisdiction of 1.4.2, he does not explicitly discuss *nitya-anitya* and *antaraṅga-bahiraṅga* in the context of *tulyabala*.

Most importantly, even though Kātyāyana does use *anavakāśa* 'without scope (to apply elsewhere)' and *apavāda* 'exception' as conflict-resolution tools, he does not use *nitya* and *antaraṅga* as conflict-resolution tools. We have seen that this changes in the *Mahābhāṣya* where both *nitya* and *antaraṅga* are explicitly interpreted as conflict-resolution tools by Patañjali. Later scholars follow Patañjali's approach to these two terms.

What both Kātyāyana and Patañjali have in common is that they do not use the term *tulyabala* in the context of *nitya* and *antaraṅga*. However, the *Kāśikā* does exactly that. On 1.4.2 it says:

> *yatra dvau prasaṅgāv anyārthāv ekasmin yugapat prāpnutaḥ sa tulyabalavirodho vipratiṣedhaḥ. tasmin vipratiṣedhe paraṁ kāryaṁ bhavati. utsargāpavādanityānityāntaraṅgabahiraṅgeṣu tulyabalatā nāstīti nāyam asya yogasya viṣayaḥ, balavataiva tatra bhavitavyam.*
>
> When two operations that can be applied at other sites become simultaneously applicable at one [and the same site], this is called a conflict of equal strength or *vipratiṣedha*. In the event of *vipratiṣedha*, the rule that comes later [in the serial order of the *Aṣṭādhyāyī*] prevails. A general rule (*utsarga*) and its exception (*apavāda*), or a *nitya* rule and an *anitya* rule, or an *antaraṅga* and a *bahiraṅga* rule, are not rules of equal strength. These pairs do not fall under the jurisdiction of this rule. In these cases, the stronger rule wins.

Notice that, unlike Kātyāyana and Patañjali, the authors of the *Kāśikā* explicitly exclude *nitya-anitya, antaraṅga-bahiraṅga*, and *apavāda-utsarga* pairs from the ambit of *vipratiṣedha* by calling them 'not *tulyabala*'. Thereafter, in both Pāṇinian and non-Pāṇinian *paribhāṣā* literature, we find multiple versions of the same *paribhāṣā*, which compares the 'strengths' of the tools mentioned above. The earliest Pāṇinian *paribhāṣā* treatise to include it is the *Paribhāṣāpāṭha* of Puruṣottamadeva written in the twelfth century. It reads: *pūrvaparanityāntaraṅgāpavādānām uttarottaraṁ balīyaḥ* (Pbh. 39). 'Of [these five kinds of rules,—viz.] a preceding [rule], a subsequent [rule], a *nitya* [rule], an *antaraṅga* [rule], and an *apavāda* [rule],—each following [rule] possesses greater force [than any one of, or all, the rules that are mentioned before it]' (Abhyankar 1967, 160a).

In sum, the relationships among *tulyabala, vipratiṣedha, nitya, antaraṅga, para, apavāda*, and so on were fully and concretely established by the twelfth century. Alongside the *paribhāṣā*s teaching these tools, dozens of *paribhāṣā*s teaching exceptions to these tools were also written by the *paribhāṣākāra*s. On this account, given its unwieldy and complicated nature, the traditional solution completely fails the Occam's razor test. Additionally, the flexibility of ideas, free thinking, willingness to consider a wide variety of possibilities and alternatives, which, as stated earlier, are so characteristic of the early tradition, that is, Kātyāyana's and Patañjali's work, came to be replaced by a willing acceptance of rigid, ossified, established, and widely accepted 'facts' and 'truths' in the later tradition—in particular, in *paribhāṣā* literature. It is noteworthy that many of these *paribhāṣā*s are *anitya* 'not always applicable' by the tradition's own admission!

Here, one may ask: Why do the *Kāśikā* and the *paribhāṣā* texts not question the correctness of Kātyāyana's interpretation of the term *para* in 1.4.2? I think the first broad reason is that, along with Pāṇini, who composed the foundational treatise of the tradition, Kātyāyana and Patañjali too came to be worshipped in the tradition, which might have made it almost unthinkable for subsequent scholars to disagree with Kātyāyana or Patañjali over such fundamental aspects of the grammar as the meaning of *para* in 1.4.2.[32] It must be noted that even though the *Kāśikā* does present an alternative viewpoint to that of the *Mahābhāṣya* on many occasions, it completely embraces Patañjali's ideas on this subject. Secondly, even amongst the three *muni*s, Patañjali's word superseded Kātyāyana's and Kātyāyana's word superseded

Pāṇini's, right from the time of Kaiyaṭa, who famously stated: *yathottaraṁ hi munitrayasya prāmāṇyam*[33] 'Among the three *munis*, the authority of later *muni* supersedes that of his predecessor(s)'.[34] Thus, Patañjali became the most important person in the tradition, surpassing Pāṇini himself, whose work he had set out to expound on. So, hypothetically speaking, even if a traditional scholar had discovered that Patañjali had misinterpreted *para* in 1.4.2, he would have preferred Patañjali's interpretation to Pāṇini's in all likelihood!

One would have expected the tradition to start paying ever closer attention to the topic of rule conflict with the writing of the *Kaumudī* texts, the main goal of which was to teach students how to perform derivations. To achieve this goal, the *Kaumudī* texts took the radical decision to reorder the rules of the *Aṣṭādhyāyī* so that a rule would be taught in the *Kaumudī* only when it applied at some step in a certain derivation. Unfortunately, these texts did not challenge the existing interpretation of *para* in 1.4.2 and, like previous texts, performed derivations using the traditional tools for conflict resolution. In fact, not only did the *Kaumudī* texts fail to discover the correct meaning of 1.4.2, but they also unwittingly ensured that coming generations would not decipher the same.

They did this by shifting the focus of the tradition from the comprehensive functioning of the Pāṇinian machine to the many individual products of the machine, namely, individual derivations of various forms. Over time, students of the *Kaumudī* got so familiar with these derivations that now they do not have to and, consequently, do not stop at most steps of the derivation to ask themselves: Which rules are applicable at this step? Which of these rules should I apply? And why? And if pupils do apply conflict-resolution tools of their own accord and end up getting the wrong form, they are not encouraged by their teachers to ask why. Instead, they are advised to consult the *Kaumudī* texts to 'correct' themselves, that is, to memorize the explanation offered by their authors.

This chain of accepting what previous scholars have said was finally broken by many modern Indologists, including Houben (2003), who asked if Pāṇini's grammar is meant to function like a machine at all[35] and Bronkhorst (2004) who questioned the 'linearity' of Pāṇinian derivations. Others have tried to make changes in some parts of the traditional conflict-resolution mechanism. For example, multiple scholars, starting with Faddegon (1936), have advocated restricting the jurisdiction of 1.4.2 to 1.4.2–2.2.38. Cardona (1970, 57–58) has proposed limited blocking, which essentially deals with more complex cases of SOI, even though he does not state this explicitly.

Joshi and Kiparsky interpret *vipratiṣedha* as 'mutual blocking' and state that 'for . . . so-called *vipratiṣedha*, no general solution has been found' (Kiparsky 1987, 295) by them.[36] However, they do propose a solution for those cases that involve unidirectional blocking, namely the *siddha* principle. What it essentially does is resort to the *nitya* principle to solve not only these cases that the tradition solves using *nityatva*, but also those that it solves using *antaraṅgatva* (Kiparsky 1982, 84–85). Bronkhorst (1984, 310–13) and Cardona (1999, 154–61) have correctly criticized the reasoning behind this principle.[37]

Even though none of these scholars has been able to offer a radically different interpretation of 1.4.2, their willingness to ask questions, to propose new ideas, and to challenge the traditional method of conflict resolution inspired me to do the same, eventually leading me to the interpretation of 1.4.2 I have presented.

CHAPTER EIGHT

Pāṇinian Studies and Other Disciplines

In this closing chapter, I discuss why the novel understanding of Pāṇini's grammar presented in this book constitutes a watershed moment in Pāṇinian studies. I dwell on the future of the discipline as well as that of related disciplines in the light of my findings.

8.1 The Philosophy of Pāṇinian Studies

The traditional way of performing Pāṇinian derivations is wrought with intractable problems, some of which I have underscored in the preceding chapters of this book. In some of these chapters, I have also outlined how these problems, especially those surrounding rule conflict, might have arisen. However, I have not touched upon the whys: Why did these problems arise at all?

This question can be answered in multiple ways, many of which could perhaps afford us valuable insights into Pāṇini's grammar. But here, when I say 'why' I mean: Why did it become possible for such problems to arise and why did the discipline allow these problems to keep cropping up, and subsequently piling up, almost unchecked? Could it be the case that the underlying philosophy of Pāṇinian studies itself has contributed towards the creation of these problems?

To answer these questions, we have to rely on our understanding of the practices prevalent in the field of Pāṇinian studies. Answering the following questions might throw some light on the 'why's: How do students get introduced to the field? Which scholarly opinions and texts mediate their relationship with the *Aṣṭādhyāyī*? In what order and manner do they internalize the rules of Pāṇini's grammar? Perhaps more importantly, what else are they reading and memorizing while they are still studying Pāṇini's rules?

Like in every other field, pedagogical tools, conventions, practices, and approaches in the field of Pāṇinian studies are heterogenous: different settings permit and/or require varying strategies, all of which nevertheless reveal to us much about the philosophy of the classroom in which they are found and, more accurately, about the mind-set of the teacher imparting 'knowledge' therein. Despite these noteworthy differences, there are certain common threads running through all Pāṇinian studies: the very presence of secondary Sanskrit texts in the classroom and their ability to populate the imagination of both pupils and teachers suffice to produce a common set of outcomes across educational institutions and settings. By secondary Sanskrit texts, I mean everything that was written about Pāṇini's grammar in Sanskrit, including Kātyāyana's *vārttikas*, Patañjali's *bhāṣya*, the *Kāśikāvrtti*, *paribhāṣā* literature, and so on.

I have been able to identify two fundamental philosophical undercurrents informing the field of Pāṇinian studies, which, if examined closely, can reveal the answers to our pressing 'why' questions. The first one involves the secondary Sanskrit texts themselves—not their contents but their contemporary status and how they are treated and used by scholars of the discipline. In other words, what kind of 'knowledge' are secondary Sanskrit texts thought to have produced? What role have they played in laying the epistemological foundations of Pāṇinian studies?

One might argue that the answer to this question depends on the goal of the student or researcher: for example, if the student wishes to study or scrutinize the *Kāśikā* as a text in its own right, even though it is a kind of commentary of the *Aṣṭādhyāyī*, then the *Kāśikā* should receive more importance than all other Pāṇinian texts, perhaps including the *Aṣṭādhyāyī* itself, during such an investigation. While such an argument can certainly be defended, the goal of the student cannot exist and thus cannot be considered in isolation: it is bound to influence and be influenced by the goal(s) of the discipline of Pāṇinian studies itself. Which of the following broad themes could be considered as one of the goals or alternatively the only goal of Pāṇinian studies?

1. Clearly understanding the *Aṣṭādhyāyī*
2. Using secondary Sanskrit sources to understand the *Aṣṭādhyāyī*
3. Studying not only the *Aṣṭādhyāyī* but also secondary Sanskrit sources

As I have argued in chapter 7, both traditional and modern Western scholarship have focused on (2) and (3), almost at the expense, if not to the complete exclusion, of (1). It is not possible to argue that (1) is a more worthy or legitimate endeavour than (2) or (3). Yet, one must not overlook the fact that the very reason the Pāṇinian grammatical tradition—to which all these secondary sources owe their existence—arose was to achieve goal (1), namely a clear understanding of the *Aṣṭādhyāyī*. And thus, if these secondary sources are not playing a productive role in helping us understand certain aspects of the functioning of the *Aṣṭādhyāyī*, or if they are creating obstacles in our path—which I have shown they unfortunately do—then we should pursue goal (1) with much more passion and dedication than we should the rest.

Since the ultimate goal of the discipline of Pāṇinian studies was, at the beginning, and should be today, achieving a clear understanding of Pāṇini's grammar, we can conclude that the epistemological status of secondary texts should not be dependent on the goals of individual students and teachers. With that established, we can now ask: What should constitute the epistemological foundation of any enquiry into Pāṇini's derivational system? Should we accept the answers, explanations, and logical frameworks offered by both Pāṇini's *sūtra*s and secondary sources like Kātyāyana's *vārttika*s, Patañjali's *bhāṣya*, the *Kāśikāvrtti*, *paribhāṣā* literature, and so on, or should we rely exclusively on those offered by Pāṇini's *sūtra*s? In the latter case, we could treat secondary sources merely as supplementary and confirmatory sources of information.

I argue that the latter approach is the more optimal one not only because it is perfectly aligned with what I have argued is the ultimate goal of Pāṇinian studies, but also because the former approach is riddled with major conceptual and methodological issues that can be encapsulated by the following question: Can so many distinct sources of information—which are all written centuries apart with different goals and which often contradict one another—contribute towards the running of the same grammatical machine? And if they cannot provide one, unified, internally consistent model or epistemological paradigm, then how useful are they? The tradition might benefit from honestly answering these questions, without worrying about how the answers might impact the 'status' and 'importance' of the authors of secondary texts in the eyes of contemporary Indians, Hindus, Sanskritists, and so on.

Of the two philosophical undercurrents mentioned above, the second one too revolves around internal consistency, only, in this case, not consistency among different texts but among the different concepts and tools fashioned, invented, and subsequently improvised by traditional scholars. Traditional pundits have claimed to rely on *jñāpaka*s 'hints' left behind by Pāṇini in his work to justify the changes they make to his system. By assuming that Pāṇini intended for them to make these leaps of logic, they have introduced radically different technicalities to his grammar from those already present in it, even though traditional scholars might not view such conceptual tampering as anything more than 'interpretating the *Aṣṭādhyāyī* as intended by Pāṇini'. Where does one draw the line between merely 'interpreting what Pāṇini is trying to say', which is what traditional scholars claim to be doing, and adding new tools to the Pāṇinian toolkit? And if traditional scholars are willing to admit that the tradition is doing more than just 'liberally' interpreting Pāṇini, how legitimate is it to add such radically new ideas to the Pāṇinian corpus?

This could be viewed as a problem of the ontology of Pāṇinian studies, whereby technical concepts constitute categories and interact with one another in ways consequential for the functioning of Pāṇinian grammar. Is it acceptable to modify Pāṇini's ontological infrastructure by introducing new categories like *nitya*, *antaraṅga*, *niravakāśa*, *pūrvavipratiṣedha*, and so on—which the tradition unabashedly does? Since these tools override Pāṇini's rule 1.4.2 *vipratiṣedhe paraṁ kāryam* on several if not most occasions of rule conflict, they are much more than mere products of attempts to interpret Pāṇini's grammar using *jñāpaka*s 'hints': they transform the Pāṇinian mechanism altogether. But even if we are to assume that this is acceptable, if there are no qualitative or quantitative limits on the introduction of such post-Pāṇinian categories—as is the case within the Pāṇinian tradition—what yardstick can be employed to ascertain the correctness of our understanding of Pāṇini's grammar?

As I have said before, to get instructions about dealing with rule conflict, I try to rely, as much as possible, upon 'internal metarules', that is, those metarules that Pāṇini has taught in his work, setting aside any 'external metarules', that is, those metarules that are not found in the *Aṣṭādhyāyī,* such as *nitya*, *antaraṅga*, post-Pāṇinian *paribhāṣās* from various texts, and so on. In other words, I treat Pāṇini's ontological paradigm as a closed one, which cannot and should not be edited. This has borne rich fruits for me in the form of the findings presented in this book, which not only presents the solution to a hitherto intractable, central problem of Pāṇinian studies but also demonstrates that the philosophy underlying a discipline, which manifests through its various pedagogical practices, has the potential to clarify or obfuscate our conception of its research problems and their possible solutions.

8.2 Pāṇinian Computational Linguistics

The question of the ontology of Pāṇini's grammar provides the perfect segue into the question of computation: How does our understanding of these interlinked categories help or obstruct our efforts to teach Pāṇini's grammar to the computer?

Although a relatively new field, Sanskrit computational linguistics has attracted the attention of several scholars from the fields of Indology, computer science, linguistics, and so on. As is predictable, one of the key points of interest for the scholars of this field has been Pāṇini's ingenious grammar.[1]

So far, scholars publishing in these journals have focused on using the traditional approach to Pāṇini's grammar, including the traditional understanding of rule conflict, to teach Pāṇini's grammar to the computer and subsequently apply those models for word generation, sentence parsing, and so on. It is understandable that efforts to deal with rule conflict have not made much progress for the simple reason that traditional methods are so incredibly convoluted that it is almost impossible to teach the entire corpus of external metarules to logically minded youths, let alone to the computer.

Scholars have attempted to teach different sets of Pāṇinian rules to the computer. The lack of attempts to teach the computer all four thousand or so rules of the Pāṇinian corpus as one integrated system can be attributed to the fact that the resolution of conflict, which arises far too often, can simply not be achieved using the traditional model, as I have stated several times in this book. By bringing simplicity, clarity, consistency, and elegance to our understanding of the Pāṇinian algorithm of conflict resolution, my work provides the groundwork for teaching the entire *Aṣṭādhyāyī* as a self-governing set of rules to the computer—without making any changes to its contents or any structural changes to its infrastructure whatsoever.

Given that I do not have expertise in the computational aspects of this field, I will focus on the conceptual contribution my work has made. The first question that must be considered is: Why is it better to teach the whole Pāṇinian system to the computer rather than teaching individual derivations, following the *Kaumudī* method, or teaching individual sections of the *Kaumudī* or the *Aṣṭādhyāyī*? This is because Pāṇini has designed his system in such a way that the key to understanding and implementing operational rules, which actually participate in Pāṇinian derivations, lies in the metarules, which are applicable throughout the *Aṣṭādhyāyī*. For this simple reason, it makes sense to let the computer benefit from this comprehensive feature of Pāṇini's grammar.

Of these metarules, the one that I have focused on, namely 1.4.2, is particularly pertinent, given that unlike other metarules, which mostly tell us how to interpret operational rules, 1.4.2 actually monitors interactions between operational rules and therefore has a direct, consequential bearing on the outcome of the derivation. More broadly, SSRI itself, be it SOI or DOI, arises on several occasions in the vast majority of Pāṇinian derivations, so it would make a lot of sense to teach consistently applicable universal solutions to the computer rather than dealing with issues on a case-by-case basis. Put differently, there is no point in catching small batches of fish if you can harvest all of them at once from the entire ocean.

Let us revisit the traditional method of conflict resolution to understand the implications of its complexity for the computerization of the *Aṣṭādhyāyī*. The traditional method stipulates the employment of the following maxim to resolve issues of rule conflict: *pūrva-para-nitya-antaraṅga-apavādānām uttarottaraṁ balīyaḥ* (Pbh 38, *Paribhāṣenduśekhara*) 'a *para sūtra* is stronger than a *pūrva sūtra*; a *nitya sūtra* is stronger than a *para sūtra*; an *antaraṅga sūtra* is stronger than a *nitya sūtra*; and an *apavāda sūtra* is stronger than an *antaraṅga sūtra*'. In practical terms this means:

First try establishing the relationship taught in step a:

a. *apavāda* > *utsarga*: an *apavāda* 'exception' *sūtra* is more powerful than, and wins when competing with, an *utsarga* 'general rule' *sūtra*.

   If and only if this step does not yield the correct result, try establishing the relationship taught in step b:

b. *antaraṅga* > *bahiraṅga*: an *antaraṅga sūtra* is more powerful than and wins when competing with a *bahiraṅga sūtra*.

   If and only if this step does not yield the correct result, try establishing the relationship taught in step c:

c. *nitya* > *anitya*: a *nitya* rule is more powerful than and wins when competing with an *anitya* rule.

   If and only if this step does not yield the correct result, apply 1.4.2 *vipratiṣedhe paraṁ kāryam*, which we call step d here:

d *para* > *pūrva*: a *para sūtra* (a later rule in the *Aṣṭādhyāyī*'s serial order) is more powerful than and wins when competing with a *pūrva sūtra* (which appears before the *para sūtra*).

Firstly, as is evident, the computer would have to jump through too many hoops to deal with each case of conflict if this method were to be adopted. But more importantly, what would happen if at the first step, for example, the computer applied the *apavāda* tool and produced the wrong answer? Obviously, the computer would not be able to decide for itself whether the answer is correct. The only way to overcome this problem would be for the human involved in this activity to check whether the answer produced at that stage is correct and then instruct the computer to halt the process or move to the next step accordingly.

Now, let us go through each tool to understand the problems that would arise at that stage. I will not present the traditional explanations of tools again, for which one can go to section 1.2 of chapter 1:

1. The *apavāda* tool has not been clearly defined. As I have said in section 2.2 of chapter 2, the tradition does not draw a clear dis-

tinction between SOI and DOI and in fact uses the *apavāda* tool indiscriminately for both these types of SSRI. In cases of SOI, where the operands of one rule are clearly a subset of the other, it would be easy to instruct the computer to choose the *apavāda* rule. But for other cases of SOI and all those cases of DOI where the tradition has opted for the *apavāda* tool, it seems impossible to even describe—let alone implement—the *apavāda* tool for the computer in a coherent manner.

2. The *antaraṅga* tool, defined in a highly convoluted manner, requires several *paribhāṣā*s worth of clarification and yet gives incorrect outcomes on so many occasions.[2] It requires one to determine how many triggers (causes) there are for each rule, then check if they lie to the right-hand side of the operand and are mentioned in the locative case for each rule, and then decide which rule is *antaraṅga*. As I have said before, it is hardly possible to bring critically minded students to digest such unjustifiably complex methods, let alone the computer, who would need to be given far too many commands to execute such procedures. And this is without taking into account all the mind-bending metarules that have been written as exceptions to the main *antaraṅga* metarule.[3] How would we teach all those to the computer?
3. Admittedly, the *nitya* tool is more clearly defined than the *antaraṅga* tool. The *nitya* tool runs into a different problem though: it requires the computer to look ahead, that is, check if the rule is applicable at the following step after the other rule has applied—albeit only hypothetically—at the present step. This would require the computer to run two secondary derivations parallel to the main, actual derivation—to check if R_1 can be applied after R_2 and if R_2 can be applied after R_1. Again, I have not mentioned yet the many metarules that have been dedicated by the Pāṇinīyas to state 'exceptions' of the *nitya* tool or to tweak it in clever but confusing ways for addressing different issues.
4. Finally, we come to the *para* tool. It would be easy to teach the computer to pick the rule that comes later in the serial order of the *Aṣṭādhyāyī*. Except, this would give the wrong answer in

> several cases, all of which would have to be taught to the computer. Some of these have been collected in what are called the '*pūrvavipratiṣiddha vārttikas*', which I have discussed in this book in various contexts.

In contrast with this, my method can be taught to the computer in an almost effortless manner. At the first step, the computer must solicit an input from the user: the base and the affix. Once this is done, it can commence the derivation. Where two rules become simultaneously applicable, the computer should first determine whether it is a case of SOI or DOI, depending on whether the two rules are applicable to the same operand or different ones. If it is a case of DOI, the computer should pick the RHS rule per my interpretation of 1.4.2. If it is a case of SOI, the computer must first check if it is a case of SOL-L by comparing the relevant subrules (see section 2.8 of chapter 2, for details and examples) to see which one is more specific. It must choose the more specific subrule. However, if both subrules in question look exactly the same, then it must compare the two rules themselves and pick the one that constitutes a subset of the other. This is called SOI-M. This is all the computer needs to do to construct grammatically correct words.[4]

For the first time, it has become possible to actually teach the computer the algorithm that Pāṇini himself designed for his system—because it is so simple to learn and teach! All other methods to teach the *Aṣṭāḍhyāyī* to computers and humans alike fail to emulate, let alone surpass, the efficacy of Pāṇini's own ingenious method. In the near future, I hope that computational linguists will use my findings to teach the entire *Aṣṭādhyāyī* to the computer following Pāṇini's teachings alone, for as I have argued in this book, they are not only sufficient but also superior.

8.3 Pāṇini and Computational Theory

Whilst important, teaching Pāṇini's grammar to the computer is not the only computational application of my findings: my work can actually help us gauge the complexity of human language. In computational theory, attempts have been made to understand how complex a formal language (i.e., an artificial language used in computer science) is using the Chomskyan hierarchy (based on Chomsky 1959), which consists of four different levels of formal language grammars and the 'machines' that correspond with them. Linguists have also tried to situate natural languages in this hierarchy. Let us look at the hierarchy before we discuss this topic further.

Language	Least powerful grammar that can generate it	Machine equivalent to this grammar	Production rule(s)
recursively enumerable	Type 0	Turing Machine	$\delta \rightarrow \theta$
context-sensitive	Type 1	Linear Bounded Automaton	$\alpha A\beta \rightarrow \alpha\gamma\beta$
context-free	Type 2	Pushdown Automaton	$A \rightarrow \gamma$
regular	Type 3	Finite State Automaton	$A \rightarrow a$ $A \rightarrow aB$

Key
a = terminal symbol
A, B = nonterminal symbol
$\alpha, \beta, \gamma, \delta, \theta$ = string of symbols[5]

Please read the following three statements carefully in the context of the table presented above:

1. In $A \rightarrow \gamma$ (Type 2), if the string γ contains only one symbol, namely the terminal symbol a, then this rule can be rewritten as $A \rightarrow a$ (Type 3). Similarly, if the string γ contains only two symbols, namely aB, then this rule can be rewritten as $A \rightarrow aB$ (Type 3). These are only two of many possibilities. Thus, regular grammars (Type 3) constitute a subset of context free grammars (Type 2).
2. In $\alpha A\beta \rightarrow \alpha\gamma\beta$ (Type 1), if both α and β are empty, then this rule can be written as $A \rightarrow \gamma$ (Type 2). This is only one of many possibilities. Thus, context-free grammars (Type 2) constitute a subset of context sensitive grammars (Type 1).
3. In $\delta \rightarrow \theta$ (Type 0), if the string δ is $\alpha A\beta$ and if the string θ is $\alpha\gamma\beta$, then this rule can be rewritten as $\alpha A\beta \rightarrow \alpha\gamma\beta$ (Type 1). This is only one of many possibilities. Thus, context-sensitive grammars (Type 1) constitute a subset of recursively enumerable grammars (Type 0).

Therefore, we can represent these grammars as follows:

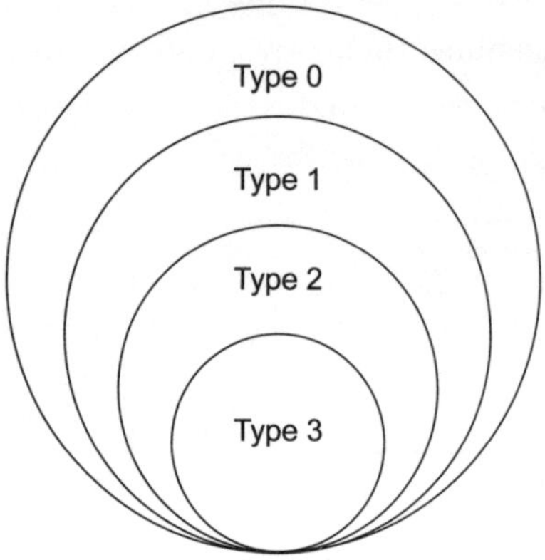

Type 0

Type 1

Type 2

Type 3

As can be seen from the diagram above:

1. Type 3 grammars can produce Type 3 languages.
2. Type 2 grammars can produce Type 3 and Type 2 languages.
3. Type 1 grammars can produce Type 3, Type 2, and Type 1 languages.
4. Type 0 grammars can produce Type 3, Type 2, Type 1, and Type 0 languages.

Note that in terms of productive power, the grammars can be compared as follows (where $G_1 > G_2$ stands for 'G_1 is more powerful than G_2'):

Type 0 > Type 1 > Type 2 > Type 3

As stated above, even though this hierarchy is primarily meant for formal languages, linguists have attempted to situate natural languages within it. They have shown that Dutch (Bresnan et al. 1982), Swiss German (Shieber 1985), and Bambara (Culy 1985) are neither regular (Type 3) nor context free (Type 2). Scholars like Fowler (1965), Staal (1965, 1966), Hyman (2007), and Penn and Kiparsky (2012) have discussed the *Aṣṭādhyāyī*'s computational ability, the characteristics of the language it produces, and whether and how we can situate such a language, that is, Pāṇinian Sanskrit, in the Chomskyan hierarchy.

I think that there are several loopholes in the thesis that we can meaningfully situate natural languages—which are significantly different in their nature, composition, and purpose from formal languages—in a hierarchy meant for formal languages. However, the outcome of my research has an interesting parallel with one aspect of the Chomskyan hierarchy, which I think merits further exploration. The following diagram illustrates how a Pāṇinian derivation would look in the absence of Pāṇini's algorithm for dealing with SSRI. Let us assume, for the sake of this discussion, that two rules are applicable at every step of the derivation. The derivation starts at State 1 and the correct final form is State 4h.

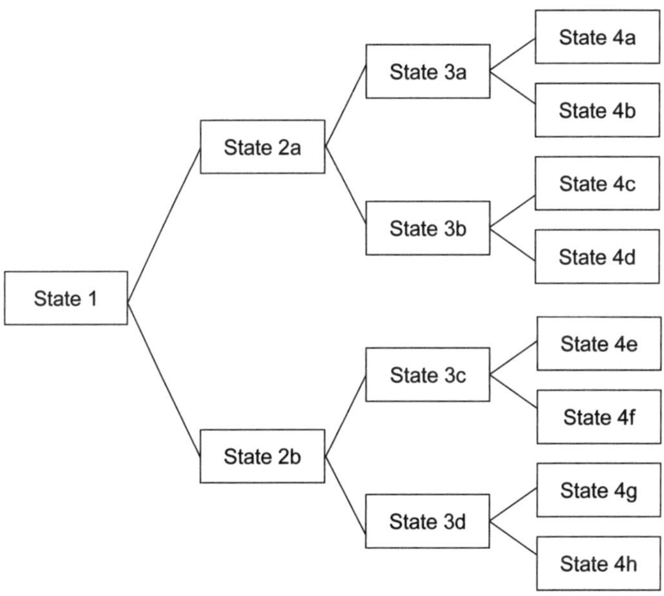

This is a three-step derivation. Step 1 takes us from State 1 to State 2, step 2 from State 2 to State 3, and lastly step 3 from State 3 to State 4. To reach State 4h, one has to make three correct decisions: one has to choose State 2b in step 1, State 3d in step 2, and State 4h in step 3. But if there had existed no internal algorithm in Pāṇini's machine, one could have ended up with any of the eight final answers (cf. State 4), and the probability of getting the correct answer would have been one in eight. However, by teaching his solution for SSRI, Pāṇini has converted the above machine into the following machine:

To borrow terms from computational theory, Pāṇini has converted his 'nondeterministic machine', which could potentially proceed along multiple derivational paths, into a deterministic one, which proceeds along a single path dictated by the algorithm. A deterministic machine is desirable because it produces only correct forms whereas a nondeterministic machine is not desirable because it produces both correct and incorrect forms. Penn and Kiparsky (2012) say: 'through the lens of contemporary NLP [Natural Language Processing], the most amazing fact about the *Aṣṭādhyāyī* is not that it produces so many correct derivations, after all, but that it simultaneously avoids so many incorrect ones'.

Now, let us use this information to situate Pāṇinian Sanskrit in this hierarchy. We already know that we find rules that resemble context-sensitive rules (cf. $\alpha A\beta \rightarrow \alpha\gamma\beta$) in Pāṇini's grammar. Since regular (Type 3) and context-free (Type 2) grammars do not contain such rules, we can infer that Pāṇini's grammar is neither regular nor context free. But does the presence of context-sensitive rules make Pāṇini's grammar context sensitive (Type 1)? Context-sensitive grammars in the Chomskyan hierarchy correspond with *nondeterministic* linear-bounded automata. But as I said, Pāṇini's grammar is *deterministic*. Thus, we cannot call the *Aṣṭādhyāyī* a Type 1 (context-sensitive) grammar. What kind of grammar is the *Aṣṭādhyāyī* then? I trust that scholars of computational theory will be able to answer this question in the future with the help of the information I have provided above.

8.4 Pāṇini and Theoretical Phonology

Alongside influencing our understanding of the complexity of human language, my work also opens up new avenues for engaging theoretically with sound patterns in our languages. But to understand how it makes this contribution, we must first examine the similarities and differences between the two systems, namely Western and Pāṇinian. Unlike Western linguistic theory, especially generative linguistics, wherein the goal is to find ways that efficiently help describe a variety of languages, Pāṇini's goal was to focus on one language and produce not necessarily the most transparent description but the most optimal way of deriving grammatically correct words from their constituent parts, namely bases and affixes.

This stands in stark contrast with the Western linguistic tradition where the derivation of the final form does not receive much attention—perhaps because it is already known. Once could say this is true of Pāṇini's grammar too, but despite the correct form being possibly known to the student, the grammar is expected to function like a machine and produce it all the same without expecting the user to be cognizant of it. For Pāṇini, the derivation of the final form is arguably more important than describing the sounds and structures of the target language through his rules.

Given these differences, it is only natural that the methods and approaches of Pāṇinian and Western linguistic systems should also differ. However, since both deal to a great extent with the question of rule interaction,[6] we do find overlaps between them. In 1968, Chomsky and Halle published their path-breaking work, *The Sound Pattern of English* (henceforth SPE). Like Pāṇini's grammar, Chomsky and Halle too start with a hypothesized abstract or underlying representation, which, upon the application of a series of rules, undergoes multiple changes to give the final form found in human speech.[7] The two main types of rules found in their grammar are stress-change rules and vowel-change rules.

This approach, wherein the order of rule application is determined simply by the demands of target language data, came to be called extrinsic ordering, since the order of rule application is influenced by external factors that have nothing to do with individual rules themselves. In contrast with this, Kiparsky (1968) introduced the idea of intrinsic ordering: he proposed that the order of rule application could be viewed as being dependent on the formal relationships between rules, namely, whether one rule feeds or bleeds the other rule.

A feeds B if the application of A facilitates the subsequent application of B ('feeding order'), and P bleeds Q if the application of P obstructs the subsequent application of Q ('bleeding order'). If A is applied after, rather than before, B, such an order is called counterfeeding order. Similarly, if P is applied after, rather than before, Q, such an order is called counterbleeding order.

It is noteworthy that Kiparsky spent a considerable amount of time in Pune, India, in the late 1960s, during which time he also published his work on intrinsic ordering. The Pāṇinian tradition is likely to have influenced or inspired the aforementioned ideas. Kiparsky writes about Pāṇini's grammar: 'As far as feeding is concerned, this really goes without saying. In almost any derivation, the application of one rule creates scope for another rule to apply, that rule applies creating scope for a third rule and so on. That all rules in such a chain of rules are to be applied is taken for granted in the tradition' (1982, 790).

Kiparsky adds, 'By this point anyone familiar with the topic will already have recognized that the principle of bleeding order is simply equivalent to the *nitya*-principle in the traditional inventory of the *paribhāṣās*' (1982, 84–85). In order to avoid feeding or bleeding where they are not desirable, Pāṇini uses the *asiddha*(*vat*) tool, thereby ensuring that rules apply in the counterfeeding or counterbleeding order, as the case may be. Kiparsky writes: 'to use terms common in linguistics, *asiddhatva* blocks bleeding and feeding between rules' (1982, 77).

Notice that neither Chomsky and Halle nor Kiparsky seek to produce closed, mechanistic grammars, as Pāṇini does. In both these contributions to Western phonological theory, we find no mention of steps or rule conflict and abundant references to rule ordering. In other words, they do not ask which rules are applicable at a given step and which one of them must be chosen but instead focus on the order in which a set of rules should apply. This is because, in both these Western paradigms, the form to be achieved at the end of the derivation is and must be known, and the goal of the derivation is to apply rules in such an order that this desired form can be produced. On the other hand, Pāṇini's grammar does not require us to know the correct form and produces it automatically—for which all applicable rules are considered at each step and cases of SSRI (colloquially, conflict) are tackled using Pāṇini's ingenious algorithm.

Although the tradition uses the *nitya* tool (equivalent to bleeding order) to deal with conflict in Pāṇini's grammar, through my work, I have shown that Pāṇini's derivations are actually neither extrinsically nor intrinsically ordered. In fact, one need not worry about the concept of rule order at all when performing Pāṇinian derivations. This is because determining which rule should apply at any given step depends neither on whether it feeds or bleeds another rule, nor on any language-specific, predetermined order of application. Instead, this decision is made by the ingenious algorithm devised by Pāṇini to deal with SSRI. Perhaps modern linguistics can overcome certain shortcomings of extrinsic and intrinsic ordering by experimenting with Pāṇini's model.

8.5 Concluding Remarks

Having discussed the applications and impact of my work on other, related fields, I will conclude this chapter and this book by underscoring how my work could potentially alter the course of Pāṇinian studies itself as a discipline. This discipline, as I have said at several junctures in this book, has relied so heavily on secondary Sanskrit literature to teach Pāṇini's grammar that it has become difficult even for traditional scholars to differentiate what Pāṇini has actually taught from what the Pāṇinīyas have made of his teachings. And my work has demonstrated that this can cause serious misunderstandings—including those that can completely alter the path of the Pāṇinian tradition.[8] These misunderstandings are related to and arguably even the root cause of the labyrinthine nature of conflict-resolution procedures devised and followed by the tradition. This has played a key role in discouraging young, logically minded Indians, the vast majority of whom go to modern schools, from studying Pāṇini's grammar.

My work shows not only that Pāṇini's grammar works perfectly well in an independent capacity but also that any attempts to tamper with it in the hopes of making it 'better', as the tradition has sought to do, are bound to fail and make things much worse. My work bears testimony to the fact that Pāṇini's grammar thrives on its transparency, consistency, and simplicity, and all these qualities should be cherished rather than suppressed. In keeping with these ideas, I hope that, in the future, students will learn and be taught Pāṇini's grammar using his rules alone. Now that I have found a surprisingly simply solution to the problem of rule conflict, which has been taught to us by Pāṇini himself, it is not essential to formally introduce students to conflict-resolution *paribhāṣā*s from *paribhāṣā* literature—unless a student wants to conduct research on the intellectual history of the tradition.

In fact, I would go so far as to say that as a beginner, or at some point in a student's Pāṇinian journey, he or she would do well to ignore all post-Pāṇinian *paribhāṣā*s, study Pāṇini's grammar through the lens of his own rules, and then come up with his or her own '*paribhāṣā*s'—based on and backed by the evidence gathered during the student's own study of the subject at hand. This would enrich the student intellectually much more than reading *paribhāṣā*s written by others ever could. Of course, the goal of such a *paribhāṣā*-writing experiment should not be to change Pāṇini's grammar in any way but only to commit to writing one's observations about his styles and methods.

One could argue that it would be unwise to completely ignore secondary Sanskrit sources. Admittedly, ignoring them could deprive us of precious facts and ideas that could aid our investigations. But the point here is, even if one does not want to ignore such traditional secondary sources, one should give oneself at least some time with the *Aṣṭādhyāyī* alone—enough to form one's own opinions—before reading Kātyāyana's *vārttika*s, Patañjali's *Mahābhāṣya*, or Bhaṭṭojī's *Kaumudī*, with which one can then confidently agree or disagree on various issues based on one's own understanding of Pāṇini's work.

Upon adopting this approach, students will benefit in one obvious way: they will find their study of the *Aṣṭādhyāyī* much more exciting than they would if they were to go down the conventional, traditional path. However, an arguably more consequential benefit will be that this method will truly sharpen their critical minds and hone their logical-thinking abilities—which they can then apply to all their endeavours, intellectual or otherwise, and which will enable them to lead more informed and enlightened lives.

As well as encouraging young scholars to don their own thinking hats when reading the *Aṣṭādhyāyī*, I hope the success of my work will serve as a small example of how, with ambition, enterprise, faith, and conviction, one can follow one's passion and inquisitiveness to their logical conclusion: discovery. As I conclude this book, I bear steadfastly in my mind one singular goal: to propel young scholars, through my research, to explore Indology, linguistics, the humanities at large, or anything else that piques their interest for that matter, with boldness, individuality, and determination. Without exception, such initiatives always reap rich dividends.

POSTFACE

Responding to the Reception

In December 2022, my thesis, on which this book is based, received extensive attention from the global press, with hundreds of newspapers, electronic portals, TV channels, YouTube shows, radio stations, and so on reporting on my work—including the BBC (online and radio), the *Daily Mail*, the *Independent*, the *Telegraph*, Fox News, Vice, CTV (Canadian state-funded radio), CGTN (Chinese state-funded portal), *El Mundo* (Spain), *Jerusalem* Post (Israel), *Folha* (Brazil), *El Observador* (Uruguay), the *Hindu*, *Hindustan Times*, *Times of India*, the *Indian Express*, Wion, NDTV, Republic TV, Aaj Tak, Zee TV, and *Times Now*.

I feel very fortunate to have garnered praise from top scholars in the fields of linguistics and Indology—including open-minded Brahmin pundits based in India. The general public—including CEOs, politicians, engineers, lawyers, authors, and intellectuals—in India and other countries showered me with such warm, disarming affection, and kindness, for which I will remain ever grateful. I was truly delighted to receive congratulatory messages from people belonging to many different socioeconomic backgrounds—all of whom seemed to share a deep appreciation for Sanskrit, ancient Indian culture, and Hinduism.

However, my work was also attacked, especially by certain cultural groups in India who were essentially upset about the fact that I have proposed a new way of looking at Pāṇini's grammar, which disagrees with and argues against certain ideas found in the writings of early commentators like Kātyāyana and Patañjali. I harbour no personal enmity towards these early commentators, and my disagreement with them is strictly based on the evidence I have presented in this book. It is very unfortunate that these cultural groups have not spent as much time studying my work and refuting it as they have badmouthing it on WhatsApp and X (formerly Twitter).

Only two serious rebuttals of my work have been written,[1] both of which claim to have proven me wrong: one by Peter Scharf, who is a Western scholar with a strong affinity for traditional Hinduism, and Neelesh Bodas, who comes from a Brahmin family that has produced, if I am not wrong, multiple generations of traditional Sanskrit pundits. Both of them are very well versed in and seem to be overly attached to the tradition, always defending it zealously, as though holding down the fort in the absence of Kātyāyana and Patañjali. I had sent my thesis to both of them, among many other experts, several months if not a year before it made the news. Both Bodas and Scharf ultimately published shoddy reviews within a couple of days of the media coverage of my thesis. When I got a chance to read them, I realized that they were single-mindedly determined to discredit my work, to make it look flawed in the eyes of the general public and Sanskritists, too, for that matter—most of whom are not experts on Pāṇini's grammar.

I responded a couple of months later and showed that both scholars had made tall claims but had failed to provide evidence disproving my work. By then the damage had been done. Crazy, traditionalist internet warriors (who anyway ignored my responses to these reviews) were celebrating the victory of the tradition, as if this were some sort of battle between me and the tradition. Perhaps it is a battle—for me, it is a battle against illogical, rigid ways of approaching ancient texts which defy all rational thinking and critical analysis. I have seen no group so self-defeating as this one: I have shown Pāṇini, whom they also worship, to be much more sophisticated than their own tradition made him out to be, but they are attacking me saying: 'We still prefer the traditional version!'

Now, let me talk about the two reviews individually. In what was evidently a hastily written review, Scharf complained that in my thesis, his publications had not been given as much attention as he would have liked (This might well have been his biggest problem with my work!) and offered only three examples to support his claim that my 'proposed solutions were largely ineffective'. In my reply to him, I rebutted all three of his so-called counterexamples and showed that none of them was able to disprove my claims. Scharf very conveniently misrepresented my work through his three examples, rebutted them, and then concluded I had been proven wrong—a classic case of what is called 'strawman fallacy'. When I pointed this out through my reply, Scharf summarily dismissed my reply saying my work had 'received more attention than it deserves already'—essentially running away from the argument, which he realized he had lost.

Like his mentor and teacher George Cardona, Scharf has consistently opposed all new ideas that S.D. Joshi and Paul Kiparsky have introduced to the field of Pāṇinian studies. No matter how convincing Joshi and Kiparsky's arguments might have been, Cardona and his student Scharf have always found reasons not to accept their work or for that matter anything that deviates from or contradicts the traditional line—which they ever so religiously tow.

Now, onto Neelesh Bodas, who writes: 'I sincerely wish Dr. Rishi was more careful with his words in his media interactions, and was extra cautious while talking about the tradition, which is deeply respected by millions of Sanskrit lovers, including myself'."It is no surprise that Bodas, who has studied Pāṇini's grammar through a traditional lens since he was just ten years old, comes across as someone who is emotionally invested in defending the tradition at any cost. As a result, he spends all his energy proving me wrong and none dwelling on the fundamental, philosophical questions that I raise throughout my work: Why does Pāṇini's grammar not work without the help of post-Pāṇinian tools? Why does the tradition take the liberty to interfere with Pāṇini's grammar?[2] Would it not be amazing if we could envision Pāṇini's grammar as a closed machine and actually make it work? Far from showing excitement over the potential achievement of these lofty goals, Bodas insists that 'there is no such puzzle' to solve. All is well and there is no need to find anything new, for everything that had to be found has been found.

Bodas did point out minor mistakes in my doctoral thesis, and I have corrected those mistakes in this book. In chapter 5, I have also addressed some of the interesting technical questions he broaches. On so many occasions though, he simply parrots the traditional line, mainly by reiterating the tradition's myopic, band-aid solutions that serve as quick fixes for the problem at hand but lack consistent and universal applicability. Even as he does this, he pretends as though they are hitherto unknown insights or as though his repeating them will make me accept them. In my reply, I have rebutted each of the so-called counterexamples that he has cited and have shown conclusively that none of them succeeds in falsifying my findings. Bodas too, like Scharf, misrepresented my arguments in his brief and rude reply to my reply and said he had decided not to engage any further with me. To show how egregiously wrong I am, he tries to calculate the number of derivations that would not produce grammatically correct results if we used my interpretation of Pāṇini's grammar. He comes up with this number based on *one* counterexample saying:

'This single pattern thus accounts for 3.6 *lac* [i.e., 0.36 million] incorrect forms: 2000 *dhatus* [roots] X 2 *pada* [active, middle] X 10 *lakaar* [Pāṇinian tense and aspect] X 9 forms for each *lakaar* [three numbers *three persons] = 3.6 *lacs*'.[3] In my reply, I have shown that the counterexample in question is wrong. I want to highlight the deceitful nature of the argument: Bodas neglects to give readers a sense of the proportion (3.6 *lacs* out of how many?). He thereby intentionally leads them to think that my interpretation is so erroneous that it fails to account for a whopping 3.6 *lac* examples!

Through the publication of this book, I aim to reassert my claims which have remained unrefuted despite the two attempts discussed here. That said, I remain open to criticism and am willing to correct myself and modify my proposition upon being confronted with solid evidence. I am of the conviction that scholarship cannot flourish in isolation: academic dialogue alone can pave the way for intellectual progress. May our discipline overcome its obstacles and scale new heights.

APPENDIX A

Tables of Concordance

In this book, I have examined some derivational examples that have been previously discussed by prominent modern scholars such as Kiparsky (1982), Bronkhorst (2004), and Joshi and Kiparsky (2005). Below, I give two tables of concordance.

Kiparsky, P. (1982). The Ordering of Rules in Pāṇini's Grammar. In *Some Theoretical Problems in Pāṇini's Grammar* (pp. 77–120). Pune, India: Bhandarkar Oriental Research Institute.

Note that:

C4 S3 E01 = chapter 4, section 4.3, example 1

App C E20 = Appendix C, example 20

Example	Kiparsky's example number	My example number
śvayitvā	01	C4 S3 E01
tad	02	C2 S7 E08
āghnīya	06	App C E20
hata	07	C4 S3 E02
vanitvā	08	App C E19
kramitvā	09	C4 S3 E04
atikramya	10	C4 S3 E05
asmai	16	C2 S7 E11
śiṣṭāt	17	C4 S3 E08
aupyata	19	C4 S2 E04
dadhati	20	C4 S2 E02
pratīcaḥ	27	C3 S1 E01
seduṣaḥ	28	C3 S1 E02
prasthāya	30	C4 S3 E06
adhītya	55	C6 S2 E01
6.1.77, 6.1.101, 6.1.87	58	C2 S8 E03, E05
tarati	after Ex. 60, pp. 117-118.	C4 S4 E03

Joshi, S. D., & Kiparsky, P. (2005). The Extended Siddha-Principle. *Annals of the Bhandarkar Oriental Research Institute*, *86*, 1–26.

Bronkhorst, J. (2004). *From Pāṇini to Patañjali: The Search for Linearity.* Pune, India: Bhandarkar Oriental Research Institute.

(Bronkhorst frequently quotes an unpublished draft of Joshi and Kiparsky in his paper. I think this draft is the aforementioned paper that was published in 2005, after the publication of Bronkhorst's paper in 2004. It is for this reason that I have mentioned both papers here).

Example	Joshi & Kip. (Pg. no)	Bronkhorst (Pg. no.)	My thesis
devaiḥ / vṛkṣaiḥ	-	15	C2 S7 E01
dadhati	16-17	17	C4 S2 E02
gārgīyāḥ	-	18-19	C3 S1 E05
aupyata	13-14	20	C4 S2 E04
rājabhiḥ	2-3	-	C6 S2 E03
tad	5-6	-	C2 S7 E08
adhītya	9-10	-	C6 S2 E01
seduṣaḥ	11-12	-	C3 S1 E02
śvayitvā	15-16	-	C4 S3 E01
asmai	18-19	-	C2 S7 E11

APPENDIX B

List of Sūtras Containing the Term *Para*

Group A (nontechnical)

1.1.34 *pūrvaparāvaradakṣiṇottarāparādharāṇi vyavasthāyām asaṁjñāyām*

1.4.109 *paraḥ saṁnikarṣaḥ saṁhitā*

3.2.39 *dviṣatparayostāpeḥ*

3.3.138 *parasmin vibhāṣā*

3.4.20 *parāvarayoge ca*

4.3.5 *parāvarādhamottamapūrvāc ca*

5.2.92 *kṣetriyac parakṣetre cikitsyaḥ*

5.3.29 *vibhāṣā parāvarābhyā*

6.3.8 *parasya ca*

Group B (technical)

1.1.47 *mid aco 'ntyāt paraḥ*

1.1.51 *ur aṇ raparaḥ*

1.1.54 *ādeḥ parasya*

1.1.57 *acaḥ parasmin pūrvavidhau*

1.1.70 *taparas tatkālasya*

1.2.40 *udāttasvaritaparasya sannataraḥ*

1.4.2 *vipratiṣedhe paraṁ kāryam*

1.4.62 *anukaraṇaṁ cānitiparam*

1.4.81 *chandasi pare'pi*

2.1.2 *sub āmantrite parāṅgavat svare*

2.2.31 *rājadantādiṣu param*

2.4.26 *paravalliṅgaṁ dvandvatatpuruṣayoḥ*

3.1.2 *paraś ca*

6.1.84 *ekaḥ pūrvaparayoḥ*
6.1.94 *eṅi pararūpam*
6.1.112 *khyatyāt parasya*
6.1.115 *prakṛtyā 'ntyaḥpādam avyapare*
6.1.120 *anudātte ca kudhapare*
6.2.199 *parādiś chandasi bahulam*
6.4.156 *sthūladūrayuvahrasvakṣiprakṣudrāṇāṁ yaṇādiparaṁ pūrvasya ca guṇaḥ*
7.3.22 *na indrasya parasya*
7.3.27 *nātaḥ parasya*
7.4.80 *oḥ puyaṇjy apare*
7.4.88 *ut parasyātaḥ*
7.4.93 *sanval laghuni caṅpare 'naglope*
8.1.2 *tasya param āmreḍitam*
8.1.56 *yaddhituparaṁ chandasi*
8.2.92 *agnīt preṣaṇe parasya ca*
8.3.4 *anunāsikāt paro 'nusvāraḥ*
8.3.6 *pumaḥ khayy ampare*
8.3.26 *he mapare vā*
8.3.27 *napare naḥ*
8.3.35 *śarpare visarjanīyaḥ*
8.3.87 *upasargaprādurbhyām astir yacparaḥ*
8.3.110 *na raparasṛpisṛjispṛśispṛhisavanādīnām*
8.3.118 *sadisvañjyoḥ parasya liṭi*
8.4.28 *upasargād anotparaḥ*
8.4.58 *anusvārasya yayi parasavarṇaḥ*

APPENDIX C

More Examples of DOI conflict

As stated in chapter 4, here I present more examples of DOI conflict.

Example #1. *glai* + *tiP*—'to become tired', present third-person singular

glai + *tiP*

6.1.45 3.1.68

6.1.45 *ād eca upadeśe'śiti*: the final sound of a verbal root that ends in *eC* when taught in the *Dhātupāṭha* is replaced with *ā*, when an affix that is not marked with *Ś* follows.

3.1.68 *kartari śap*: affix *ŚaP* occurs after a verbal root when a *sārvadhātuka* affix that denotes *kartṛ* 'agent' follows.

If we apply 6.1.45 at this step, 3.1.68 will be applicable at the following step. But if we add the affix *ŚaP* at this step by 3.1.68, then 6.1.45 will not be applicable at the following step.

This is a case of unidirectional blocking and thus of DOI conflict.

By my application of 1.4.2, we apply the RHS rule 3.1.68 and get the correct form: *glai* + *a* + *ti* → *glāyati* (6.1.78 *eco'yavāyāvaḥ*).

Example #2. *bhū* + *tiP*—'to be', aorist third-person singular

3.1.43 *cli luṅi*: affix *cli* is added to a verbal root when *LUṄ* follows.

3.4.100 *itaś ca*: the *i* of a replacement of any *lakāra* marked with *Ṅ* is replaced with *LOPA*.

There is no conflict between the two rules. By my interpretation of 1.4.2, we apply the RHS rule 3.4.100 and get: *bhū* + *t*. At this step, only one rule, namely 3.1.43, is applicable. On applying this rule, we get *bhū* + *cli* + *tiP*. Since *bhū* is an *aṅga* with respect to *cli*, 7.3.84 from the *aṅgādhikāra* is applicable here, and so is 3.1.44:

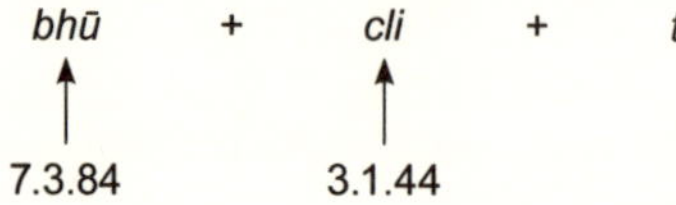

7.3.84 *sārvadhātukārdhadhātukayoḥ*: *guṇa* replaces the final sound *iK* of a verbal base when a *sārvadhātuka* or *ārdhadhātuka* affix follows.

3.1.44 *cleḥ sic*: *cli* is replaced with *sIC*.

There is no conflict between these two rules. By my interpretation of 1.4.2, we apply the RHS rule 3.1.44 and get *bhū* + *sIC* + *t*. Here, three rules are applicable:

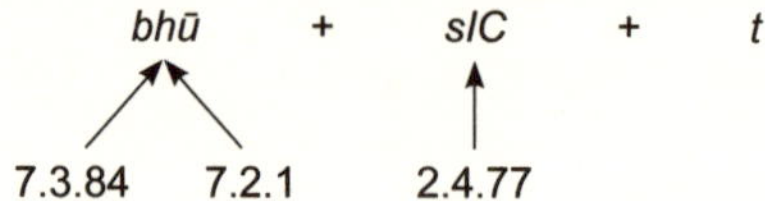

7.3.84 *sārvadhātukārdhadhātukayoḥ*: same as above.

7.2.1 *sici vṛddhiḥ parasmaipadeṣu*: the final sound *iK* of a verbal base is replaced with its *vṛddhi* counterpart before a *sIC* that is followed by a *parasmaipada* affix.

2.4.77 *gātisthāghupābhūbhyaḥ sicaḥ parasmaipadeṣu*: affix *sIC* is replaced with *LUK* when it is located after *gā* 'to go', *sthā* 'to stand', *ghu* 'a root termed *ghu*', *pā* 'to drink', or *bhū* 'to be, become' and before a *parasmaipada* affix.

There is an SOI relationship between 7.3.84 and 7.2.1. Since 7.2.1 has been taught for bases followed by *sIC*, it is more specific and thus wins. Now let us look at the relationship between 7.2.1 and 2.4.77.

If we apply 7.2.1 at this step, 2.4.77 will be applicable at the following step. But if we apply 2.4.77 at this step, 7.2.1 will not be applicable at the following step. This is a case of unidirectional blocking and thus of DOI conflict.

By my interpretation of 1.4.2, we apply the RHS rule 2.4.77 and get *bhū* +

t. *bhū* can now be called an *aṅga* with respect to *t*. Note that *t* cannot trigger *guṇa* of the *ū* of *bhū* due to the following rule:

7.3.88 *bhūsuvos tiṅi*: a *guṇa* vowel does not replace the *iK* of *bhū* 'to be' and *sū* 'to give birth to' when a *sārvadhātuka tiṄ* affix follows.

So only one rule from the *aṅgādhikāra*, namely 6.4.71 *luṅlaṅlṛṅṣv aḍ udāttaḥ*, which is triggered by *t*, is applicable. It teaches that the *udātta* augment *aṬ* is attached to a verbal base when affixes *LUṄ*, *LAṄ*, and *LṚṄ* follow. On applying this rule, we get the correct form: *abhūt*.

Example #3. *grah* + *tiP*—'to obtain', aorist third-person singular

The first couple of steps of this derivation are similar to the previous one. I will mention them in brief here and focus on the step that involves conflict.

grah + *tiP* → *grah* + *t* (3.4.100 *itaś ca*) → *grah* + *cli* + *t* (3.1.43 *cli luṅi*) → *grah* + *sIC* + *t* (3.1.44 *cleḥ sic*).

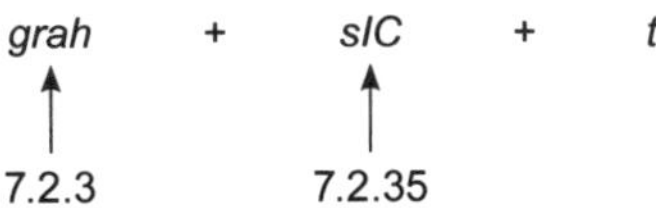

7.2.3 *vadavrajahalantasyācaḥ*: a vowel termed *vṛddhi* replaces the vowel of *vad* 'to speak', *vraj* 'to wander', and a verbal base ending in a consonant, before a *sIC* that is followed by a *parasmaipada* affix.

7.2.35 *ārdhadhātukasyeḍ valādeḥ*: augment *iṬ* is attached to an *ārdhadhātuka* affix beginning with *vaL* (any consonant except *y*).

If we apply 7.2.3 at this step, 7.2.35 will be applicable at the following step. But if we attach the augment *iṬ* to *sIC* by 7.2.35 at this step, 7.2.3 will not be applicable at the following step, due to 7.2.5:

7.2.5 *hmyantakṣaṇaśvasajāgṛṇiśvyeditām*: a vowel termed *vṛddhi* does not come in place of the vowel of verbal bases (i) ending in *h*, *m*, *y*; or (ii) *kṣaṇA* 'to harm', *śvasA* 'to breathe', and *jāgṛ* 'to wake up'; or (iii) ending in the affix *Ṇi*; or (iv) *śvi* 'to swell'; or (v) marked with *E*; before an *iṬ*-initial *sIC* that is followed by a *parasmaipada* affix.[1]

In conclusion, if we apply 7.2.35 at this step, 7.2.3 will not be applicable at the following step. This is a case of unidirectional blocking and thus of DOI conflict.

By my interpretation of 1.4.2, we apply the RHS rule 7.2.35 and get *grah* + *is* + *t*. *grah* and *is* cannot undergo any other operations that are not triggered by *t*, thus we can write *grah* + *is* as *grahis*. *grahis* is an *aṅga* with respect to *t*. The following rules from the *aṅgādhikāra* become applicable:

grahis + *t*
↑ ↑
6.4.71 7.3.96

6.4.71 *luṅlaṅlṛṅṣv aḍ udāttaḥ*: same as above.

7.3.96 *astisico'pṛkte*: augment *īṬ* is attached to a consonant-initial *sārvadhātuka* affix that consists of only one sound and occurs after the verbal base *as* or affix *sIC*.

There is no conflict between these rules. By my interpretation of 1.4.2, we apply the RHS rule 7.3.96 and get *grahis* + *īt*. At this step, we apply 6.4.71 and get *agrahis* + *īt*. Now that all possible rules from the *sapādasaptādhyāyī* have been applied, we apply 8.2.28 *iṭa īṭi* from the *tripādī*, which replaces the *s* between *iṬ* and *īṬ* with *LOPA*. This gives us the correct form: *agrahiīt* → *agrahīt* (6.1.101 *akaḥ savarṇe dīrghaḥ*).[2]

Example #4. *gupU* + *tiP*—'to hide', aorist third-person singular[3]

3.1.43 *cli luṅi*: same as above.

3.4.100 *itaś ca*: same as above.

There is no conflict between these two rules. By my interpretation of 1.4.2, we apply the RHS rule 3.4.100 and get *gup* + *t*. By my interpretation of 1.4.13, *gup* is not an *aṅga* with respect to *t*, so rules like 7.3.86 *pugantalaghūpadhasya ca*, which are taught in the *aṅgādhikāra* and which are triggered by *t*, cannot apply here. By applying 3.1.43, we get *gup* + *cli* + *t*. Here, the following rules are applicable:

gup + *cli* + *t*
↑ ↑
7.3.86 3.1.44

7.3.86 *pugantalaghūpadhasya ca*: *guṇa* replaces the *iK* (*i*, *u*, *r̥*, *l̥*) of a verbal base that ends in the augment *pUK* or that has a *laghu* 'light' vowel as its penultimate sound when a *sārvadhātuka* or *ārdhadhātuka* affix follows.

3.1.44 *cleḥ sic*: same as above.

There is no conflict between the two rules. By my interpretation of 1.4.2, we apply the RHS rule 3.1.44 and get: *gup* + *sIC* + *t*. Here, multiple rules are applicable:

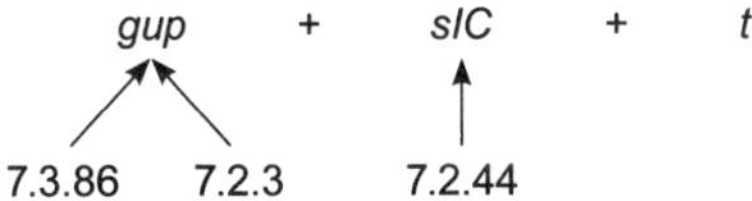

7.3.86 *pugantalaghūpadhasya ca*: same as above.

7.2.3 *vadavrajahalantasyācaḥ*: same as above.

7.2.44 *svarati-sūti-sūyati-dhūñ-ūdito vā*: augment *iṬ* is introduced to an *ārdhadhātuka* affix that begins with *vaL* (any consonant except *y*), provided the same occurs after *svr̥* 'resound', *ṣūṄ* (*adādi*) 'give birth to', *ṣūṄ* (*divādi*) 'give birth to', *dhūÑ* 'to shake', and roots marked with *Ū*.

There is an SOI relationship between 7.3.86 and 7.2.3. 7.2.3 has been taught specifically for a set of verbs followed by *sIC* and thus wins. Now, let us look at the DOI relationship between 7.2.44 and 7.2.3.

If we apply 7.2.3 at this step, 7.2.44 will be applicable at the following step. But if we apply 7.2.44 at this step, then 7.2.3 will not be applicable at the following step because of 7.2.4 *neṭi*, which prohibits *vr̥ddhi* of the vowel of a consonant-final base when the following *sIC* has taken the augment *iṬ*.

This is a case of unidirectional blocking and thus of DOI conflict. By my interpretation of 1.4.2, we apply the RHS rule 7.2.44 and get *gup* + *is* + *t*. By 7.3.86 *pugantalaghūpadhasya ca*, we get *gop* + *is* + *t*. Note that *gop* and *is* cannot undergo any other operations that are not triggered by *t*. Thus, we can write *gop* + *is* as *gopis*. *gopis* is an *aṅga* with respect to *t*.

I will not go into the depth of the remaining steps of this derivation because we have seen these steps in a similar derivation above: *gopis* + *t* → *gopis* + *īt* (7.3.96 *astisico'pr̥kte*) → *agopis* + *īt* (6.4.71 *luṅlaṅlr̥ṅṣv aḍ udāttaḥ*) → *agopi* + *īt* (8.2.28 *iṭa īṭi*) → *agopīt* (6.1.101 *akaḥ savarṇe dīrghaḥ*), which is the correct form.

If we do not implement the optional rule 7.2.44, we get: *gup* + *s* + *t* → *gaups* + *t* (7.2.3 *vadavrajahalantasyācaḥ*) → *gaups* + *īt* (7.3.96 *astisico'pr̥kte*) → *agaupsīt* (6.4.71 *luṅlaṅlr̥ṅṣv aḍ udāttaḥ*), which is also correct.

Example #5. *bhid* + *ta*—'to break', aorist third-person singular
bhid + *ta* → *bhid* + *cli* + *ta* (3.1.43 *cli luṅi*)

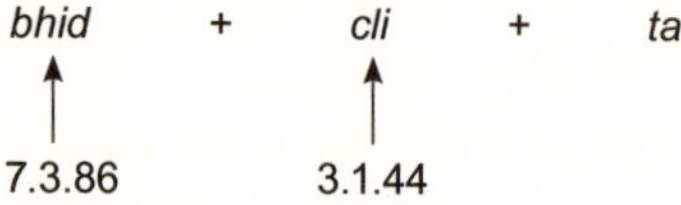

3.1.44 *cleḥ sic*: same as above.

7.3.86 *pugantalaghūpadhasya ca*: same as above.

If we apply 7.3.86 at this step, 3.1.44 will be applicable at the following step. But, if we apply 3.1.44 at this step, 7.3.86 will not be applicable at the following step because of 1.2.11:

1.2.11 *liṅsicāv ātmanepadeṣu*: a *LIṄ* or *sIC* affix which begins with a *jhaL* (a non-nasal stop or a fricative) and occurs after a consonant preceded by an *iK* (*i, u, ṛ, ḷ*) is treated as if marked with *K*, before *ātmanepada* endings.

By 1.2.11 *sIC* is treated as marked with *K*. So, if we apply 3.1.44 at this step, *sIC*, marked by *K*, will not trigger *guṇa* (here, 7.3.86), thanks to 1.1.5 *kṅiti ca*, at the following step.

This is a case of unidirectional blocking, and thus of DOI conflict.

By my interpretation of 1.4.2, we apply the RHS rule 3.1.44 and get *bhid* + *s* + *ta* → *bhids* + *ta* → *abhids* + *ta* (6.4.71 *luṅlaṅḷṛṅṣv aḍ udāttaḥ*) → *abhidta* (8.2.26 *jhalo jhali*) → *abhitta* (8.4.55 *khari ca*), which is the correct form.

Example #6. *ūrṇuÑ* + *tiP*—'to cover', simple future third-person singular
ūrṇuÑ + *tiP* → *ūrṇuÑ* + *sya* + *tiP* (3.1.33 *syatāsī ḷṛluṭoḥ*).

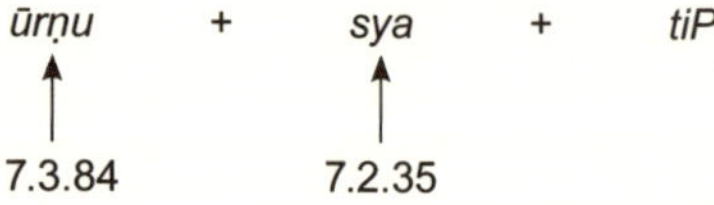

7.3.84 *sārvadhātukārdhadhātukayoḥ*: *guṇa* replaces the final *iK* (*i, u, ṛ, ḷ*) of a verbal base when a *sārvadhātuka* or *ārdhadhātuka* affix follows.

7.2.35 *ārdhadhātukasyeḍ valādeḥ*: augment *iṬ* is attached to an *ārdhadhātuka* affix beginning with *vaL* (any consonant except *y*).

If we apply 7.3.84 at this step, 7.2.35 will be applicable at the following step. But if we apply 7.2.35 at this step, 7.3.84 will not be applicable at the following step due to 1.2.3:

1.2.3 *vibhāṣorṇoḥ*: an affix with initial augment *iṬ* is optionally treated as marked with *Ṅ* when it occurs after *ūrṇuÑ*.

So, if we apply 7.2.35 and treat the resultant *iṣya* as marked with *Ṅ*, then by 1.1.5 *kṅiti ca*, 7.3.84 will not be applicable at the following step.

This is a case of unidirectional blocking and thus of DOI conflict.

By my interpretation of 1.4.2, we apply the RHS rule 7.2.35 and get: *ūrṇu* + *iṣya* + *ti* → *ūrṇuviṣyati* (6.4.77 *aci śnudhātubhruvāṁ yvor iyaṅuvaṅau*[4]).

On the other hand, if we do not implement the optional rule 1.2.3, then the derivation proceeds as follows: *ūrṇu* + *iṣya* + *tiP* (7.2.35 *ārdhadhātukasyeḍ valādeḥ*) → *ūrṇo* + *iṣya* + *tip* (7.3.84 *sārvadhātukārdhadhātukayoḥ*) → *ūrṇaviṣyati* (6.1.78 *eco'yavāyāvaḥ*).

Example #7. *bhū* + *tiP*—'to be', *āśīrliṅ* (benedictive) third-person singular

Since no *vikaraṇa* is added between *bhū* and *tiP* in *āśīrliṅ* forms, at this step, *bhū* can be called an *aṅga* with respect to *tiP*.

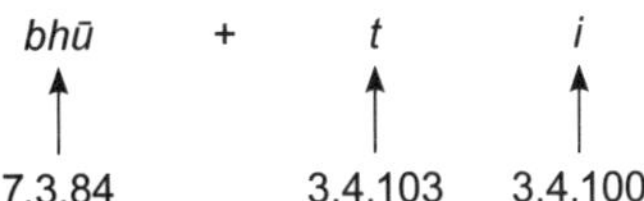

7.3.84 *sārvadhātukārdhadhātukayoḥ*: same as above.

3.4.103 *yāsuṭ parasmaipadeṣūdātto ṅic ca*: *udātta* 'high-pitched' augment *yāsUṬ* is attached to *parasmaipada* substitutes of *LIṄ*, and is treated as marked with *Ṅ*.

3.4.100 *itaś ca*: the *i* of a replacement of any *lakāra* marked with *Ṅ*, is replaced with *LOPA*.

3.4.100 neither blocks nor is blocked by the other two rules. By my interpretation of 1.4.2, we apply the right-most rule 3.4.100 and get *bhū* + *t*. Here, two rules are applicable:

bhū + t

7.3.84 3.4.103

If we apply 7.3.84 at this step, 3.4.103 will be applicable at the following step. But if we apply 3.4.103 at this step, 7.3.84, which prescribes *guṇa* of *ū*, will not be applicable at the following step. This is because *yāsUṬ* is marked with *Ṅ*, and thus by 1.1.5 *kṅiti ca*, *guṇa* is blocked.

This is a case of unidirectional blocking and thus of DOI conflict.

By my interpretation of 1.4.2, we apply the RHS rule 3.4.103 and get *bhū* + *yāst*. Here, again, two rules are applicable:

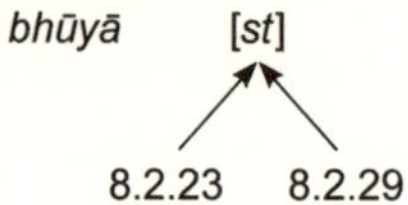

8.2.23 *saṁyogāntasya lopaḥ*: the final sound of a conjunct that occurs at the end of a *pada* is replaced with *LOPA*.

8.2.29 *skoḥ saṁyogādyor ante ca*: the initial *s* and *k* of a conjunct that occurs at the end of a *pada* or is followed by *jhaL* (a non-nasal stop or a fricative) is replaced with *LOPA*.

Note that both 8.2.23 and 8.2.29 belong to the *tripādī* section. So, 8.2.29 is *asiddha* with respect to 8.2.23. However, this does not impact our method of resolving the SOI between them. I discuss this in chapter 6.

8.2.29 has been taught for a specific set of conjuncts and thus wins, thereby leading to the correct form: *bhūyāt*.

Example #8. *naś* + *tavyaT*—'to perish', optative passive participle

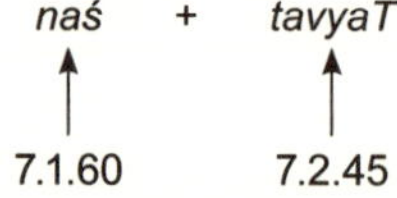

7.1.60 *masjinaśor jhali*: augment *nUM* is attached to *ṬUmasjI* 'to sink, immerse' and *naś* 'to perish' when an affix beginning with *jhaL* (a non-nasal stop or a fricative) follows.

7.2.45 *radhādibhyaś ca*: augment *iṬ* is optionally attached to *ārdhadhātuka* affixes beginning with *vaL* (any consonant except *y*) and occurring after the set of verbal roots beginning with *radhA* 'to be subdued'.[5]

If we apply 7.1.60 at this step, 7.2.45 will still be applicable at the following step. But if we apply 7.2.45 at this step, then the affix no longer begins with a *jhaL* sound, so 7.1.60 will not be applicable at the following step. This is a case of unidirectional blocking and thus of DOI conflict. By my interpretation of

1.4.2, we apply the RHS rule 7.2.45 and get: *naśitavya*, which is the correct form. If we do not implement the optional rule 7.2.45, we get: *naṁṣṭavya*, which is also correct.

Example #9. *divU + Ktvā*—'to gamble', absolutive

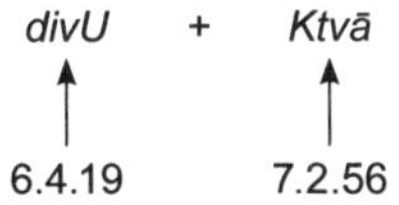

divU + *Ktvā*
↑ ↑
6.4.19 7.2.56

6.4.19 *chvoḥ śūḍ anunāsike ca*: *ch* and *v* of a base are replaced with *ś* and *ūṬH*, respectively, when *KvI* or an affix beginning with *jhaL* (a non-nasal stop or a fricative) and marked with *K* or *Ṅ* or beginning with a nasal follows.

7.2.56 *udito vā*: augment *iṬ* is optionally attached to affix *Ktvā* when it follows a verbal root marked with *U*.

If we apply 6.4.19 at this step, 7.2.56 will be applicable at the following step. If we attach augment *iṬ* to *tvā* by 7.2.56 at this step, then by 1.2.18 *na ktvā seṭ*[6], *Ktvā* cannot be treated as marked with *K*. Thus, 6.4.19 will not be applicable at the following step. This is a case of unidirectional blocking and thus of DOI conflict.

By my interpretation of 1.4.2, we apply the RHS rule 7.2.56 and get: *div + itvā*. Since *itvā* cannot be treated as marked with *K*, it can no longer block *guṇa* and *vr̥ddhi* (i.e., 1.1.5 *kṅiti ca* does not hold). Thus, by 7.3.86 *pugantalaghūpadhasya ca*, we get *devitvā*, which is the correct form. If we do not implement the optional rule 7.2.56, we get: *div + tvā* → *diū + tvā* (6.4.19 *chvoḥ śūḍ anunāsike ca*) → *dyūtvā* (6.1.77 *iko yaṇ aci*), which is also correct.

Example #10. *khanU + Ktvā*—'to dig', absolutive

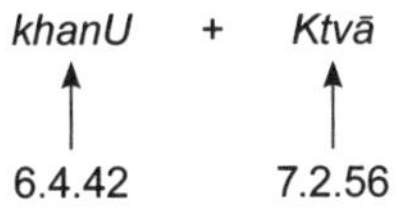

khanU + *Ktvā*
↑ ↑
6.4.42 7.2.56

6.4.42 *janasanakhanāṁ sañjhaloḥ*: the final sound of *janA* 'to generate', *sanA* 'to gain', and *khanU* 'to dig' is replaced with *ā* when *saN* or an affix beginning with *jhaL* (a non-nasal stop or a fricative) and marked with *K* or *Ṅ* follows.

7.2.56 *udito vā*: same as above.

If we apply 6.4.42 at this step, 7.2.56 will be applicable at the following step. But if we apply 7.2.56 at this step, the affix will no longer begin with *jhaL* and so 6.4.42 will not be applicable at the following step. This is a case of unidirectional blocking, and of DOI conflict.

By my interpretation of 1.4.2, we apply the RHS rule 7.2.56 and get *khanitvā*, which is the correct form. If we do not implement the optional rule 7.2.56, we get *kha-ā* + *tvā* → *khātvā* (6.1.101 *akaḥ savarṇe dīrghaḥ*), which is also correct.

Example #11. *kr̥* + *siP*—'to make', imperative second-person singular

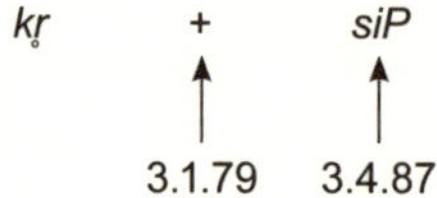

3.1.79 *tanādikr̥ñbhya uḥ*: affix *u* is added after verbal roots belonging to the set headed by *tanU* 'to stretch' and also after *kr̥Ñ* 'to make' when a *sārvadhātuka* affix which denotes *kartr̥* follows.

3.4.87 *ser hy apic ca*: a *siP* replacement of *LOṬ* is replaced with *hi* and is treated as if not marked with *P*.

There is no conflict between these rules.

By my interpretation of 1.4.2, we apply the RHS rule 3.4.87 and get *kr̥* + *hi*. Thereafter, the derivation proceeds as follows *kr̥* + *hi* → *kr̥* + *u* + *hi* (3.1.79 *tanādikr̥ñbhya uḥ*) → *karu* + *hi* (7.3.84 *sārvadhātukārdhadhātukayoḥ*). *karu* is an *aṅga* with respect to *hi*, so the following rules from the *aṅgādhikāra* are applicable:

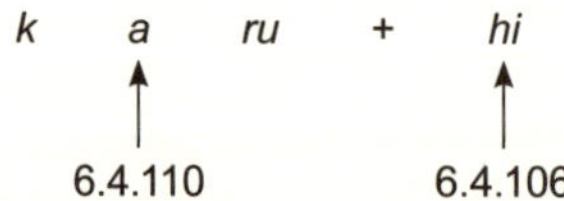

6.4.110 *ata ut sārvadhātuke*: the *a* of base that is constituted by *kr̥* and ends in affix *u* is replaced with *u* when a *sārvadhātuka* affix marked with *K* or *Ṅ* follows.

6.4.106 *utaś ca pratyayād asaṁyogapūrvāt*: *hi* is replaced with *LUK* when it is preceded by a base that ends in affix *u*, such that *u* is not preceded by a conjunct.

Note that both these rules fall under the heading rule 6.4.22 *asiddhavat atrābhāt*. I interpret this rule as: till 6.4.129 *bhasya*, any rule will treat any other rule here (i.e., in this section) as *asiddhavat*. In my opinion, if A treats B as *asiddhavat*, A acknowledges the existence of B but not the outcome of the application of B. I have discussed this interpretation in detail in chapter 6.

Since 6.4.110 and 6.4.106 acknowledge each other's existence, we can use 1.4.2 to deal with this case of DOI.

If we apply 6.4.110 at this step, 6.4.106 will be applicable at the following step. But if we replace *hi* with *LUK* by 6.4.106, 6.4.110 will not be applicable at the following step.[7] This is a case of unidirectional blocking and thus of DOI conflict.

By my interpretation of 1.4.2, we apply the RHS rule 6.4.106 and get *karu*. Since 6.4.106 is *asiddhavat* with respect to 6.4.110, 6.4.110 does not acknowledge the outcome of the application of 6.4.106. Thus, 6.4.110 applies, and we get the correct form: *kuru*.

Example #12. *as* + *siP*—'to be', imperative (*āśiṣi* 'benediction') second-person singular

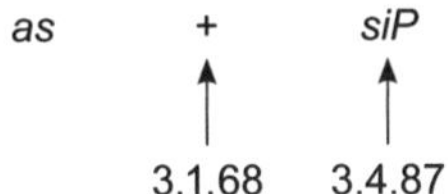

3.1.68 *kartari śap*: affix *ŚaP* occurs after a verbal root when a *sārvadhātuka* affix that denotes *kartr̥* 'agent' follows.

3.4.87 *ser hy apic ca*: same as above.

There is no conflict between these rules.

By my interpretation of 1.4.2, we apply the RHS rule 3.4.87 and get *as* + *hi*. Then, the derivation proceeds as follows: *as* + *hi* → *as* + *ŚaP* + *hi* (3.1.68 *kartari śap*) → *as* + *hi* (2.4.72 *adiprabhr̥tibhyaḥ śapaḥ*). Since *as* is an *aṅga* with respect to *hi*, the following rules from the *aṅgādhikāra* are applicable:

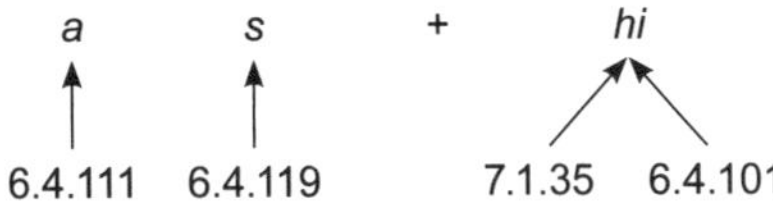

6.4.111 *śnasor allopaḥ*: the *a* of affix *ŚnaM* and of root *as* is replaced with *LOPA* when a *sārvadhātuka* affix marked with *K* or *Ṅ* follows.

6.4.119 *ghvasor ed dhāv abhyāsalopaś ca*: the final sound of a verbal base termed *ghu* or of *as* is replaced with *e* when affix *hi* follows, and *abhyāsa* (first of two reduplicated syllables) is replaced with *LOPA*.

7.1.35 *tuhyos tātaṅ āśiṣy anyatarasyām*: affixes *tu* and *hi* are optionally replaced with *tātAṄ*, provided benediction (*āśiḥ*) is denoted.

6.4.101 *hujhalbhyo her dhiḥ*: *hi* is replaced with *dhi* when it occurs after root *hu* or after a verbal base ending in *jhaL* (a non-nasal stop or a fricative).

There is no conflict between 6.4.111 and 6.4.119.

There is an SOI between 7.1.35 and 6.4.101. 7.1.35 is more specific because it has been taught with respect to benedictive forms.

So now let us look at the relationship between 6.4.119 and 7.1.35. If we apply 6.4.119 at this step, then 7.1.35 will be applicable at the following step. If we replace *hi* with *tātAṄ* by 7.1.35 at this step, 6.4.119 will not be applicable at the following step. This is a case of unidirectional blocking and thus of DOI conflict.

By my interpretation of 1.4.2, we perform the right-most operation 7.1.35 (which defeats 6.4.101 in SOI, as seen above) and get: *as* + *tāt* → *stāt* (6.4.111 *śnasor allopaḥ*), which is the correct form.

If we do not implement the optional rule 7.1.35, the derivation proceeds as follows:

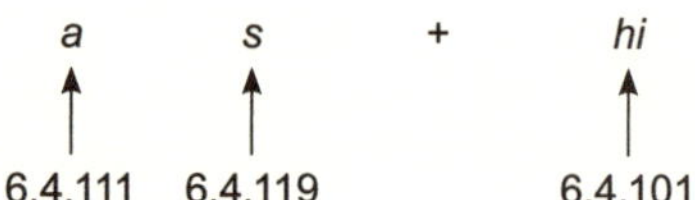

There is no conflict between 6.4.111 and 6.4.119. Let us look at the relationship between 6.4.119 and 6.4.101.

If we apply 6.4.119 at this step, then 6.4.101 will not be applicable at the following step. If we apply 6.4.101 at this step, then 6.4.119 will not be applicable at the following step. This is a case of mutual blocking.

Note that all three rules belong to the *asiddhavat* section. So, each rule can see the other two rules but not the outcome of the application of the other two rules. Since these rules can see one another, we can use 1.4.2 to solve the DOI between them.

By my interpretation of 1.4.2, we apply the right-most rule 6.4.101 and get *as* + *dhi*. The other two rules cannot see the outcome of the application of 6.4.101. They are still applicable:

By my interpretation of 1.4.2, we apply the RHS rule 6.4.119 and get *ae* + *dhi*. Here, 6.4.111 applies, and we get the correct form *edhi*.

Example #13. *bhū* + *ta*—'to be', passive aorist third-person singular

bhū + *ta* → *bhū* + *cli* + *ta* (3.1.43 *cli luṅi*[8])

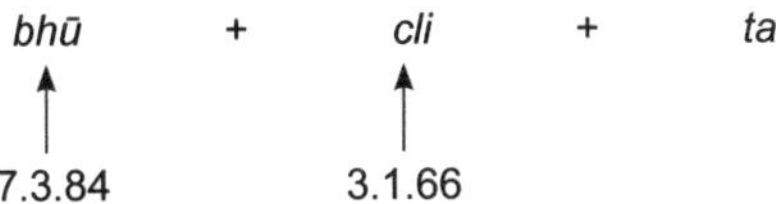

7.3.84 *sārvadhātukārdhadhātukayoḥ*: *guṇa* replaces the final *iK* (*i, u, ṛ, ḷ*) of a verbal base when a *sārvadhātuka* or *ārdhadhātuka* affix follows.

3.1.66 *ciṇ bhāvakarmaṇoḥ*: *CiṆ* occurs in place of affix *cli* after a verbal base when the *LUṄ* substitute *ta* denoting *bhāva* 'action' or *karman* 'object' follows.

There is no conflict between these two rules. By my interpretation of 1.4.2, we apply the RHS rule 3.1.66 and get *bhū* + *CiṆ* + *ta*. Thereafter, the derivation proceeds as follows: *bhū* + *CiṆ* + *ta* → *bhau* + *CiṆ* + *ta* (7.2.115 *aco ñṇiti*[9]) → *bhāv* + *CiṆ* + *ta* (6.1.78 *eco'yavāyāvaḥ*). Since *bhāv* and *CiṆ* cannot undergo any other operations that are not triggered by *ta*, we can write *bhāv* + *CiṆ* as *bhāvi*. By my interpretation of 1.4.13, *bhāvi* is an *aṅga* with respect to *ta*. Here, multiple rules from the *aṅgādhikāra* become applicable:

bhāvi + ta
↑ 6.4.71 ↑ 6.4.104

6.4.71 *luṅlaṅḷṛṅṣv aḍ udāttaḥ*: the *udātta* 'high-pitched' augment *aṬ* is attached to a verbal base when affixes *LUṄ*, *LAṄ*, and *LṜṄ* follow.

6.4.104 *ciṇo luk*: an affix that occurs after *CiṆ* is replaced with *LUK*.

Note that both these rules fall under the heading rule 6.4.22 *asiddhavad atrābhāt*. They are *asiddhavat* with respect to each other. That is, each rule acknowledges the existence of the other rule but not the outcome of the application of the other rule.

Since 6.4.71 and 6.4.104 acknowledge each other's existence, we can use 1.4.2 to deal with this case of DOI.

If we apply 6.4.71 at this step, 6.4.104 will be applicable at the following step. But if we apply 6.4.104 at this step, the affix will be replaced with *LUK*, and so 6.4.71 will not be applicable at the following step.[10] This is a case of unidirectional blocking and thus of DOI conflict. By my interpretation of 1.4.2, we apply the RHS rule 6.4.104 and get: *bhāvi*. Since 6.4.104 is *asiddhavat* with respect to 6.4.71, 6.4.71 does not acknowledge the outcome of the application of 6.4.104. Consequently, 6.4.71 applies, and we get the correct form: *abhāvi*.

Example #14. *krī* + *jhi*—'to buy', present third-person plural

krī + *jhi* → *krī* + *Śnā* + *jhi* (3.1.81 *kryādibhyaḥ śnā*[11]) → *krīnā* + *jhi*. Now that *krīnā* is an *aṅga* with respect to *jhi*, the following rules from the *aṅgādhikāra* become applicable:

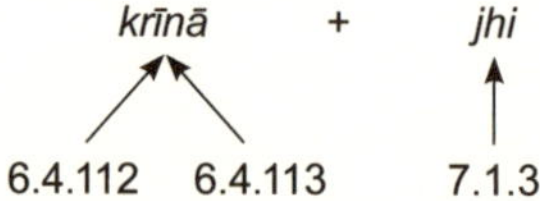

6.4.112 *śnābhyastayor ātaḥ*[12]: the final *ā* of a base that ends in *Śnā* or of a reduplicated base (*abhyasta*) is replaced with *LOPA* when a *sārvadhātuka* affix marked with *K* or *Ṅ* follows.

6.4.113 *ī haly aghoḥ*: the final *ā* of a base that ends in *Śnā* or of a reduplicated base (*abhyasta*), excluding items termed *ghu*, is replaced with *ī* when a *sārvadhātuka* affix beginning with a consonant and marked with *K* or *Ṅ* follows.

7.1.3 *jho'ntaḥ*: *jh*, which is the initial sound of an affix, is replaced with *ant*.

There is an SOI between 6.4.112 and 6.4.113. First, let us identify the more specific, that is, winning rule. Then we will examine the DOI between the winning rule and 7.1.3.

6.4.113 is more specific because it is applicable only when the affix begins with a consonant and thus wins. Now, let us look at the DOI relationship between 6.4.113 and 7.1.3.

If we apply 6.4.113 at this step, 7.1.3 will be applicable at the following step. However, if we apply 7.1.3 at this step, *jhi* will no longer begin with a consonant. Thus, 6.4.113 will not be applicable at the following step.

This is a case of unidirectional blocking and thus of DOI conflict.

By my interpretation of 1.4.2, we apply the RHS rule 7.1.3 and get: *krīnā+ anti*. Here, 6.4.112 applies, and we get *krīṇanti*,[13] which is the correct form.

Example #15. *udvij + ta*—'to fear', simple future third-person singular

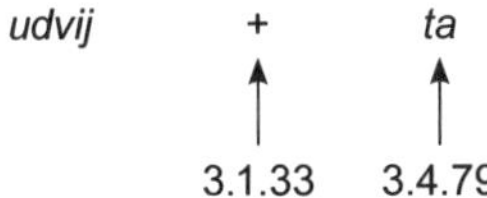

3.1.33 *syatāsī lṛluṭoḥ*: affixes *sya* and *tāsI*, respectively, occur after verbal bases when *LṚ* and *LUṬ* follow.

3.4.79 *ṭita ātmanepadānāṁ ṭer e*: the part that begins with the last vowel (*ṭi*)[14] of an *ātmanepada* replacement of a *lakāra* marked with *Ṭ* is replaced with *e*.

There is no conflict between these rules.

By my interpretation of 1.4.2, we apply the RHS rule 3.4.79 and get *udvij + te*. Thereafter, we apply 3.1.33 and get *udvij + sya + te*. Here, two rules are applicable:

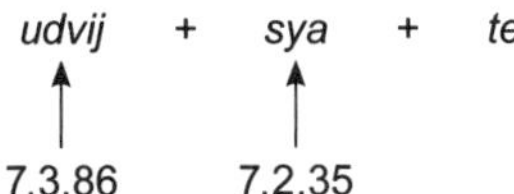

7.3.86 *pugantalaghūpadhasya ca*: *guṇa* replaces the *iK* (*i, u, ṛ, ḷ*) of a verbal base that ends in the augment *pUK* or that has a *laghu* 'light' vowel as its penultimate sound when a *sārvadhātuka* or *ārdhadhātuka* affix follows.

7.2.35 *ārdhadhātukasyeḍvalādeḥ*: augment *iṬ* is attached to an *ārdhadhātuka* affix beginning with *vaL* (any consonant except *y*).

If we apply 7.3.86 at this step, 7.2.35 will be applicable at the following step. But if we apply 7.2.35 at this step, 7.3.86 will not be applicable at the following step because of the following rule:

1.2.2 *vija iṭ*: an affix with initial augment *iṬ* is treated as if marked with *Ṅ* when it occurs after *OvijI* 'to fear'.

So, if we apply 7.2.35 at this step, the resultant *isya*, by 1.2.2, will be treated as marked with *Ṅ*. Consequently, thanks to 1.1.5 *kṅiti ca*, 7.3.86 will not be applicable at the following step.

This is a case of unidirectional blocking and thus of DOI conflict.

By my interpretation of 1.4.2, we apply the RHS rule 7.2.35 and get: *udvijisya* + *te* → *udvijiṣyate* (8.3.59 *ādeśapratyayoḥ*), which is the correct form.

Example #16. *bhī* + *jhi*—'to be afraid', present third-person plural

bhī + *jhi* → *bhī* + *ŚaP* + *jhi* (3.1.68 *kartari śap*) → *bhī* + *ŚLU* + *jhi* (2.4.75 *juhotyādibhyaḥ śluḥ*) → *bhībhī* + *ŚLU* + *jhi* (6.1.10 *ślau*) → *bhibhī* + *ŚLU* + *jhi* (7.4.59 *hrasvaḥ*[15]).

At this point, *bhibhī* and *ŚLU* cannot undergo any other operations that are not triggered by *jhi*. Thus, we can write *bhibhī* + *ŚLU* as *bhibhī*. In *bhibhī* + *jhi*, *bhibhī* can now be called an *aṅga* with respect to *jhi*. Thus, the following rules from the *aṅgādhikāra* become applicable:

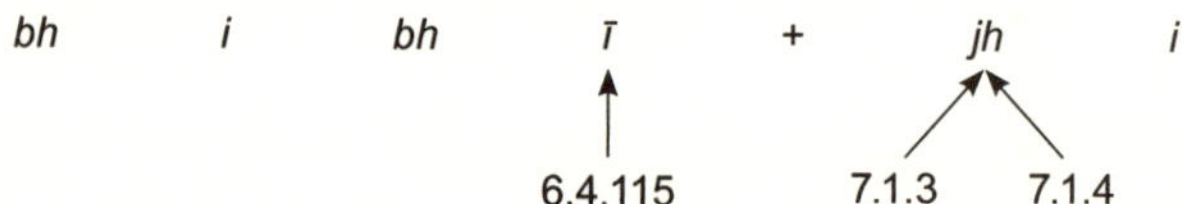

6.4.115 *bhiyo'nyatarasyām*: the final *ī* of *bhī* is optionally replaced with *i* when an affix beginning with a consonant and marked with *K* or *Ṅ* follows.[16]

7.1.3 *jho'ntaḥ*: a *jh* that is the initial sound of an affix is replaced with *ant*.

7.1.4 *ad abhyastāt*: when preceded by a reduplicated base, a *jh* that is the initial sound of an affix is replaced with *at*.

There is an SOI relationship between 7.1.3 and 7.1.4. Since 7.1.4 has been taught specifically for reduplicated bases, it is more specific and thus wins.

Let us consider the relationship between 7.1.4 and 6.4.115. If we apply 6.4.115 at this step, 7.1.4 will be applicable at the following step. But if, by 7.1.4, we replace *jh* with *at*, which starts with a vowel, 6.4.115 will not be applicable at the following step. This is a case of unidirectional blocking and thus of DOI conflict.

By my interpretation of 1.4.2, we apply the RHS rule 7.1.4 (which defeats 7.1.3 in SOI, as seen above) and get: *bhibhī* + *ati* → *bhibhy* + *ati* (6.4.82 *eranekāco'saṁyogapūrvasya*). Now that all rules from the *sapādasaptādhyāyī* have applied, we can apply 8.4.54 *abhyāse car ca* from the *tripādī*. This gives us *bibhyati*, which is the correct form.

Note that the optional rule 6.4.115 *bhiyo'nyatarasyām*, despite being applicable, does not actually end up applying in this derivation. So even if we had not implemented the optional rule 6.4.115, we would still have got the same form, that is, *bibhyati*.

Example #17. *ṇijIR* + *tiP*—'to purify', aorist third-person singular

6.1.65 *ṇo naḥ*: the initial *ṇ* of a verbal root when taught in the *Dhātupāṭha* is replaced with *n*.

3.1.43 *cli luṅi*: affix *cli* is added to a verbal root when *LUṄ* follows.

3.4.100 *itaś ca*: the *i* of a replacement of any *lakāra* marked with *Ṅ* is replaced with *LOPA*.

There is no conflict between these rules. By my interpretation of 1.4.2, we apply the right-most rule 3.4.100 and get: *ṇijIR* + *t*. Here, the following rules are applicable:

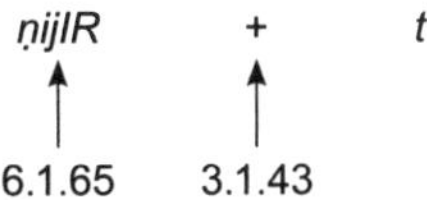

There is no conflict between these rules. By my interpretation of 1.4.2, we apply the RHS rule 3.1.43 and get *ṇij* + *cli* + *t*. Here, the following rules are applicable:

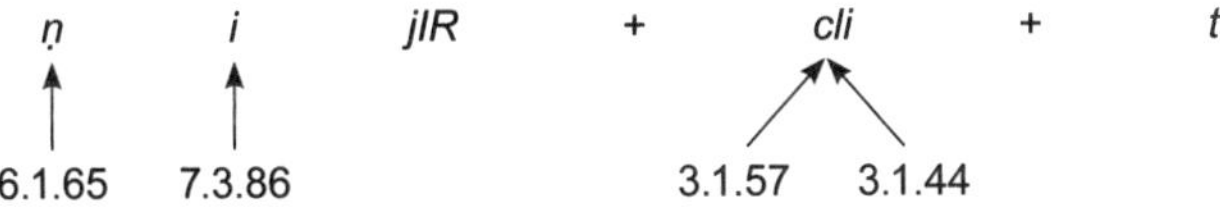

6.1.65 *ṇo naḥ*: same as above.

7.3.86 *pugantalaghūpadhasya ca*: same as above.

3.1.44 *cleḥ sic*: *cli* is replaced with *sIC*.

3.1.57 *irito vā*: affix *cli* is optionally replaced with *aṄ* after verbal roots marked with *IR* when a *parasmaipada* replacement of *LUṄ*, which denotes *kartṛ* follows.

6.1.65 is not in conflict with the other rules. There is an SOI relationship between 3.1.44 and 3.1.57. Since 3.1.57 has been specifically taught for roots marked with *IR*, it wins.

Let us consider the DOI relationship between 7.3.86 and 3.1.57. If we apply 7.3.86 at this step, 3.1.57 will be applicable at the following step. But if we replace *cli* with *aṄ* by 3.1.57, then by 1.1.5 *kṅiti ca*, 7.3.86 will not be applicable at the following step. This is a case of unidirectional blocking and thus of DOI conflict.

By my interpretation of 1.4.2, we perform the right-most operation 3.1.57 (which defeats 3.1.44 in SOI, as seen above). We get: *ṇij* + *aṄ* + *t* → *nij* + *aṄ* + *t* (6.1.65). *nij* and *aṄ* cannot undergo any other operations that are not triggered by *t*, so we can write *nij* + *aṄ* as *nija*. *nija* is an *aṅga* with respect to *t*. Thus, we apply 6.4.71 *luṅlaṅlr̥ṅṣv aḍ udāttaḥ* and get *anijat*, which is the correct form. If we do not implement the optional rule 3.1.57 *irito vā*, the derivation proceeds as follows: *ṇij* + *cli* + *t* → *ṇij* + *sIC* + *t* (3.1.44) → *ṇaij* + *s* + *t* (7.2.3 *vadavrajahalantasyācaḥ*) → *naij* + *s* + *t* (6.1.65 *ṇo naḥ*) → *naijs* + *īt* (7.3.96 *astisico'pr̥kte*) → *anaikṣīt* (6.4.71 *luṅlaṅlr̥ṅṣv aḍ udāttaḥ*),[17] which is also correct.

Example #18. *sic* + *tiP*—'to sprinkle', aorist third-person singular

This derivation is very similar to the previous one, so I will simply focus on the part involving DOI conflict. In the rest of the steps, if two rules are simultaneously applicable, I choose the RHS rule in the case of DOI and the more specific rule in the case of SOI.

sic + *tip* → *sic* + *t* (3.4.100 *itaś ca*) → *sic* + *cli* + *t* (3.1.43 *cli luṅi*)

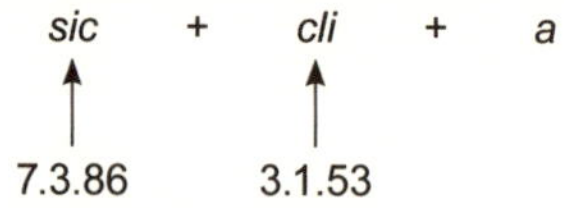

7.3.86 *pugantalaghūpadhasya ca*: same as above.

3.1.53 *lipisicihvaś ca*: affix *cli* is replaced with *aṄ* after verbal roots *lip* 'to coat, smear', *sic* 'to pour out, sprinkle' or *hveÑ* 'to call' when *LUṄ* that denotes *kartr̥* follows.

If we apply 7.3.86 at this step, 3.1.53 will be applicable at the following step. But if we apply 3.1.53 at this step, then by 1.1.5 *kṅiti ca*, 7.3.86 will not be applicable at the following step. This is a case of unidirectional blocking and thus of DOI conflict.

By my interpretation of 1.4.2, we apply the RHS rule 3.1.53 and get *sic* + *aṄ* + *t*. *sic*, and *aṄ* cannot undergo any other operations that are not triggered by *t*.

Thus, *sic* + *aṄ* can be written as *sica*. Thereafter, 6.4.71 *luṅlaṅl̥ṛṅṣv aḍ udāttaḥ* from the *aṅgādhikāra* applies, leading to the correct form, *asicat*.

Example #19. *vanU* + *Ktvā*—'to desire', absolutive

6.4.15 *anunāsikasya kvijhaloḥ kṅiti*: the penultimate vowel of a base that ends in a nasal (*anunāsika*), is replaced with its long counterpart when affix *KvI*, or an affix beginning with *jhaL* (a non-nasal stop or a fricative) and marked with *K* or *Ṅ* follows.

6.4.37 *anudāttopadeśavanatitanotyādīnām anunāsikalopo jhali kṅiti*: the final nasal of a base marked with *anudātta* when taught in the *Dhātupāṭha*, as well as of *vanA* 'to like' and the roots headed by *tanU* 'to extend', is replaced with *LOPA* when an affix beginning with *jhaL* (a non-nasal stop or a fricative) and marked with *K* or *Ṅ* follows.

7.2.56 *udito vā*: augment *iṬ* is optionally attached to affix *Ktvā* when it follows a verbal root marked with *U*.

Let us consider the relationship of 7.2.56 with the other two rules. If we apply 6.4.15 or 6.4.37 at this step, 7.2.56 will be applicable at the following step. But if we apply 7.2.56 at this step, then then both 6.4.14 and 6.4.37 will not be applicable at the following step. Thus, 7.2.56 unidirectionally blocks both 6.4.15 and 6.4.37 and is in a DOI conflict with both of them.

By my interpretation of 1.4.2, we apply the right-most rule 7.2.56 and get *vanitvā*, which is the correct form.

If we do not implement the optional rule 7.2.56, the derivation proceeds as follows:

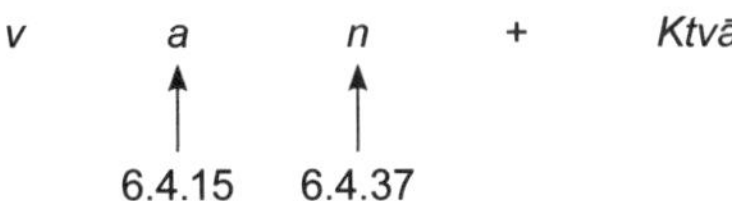

If we apply 6.4.15 at this step, 6.4.37 will be applicable at the following step. But if we apply 6.4.37 at this step, 6.4.15 will not be applicable at the following step. This is a case of unidirectional blocking and of DOI conflict.

By my interpretation of 1.4.2, we apply the RHS rule 6.4.37 and get *vatvā*, which is also correct.

Example #20. *āhan* + *iṬ*—'to hit', optative first-person singular

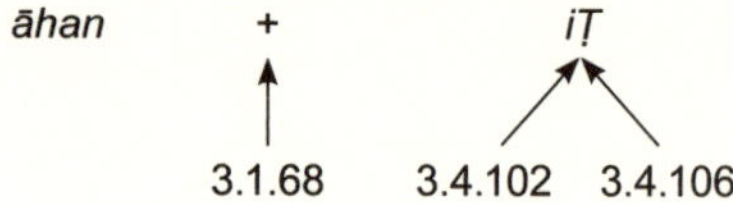

3.1.68 *kartari śap*: affix *ŚaP* occurs after a verbal root when a *sārvadhātuka* affix that denotes *kartṛ* 'agent' follows.

3.4.102 *liṅas sīyuṭ*: a substitute of *LIṄ* receives the augment *sīyUṬ*.

3.4.106 *iṭo't*: *iṬ*, which is the first-person singular *ātmanepada* substitute of *LIṄ*, is replaced with *aT*.

3.1.68 neither blocks nor is blocked by the other rules. There is an SOI relationship between 3.4.106 and 3.4.102, and 3.4.106 wins because it has been specifically taught for *iṬ*.

By my interpretation of 1.4.2, we apply the RHS rule 3.4.106 (which defeats 3.4.102 in SOI, as stated above) and get *āhan* + *aT*. Here, two rules are applicable:

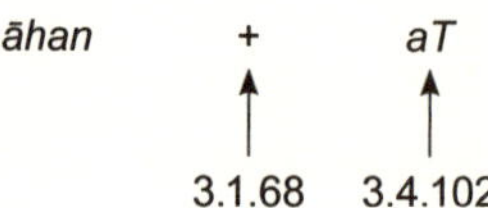

As stated before, there is no conflict between these two rules. By my interpretation of 1.4.2, we apply the RHS rule 3.4.102 and get *āhan* + *sīya*. Thereafter, the derivation proceeds as follows: *āhan* + *sīya* → *āhan* + *ŚaP* + *sīya* (3.1.68 *kartari śap*) → *āhan* + *sīya* (2.4.72 *adiprabhṛtibhyaḥ śapaḥ*). Now *āhan* can be called an *aṅga* with respect to *sīya*. Thus, the following rules from the *aṅgādhikāra* are applicable:

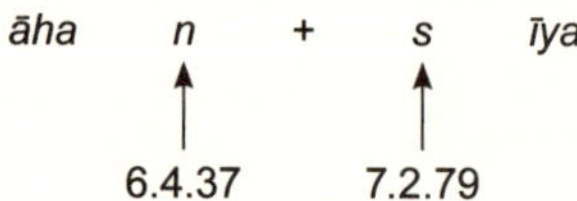

6.4.37 *anudāttopadeśavanatitanotyādīnām anunāsikalopo jhali kṅiti*: same as above.

7.2.79 *liṅaḥ salopo'nantyasya*: the nonfinal *s* of a *sārvadhātuka* substitute of *LIṄ* is replaced with *LOPA*.

If we apply 6.4.37 at this step, 7.2.79 will still be applicable at the following step. But if we apply 7.2.79 at this step, *āhan* will no longer be followed by a *jhaL* sound, and thus 6.4.37 will not be applicable at the following step. This is a case of unidirectional blocking and thus of DOI conflict.

By my interpretation of 1.4.2, we apply the RHS rule 7.2.79 and get *āhan* + *īya*. Thereafter, the derivation proceeds as follows: *āhn* + *īya* (6.4.98 *gamahanajanakhanaghasāṁ lopaḥ kṅity anaṅi*) → *āghnīya* (7.3.54 *ho hanter ñṇinneṣu*), which is the correct form.

Example #21. *vyadh* + *Ktvā*—'to hurt', absolutive

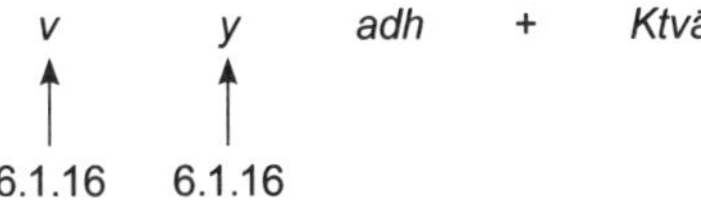

6.1.16 *grahijyāvayivyadhivaṣṭivicativṛścatipṛcchatibhṛjjatīnāṁ ṅiti ca*: verbal roots *grahA* 'to grab, seize', *jyā* 'to decay, grow old', *vay* (a substitute of *veÑ* 'to weave' by 2.4.41 *veño vayiḥ*), *vyadhA* 'to pierce, hurt', *vaśA* 'to shine', *vyacA* 'to deceive', *OvraścŪ* 'to cut', *pracchA* 'to ask', and *bhrasjA* 'to roast' undergo *samprasāraṇa* when an affix marked with *K* and *Ṅ* follows.

Note that both *v* and *y* can potentially undergo *samprasāraṇa* by 6.1.16. If we apply 6.1.16 to *v* at this step, 6.1.16 will be applicable to *y* at the following step. But if we apply 6.1.16 to *y* at this step, then by 6.1.37 *na samprasāraṇe samprasāraṇam*, 6.1.16 will not be applicable to *v* at the following step. This is a case of unidirectional blocking and thus of DOI conflict.

By my interpretation of 1.4.2, we apply the RHS rule 6.1.16 to *y* and get *viadh* + *tvā*. Thereafter, the derivation proceeds as follows: *vidh* + *tvā* (6.1.108 *samprasāraṇāc ca*) → *vidhdhvā* (8.2.40 *jhaṣas tathor dho'dhaḥ*) → *viddhvā* (8.4.53 *jhalāṁ jaś jhaśi*), which is the correct form.

NOTES

Chapter 1

1. In the modern literature on the Pāṇinian grammatical tradition, it is customary to use the verb 'to derive' and its derivatives (e.g., derivation) to simply mean 'to construct'. The verb 'to derive' is used in the context of not only derivational but also inflectional morphology. I shall abide by this convention in this book.
2. Metarules teach us how rules should be interpreted, how certain operations should be undertaken, and how rules interact with one another.
3. Note that the whole base does not undergo reduplication; instead, only one syllable does. See 6.1.1 *ekāco dve prathamasya* 'The first syllable of the root undergoes reduplication,' and 6.1.2 *ajāder dvitīyasya* 'The second syllable of vowel-initial roots undergoes reduplication'.
4. In this book, I use capital letters in Pāṇinian morphemes to represent *itsaṁjñakas* (taught in 1.3.2 *upadeśe'j anunāsika it* and following *sūtras*). Such *its* (commonly called *anubandhas* in post-Pāṇinian grammatical literature) are used to mark certain properties of the item to which they are added and are not actually part of the item. Their unconditional deletion is taught by 1.3.9 *tasya lopaḥ*.
5. Note that, in this book, I have used English translations of Pāṇini's rules by Sharma (1987–2003) and Katre (1987) for many but not all rules. I have taken the liberty to edit their translations as required. For the remaining rules, I have presented my own translations.
6. Besides, it is not possible to arrange rules on the basis of the derivations in which they participate because most rules participate in umpteen different derivations.
7. *Tip-tas-jhi-sip-thas-tha-mib-vas-mas-t*(*a*)*-ātāṁ-jha-thās-āthāṁ-dhvam-iḍ-vahi-mahiṅ.*
8. I think that there was a break in the transmission of the *Aṣṭādhyāyī* between Pāṇini and Kātyāyana, since Kātyāyana seems to be in the process of understanding the *Aṣṭādhyāyī* without much help from anyone else. I shall furnish evidence to support this statement in chapter 7.
9. The two major commentaries on the *Mahābhāṣya* are the *Pradīpa* of Kaiyaṭa and the *Uddyota* of Nāgeśa.
10. K. V. Abhyankar has edited and compiled many Pāṇinian and non-Pāṇinian *paribhāṣā* treatises in his *Paribhāṣāsaṁgraha* (1967).
11. The two major commentaries on the *Kāśikā* are the *Nyāsa* of Jinendrabuddhi and the *Padamañjarī* of Haradatta.
12. The earliest reordered commentary was the *Rūpāvatāra* of Dharmakīrti (tenth century), but its influence on the later *Kaumudī* literature is uncertain.

13. It is accompanied by Bhaṭṭojī's autocommentary on the *Siddhāntakaumudī* called *Prauḍhamanoramā*. Two commentaries on the *Siddhāntakaumudī* are widely used to study it, namely Vāsudeva Dīkṣita's elaborate and beginner-friendly *Bālamanoramā* (*bāla* means 'child', the title literally means 'pleasant to children') and Jñānendra Sarasvatī's concise and advanced *Tattvabodhinī* (Cardona 1976, 285–86).
14. I have translated *para kārya* as understood by the tradition.
15. Perhaps Vasu intended to say 'sound' and not 'letter'.
16. This example in the *Kāśikā* is borrowed from the *Mahābhāṣya* on 1.4.2 (Mbh I.304.15). Note that Mbh I.304.15 stands for volume I of the *Mahābhāṣya* edited by Kielhorn, page number 304, line number 15.
17. Another version of this *paribhāṣā* is *balavan nityam anityāt* (92, *Bhojaparibhāṣāsūtra*).
18. Another version of this *paribhāṣā* is (*balavad*) *antaraṅgaṁ bahiraṅgāt* (93, *Bhojaparibhāṣāsūtra*), where *balavat* is *anuvṛtta* from the previous *paribhāṣā*.
19. It is not clear why the word *pūrva* has been mentioned in the *paribhāṣā*.
20. Patañjali and Nāgeśa hold the *antaraṅga paribhāṣā* true for both conflict and other situations. See the *Mahābhāṣya* on 1.4.2 (Mbh I.309.24 onwards) and *paribhāṣā* 50 of the *Paribhāṣenduśekhara, asiddham bahiraṅgam antaraṅge.*
21. See the entry on *vipratiṣedha* in Apte's Sanskrit dictionary.
22. The terms in brackets are *anuvṛtta* 'continued' from previous *sūtras*.
23. From here on, nearly all asterisks signal a form that is grammatically incorrect.
24. This is one of only two *sūtras* that refer to an ancillary text known as *Uṇādisūtras*, which provide for introducing certain affixes after verb roots to derive nominal bases (Cardona 1976, 170). There is no clear consensus about whether or not Pāṇini himself wrote the *Uṇādisūtras* (Cardona 1976, 174). I personally do not think he did, and so I do not consider this derivation 'Pāṇinīya'. But because the commentarial tradition uses this as an example in the present context, I discuss it, nonetheless. The relevant *Uṇādi sūtra* here is 289 *siveṣ ṭer yū ca.*
25. I am aware that the tradition reads this rule as *cchvoḥ* and not as *chvoḥ*. However, I think that the original version must have been *chvoḥ*. See Kiparsky 1982, 89.
26. 5.2.123 *ūrṇāyā yus* 'The *taddhita* suffix *yuS* occurs to denote the sense of *matUP* after syntactically related nominal stem *ūrṇā* "wool"'.
27. I agree with Cardona's explanation for this: 'Consider now 1.4.16. There are only four affixes marked with *S* in Pāṇini's grammar: *ghaS* (→ *iya* by 7.1.2) introduced by 5.1.106, *chaS* (→ *īya*, 7.1.2) by 4.2.114–5, *yaS* (*ya*) by 5.2.138, and *yuS* (→ *aka*, 7.1.1) by 5.2.123, 138, 140. For example, *ṛtviya-* "tempestivus" (<*ṛtu* "appropriate time, season") contains *ghaS*. All such affixes are *taddhita* (4.1.76: *taddhitāḥ*), included among the affixes referred to in 1.4.17-8, and all also begin with *y* or a vowel. Hence, items occurring before these are eligible for being *bha* by 1.4.18' (1970, 46). With the help of this information, we can infer that 1.4.18 is applicable wherever 1.4.16 is applicable, but 1.4.16 is not always applicable where 1.4.18 is. 1.4.16 is more specific than 1.4.18 and thus wins.
28. For example, consider Pbh 52 of the *Paribhāṣenduśekhara, antaraṅgān api vidhīn bahiraṅgo lug bādhate* (A *bahiraṅga* rule teaching *LUK* deletion defeats an *antaraṅga* rule [in case of conflict]), which is an exception of Pbh 50 *antaraṅge bahiraṅgam asiddham* (An *antaraṅga* rule treats a *bahiraṅga* rule as suspended).
29. 1.4.2 *vipratiṣedhe paraṁ kāryam*: 'The rule that comes later in the serial order of the *Aṣṭādhyāyī* wins the rule conflict between two equally powerful rules'.

30. Let us say that there is a conflict between rules A and B. A is called *nitya* with respect to B if A is applicable (both before and) after the application of B (cf. Pbh 117 *kṛtākṛtaprasaṅgī yo vidhiḥ sa nityaḥ, Vyāḍiparibhāṣāpāṭha*). B is called *anitya* with respect to A, if B is applicable before, but not after the application of A. The *nitya* rule A is stronger than and defeats the *anitya* rule B.
31. *Paribhāṣenduśekhara* describes *antaraṅga* as follows: *antarmadhye bahiraṅgaśāstrīyanimittasamudāyamadhye' ntarbhūtāny aṅgāni nimittāni yasya tad antaraṅgam.* Kielhorn translates it as follows: '*antaraṅga* is (a rule) the causes (of the application) of which lie within (or before) the sum of the causes of a *bahiraṅga* rule'. See Abhyankar's reprint (second edition) of Kielhorn's work (1960, 221–22).
32. An *apavāda* 'exception' is stronger than, and thus defeats, the *utsarga* 'general' rule in case of conflict.
33. The contents in brackets have been added by me.
34. Patañjali says that *para* may mean *iṣṭa* 'desirable' in his commentary on 1.4.1 (*iṣṭavācī paraśabdaḥ. vipratiṣedhe paraṁ yad iṣṭaṁ tad bhavati*; Mbh I.306.9–10). According to Bronkhorst, by *iṣṭa*, Patañjali means 'the rule that he thinks should be applied'. I disagree with Bronkhorst's interpretation. I think by *iṣṭa,* Patañjali means 'the rule that should be applied so as to get the correct final form'. This means that, in order to determine which rule is *iṣṭa*, one is required to know the final form. And to know the final form, one needs to look ahead into the derivation. So, in my opinion, this is an instance where Patañjali repudiates his linear reading of the *Aṣṭādhyāyī.*
35. A is *siddha* with respect to B if B recognizes the existence of A. Likewise, A is *asiddha* 'not *siddha*' with respect to B if B does not recognize the existence of A.
36. The contents in brackets have been added by me. Rule A bleeds rule B if B, which was applicable before the application of A, is no longer applicable after the application of A. A feeds B, if B, which was not applicable before the application of A, becomes applicable after the application of A.
37. Sometimes, though, the *apavāda* precedes the *utsarga* rule when the former constitutes an a priori exception.
38. A single replacement of the preceding and the following sounds is suspended (*asiddha*) with respect to rules teaching replacement with *ṣ* (*ṣatva*) and the introduction of augment *tUK.*
39. According to the *Kāśikā* and, broadly, the tradition, the scope of 6.4.22 continues up to the end of 6.4. I will discuss this in detail in chapter 6.
40. The contents in brackets have been added by me to clarify what the author means.
41. However, note that the positioning of rules teaching compounds in the *Aṣṭādhyāyī* poses a challenge to Roodbergen's proposition.
42. On this, Joshi makes an interesting remark: 'in his 1936 publication on Pāṇini's grammar (p. 26–27) B. Faddegon casually notes that P. 1.4.2 is a *paribhāṣā* and that it is valid up to the end of P. 2.2, as if there never had been any doubt. Compare further Cardona 1976, p. 190' (1998, 58).
43. Up to 2.2.38 *kaḍārāḥ karmadhāraye*, each item can take only one *saṁjñā.*
44. Up to 2.2.38 *kaḍārāḥ karmadhāraye*, the rule that comes later in the *Aṣṭādhyāyī*'s serial order prevails.
45. In the *Aṣṭādhyāyī*'s serial order, 1.2.64 *sarūpāṇām ekaśeṣa ekavibhaktau* comes before 1.4.1 *ā kaḍārād ekā saṁjñā.* So, one may wonder how Patañjali would be able to continue *ekā* from

1.4.1 into 1.2.64 by *anuvṛtti*. I want to clarify here that Patañjali is proposing to reorder the rules such that *ā kaḍārād ekā saṁjñā* comes before *sarūpāṇām ekaśeṣa ekavibhaktau*, so that he may be able to continue *ekā* from the former into the latter by *anuvṛtti*. I do not see how doing this would be justified or useful.

46. Note that there is no evidence that Kātyāyana was aware of these two versions. Vt. 2 *tatraikasaṁjñādikāre tadvacanaṁ* (Mbh I.296.15) has been written in context of the first *vārttika* and not in the context of these supposedly different versions of 1.4.1 (and 1.4.2). The first *vārttika* reads *anyatra saṁjñāsamāveśān niyamārthaṁ vacanam*, which means 'because names coapply elsewhere, the statement is for the sake of making a restriction' (Mbh I.296.3). And so, the second *vārttika* continues to discuss this topic, *tatraikasaṁjñādikāre tadvacanaṁ*: 'In that section where one name applies, the statement of that [must be made]'. As is peculiar of Patañjali, he skilfully weaves Kātyāyana's *vārttika*s into his own discourse. But it must be borne in mind that, as far as we know, the idea of two different versions of 1.4.1 (and 1.4.2) is Patañjali's alone.
47. The presence of the word *ca* in 1.4.2 *vipratiṣedhe ca* hints at the fact that some words would become *anuvṛtta* from 1.4.1 into 1.4.2.
48. While Joshi's overall view on this topic is very different from mine, he makes some observations that resonate with my findings: 'the tradition in general is wrong . . . in thinking that *apavādatva* cannot take care of the designations introduced in the *ekā saṁjñā* section' (1998, 45).
49. Besides, there are some cases that may appear to be conflicts between rules teaching *kāraka saṁjñā*s but that, according to me, are not conflicts at all. For example, whether one says *geham praviśati* (cf. 1.4.49 *kartur īpsitatamaṁ karma* → 2.3.2 *karmaṇi dvitīyā*) or *gehe praviśati* (cf. 1.4.45 *ādhāro'dhikaraṇam* → 2.3.36 *saptamy adhikaraṇe ca*) depends entirely on the nonlinguistic feature that the speaker wishes to express, that is, whether he or she wants to express *kartur īpsitatama* or *ādhāra*. So, this choice lies outside the domain of Pāṇini's *Aṣṭādhyāyī*. In conclusion, in my opinion, rule conflict does not arise between 1.4.45 and 1.4.49.
50. We shall look at limited blocking (Cardona) in chapter 4 and *siddha* principle (Joshi and Kiparsky) in chapter 5.

Chapter 2

1. Cardona does recognize this distinction: 'the general condition for *vipratiṣedha* is, as noted . . . that two rules tentatively apply to provide operations which cannot possibly take place concurrently. The two operations can involve (a) a single operand or (b) different operands' (1970, 48). But he does not develop this intuition, relying instead on the traditional approach to rule interaction.
2. Since our focus is not on this group, I have not listed certain rules in which we find compounds or secondary derivatives containing *para*. Examples include *parasmaipada*, *parokṣa*, *aparokṣa*, *parovara*, *parama*, and *paraspara*.
3. The original rule is *upasargād anotparaḥ*, but Patañjali has suggested that it should be read as *upasargād bahulam*. We find the latter version in many recensions.
4. See Appendix B for the list of *sūtras*.
5. Here, *uttara* is a synonym of *para*.
6. These are the traditional interpretations of these two rules. I discuss my interpretations of them towards the end of chapter 5.

7. While I will discuss this in detail in chapter 7, I must mention here that Kātyāyana mentions that *para* in 1.4.2 could mean 'RHS' in vt. 12 on 6.1.158 *anudāttaṁ padam ekavarjam.* He says: *śāstraparavipratiṣedhāniyamād vā śabdaparavipratiṣedhāt siddham* '[in the event of *vipratiṣedha* between two operations] because it has not been [explicitly] mandated that *paratva* of rules [alone should be used to resolve] *vipratiṣedha*, alternatively *paratva* of sounds [may also be used to] accomplish [the task of resolving] *vipratiṣedha*' (Mbh III.100.12).
8. 5.3.10 *saptamyās tral.*
9. *Pūrvatra* stands for 'with respect to a rule which comes earlier in the *Aṣṭādhyāyī*'s serial order'.
10. When I make the distinction between Pāṇinian and post-Pāṇinian approaches in the following pages, it must be understood that by Pāṇinian approach, I mean my interpretation of the Pāṇinian approach.
11. So, going by the definition of blocking, Y does not block X.
12. In the previous chapter, I have discussed the hierarchy of these rules (Pbh 38 of the *Paribhāṣenduśekhara*), so I do not discuss it here again. This hierarchy is not of much consequence, practically speaking.
13. 7.3.111 *gher ṅiti.*
14. 7.2.115 *aco ñṇiti.*
15. 7.3.119 *ac ca gheḥ.*
16. 7.1.95 *tr̥jvat kroṣṭuḥ.*
17. 7.1.54 *hrasvanadyāpo nuṭ.*
18. 7.1.73 *iko'ci vibhaktau.*
19. 7.2.100 *aci ra r̥taḥ.*
20. 7.1.95 *tr̥jvat kroṣṭuḥ.*
21. *niravakāśā hi vidhayaḥ sāvakāśān vidhīn bādhante* '*niravakāśa* operations defeat *sāvakāśa* operations' (Pbh 11 of *Vyāḍiparibhāṣāpāṭha*).
22. Note that examples from nominal inflection are simpler than those from verbal inflection. One of the many reasons behind this is that, while nominal inflection involves only two items, that is, a base and affix, verbal inflection generally involves at least three items, that is, a base followed by two affixes. We will look at examples from verbal inflections as well as primary and secondary derivatives in the following chapters.
23. *n* > *ṇ*, by 8.4.2 *aṭkupvāṅnumvyavāye'pi.*
24. In my doctoral thesis, I had argued that the SSRI between 6.1.77 and 7.1.73 could be treated as a case of DOI. This is because I had wrongly assumed that the use of *para* in 1.1.47 *mid aco 'ntyāt paraḥ* implies that we could use 1.4.2 *vipratiṣedhe paraṁ kāryam* to deal with such cases of SSRI. In other words, I had assumed this is a case of DOI. However, since augments become part of the item to which they are attached, cases of SSRI between an augmentation rule (be it a *Ṭ*-marked, *K*-marked, or *M*-marked augment) and any other rule should be treated as SOI if the two rules share a common operand. Thus, I have concluded that the SSRI between 6.1.77 and 7.1.73 is a case of SOI. I have followed this principle throughout this book.
25. Note that this is one of the rare cases in which even if we had applied another rule, namely 7.1.73, we would still have got the correct form.
26. *n* > *ṇ*, by 8.4.2 *aṭkupvāṅnumvyavāye'pi.*
27. *n* > *ṇ*, by 8.4.2 *aṭkupvāṅnumvyavāye'pi.*

28. Note that both augments, that is, *nUM* and *nUṬ*, essentially refer to the same sound *n*. However, if we applied the rule prescribing *nUM*, we would get *vārin* + *ām* (1.1.47 *mid aco'ntyāt paraḥ*). In such a situation, we would not be able to elongate the *ī* of *vārin* because 6.4.3 *nāmi* would not apply here.
29. Note that this is not actually an operational rule but an *atideśa sūtra* or extension rule. For the sake of studying conflict, we may treat it as an operational rule that teaches that the *u* of *kroṣṭu* changes to *ṛ*.
30. This is discussed in *Pradīpa* on vt. 11, 7.1.96.
31. Note that 7.2.102 is not applicable at this point, thanks to 1.1.63 *na lumatāṅgasya.*
32. Affixes *sU* and *am* occurring after a neuter base ending in *a* are replaced with *am.*
33. 8.2.7 is *asiddha* with respect to 6.4.8 and 6.1.68, so it cannot be applied before them.
34. The augment *nUṬ* is added at the beginning of *ām* by 1.1.46 *ādyantau ṭakitau.*
35. The *ṛ* of *tisṛ* does not undergo elongation by 6.4.3 *nāmi* because this is prohibited by the following rule 6.4.4 *na tisṛcatasṛ*. The *n* of *nām* becomes *ṇ* in *tisṛṇām.* There is no rule in the *Aṣṭādhyāyī* that explicitly teaches this. However, there is a *vārttika* on 8.4.1 *raṣābhyāṁ no ṇaḥ samānapade* that correctly teaches this operation: *raṣābhyāṁ ṇatvam ṛkāragrahaṇam* 'it should be added that [not only] after *r* and *ṣ*, [but after] *ṛ* [too], [*n* is replaced with] *ṇ*' (Mbh III.452.1–6).
36. The tradition translates *maparyantasya* as 'up to *m*', but I think that Pāṇini means 'up to *ma*'. Both interpretations lead to correct answers for all forms of *yuṣmad-asmad.* My interpretation makes derivations simpler and shorter.
37. Given that *sU* has been replaced with *am*, how will 7.2.94 apply at the following step? This is because, by 1.1.56 *sthānivadādeśo'nalvidhau, am* is treated like *sU.* How do we know this is not an *aL-vidhi*? *asma* and *am* are not adjacent to each other (*d* sits in the middle of the two), and so this is not an *aL* operation.
38. Note that, here, the affix *sU* has undergone *ādeśa* 'substitution' with *am.* So, 7.2.86, which can only apply to *asmad* when followed by a nonsubstituted and consonant initial affix and which was applicable in the previous step is no longer applicable at this step. Instead of that rule, 7.2.90 has become applicable.
39. An *a* that is not at the end of a *pada* and the *guṇa* vowel following it are both replaced with the latter.
40. Note that both 6.1.87 and 6.1.88 belong to the *ekādeśa-adhikāra*, that is, the section headed by the *sūtra* 6.1.84 *ekaḥ pūrvaparayoḥ*, which teaches that both the LHS and the RHS item are replaced with a single substitute.
41. Another way of comparing the two rules is to simply compare the RHS item of each. For example, for 6.1.77, the RHS item is *aC* (any vowel), while for 6.1.101, it is specifically a *savarṇa* sound. This leads us to the correct conclusion that 6.1.101 is more specific than 6.1.77.
42. The base *eka* is listed in the *sarvādigaṇa*, referred to in 1.1.27 *sarvādīni sarvanāmāni.*
43. See Staal's *A Reader on the Sanskrit Grammarians* (1972, 115).

Chapter 3

1. I use the plus (+) sign between a base and an affix. Since *ac* is not an affix with respect to *prati*, I put a minus sign (–) instead of a plus (+) between *prati* and *ac.*
2. Among other things, this rule teaches that *KvIN* occurs after the root *añcU* 'to bend' when this root co-occurs with a *pada* ending in *sUP.*

3. *LOPA* replaces the penultimate *n* of a verbal base ending in a consonant and not marked with *I* (in the *Dhātupāṭha*) when an affix marked with *K* or *Ṅ* follows.
4. Affix *vI* unaccompanied [by any other sound] is replaced with *LOPA*.
5. We know this because of a *paribhāṣā* it mentions, which I will discuss below.
6. Another version of this, which we occasionally find in *paribhāṣā* texts, is *nimittāpāye naimittikasyāpy apāyaḥ*.
7. SK 417 (6.3.138 *cau*).
8. This rule teaches all the declensional affixes. The affix that is applicable here is the genitive singular *Ṅas*.
9. We know this because of the use of the *paribhāṣā*, *akṛtavyūhāḥ pāṇinīyāḥ* on SK 435 (6.4.131 *vasoḥ samprasāraṇam*). I will discuss this later in the example.
10. The affix *LIṬ* is optionally replaced with *KvasU* in classical Sanskrit after the roots *sadA* 'to sit', *vasA* 'to inhabit', and *śru* 'to listen' when the action has taken place in the past.
11. An *a*, which occurs in between two single consonants of a verbal base whose initial sound has not undergone replacement, is replaced with *e*, when a *LIṬ* affix marked with *K* or *Ṅ* follows. In such cases, the *abhyāsa* (i.e., the first of the two reduplicated syllables) is also deleted.
12. I interpret this rule differently. I will discuss my interpretation later in this example.
13 Note that the whole base does not undergo reduplication. Instead, only one syllable does. See 6.1.1 *ekāco dve prathamasya* and 6.1.2 *ajāder dvitīyasya*.
14. The tradition interprets this rule as follows: augment *iṬ* is introduced to *vasU* when it occurs after a root that, *after doubling*, either consists of a single syllable, or ends in *a*, or else, is constituted by *ghas* 'to eat'. Note that Pāṇini does not say 'after doubling' anywhere in his rule, and 'after doubling' cannot be inferred by *anuvṛtti* either. The tradition takes the liberty to read this phrase into this rule purely on the basis of certain derivational considerations. I do not think we should make such assumptions, and therefore I do not include 'after doubling' in my interpretation.
15. 1.2.46 *kṛttaddhitasamāsāś ca.*
16. 1.4.18 *yaci bham.*
17. I give a reference later in the example.
18. The *taddhita* affix *yaÑ* is added to the syntactically related genitive form of any base included in the list starting with *garga* to construct a form that means *gotra*-descendant of that individual.
19. A *suP* undergoes *LUK* deletion when it occurs inside a *dhātu* 'verbal base' or a *prātipadika* 'nominal base'.
20. The *a*, *i*, or *u* at the end of the base and the following vowel, which constitutes the first sound of nominative and accusative affixes, are together replaced with the long equivalent of the former.
21. I give a reference later in the example.
22. Note that, in all the derivations that I have performed using my method in this chapter, I apply 2.4.71 *supo dhātuprātipadikayoḥ* before actually starting the derivation. I do this to avoid making the derivations unnecessarily lengthy and to avoid monotony. I take this liberty because the correctness of the form we get at the end of the derivation does not depend on the step at which we apply 2.4.71. Ideally, one should apply this rule only when it ought to be applied.

23. 4.1.83 *prāg dīvyato'ṇ*–4.4.2 *tena dīvyati khanati jayati jitam.*
24. He focuses on the question: should the *ya* of *gārgya* be deleted by 2.4.64 *yañañoś ca* before a plural declensional affix is introduced to the derivation? I think this question is invalid because, in my view, 2.4.64 should only apply to a base when a plural affix is present.
25. Note that our sentence is *adya puṣyaḥ* wherein the time mentioned is *adya*, which is not specific (unlike for example, *rātri*, which is specific); thus 4.2.4 is applicable here.
26. A form is termed *pada* when a *svādi* (affixes enumerated under 4.1.2 *svaujas...* through 5.4.151 *uraḥ prabhṛtibhyaḥ kap*) affix that is not a *sarvanāmasthāna* (*sU, au, Jas, am, auṬ*; see 4.1.2 *svaujas...*) follows.
27. For a detailed study, see Deo (2007).

Chapter 4

1. Affix *LAṬ* occurs after a verbal root when the action is denoted at the current time (*vartamāna*).
2. *Tip-tas-jhi-sip-thas-tha-mib-vas-mas-ta-ātāṁ-jha-thās-āthāṁ-dhvam-iḍ-vahi-mahiṅ.*
3. Though the tradition does not explicitly state this, it becomes clear from the derivations we will examine below that such is indeed the case.
4. Affix *ŚaP* occurs after a verbal root when a *sārvadhātuka* affix, which denotes *kartṛ* 'agent', follows.
5. *Guṇa* replaces the *iK* of a verbal base, which ends in the augment *pUK* or which has a *laghu* 'light' vowel as its penultimate sound, when a *sārvadhātuka* or *ārdhadhātuka* affix follows.
6. I must clarify that, in my view, the modified version of an *aṅga* can, too, be called an *aṅga*, thanks to 1.1.56 *sthānivad ādeśo'nalvidhau*, which teaches that the substitute is treated like the substituendum, except when an operation relative to the original sound is to be performed. So, for example, in *deva* + *bhyām*, *deva* is an *aṅga* with respect to *bhyām*. By applying 7.3.102 *supi ca*, we get *devā* + *bhyām*. *devā* too can be called an *aṅga* with respect to *bhyām* by 1.1.56 *sthānivad ādeśo'nalvidhau.*
7. See section 5.4 or chapter 5 for the continuation of this discussion.
8. Unless I explicitly state that the form being derived is passive, it must be assumed that it is active.
9. 1.1.64 *aco'ntyādi ṭi.*
10. When a short *a* that is not *pada*-final (word-final) is followed by a *guṇa* vowel, that is, *a*, *e*, or *o*, then both *a* and the following *guṇa* are replaced with the latter.
11. When the affix *ŚaP* is preceded by any verbal root belonging to the list headed by *hu* 'to perform sacrifice', it is replaced with *ŚLU* (cf. 1.1.61 *pratyayasya lukślulupaḥ*).
12. A verbal base that has not already undergone reduplication undergoes reduplication when it is followed by *ŚLU.* (Note that the whole base does not undergo reduplication. Instead, only one syllable does. See 6.1.1 *ekāco dve prathamasya* and 6.1.2 *ajāder dvitīyasya*. Unless necessary, I will not repeat this clarification in this chapter.)
13. The vowel of the *abhyāsa* 'first of two reduplicated syllables' is replaced with its short counterpart.
14. 8.2.1 *pūrvatrāsiddham* teaches that from this rule onwards, a following rule is *asiddha* 'suspended' with respect to a preceding rule. So, if 8.4.54 and any rule that precedes it in the *Aṣṭādhyāyī*'s serial order are simultaneously applicable, then the latter will not acknowledge 8.4.54 and will thus apply at that step. 8.4.54 can apply only after this. I will demonstrate this more elaborately in chapter 6, which is devoted to the concepts *asiddha* and *asiddhavat*.

15. *Paribhāṣās* 62 and 63 are found mentioned together on numerous occasions in the *Mahābhāṣya* (see Bronkhorst 2004, 18).
16. A *siP* replacement of *LOṬ* is replaced with *hi* and is treated as if not marked with *P*.
17. The *tas, thas, tha,* and *miP* replacements for any *lakāra* marked with *Ṅ* are replaced with *tām, tam, ta,* and *am*, respectively.
18. Note that I will use the word *implement* henceforth in relation with optionality.
19. Note that this rule is applicable because *ta*, by virtue of being an *apit sārvadhātuka*, can be treated as marked with *K*, by 1.2.4 *sārvadhātukam apit*.
20. A *samprasāraṇa* vowel and the following vowel are together replaced with the former.
21. A single *vr̥ddhi* vowel replaces both *āṬ* and the vowel following it.
22. *Iha aijyata, aupyata, auhyata iti laṅi kr̥te lāvasthāyām aḍāgamād antaraṅgatvāl lādeśaḥ kriyate, tatra kr̥te vikaraṇo nityatvād aḍāgamaṁ bādhate*: 'Here [with reference to the derivation of the forms] *aijyata, aupyata, auhyata*, after the addition of the affix *LAṄ*, in that state of the *lakāra*, by *antaraṅgatva*, the substitution of the *lakāra* is done [rather than] the addition of the augment *aṬ*, and thereafter, by *nityatva*, the [addition of] *vikaraṇa* defeats [the insertion of] augment *aṬ*.'
23. I have included the *kr̥danta* derivation *sad* + *KvasU* + *Ṅas* in the previous chapter because there nominal inflection plays a crucial role in helping us obtain the correct form.
24. *Guṇa* replaces the final sound *iK* (*i, u, r̥, l̥*) of a verbal base when a *sārvadhātuka* or *ārdhadhātuka* affix follows.
25. Affix *ŚaP* occurs after a verbal root when a *sārvadhātuka* affix that denotes *kartr̥* 'agent' follows.
26. Affix *ŚaP* is replaced with *LUK* when it occurs after one of the roots headed by *adA* 'to eat' in the *Dhātupāṭha*.
27. The penultimate sound of *gam* 'to go', *han* 'to kill', *jan* 'to be born', *khan* 'to dig', and *ghas* 'to eat' is replaced with *LOPA* when an affix beginning with a vowel and marked with *K* or *Ṅ*, except *aṄ*, follows.
28. The *h* of *han* 'to harm, kill' is replaced with a velar stop when an affix marked with *Ñ* and *Ṇ*, or simply *n* (i.e., after *LOPA* of *a*) follows.
29. The tradition too takes cognizance of this. Vyāḍi suggests that an operation involving the *upasarga* and the verbal base is *antaraṅga*: *dhātūpasargayor antaraṅgaṁ kāryam bhavati* (Pbh 37 of *Paribhāṣāsūcanam*). We know that an *antaraṅga* operation gets precedence over a *bahiraṅga* operation.
30. The final nasal of a root marked with *anudātta* when taught in the *Dhātupāṭha* (cf. *upadeśe*), as well as of *vanA* 'to like' and the roots headed by *tanU* 'to extend', is optionally replaced with *LOPA* before the substitute *LyaP*.
31. Augment *tUK* is attached to a root ending in a short vowel when a *kr̥t* affix marked with *P* follows.
32. Affix *ŚaP* is replaced with *LUK* when it occurs after one of the roots headed by *adA* 'to eat' in the *Dhātupāṭha*.
33. *hi* is an *apit* (cf. 3.4.87 *ser hy apic ca*) *sārvadhātuka*, and so by 1.2.4 *sārvadhātukam apit*, it can be treated as marked with *K* or *Ṅ*. Thus, 6.4.34 is applicable here.
34. For a discussion on how this rule should be interpreted using Pāṇini's metarules, see section 5.9 of chapter 5.
35. The operand of 6.4.34 is a part of the operand of 6.4.35, and so, like in the previous chapters, here too we classify such interactions as Type 1 (SOI).

36. Note that 6.4.35 is *asiddhavat* with respect to 6.4.34, but in my view, this does not affect the way in which we deal with SOI. I will discuss this further in chapter 6.
37. Since *hi* is an *apit sārvadhātuka*, it can be treated as marked with *K* by 1.2.4 *sārvadhātukam apit*. Thus, 6.4.37 is applicable.
38. As pointed out by Kiparsky, Cardona means the exact opposite, that is, '7.3.84 will counter 7.1.100'.

Chapter 5

1. In my doctoral thesis, I had included another example under this section, namely the derivation of *kālimmanyā*, which I thought involved DOI. However, I no longer believe that it is a case of DOI. For more, please see note 24 of chapter 2 where I discuss whether SSRI between rules teaching *M*-marked augments and other rules should be treated as SOI or DOI.
2. This example has been given in the *Kāśikā* on 7.1.53. Another example is: *mahi trīṇām avo'stu dyukṣam mitrasyāryamṇaḥ* (*Maṇḍala* 10, *Sūkta* 185, *Ṛk* 1).
3. Observe its similarity with *trayaḥ*, the nominative plural form of *tri* (masculine). It is likely that the presence of *traya* here rubbed off on the genitive plural.
4. When a short *a*, that is not *pada*-final (word-final) is followed by a *guṇa* vowel, that is, *a, e,* or *o*, then both *a* and the following *guṇa* are replaced with the latter.
5. The consonant of the vocative singular affix *sU* is elided after a nominal-stem ending in *e, o,* or a short vowel.
6. *v* and *y* are replaced with *LOPA* when followed by any consonant except *y*.
7. Affix *vI* unaccompanied (by any other sound) is replaced with *LOPA*.
8. *jarā* can optionally be replaced with *jaras* before a vowel-initial inflectional affix.
9. For the exact meanings of these rules and a detailed discussion on them, see section 5.9 of chapter 5.
10. Please refer to Thieme (1935) and Bronkhorst (1991) for more on this topic.
11. In fact, it is in this context that Kātyāyana hints at the meaning of 1.4.2 that I support (i.e., *śabdaparatva*, as opposed to *sūtraparatva*). See section 7.1 of chapter 7 for more.
12. Affix *Śnā* occurs after verbal roots belonging to the class headed by *ḌUkrīÑ* 'to buy, barter' when a *sārvadhātuka* affix that denotes *kartṛ* follows.
13. Before an affix marked with *Ś*, *jñā* and *jan* are replaced with *jā*'.
14. Note that we can treat *tas* as being marked with *K* or *Ṅ* thanks to 1.2.4 *sārvadhātukam apit*.
15. The substitute should be treated like the substituendum except in the case of *al-vidhi*, that is, when an operation relative to the original sound is to be performed.
16. See Pbh 50 in Abhyankar's reprint (1960, 221–22) of Kielhorn's translation of the *Paribhāṣendušekhara*.
17. The Sanskrit text is as follows: *antarmadhye bahiraṅgaśāstrīyanimittasamudāyamadhye 'ntarbhūtāny aṅgāni nimittāni yasya tad antaraṅgam. evaṁ tadīyanimittasamudāyād bahirbhūtāṅgakaṁ bahiraṅgam.* See the first two lines under Pbh 50 in *Paribhāṣenduśekhara* edited by Abhyankar (1962, 76).
18. *Antaraṅgabahiraṅgayor antaraṅgo vidhir balīyān* (Pbh 115, *Vyāḍiparibhāṣāpāṭha*).
19. The specific *Uṇādisūtra* teaching this is 289 *siveṣ ṭer yū ca*.
20. The final *i* or *a* of a *bha* item is replaced with *LOPA* when it is followed by *ī* or a *taddhita* affix.
21. Note that I have not added the nominative singular affix here for the purpose of brevity.

22. If we interpret *sanyaṅoḥ* as locative, as I think Patañjali does in this case, then this rule teaches that a verbal base that has not undergone reduplication is reduplicated when followed by *saN* or *yaṄ*. Note that the whole base does not undergo reduplication; instead, only one syllable does. See 6.1.1 *ekāco dve prathamasya* and 6.1.2 *ajāder dvitīyasya.*
23 If we interpret it as a locative, it is not possible to derive the form *aṭiṭiṣati* (Cardona 1997, xviii). Thus, we must interpret it as a genitive.
24. The whole base does not undergo reduplication; instead, only one syllable does. See 6.1.1 *ekāco dve prathamasya* and 6.1.2 *ajāder dvitīyasya.*
25. Here, the following operations take place: *ayaje indram* → *ayajay indram* (6.1.78 *eco'yavāyāvaḥ*) → *ayaja indram* (8.3.19 *lopaḥ śākalyasya*).
26. When A is suspended with respect to B, B cannot acknowledge A.
27. The *vārttika* (Mbh III.65.9) has the word *ṣatvatukor* in it, but when Kiparsky quotes the *vārttika*, he excludes this word from it.
28. The affix *Ṅe*, when occurring after a base ending in *a*, is replaced with *ya*.
29. The *a* at the end of a nominal base is replaced with its long equivalent when followed by a declensional affix starting with *yaÑ* (*y, v, r l, jh, bh*, or any nasal).
30. The affixes *Ṭā, ṄasI*, and *Ṅas*, when occurring after a base ending in *a*, are replaced with *ina, āt* and *sya* respectively.
31. The *a* at the end of a nominal base is replaced with its long equivalent when a *yaÑ*-initial declensional affix follows.
32. The *a* at the end of a nominal base is replaced with *e* when a plural declensional affix starting with *jhaL* (a non-nasal stop or a fricative) follows.
33. *Vṛddhi* (*ā, ai, au*) replaces both *a* and the *eC* vowel (*e, o, ai, au*) immediately following it.
34. The full *sūtra* reads: *tip-tas-jhi-sip-thas-tha-mip-vas-mas-t*(*a*)*-ātām-jha-thās-āthām-dhvam-iḍ-vahi-mahiṅ.*
35 *Alo'ntyasya ity asyāpavādaḥ* (SK on 1.1.54).
36. *Alo'ntyasūtrāpavādaḥ* (SK on 1.1.55).
37. *Sarvasya ity asyāpavādaḥ* (SK on 1.1.53).
38. *Aṣṭābhya auś* (7.1.21) *ityādau deḥ parasya ity etad api paratvād anena bādhyate* (SK on 1.1.55).
39. *Tātaṅi ṅitkaraṇasya sāvakāśatvād vipratiṣedhāt sarvādeśaḥ* (1) 'Because the *Ṅ* of *tātAṄ* is *sāvakāśa* 'useful elsewhere' [we can infer that] there is a *vipratiṣedha* 'conflict' (between 1.1.55 *anekālśit sarvasya* and 1.1.53 *ṅic ca*) [and thus, the *para* rule, which teaches] *sarvādeśa*, [wins]' (Mbh I.131.1).
40. *Kāśikā* on 1.1.66: *tasminn iti saptamyarthanirdeśe pūrvasyaiva kāryaṁ bhavati nottarasya.*
41. *Kāśikā* on 1.1.67: *tasmād iti pañcamyarthanirdeśa uttarasyaiva kāryaṁ bhavati na pūrvasya.*
42. Note that I have not mentioned instances of DOI and SOI at different steps of this derivation, since our focus is on the competition between *paribhāṣā* rules. Nonetheless, I follow my method of dealing with SOI and DOI in this derivation.
43. On 1.1.46, the *Kāśikā* says: *ādiḥ ṭit bhavati antaḥ kit bhavati ṣaṣṭhīnirdiṣṭasya.*

Chapter 6

1. When A is suspended with respect to B, B cannot acknowledge A.
2. *ṣatve tuki ca kartavye ekādeśo'siddho bhavati, siddhakāryaṁ na karoti ity arthaḥ.*
3. *ṣatve tuki ca kartavye ekādeśaśāstram asiddhaṁ syāt.*

4. In his commentary on 8.2.1, Rama Nath Sharma (2003, vol. 6, 476) says, 'the *asiddhatva* of 8.2.1 *pūrvatrāsiddham* is thus accepted as suspension of rules (*sāstrāsiddhatva*). *Nava-Vaiyākaraṇas* such as Nāgeśa and Bhaṭṭojī Dīkṣita accept this view. Earlier grammarians, which also includes authors of the *Kāśikāvṛtti*, accept the *kāryāsiddhatva* view'.
5. There is some controversy about the meaning of *ā bhāt*. We will examine this topic later in this chapter.
6. *Kāśikā*'s interpretation alludes to the rules that are *asiddhavat* but does not mention the rules with respect to which these rules are *asiddhavat*. We are left to answer the 'with respect to what?' question on our own.
7. *atreti samānāśrayatvapratipattyartham.*
8. Explaining why *asiddhavat* is not applicable in a certain context, Kātyāyana says (vt. 12) *samānāśrayavacanāt siddham* '[despite being placed in the section headed by 6.4.22] it (i.e., this rule) is *siddha* [and not *asiddhavat*] because [*asiddhavat* has been taught only in regard with] *samānāśrayatva*, [and here the *samānāśrayatva* condition has not been met]' (Mbh III.190.22).
9. See Vt. 2 *atragrahaṇam viṣayārtham* (Mbh III.187.11) and Patañjali's commentary on it.
10. For example, consider the form *rāga* 'colour', which is derived from the root *rañjI* 'to colour'. The derivation proceeds as follows: *rañj* + *GHaÑ* (3.3.18 *bhāve*) → *raj* + *a* (6.4.27 *ghañi ca bhāvakaraṇayoḥ*) → *rāj* + *a* (7.2.116 *ata upadhāyāḥ*) → *rāga* (7.3.52 *cajoḥ ku ghiṇṇyatoḥ*). Here, if 6.4.27 is *asiddhavat* with respect to 7.2.116, then 7.2.116 will not apply after the application of 6.4.27.
11. On vt. 2, Patañjali says: *viṣayaḥ pratinirdiśyate. atraitasminn ābhāc chāstra ā bhāc chāstram asiddhaṁ yathā syāt. iha mā bhūt. abhāji rāgaḥ upabarhaṇam iti.*
12. *yad ita ūrdhvam anukramiṣyāmaḥ ā adhyāyaparisamāpteḥ tad asiddhavat bhavati ity evaṁ veditavyam* (*Kāśikā* on 6.4.22).
13. The *Nyāsa* on 8.2.1 too says so: *śāstrasyāsiddhau ca kṛtāyām arthataḥ kāryāsiddhatvaṁ kṛtam eva bhavati tasya tannibandhanatvāt.*
14. Note that if we had started the derivation with *adhi* + *itvā*, the derivation would have proceeded as follows. Two rules are applicable here, namely 6.1.101 *akaḥ savarṇe dīrghaḥ* and 7.1.37 *samāse'nañpūrve ktvo lyap*. This is a case of DOI. By 1.4.2, the RHS rule wins, and we get *adhi* + *iya*. Here, two rules are applicable: 6.1.101 and 6.1.71 *hrasvasya piti kṛti tuk*. This is a case of SOI. 6.1.71 is more specific and thus wins. This gives us *adhi* + *itya*. Now 6.1.101 applies, giving the correct form *adhītya*. Notice that, if we start the derivation with *adhi* + *itvā*, we get the correct form without applying 6.1.86. But the fact that Pāṇini composed 6.1.86 confirms the fact that the derivation of this compound begins with *adhī* + *tvā* and not with *adhi* + *itvā*, even though the compound itself is being formed from *adhi* and *itvā* by 2.2.18 *kugatiprādayaḥ*. I have discussed this in some detail in example 5 of section 4.3, chapter 4.
15. The *s* at the end of a *pada* and the final *s* of *sajus* 'companion, together with' are replaced with *rU*.
16. An *uT* replaces a *rU* when it is both preceded and followed by a non-*pluta a*.
17. *Yadi rutvam asiddhaṁ syāt tadā sthānitvena ror āśrayaṇam anarthakaṁ syāt. kasyacid ukārānubandhaviśiṣṭasya ror asambhavāt.*
18. However, I must admit that there exist other cases of this kind that remain intractable or unexplainable. For example, see example 15 of section 4.3, chapter 4, where 6.1.101 applies after the application of 8.2.28.

19. Technically, there is a rule more specific than 8.2.1 *pūrvatrāsiddham* that teaches this *asiddhatva*. This rule is 8.2.2 *nalopaḥ supsvarasaṁjñātugvidhiṣu kr̥ti*, which teaches that the rule teaching *n*-deletion is suspended with respect to rules pertaining to declension (*suP*), accent (*svara*), technical designations (*saṁjñā*) and introduction of augment *tUK* before a *kr̥t* affix. 8.2.2 is a *niyama sūtra*, which allows *n*-deletion to be *asiddha* only in the aforementioned circumstances.
20. *Ais* replaces *bhis* when *bhis* occurs after an *a*-final base.
21. The *a* at the end of a nominal base is replaced with its long equivalent when followed by a declensional affix starting with *yaÑ* (i.e., *y, v, r l, jh, bh*, or any nasal).
22. The *a* at the end of a nominal base is replaced with *e* when followed by a plural declensional affix starting with *jhaL* (a non-nasal stop or a fricative).
23. An e*C* (*e, o, ai, au*) is replaced with *ay, av, āy, āv*, respectively, when a vowel follows.
24. A *pada*-final *v* or *y* that occurs after *a* or *ā* is, in the opinion of Śākalya, replaced with *LOPA* when *aŚ* (any voiced sound) follows.
25. 1.1.26 *ktaktavatū niṣṭhā.*
26. Even though the traditional understanding of *vipratiṣedha* is different from mine, it must be mentioned here that, in his first *vārttika* on 8.2.1, Kātyāyana says: *pūrvatrāsiddhe nāsti vipratiṣedho'bhāvād uttarasya* 'in the section headed by 8.2.1, *vipratiṣedha* does not arise because of the absence [i.e., suspension] of the rule which comes later in the *Aṣṭādhyāyī*'s serial order' (Mbh III.385.14).
27. *dah* + *tum* → *daḍh* + *tum* (8.2.31) → *daḍh* + *dhum* (8.2.40 *jhaṣas tathor dho'dhaḥ*) → *daḍh* + *ḍhum* (8.4.41 *ṣṭunā ṣṭuḥ*) → *da* + *ḍhum* (8.3.13 *ḍho ḍhe lopaḥ*) → **dāḍhum* (6.3.111 *ḍhralope pūrvasya dīrgho'ṇaḥ*).
28. The *taddhita* affix *vatI* occurs to denote the sense of *tulya* 'similar to, comparable with' after a syntactically related nominal stem ending in *tr̥tīyā* 'instrumental', provided what is *tulya* is also *kriyā* 'action'.
29. Cardona (1997, 425) too holds this opinion: 'I differ from Pāṇinīyas in my interpretation of 6.4.22 [*asiddhavad atrābhāt*]. Pāṇinīyas maintain that this too should be considered to provide for rule suspension (*śāstrāsiddhatvam*), not the suspension of what results from applying rules (*kāryāsiddhatvam*)'.
30. We have performed an almost identical derivation in chapter 4 (see example 9, section 4.3). There, we replaced *hi* with *tātAṄ*, by the optional rule 7.1.35 *tuhyos tātaṅ āśiṣy anyatarasyām.* Here, however, we will not apply 7.1.35.
31. Since *hi* is a *sārvadhātuka* that is not marked with *P*, we can say that it is marked with *K* by 1.2.4 *sārvadhātukam apit*. Thus, 6.4.37 is applicable.
32. Note that the whole base does not undergo reduplication; instead, only one syllable does. See 6.1.1 *ekāco dve prathamasya* and 6.1.2 *ajāder dvitīyasya.*
33. We have performed this derivation in chapter 4. See derivation 8 of section 4.3. There, we replaced *hi* with *tātAṄ*, by the optional rule 7.1.35 *tuhyos tātaṅ āśiṣy anyatarasyām.* Here, however, we will not do so.
34. Affix *ŚaP* is replaced with *LUK* when it occurs after roots belonging to the set headed by *adA* 'to eat' (second class).
35. *hi* is an *apit* (cf. 3.4.87 *ser hy apic ca*) *sārvadhātuka*, and so by 1.2.4 *sārvadhātukam apit*, we can say that it is marked with *K* or *Ṅ*. Thus, 6.4.34 is applicable here.
36. In contrast with other derivations, where, for brevity's sake, I start the derivation directly

with the substitute of the *lakāra*, here I have started this unconventional derivation with *LIṬ* for the sake of clarity.

37. Note that the whole base does not undergo reduplication; instead, only one syllable does. See 6.1.1 *ekāco dve prathamasya* and 6.1.2 *ajāder dvitīyasya*.
38. This is applicable because *KvasU* is a *kṛt* affix (cf. 1.2.46 *kṛttaddhitasamāsāś ca*).
39. Note that the *Mahābhāṣya* discusses two possible interpretations of 1.1.59. I have mentioned the one accepted by the *Kāśikā*. I think this is the correct interpretation. The *Kaumudī* accepts the other interpretation, which I think is incorrect. I will not discuss the same here because it is not directly related to the topic of *asiddhavat*.
40. The vowel of the *abhyāsa* 'first of two reduplicated syllables' is replaced with its short counterpart.
41. 8.3.59 *ādeśapratyayoḥ*.
42. On vt. 12 *samānāśrayatvāt siddham*, Patañjali says, *samānāśrayam asiddhaṁ bhavati vyāśrayaṁ caitat*.
43. See *Ṛgveda* 5.41.1 for the context of the phrase *paśuṣo na vājān*.
44. The derivation of *preyān* discussed under vt. 16 on 6.4.22 *ā bhād iti ced vasusamprasāraṇay alopaprasthādīnāṁ pratiṣedhaḥ* (Mbh III.193.17) also involves the same problem. Extending the jurisdiction of 6.4.22 all the way up to the end of 6.4 produces undesirable results, to deal with which Kātyāyana has composed vt. 16.
45. 3.1.26 *hetumati ca*.
46. '*Lyapi laghupūrvāt* originally was *lyapi laghupūrvasya*. The substitution of the Ablative for the Genitive case has been suggested by Kātyāyana (Vol. III. p. 204)'. See Kielhorn (1887, 178–84), reprinted in Staal's *A Reader on the Sanskrit Grammarians* (1972, 121). The original version, *lyapi laghupūrvasya*, teaches that '*Ṇi*, when preceded by a light vowel, is replaced with *ay*, provided the *ārdhadhātuka* affix *LyaP* follows'. In *praśam* + *ṆiC* + *LyaP*, even though there is a light vowel (*a* of *śam*) to the left of *Ṇi*, note that *Ṇi* is not immediately preceded by *a* (there is *m* between *a* and *Ṇi*). To lend greater clarity to this rule, Kātyāyana decided to edit it (vt. 1: *lyapi laghupūrvasyeti ced vyañjanānteṣūpasaṁkhyānam*; vt. 3: *lyapi laghupūrvād iti vacanāt siddham*). Since we are discussing an example based on Kātyāyana's *vārttika* 13 on 6.4.22 here, I have presented his version in the main text, rather than the original one.

Chapter 7

1. Some of these findings have already been published in the following papers: Rajpopat (2023) and Rajpopat (2024).
2. Note that this *vārttika* makes an incorrect statement. There is no conflict at all here: *yaK* is added to verbal roots followed by *sārvadhātuka* affixes denoting *bhāva* 'action' or *karman* 'object', whereas *ŚaP* is added when the *sārvadhātuka* affix denotes *kartṛ* 'agent'. In fact, we come across many such errors in Kātyāyana's *vārttika*s.
3. Here, Nāgeśa, in his *Uddyota*, refers to another discussion on this subject on 1.1.57 *acaḥ parasmin pūrvavidhau* by Kaiyaṭa and Nāgeśa.
4. Note that, I do not think 1.4.2 can be used to make decisions about accentuation. I explain why this is the case in section 5.4 of chapter 5.
5. An *anavakāśa* rule is one that is not applicable elsewhere, whereas a *sāvakāśa* rule is one that is applicable elsewhere.

6. It must be stated, though, that this passage is reproduced verbatim by Patañjali in his comments on vt. 3 on 6.1.85 *antādivac ca* (Mbh III.59.20–60.6).
7. See Pathak and Chitrao (1935).
8. Patañjali's statements on both are very close paraphrases of this form.
9. 'An *ātmanepada* affix occurs after *śadLṚ* 'to cut' when it is to be used with an item marked with *Ś*'.
10. 'Augment *aṬ*, concurrently marked *udātta*, is introduced to an *aṅga* when affixes *LUṄ, LAṄ* and *LṚṄ* follow'.
11. But since Pāṇini accounts for both Vedic and non-Vedic usages, Kātyāyana's dismissal of the need to write a *sūtra* that justifies a Vedic form is unacceptable. But this is beside the point here.
12. 'The *aṅga, kroṣṭu* is also treated as if ending in affix *trC*, when the denotation is feminine'.
13. 7.1.54 *hrasvanadyāpo nuṭ.*
14. 7.1.73 *iko'ci vibhaktau.*
15. 7.2.100 *aci ra ṛtaḥ.*
16. 7.1.95 *tṛjvat kroṣṭuḥ* and the following *sūtras* such as 7.1.97 *vibhāṣā tṛtīyādiṣv aci.*
17. By applying 7.1.97, 7.1.54, and, finally, 6.4.3 *nāmi*, in that order.
18. *tṛjvadbhāvaḥ kṛte nuṭy anajāditvān na prāpnotīty anityo, nuḍāgamo'pi kṛte tṛjvadbhāve sannipātaparibhāṣayā na prāpnotīty anityaḥ* (see p. 91, part 6, Caukhambā's publication [1987–1988] of the *Mahābhāṣya* with Kaiyaṭa's *Pradīpa* and Nāgeśa's *Uddyota*).
19. 'Augment *sUṬ* is introduced before *K*'.
20. 'The affix *saN* is optionally introduced after a verbal stem, the action denoted by which is the object of a verbal stem expressing desire and provided both actions have the same agent'.
21. '*ch* and *v* are replaced with *ś* and *ūṬH*, respectively, when an affix beginning with a nasal, or affix *KvI*, or one beginning with *jhaL* (a non-nasal stop or a fricative) and marked with *K* or *Ṅ*, follows'.
22. '*iK* (*i, u, ṛ, ḷ*) is replaced with *yaṆ* (*y, v, r, l*) when *aC* (any vowel) follows'.
23. If we interpret *sanyaṅoḥ* as locative, as I think Patañjali does in this case, then this rule teaches that a verbal base that has not undergone reduplication is reduplicated when followed by *saN* or *yaṄ*. Note that the whole base does not undergo reduplication; instead, only one syllable does. See 6.1.1 *ekāco dve prathamasya* and 6.1.2 *ajāder dvitīyasya.*
24. I think Kātyāyana interprets *sanyaṅoḥ* as genitive.
25. The whole base does not undergo reduplication; instead, only one syllable does. See 6.1.1 *ekāco dve prathamasya* and 6.1.2 *ajāder dvitīyasya.*
26. 'A *suP* is replaced with *LUK* when it occurs inside a *dhātu* "verbal base" or a *prātipadika* "nominal base"'.
27. 'The final *i* or *a* of a *bha* item is replaced with *LOPA* when it is followed by *ī* or a *taddhita* affix'.
28. An *aT* which replaces a *jh* that is the initial sound of an affix preceded by *śīṄ*, takes the augment *rUṬ*.
29. Augments *aṬ* and *āṬ* are introduced, in turn (*paryāyeṇa*), to affixes that replace *LEṬ*.
30. A *jh* that is the initial sound of an *ātmanepada* affix preceded by a verbal base that does not end in *a* is replaced with *at.*
31. The contents in square brackets have been added by me to Kielhorn's quote.
32. Deshpande (1998, 2019) discusses this topic in great detail.

33. Another popular version of this, also written by Kaiyaṭa is: *uttarottaraṁ munīnāṁ prāmāṇyam.*
34. See *Pradīpa* on *Mahābhāṣya* on 1.1.29.
35. I hope I have proven through this book that Pāṇini intended for his grammar to function like a well-oiled machine. But I do not want to deny that he may have made certain mistakes by virtue of being human or that interpolations and changes occurred in the *Aṣṭādhyāyī* at the hands of later scholars. I think these factors certainly had a negative impact on the functioning of Pāṇini's machine.
36. Kiparsky (1991, 349) also says, 'Joshi and I were unable to find any general way to predict which rule wins in such a situation [i.e., *vipratiṣedha*, which they interpret as mutual blocking], although solutions for some special subtypes of *vipratiṣedha* were suggested'. Note that the words in the square brackets in this quote have been added by me for the sake of clarity.
37. For my criticism of the same, please see section 5.7 of chapter 5.

Chapter 8

1. Publications in the field include Springer's *Sanskrit Computational Linguistics* and also several proceedings of the Computational Linguistics and Digital Humanities panels held at multiple World Sanskrit Conferences.
2. In fact, as I have shown in section 5.6 of chapter 5, the *antaraṅga* tool is often used to deal with faux conflict cases, which actually involve no conflict at all.
3. Many traditional scholars with whom I have spoken pride themselves over having mastered the dense and impenetrable collection of metarules dedicated exclusively to the *antaraṅga* tool. But when topics get so unnecessarily complicated that they make sense only to a small, elite group of learners, should we lament or celebrate? The attitude of these pundits betrays the reason behind the receding interest of newer generations in the field of Pāṇinian studies.
4. It is noteworthy that, unlike DOI, SOI is not a part of Pāṇini's grammar but a feature of the *sūtra* style. However, it is necessary to teach both the fundamentals of the *sūtra* style (thus SOI) and Pāṇini's grammar itself (of which DOI is part) to make the computer interpret and implement the *Aṣṭādhyāyī* correctly.
5. This information has a purely indicative value but no claim to exhaustiveness. There are some constraints on some of these strings depending on whether or not they can contain terminals, whether or not they can be empty, and so on, but I won't delve into this because it is not of much importance in the present context.
6. Western phonology has also dabbled, more recently, in 'constraints' (look up optimality theory), as opposed to 'rules', but we will not discuss this subject here.
7. Although simultaneous rather than sequential application of rules has been extensively discussed in Western linguistics, we will not dwell on it here. In both Western and Pāṇinian derivations, the question of which rule—of multiple applicable rules—must be applied at a given step arises. Pāṇini explicitly teaches us to choose one, and thus our interest lies in applying one rule per step, or put differently, in sequential application. Note that, for the tradition, rule order is not as important in cases of nonconflict as it is in cases of conflict (see section 2.5 of chapter 2 for more on this).
8. For more, see chapter 7.

Postface

1. The two reviews, my replies, and Bodas's and Scharf's emails in response to my replies can be found on mailing lists like Indology and BVP.
2. In my reply to Scharf, I wrote: 'Both traditional and modern interpretations offer no explanation about why *para* means RHS in all cases where it is used for a technical purpose except in 1.4.2 and why Pāṇini does not give us any instructions about the many kinds of conflict they exclude from the jurisdiction of 1.4.2'.
3. The glosses and explanations in brackets are mine.

Appendix C

1. One may ask: why did Pāṇini compose 7.2.5 if 7.2.4 *neṭi* already prohibits *vṛddhi* in such cases? It is true that by 7.2.4 *neṭi*, when the consonant-final base is followed by an *iṬ*-initial *sIC*, *vṛddhi* is prohibited. But 7.2.7 *ato halāder laghoḥ* makes this optional for bases which start with a consonant and contain the light vowel *a*. Thus, Pāṇini has composed 7.2.5 to negate this optionality, or in other words, to prescribe the mandatory prohibition of *vṛddhi* in the said circumstances.
2. An important question arises here: how is it possible to apply 6.1.101, after applying 8.2.28, which belongs to the *asiddha* section? Unfortunately, I have not been able to find a satisfactory explanation for this.
3. By 3.1.31 *āyādaya ārdhadhātuke vā*, *āya* can be optionally added to *gupU* here, but we will not discuss this option because it is not relevant to the present argument.
4. The final *i* and *u* of *Śnu*, and of any verbal base, and of *bhrū* 'brow' are replaced with *iyAṄ* and *uvAṄ*, respectively, when an affix beginning with a vowel (*aC*) follows.
5. This set of roots includes *naś*.
6. *Ktvā* which has taken the *iṬ* augment is not treated as marked with *K*.
7. 1.1.63 *na lumatāṅgasya*.
8. Affix *cli* is added to a verbal root when *LUṄ* follows.
9. Note that, at this step, there is an SOI between 7.2.115 *aco ñṇiti* and 7.3.84 *sārvadhātukārdhadhātukayoḥ*. However, I have not drawn a diagram to show this in the main text for the sake of brevity. Since 7.2.115 is conditioned by affixes marked with *Ñ* and *Ṇ*, it is more specific and thus wins.
10. 1.1.63 *na lumatāṅgasya*.
11. Affix *Śnā* occurs after verbal roots belonging to the class headed by *ḌUkrīÑ* 'to buy, barter' when a *sārvadhātuka* affix which denotes *kartṛ* follows.
12. 6.4.112 and 6.4.113 are applicable here because *jhi* is treated as marked with *K* / *Ṅ* by virtue of being an *apit sārvadhātuka* (cf. 1.2.4 *sārvadhātukam apit*).
13. 8.4.2 *aṭkupvāṅnumvyavāye'pi*.
14. 1.1.64 *aco'ntyādi ṭi*.
15. The vowel of the *abhyāsa* 'first of two reduplicated syllables' is replaced with its short counterpart.
16. By virtue of being an *apit sārvadhātuka*, *jhi* is treated as marked with *K* / *Ṅ* (cf. 1.2.4 *sārvadhātukam apit*).
17. In the interest of brevity, I have omitted mentioning certain phonological processes here, which lead us from *naijs* to *naikṣ*.

BIBLIOGRAPHY

Primary Sources

***Aṣṭādhyāyī* (Pāṇini)**

Dīkṣita, P. (Ed.). (2010). *Maharṣipāṇinipraṇītaḥ Aṣṭādhyāyīsūtrapāṭhaḥ*. New Delhi, India: Saṁskṛta Bhāratī.

***Bālamanoramā* (Vāsudeva Dīkṣita)**

See *Siddhāntakaumudī*.

***Dhātupāṭha* (Pāṇini)**

Dīkṣita, P. (Ed.). (2010). *Prakriyānusārī Pāṇinīyadhātupāṭhaḥ*. New Delhi, India: Saṁskṛta Bhāratī.

***Gaṇapāṭha* (Pāṇini)**

Shastri, K. (Ed.). (1967). *The Gaṇapāṭha*. Thanesar, Haryana, India: Kurukshetra University.

***Kāśikāvṛtti* (Jayāditya and Vāmana)**

Misra, S. (Ed.). (1985). *Kāśikā-vṛtti of Jayāditya-Vāmana with Vivaraṇapañjikā-Nyāsa and Padamañjarī*. Varanasi, Uttar Pradesh, India: Ratna Publications.

Sharma, A., & Deshpande, K. (Eds.). (1996). *Kāśikā: A Commentary on Pāṇini's Grammar* (Part 1 and 2). Secunderabad, Telangana , India: Sanskrit Academy, Osmania University.

***Laghusiddhāntakaumudī* (Varadarājācārya)**

Laghusiddhāntakaumudī. Gītāpresa Gorakhapura.

***Mahābhāṣya* (Patañjali)**

Kielhorn, F. (Ed.). (1880–1885). *The Vyākaraṇa-Mahābhāṣya of Patañjali* (Vols. 1–3). Bombay, India: Government Central Book Depot. Digitized version of the original volumes available at the Internet Archive Books, https://archive.org/details/internetarchivebooks.

Śāstrī, B. et al. (Eds.). (1987–1988). *Vyākaraṇamahābhāṣya with Bhāṣyapradīpa and Bhāṣyapradīpoddyota* (Vols. 1–6). Varanasi, India: Caukhambā Saṁskṛta Pratiṣṭhāna. Reprint of Nirṇaya Sāgara Press edition.

***Nyāsa* (Jinendrabuddhi)**

See Misra under *Kāśikāvṛtti*; see also www.ashtadhyayi.com.

***Padamañjarī* (Haradatta)**

See Misra under *Kāśikāvṛtti*; see also www.ashtadhyayi.com.

***Paribhāṣenduśekhara* (Nāgeśa)**

Abhyankar, K. V. (Ed.). (1962). *The Paribhāṣenduśekhara of Nāgojībhaṭṭa (with the commentary Tattvādarśa of MM. Vasudev Shastri Abhyankar) Part I*. Pune, India: Bhandarkar Oriental Research Institute.

***Pradīpa* (Kaiyaṭa)**

See Śāstrī et al. under *Mahābhāṣya*; see also www.ashtadhyayi.com.

***Prauḍhamanoramā* (Bhaṭṭojī Dīkṣita)**

Mishra, C. (Ed.). (1933). *Prauḍhamanoramā*. Sanskrit Pustak Bhandar.

Ṛgveda: https://theveda.org.in/rigveda

***Siddhāntakaumudī* (Bhaṭṭojī Dīkṣita)**

Bhaṭṭojī Dīkṣita, Vāsudeva Dīksita, & Jñānendra Sarasvatī. (2006). *Vaiyākaraṇa-siddhāntakaumudī with Bālamanoramā and Tattvabodhinī* (Vols. 1–4). New Delhi, India: Motilal Banarsidass.

***Tattvabodhinī* (Jñānendra Sarasvatī)**

See *Siddhāntakaumudī*.

***Uddyota* (Nāgeśa)**

See Śāstrī et al. under *Mahābhāṣya*; see also www.ashtadhyayi.com.

***Uṇādipāṭha* (author unknown)**

Pathak, P. S., & Chitrao, P. S. (Eds.). (1935). Uṇādisūtrapāṭha. In *Word Index to Pāṇini-Sūtra-Pāṭha and Pariśiṣṭas* (pp. 724–42). Pune, India: Bhandarkar Oriental Research Institute.

Secondary Sources

Abhyankar, K. V. (Ed.). (1960). *The Paribhāṣenduśekhara of Nāgojībhaṭṭa. Part II: Translation and Notes* (2nd ed. of translation by F. Kielhorn). Pune, India: Bhandarkar Oriental Research Institute.

———. (1961). *A Dictionary of Sanskrit Grammar*. Baroda, India: Oriental Institute.

———. (1967). *Paribhāṣāsaṁgraha: A Collection of Original Qorks on Vyākaraṇa Paribhāṣās*). Pune, India: Bhandarkar Oriental Research Institute.

Abhyankar, V. S. (1863). *Śrimadbhagavatpatañjaliviracita* Vyākaraṇamahābhāṣya (Parts 1–6) [Marathi translation]. Pune, India: Deccan Education Society.

Acharya, D. (2017). On the Meaning and Function of 'Ādeśa' in the Early Upaniṣads. *Journal of Indian Philosophy, 45* (3), 539–67.

Ajotikar, A., Kulkarni, M., & Scharf, P. (2016). On the Resolution of Conflict between Accentual Rules and Other Rules of Derivation in Pāṇini's Grammar. In G. Cardona, & H. Ogawa (Eds.), *Vyākaraṇaparipṛcchā: Proceedings of the Vyākaraṇa Section of the 16th World Sanskrit Conference* (pp. 1–22). New Delhi, India: D.K. Publishers.

———. (2016). Counter-examples (*pratyudāharaṇa*) in Pāṇinian Grammar. In G. Cardona, & H. Ogawa (Eds.), *Vyākaraṇaparipṛcchā: Proceedings of the Vyākaraṇa Section of the 16th World Sanskrit Conference* (pp. 23–52). New Delhi, India: D.K. Publishers.

Ajotikar, T., & Ajotikar, A. (2018). *Bhāṣyasammata Aṣṭādhyāyīpāṭhaḥ: An Unpublished Manuscript on Variations in the Sūtras of the Aṣṭādhyāyī (A Presentation in the Vyākaraṇa Section at the 17th World Sanskrit Conference)*. [PowerPoint slides procured through personal communication].

Ananthanarayana, H. S. (1998). Formalization of Grammar: Pāṇinian Techniques. In D. D. Mahulkar (Ed.), *Essays on Pāṇini* (pp. 26–36). Shimla, India: Indian Institute of Advanced Study.

Apte, V. S. (1957). *The Practical Sanskrit-English Dictionary* (rev. ed.). Pune, India: Prasad Prakashan. [Electronic version by DDSA: https://dsal.uchicago.edu/dictionaries/apte/].

Bahulikar, S. (1972). *Some Criteria for Determining the Insertions in the Aṣṭādhyāyī* [unpublished doctoral dissertation]. Harvard University.

Bali, S. (1976). *Bhaṭṭojī Dīkṣita: His Contribution to Sanskrit Grammar.* New Delhi, India: Munshiram Manoharlal.

Belvalkar, S. K. (1915). *An Account of the Different Existing Systems of Sanskrit Grammar.* Pune, India: Aryabhushan Press.

Benson, J. (1990). *Patañjali's Remarks on Aṅga.* Oxford, UK: Oxford University Press.

Bhandarkar, R. G. (1972). Review of Goldstücker's Pāṇini. In J. F. Staal (Ed.), *A Reader on the Sanskrit Grammarians* (pp. 72–77). Cambridge, MA: MIT Press. [Reprinted from *Native Opinion* (1864). Also reprinted in *Indian Antiquary, 6* (1877), pp. 108–13].

———. (1972*). Ācārya, the Friend of the Student, and the Relations between the Three Ācāryas. In J. F. Staal (Ed.), *A Reader on the Sanskrit Grammarians* (pp. 81–86). Cambridge, MA: MIT Press. [Reprinted from *Indian Antiquary, 5* (1876), pp. 345–50].

Bhate, S. (1987). Grammar and Lexicon. *Annals of the Bhandarkar Oriental Research Institute, 68* (1/4), 563–70.

———. (1989). *Pāṇini's Taddhita Rules.* Pune, India: Centre of Advanced Study in Sanskrit, University of Poona.

———. (1998). Economy and Generalization in Pāṇini's Grammar. In D. D. Mahulkar (Ed.), *Essays on Pāṇini* (pp. 76–82). Shimla, India: Indian Institute of Advanced Study.

———. (2002). *Pāṇini.* Delhi, India: Sahitya Akademi.

Bhate, S., & Kak, S. (1991). Pāṇini's Grammar and Computer Science. *Annals of the Bhandarkar Oriental Research Institute, 72/73* (1/4), 79–94.

Bhattacharya, R. C. (1953). Senses of 'ca'. *Poona Orientalist, 18,* 8–10.

Bloomfield, L. (1927). On Some Rules of Pāṇini. *Journal of the American Oriental Society, 47,* 61–70.

Bresnan, J., Kaplan, R., Peters, S., & Zaenen, A. (1982). Cross-Serial Dependencies in Dutch. *Linguistic Inquiry, 13* (4), 613–35.

Bronkhorst, J. (1980). "Asiddha" in the *Aṣṭādhyāyī*: A Misunderstanding among the Traditional Commentators? *Journal of Indian Philosophy, 8* (1), 69–85.

———. (1984). Review of Kiparsky (1982). *Indo-Iranian Journal, 27* (4), 309–14.

———. (1986). *Tradition and Argument in Classical Indian Linguistics.* Dordrecht, Netherlands: D. Reidel.

———. (1991). Pāṇini and the Veda Reconsidered. In M. Deshpande, & S. Bhate (Eds.), *Pāṇinian Studies: Professor S. D. Joshi Felicitation Volume* (pp. 75–122). Ann Arbor: University of Michigan Press.

———. (2004). *From Pāṇini to Patañjali: The Search for Linearity.* Pune, India: Bhandarkar Oriental Research Institute.

———.(2014). Deviant Voices in the History of Pāṇinian Grammar. *Bulletin d'Études Indiennes, 32,* 47–53.

Buiskool, H. E. (1939). *The Tripādī.* Leiden, Netherlands: E. J. Brill.

Candotti, M. P. (2012). The Role and Import of the Metalinguistic Chapters in the New Pāṇinian Grammars. In C. Watanabe, N. Desmarais, & Y. Honda (Eds.), *Saṁskṛta-sādhutā: Goodness of Sanskrit (Studies in Honour of Professor Ashok N. Aklujkar)* (pp. 86–99). New Delhi, India: D.K. Printworld.

———. (2016). Natural and Grammatical Zero: The Case of Indeclinables. In G. Cardona, & H. Ogawa (Eds.), *Vyākaraṇaparipṛcchā: Proceedings of the Vyākaraṇa Section of the 16th World Sanskrit Conference* (pp. 99–137). New Delhi, India: D.K. Publishers.

Candotti, M. P., & Pontillo, T. (2004). Substitution as a Descriptive Model in Pāṇini's Grammar: Towards an Opposition between Phonological and Morphological Levels. In R. Ronzitti, & G. Borghi (Eds.), *Atti del Secondo Incontro Genovese di Studî Vedici e Pāṇiniani* (pp. 1–45). Milan, Italy: Le Mani-Microart's Edizioni.

———. (2012). Interpreting Forms with Markers: The Morphological Approach. In G. Cardona, & M. Deshpande (Eds.), *Indian Grammars: Philology and History (Papers of the 12th World Sanskrit Conference)* (pp. 61–82). New Delhi, India: Motilal Banarsidass.

———.. (2018). From Commentary to Paribhāṣās: Kātyāyana and Patañjali vis-à-vis Vyāḍi. *Asiatische Studien/Études Asiatiques, 72* (2), 515–66.

Cardona, G. (1970). Some Principles of Pāṇini's Grammar. *Journal of Indian Philosophy, 1* (1), 40–74.

———. (1976). *Pāṇini: A Survey of Research*. Berlin, Germany: Mouton.

———. (1989). Pāṇinian Studies. In V. N. Jha (Ed.), *New Horizons of Research in Indology: Silver Jubilee Volume* (pp. 49–84). Pune, India: Centre of Advanced Study in Sanskrit, University of Poona.

———. (1997). *Pāṇini: His Work and Its Tradition. Volume I: Background and Introduction* (2nd ed.). New Delhi, India: Motilal Banarsidass.

———. (1999). *Recent Research in Pāṇinian Studies*. New Delhi, India: Motilal Banarsidass.

Chatterji, K. C. (1972). The Critics of Sanskrit Grammar. In J. F. Staal (Ed.), *A Reader on the Sanskrit Grammarians* (pp. 287–97). Cambridge, MA: MIT Press. [Reprinted from the *Journal of the Department of Letters, University of Calcutta, 24* (3) (1934), pp. 1–21].

Chomsky, N. (1959). On Certain Formal Properties of Grammars. *Information and Control, 2* (2), 137–67.

Chomsky, N., & Halle, M. (1968). *The Sound Pattern of English*. Cambridge, MA: MIT Press.

Culy, C. (1985). The Complexity of the Vocabulary of Bambara. *Linguistics and Philosophy, 8*, 345–51.

D'Avella, V. B. (2018). *Creating the Perfect Language: Sanskrit Grammarians, Poetry, and the Exegetical Tradition* [doctoral dissertation]. University of Chicago. ProQuest Dissertations & Theses.

Deo, A. (2007). Derivational Morphology in Inheritance-based Lexica: Insights from Pāṇini. *Lingua, 117* (1), 175–201.

Deshpande, M. (1983). Linguistic Presuppositions of Pāṇini 8.3.26–27. In S. D. Joshi, & S. D. Laddu (Eds.), *Proceedings of the International Seminar on Studies in the Aṣṭādhyāyī* (pp. 23–42). Pune, India: Centre of Advanced Study in Sanskrit, University of Poona.

———. (1998). Evolution of the Notion of Authority (Prāmāṇya) in the Pāṇinian Tradition. *Histoire Epistemologie Language, 20* (1), 5–28.

———.(2019). *From Pāṇini to Patañjali and Beyond: Development of Religious Motifs in Sanskrit Grammar (26th J. Gonda Lecture 2018)*. Amsterdam: Royal Netherlands Academy of Arts and Sciences.

Deshpande, M., & Bhate, S. (Eds.). (1991). *Pāṇinian Studies: Professor S. D. Joshi Felicitation Volume*. Ann Arbor: University of Michigan Press.

Deshpande, M., & Hook, P. (Eds.). (2002). *Indian Linguistic Studies: Festschrift in Honor of George Cardona*. New Delhi, India: Motilal Banarsidass.

Emeneau, M. B. (1988). Bloomfield and Pāṇini. *Language, 64* (4), 755–60.

Faddegon, B. (1936). *Studies on Pāṇini's Grammar.* Verhandelingen der Konink-lijke Akademie der Wetenschapen, Afdeeling Letterkunde, Nieuwe Reeks (38.1).

Freschi, E., & Pontillo, T. (2013). *Rule-extension Strategies in Ancient India.* Lausanne, Switzerland: Peter Lang.

Fowler, M. (1965). How Ordered are Pāṇini's Rules? *Journal of the American Oriental Society, 85* (1), 44–47.

Godse, B. S. (1973). Concept of Vipratiṣedha in Pāṇinian Grammar. *Annals of the Bhandarkar Oriental Research Institute, 54* (1/4), 250–56.

Goldstücker, T. (1861). *Pāṇini: His Place in Sanskrit Literature.* London: N. Trübner.

Houben, J. (2003). Three Myths in Modern Pāṇinian Studies. *Asiatische Studien/Études Asiatiques, 57* (1), 121–79.

Houben, J. (2008). Bhaṭṭojī Dīkṣita's "Small Step" for a Grammarian and "Giant Leap" for Sanskrit Grammar. *Journal of Indian Philosophy, 36* (5/6), 563–74.

———. (2009). Pāṇini's Grammar and Its Computerization: A Construction Grammar Approach. In A. Kulkarni, & G. Huet (Eds.), *Sanskrit Computational Linguistics: Third International Symposium* (pp. 6–25). New York: Springer.

———. (2014). Pāṇinian Grammar of Living Sanskrit: Features and Principles of the Prakriyā Sarvasva of Nārāyaṇa-Bhaṭṭa of Melputtūr. *Bulletin d'Études Indiennes, 32*, 149–70.

Hueckstedt, R. (1995). *Nearness and Respective Correlation: A History of the Interpretations of Aṣṭādhyāyī 6.1.77: iko yaṇ aci.* Wiesbaden, Germany: Harrassowitz.

———. (2002). Some Later Argument on 'iko yaṇ aci'. In M. Deshpande, & P. Hook (Eds.), *Indian Linguistic Studies: Festschrift in Honor of George Cardona* (pp. 44–72). New Delhi, India: Motilal Banarsidass.

Huet, G., Kulkarni, A., & Scharf P. (Eds.). (2009). *Sanskrit Computational Linguistics—First and Second International Symposia.* New York: Springer.

Hyman, M. (2009). From Pāṇinian Sandhi to Finite State Calculus. In G. Huet, A. Kulkarni, & P. Scharf (Eds.), *Sanskrit Computational Linguistics: First and Second International Symposia* (pp. 253–65). New York: Springer.

Iyer, S. (1983). On Variants in the *Aṣṭādhyāyī.* In S. D. Joshi, & S. D. Laddu (Eds.), *Proceedings of the International Seminar on Studies in the Aṣṭādhyāyī* (pp. 141–255). Pune, India: Centre of Advanced Study in Sanskrit, University of Poona.

Jha, G. N. (Ed.). (2010). *Sanskrit Computational Linguistics: Fourth International Symposium.* New York: Springer.

Jijñāsu, B. (2003). *Aṣṭādhyāyī Bhāṣya Prathamāvṛtti* [Hindi translation]. Rāmalāla Kapūra Trust.

Joshi, S. D. (1977). The Ordering of Rules in Pāṇini's Grammar. *Annals of the Bhandarkar Oriental Research Institute, 58/59*, 667–74.

———. (1982). *The Functions of Asiddhatva and Sthānivadbhāva in Pāṇini's Aṣṭādhyāyī.* Pune, India: Centre of Advanced Study in Sanskrit, University of Poona.

———. (1998). The Para Principle in Pāṇini's *Aṣṭādhyāyī.* In D. D. Mahulkar (Ed.), *Essays on Pāṇini* (pp. 43–58). Shimla, India: Indian Institute of Advanced Study.

Joshi, S. D., & Bhate, S. (1983). The Role of the Particle 'ca' in the Interpretation of the *Aṣṭādhyāyī.* In S. D. Joshi, & S. D. Laddu (Eds.), *Proceedings of The International Seminar on Studies in the Aṣṭādhyāyī* (pp. 167–227). Pune, India: Centre of Advanced Study in Sanskrit, University of Poona.

———. (1984). *The Fundamentals of Anuvṛtti.* Pune, India: Centre of Advanced Study in Sanskrit, University of Poona.

Joshi, S. D., & Kiparsky, P. (1979). Siddha and Asiddha in Pāṇinian Phonology. In D. Dinnsen (Ed.), *Current Approaches to Phonological Theory* (pp. 223–50). Bloomington: Indiana University Press.

———.. (2005). The Extended Siddha-Principle. *Annals of the Bhandarkar Oriental Research Institute, 86*, 1–26.

Joshi, S. D., & Laddu, S.D. (Eds.). (1983). *Proceedings of the International Seminar on Studies in the Aṣṭādhyāyī.* Pune, India: Centre of Advanced Study in Sanskrit, University of Poona.

Joshi, S. D., & Roodbergen, J. A. F. (1969–1986). *Patañjali's Vyākaraṇa-mahābhāṣya: Text, Translation and Notes* (Vols. 1–9) [English translation]. Pune, India: Centre of Advanced Study in Sanskrit, University of Poona.

———. (1983). The Structure of the *Aṣṭādhyāyī* in Historical Perspective. In S. D. Joshi, & S. D. Laddu (Eds.), *Proceedings of the International Seminar on Studies in the Aṣṭādhyāyī* (pp. 59–95). Pune, India: Centre of Advanced Study in Sanskrit, University of Poona.

———. (1987). On Siddha, Asiddha, and Sthānivat. *Annals of the Bhandarkar Oriental Research Institute, 68* (1/4), 541–49.

———. (1991–2007). *The Aṣṭādhyāyī of Pāṇini with Translations and Explanatory Notes* (Vols. 1–13). Delhi, India: Sahitya Akademi.

———. (2002). On P. 1.4.1–2: A Reconsideration. In M. Deshpande, & P. Hook (Eds.), *Indian Linguistic Studies: Festschrift in Honor of George Cardona* (pp. 112–20). New Delhi, India: Motilal Banarsidass.

Katre, S. (1987). *Aṣṭādhyāyī of Pāṇini* [English translation]. Austin: University of Texas Press.

Kawamura, Y. (2018). *The Kāraka Theory Embodied in the Rāma Story: A Sanskrit Textbook in Medieval India.* New Delhi, India: D.K. Printworld.

Keidan, A. (2014). Form, Function and Interpretation: A Case Study in the Textual Criticism of Pāṇini's *Aṣṭādhyāyī. Bulletin d'Études Indiennes, 32*, 171–203.

Kielhorn, F. (1876). *Kātyāyana and Patañjali: Their Relation to Each Other, and to Pāṇini.* Bombay, India: Education Society's Press, Byculla.

———. (1972). The Text of Pāṇini's Sūtras, as Given in the Kāśikā-Vṛtti Compared with the Text Known to Kātyāyana and Patañjali. In J. F. Staal (Ed.), *A Reader on the Sanskrit Grammarians* (pp. 115–23). Cambridge, MA: MIT Press. [Reprinted from *Indian Antiquary, 16* (1887), pp. 178–84].

———. (1972). Some Devices of Indian Grammarians. In J. F. Staal (Ed.), *A Reader on the Sanskrit Grammarians* (pp. 123–34). Cambridge, MA: MIT Press. [Reprinted from *Indian Antiquary, 16* (1887), pp. 244–52].

Kiparsky, P. (1968). Linguistic Universals and Linguistic Change. In E. Bach, & R. T. Harms (Eds.), *Universals in Linguistic Theory* (pp. 170–202). New York: Holt, Rinehart, and Winston.

———. (1979). *Pāṇini as a Variationist.* Pune, India/Cambridge, MA: Poona University Press/ MIT Press.

———. (1982). The Ordering of Rules in Pāṇini's Grammar. In *Some Theoretical Problems in Pāṇini's Grammar* (pp. 77–120). Pune, India: Bhandarkar Oriental Research Institute.

———. (1987). What Is Siddha? *Annals of the Bhandarkar Oriental Research Institute, 68* (1/4), 295–303.

———. (1991). On Pāṇinian Studies: A Reply to Cardona. *Journal of Indian Philosophy, 19* (4), 331–67.

———.(1991). Economy and the Construction of the Śivasūtras. In M. Deshpande, & S. Bhate (Eds.), *Pāṇinian Studies: Professor S. D. Joshi Felicitation Volume* (pp. 239–62). Ann Arbor: University of Michigan Press.

———. (2007). Pāṇini Is Slick, but He Isn't Mean. *Nagoya Studies in Indian Culture and Buddhism: Saṁbhāṣā, 26*, 1–28.

———. (2009) On the Architecture of Pāṇini's Grammar. In G. Huet, A. Kulkarni, & P. Scharf (Eds.), *Sanskrit Computational Linguistics: First and Second International Symposia* (pp. 33–94). Springer.

Kulkarni, A., & Huet, G. (Eds.). (2009). *Sanskrit Computational Linguistics: Third International Symposium*. New York: Springer.

Lahiri, P. C. (1935). *Concordance Pāṇini-Patañjali*. Breslau, Poland: Verlag von M. & H. Marcus.

Lowe, J. (in press). Revisiting Pāṇini's Generative Power. In G. Sharma, & J. Lowe (Eds.), *Trends in South Asian Linguistics*. Berlin, Germany: De Gruyter.

Macdonell, A. A. (1893). *A Sanskrit-English Dictionary*. London: Longmans, Green. [Electronic version by DDSA: https://dsal.uchicago.edu/dictionaries/macdonell/].

Mahulkar, D. D. (1998). Pāṇini in a New Setting. In D. D. Mahulkar (Ed.), *Essays on Pāṇini* (pp. 13–25). Shimla, India: Indian Institute of Advanced Study.

———. (1998). *Essays on Pāṇini*. Shimla, India: Indian Institute of Advanced Study.

Monier-Williams, M. (1963). *A Sanskrit-English Dictionary* (rev. ed.). Oxford, UK: Clarendon Press. [Electronic version by GRETIL: https://www.sanskrit-lexicon.uni-koeln.de/scans/MWScan/2020/web/webtc2/index.php].

Nooten, B. A. van (1967). Pāṇini's Replacement Technique and the Active Finite Verb. *Language, 43* (4), 883–902.

Ogawa, H. (1987). The Use of the Particle Eva in the *Aṣṭādhyāyī*. *Journal of Indian and Buddhist Studies, 35* (2), 12–15.

Palsule, G. (1991). A Glimpse into a Pre-Pāṇinian View about Vikaraṇas. In M. Deshpande, & S. Bhate (Eds.), *Pāṇinian Studies: Professor S. D. Joshi Felicitation Volume* (pp. 283–88). Ann Arbor: University of Michigan Press.

Pandit, M. D. (1966). *Mathematical Representation of Some Pāṇinian Sūtras*. Pune, India: Centre of Advanced Study in Sanskrit, University of Poona.

Pataskar, B. (1985). *Utsargāpavāda Relation in the Aṣṭādhyāyī* [unpublished doctoral dissertation]. Centre of Advanced Study in Sanskrit, University of Poona.

Pathak, P. S., & Chitrao, P. S. (1927). *Word Index to Patañjali's Vyākaraṇa Mahābhāṣya*. Pune, India: Bhandarkar Oriental Research Institute.

———. (1935). *Word Index to Pāṇini-Sūtra-Pāṭha and Pariśiṣṭas*. Pune, India: Bhandarkar Oriental Research Institute.

Penn, G., & Kiparsky, P. (2012). On Pāṇini and the Generative Capacity of Contextualized Replacement Systems. *Proceedings of COLING 2012*, 943–50.

Rajpopat. R. (2023). The Evolution of Conflict Resolution Tools in the Early Pāṇinian Grammatical Tradition. *Bhāṣā: Journal of South Asian Linguistics, Philology and Grammatical Traditions, 2* (1), 31–58.

———. (2024). The Historical Reception of Panini's Sanskrit Grammar. In L. Vemsani (Ed.), *Handbook of Indian History*. Singapore: Springer.

Roodbergen, J. A. F. (1991). Time For a Little Something. In M. Deshpande, & S. Bhate (Eds.), *Pāṇinian Studies: Professor S. D. Joshi Felicitation Volume* (pp. 293–322). Ann Arbor: University of Michigan Press.

———. (1998). On P. 1.4.2, Vipratiṣedhe Paraṁ Kāryam. In D. D. Mahulkar (Ed.), *Essays on Pāṇini* (pp. 68–75). Shimla, India: Indian Institute of Advanced Study.

———. (2008). *Dictionary of Pāṇinian Grammatical Terminology*. Pune, India: Bhandarkar Oriental Research Institute.

Scharf, P. (2009). Modelling Pāṇinian Grammar. In G. Huet, A. Kulkarni, & P. Scharf (Eds.), *Sanskrit Computational Linguistics: First and Second International Symposia* (pp. 95–126). New York: Springer.

———. (2009*). Levels in Pāṇini's *Aṣṭādhyāyī*. In A. Kulkarni, & G. Huet (Eds.), *Sanskrit Computational Linguistics: Third International Symposium* (pp. 66–77). New York: Springer.

———.(2011). On the Semantic Foundation of Pāṇinian Derivational Procedure: The Derivation of Kumbhakāra. *Journal of the American Oriental Society, 131* (1), 39–72.

———.(2016). On the Status of Nominal Terminations in Upapada Compounds. In G. Cardona, & H. Ogawa (Eds.), *Vyākaraṇaparipṛcchā: Proceedings of the Vyākaraṇa Section of the 16th World Sanskrit Conference* (pp. 291–320). New Delhi, India: D.K. Publishers.

Scharfe, H. (1983). Secondary Noun Formation in Pāṇini's Grammar: What Was the Great Option? In S. D. Joshi, & S. D. Laddu (Eds.), *Proceedings of the International Seminar on Studies in the Aṣṭādhyāyī* (pp. 53–57). Pune, India: Centre of Advanced Study in Sanskrit, University of Poona.

———. (2009). A New Perspective on Pāṇini. *Indologica Taurinensia, 35*.

Sharma, G. P. (2015). *The Laghusiddhāntakaumudī of Śrī Varadarājācārya* [Hindi translation and commentary]. Varanasi, India: Caukhambā Surabhāratī Prakāśana.

Sharma, R. N. (1987–2003). *The Aṣṭādhyāyī of Pāṇini* (Vols. 1–6) [English translation and commentary]. New Delhi, India: Munshiram Manoharlal.

———. (2010). Rule Interaction, Blocking and Derivation in Pāṇini. In G. N. Jha (Ed.), *Sanskrit Computational Linguistics: Fourth International Symposium* (pp. 1–20). New York: Springer.

Śāstrī, B. (1993–2009). *Laghusiddhāntakaumudī: Bhaimī Vyākhyā* (3rd ed.) [Hindi translation and commentary]. Bhaimī Prakāśana.

Shieber, S. (1985). Evidence Against the Context-Freeness of Natural Language. *Linguistics and Philosophy, 8* (3), 333–43.

Singh, U. (2008). *A History of Ancient and Early Medieval India*. London: Pearson.

Staal, J. (1965). Context-Sensitive Rules in Pāṇini. *Foundations of Language, 1* (1), 63–72.

———. (1966). Pāṇini Tested by Fowler's Automaton. *Journal of the American Oriental Society, 86* (2), 206–9.

———. (Ed.). (1972). *A Reader on the Sanskrit Grammarians*. Cambridge, MA: MIT Press.

Thieme, P. (1935). *Pāṇini and the Veda: Studies in the Early History of Linguistic Science in India*. Allahabad, India: Globe Press.

———. (1956). Pāṇini and the Pāṇinīyas. *Journal of the American Oriental Society, 76* (1), 1–23.

———. (1972). On the Identity of the Vārttikakāra. In J. F. Staal (Ed.), *A Reader on the Sanskrit Grammarians* (pp. 332–56). Cambridge, MA: MIT Press. [Reprinted from *Indian Culture, 4* (1937–1938), pp. 189–209].

Vasu, S. C. (1897). *The Aṣṭādhyāyī of Pāṇini* (Parts 1 and 2) [English translation and commentary]. Sindhu Charan Bose, Pāṇini Office.

———. (1905–1907). *The Siddhāntakaumudī of Bhaṭṭojī Dīkṣita* (Vols. 1–3) [English translation and commentary]. Bhuvaneshwari Ashram, Pāṇini Office.

Vergiani, V. (1993). The Negative Asamarthasamāsas in the Pāṇinian Tradition. *Rivista Degli Studi Orientali, 67* (1/2), 65–81.

———. (2011). Dealing with Conflicting Views Within the Pāṇinian Tradition: On the Derivation of Tyadṛś etc. In F. Squarcini (Ed.), *Boundaries, Dynamics and Construction of Traditions in South Asia* (pp. 411–33). London: Anthem Press.

———. (2020). Pāṇini's *Aṣṭādhyāyī*: A Turning Point in Indian Intellectual History. *Rivista Degli Studi Orientali, 92* (3–4), 11–35.

Weber, A. (1872). Das Mahābhāṣya des Patañjali. *Indische Studien, 13* (2–3), 293–496.

Whitney, W. D. (1972). The Study of Hindu Grammar and the Study of Sanskrit. In J. F. Staal (Ed.), *A Reader on the Sanskrit Grammarians* (pp. 142–54). Cambridge, MA: MIT Press. [Reprinted from the *American Journal of Philology, 5* (1884), pp. 279–97].

Wujastyk, D. (1983). Do Paribhāṣās Wrongly Immunize Pāṇini's Theory Against Criticism? In S. D. Joshi, & S. D. Laddu (Eds.), *Proceedings of the International Seminar on Studies in the Aṣṭādhyāyī* (pp. 97–103). Pune, India: Centre of Advanced Study in Sanskrit, University of Poona.

Wujastyk, D. (2017). *Metarules of Pāṇinian Grammar: The Vyāḍīyaparibhāṣāvṛtti* [English translation]. New Delhi, India: Motilal Banarsidass.

Yagi, T. (1992). The Asiddha/Asiddhavat Reconsidered. *Vienna Journal of South Asian Studies 36* (Suppl.): *Proceedings of the Eighth World Sanskrit Conference*, 49–58.

ACKNOWLEDGMENTS

First and foremost, I want to thank the lady who helped me take my baby steps in the field of Sanskrit studies. Ranjana Deshpande, who taught me Sanskrit from scratch, was one of the warmest teachers I have known. She loved us like grandmothers love their grandchildren. Whenever I visited her, she would tell me how proud she was that I was studying Pāṇini's grammar. She is no longer with us, but her memory will live on in the hearts of all her students. If only I could present a copy of this book to her—I know it would have made her extremely happy.

Geetaben Gandhi, a retired professor at Uttar Gujarat University, taught me Pāṇini for about three years at her home in Mumbai without charging a single penny. She has given her selfless service to the cause of Pāṇinian education for several years now—touching the lives of hundreds of students with her generosity and passion. Geetaben always encouraged me to ask questions and engaged in spirited debates with me about the nature and role of the tradition. Her unique personality will never cease to inspire me, nor will her spirit of learning through the art of teaching.

No one deserves more gratitude than my doctoral supervisor, Vincenzo Vergiani. His insights into the evolution of the Indian grammatical tradition helped me develop and articulate my thoughts in a cogent manner. It would be no exaggeration to say that, were it not for his perceptiveness, knowledge, wisdom, magnanimity, and liberal attitude, I would never have been able to produce this book. From mentoring and encouraging me, to having faith in my abilities, to challenging and criticizing me, he did everything that was necessary for me to thrive at Cambridge. Given that he has single-handedly overseen my growth as a researcher for the last four years, he deserves no less than a lion's share of credit for this book.

Another key figure who played a major role in my journey is Maria Piera Candotti, who engaged critically with me on various topics in Pāṇinian studies over the years. She has been extremely kind, generous, and magnanimous and has helped me at every step of my journey. I am indebted to her also for her wisdom, acuity, perspicacity, and eye for detail—all of which have influenced me significantly as a researcher.

I also want to thank Tiziana Pontillo, who has been extremely gracious, generously helping me and encouraging me to pursue my research with passion and commitment. My conversations with her have been instructive and enriching—thanks to her intelligence, versatility, erudition, and thoroughness.

I have also benefited from the support and advice of Paul Kiparsky, with whom I have had multiple thought-provoking discussions over the years. Despite our disagreements, he has shown the sort of big-heartedness that makes one stand out as a scholar, leader, and pioneer. I am very grateful for his generosity and encouragement.

I must also thank Saroja Bhate, Balram Shukla, Diwakar Acharya, Brendan Wolfe, Peter Bisschop, Ankur Barua, James Benson, and Tilak Rao for their support, advice, and suggestions. The enlightening discussions I have had with them have greatly helped me to hone and advance my views.

For helping me put together this book, I offer my heartfelt gratitude to Sharmila Sen, Joseph Pomp, Sana Mohtadi, Eric Mulder, Kate Mueller, and Peter Holm. I would not have been able to accomplish this task without their advice, support, and patience.

There are many other colleagues and seniors whom I would like to thank, but mentioning them all would prove to be a daunting task and would risk hurting those whose names were omitted by mistake—given the limitations of my memory. I would not have succeeded in this endeavour without them and remain very grateful to them.

I am very grateful to my family and friends for their unwavering support and affection, for their presence in both trying times and moments of celebration. Their love and solidarity mean a lot to me.

Finally, but most importantly, I remain perennially indebted to Bhagavān, who has blessed me with the curiosity and enthusiasm that enable me to conduct such studies. I feel humbled by this divine presence in my life.

INDEX

ābhīya, 162, 172, 173
Abhyankar, K.V., 6, 7, 15, 38, 195
accent, 4, 122-124
accentuation, 97, 105, 121-124
active, 11
adhikāra, 18, 82, 162
adhyāya, 1, 17, 162
algorithm, 111, 178, 203, 206, 209, 210, 212
anavakāśa, 13, 39, 42, 178, 179, 194. *See also* *niravakāśa*
aṅgādhikāra, 82, 84, 85-92, 94, 99, 100, 125, 164, 167
anudātta, 94, 98, 100, 122-125, 164, 177
anuvṛtta, 2, 3, 60, 115, 116,
anuvṛtti, 2, 3, 19, 60, 113, 149, 180
apavāda sutra, 10, 17, 61, 204
asymmetrical (blocking), 34
atulyabala, 13, 22

balābala, 7
Bālamanoramā, 44
Bhaimī, 44, 73, 75, 78
bhāṣya, 6, 116, 153, 162, 199, 200
bleeding, 16, 132-135, 211, 212
Bloomfield, L., 3
Bronkhorst, J., 14, 15, 17, 106, 176, 196, 197

Cāndra, 6
Cardona, G., 1, 2, 5, 16, 17, 22, 63, 103, 104, 106, 197
Chomsky, N., 207, 211, 212
Chomskyan, 207-210
computation, 202
computational, 24, 202, 203, 206, 208, 210
conflict resolution, 24, 177, 186, 196, 197, 203. *See also* rule conflict resolution
continued, 2, 3, 19, 115, 149. *See also anuvṛtti* and *anuvṛtta*
counterbleeding, 211, 212
counterfeeding, 211, 212

definition rule, 2, 17, 31, 141. *See also saṁjñā sūtra*
descriptive, 4, 14, 136, 210
deterministic, 210
Dhātupāṭha, 11, 94, 98, 100, 117, 130, 164, 174
Different Operand Interaction, 23, 26, 105
Dīkṣita, Bhaṭṭojī, his *Siddhāntakaumudī*, 7, 16

epistemological, 199-201
equal strength, 8, 9, 10, 11, 38, 179, 189, 194
exception rule, 10, 17, 26, 30, 31, 38, 54, 159
extended *siddha* principle, 16, 135

Faddegon, B., 18, 21, 196
feeding, 15, 16, 132, 133, 135, 211, 212
finite verb, 3, 29, 48, 82, 92, 104, 114
Freschi, E., 26
functional, 3
functioning, 5, 14, 17, 18, 24, 136, 137, 196, 200, 201

general rule, 8, 10, 17, 24, 26, 31, 38, 88, 159, 160, 179, 194, 204
grammarian: early, 3; fellow, 192; great, 15; traditional, 137
grammatical, 5, 60, 180; derivation, 15; gender, 107, 138; machine, 3, 7, 18, 23, 82, 136, 200; tradition, 4, 200
grammatically, 2; correct, 5, 117, 136, 188, 206, 210

Haima, 6
Halle, M., 211, 212
hierarchy, 9, 13, 17, 207-210
Houben, J., 16, 196
hypothesized, 211
hypothetical application, 32, 47
hypothetically, 135, 196, 205

Indian, 1, 4, 124, 201, 213
inflection, 7, 24, 41, 68, 82, 110, 137, 141
inflectional, 2, 127, 191

Jayāditya, 7
jñāpaka, 13, 201
Joshi, S. D., 16, 17, 22, 63, 105, 106, 131-133, 135, 136, 176, 197

Kaiyaṭa, 187, 196
kāryāsiddhi, 152-155, 161, 163
Kāśikā, 7-11, 13, 58, 60, 64, 81, 91, 106, 143, 150, 152-154, 160-162, 171-172, 194, 195, 199
Kāśikāvṛtti, 199, 200
Kātantra, 6, 7
Kaumudī, 7, 121, 196, 203, 214
Kielhorn, F., 66, 87, 187, 193
Kiparsky, P, 2, 16-18, 20-22, 103-106, 131-136, 197, 208, 210-212
kṛdanta, 68, 81, 84, 92, 93, 106, 107, 109, 110

Laghusiddhāntakaumudī, 44, 73, 75, 78, 105
lakāra, 3, 15, 84, 85, 101, 108, 123, 182
left-hand side, 23, 65, 149
left-to-right, 18, 29
limited blocking, 103, 104, 197
linear, 14, 16, 17, 207, 210
linearity, 16, 17, 196
linearly, 15, 18
linguist, 3, 207, 208
linguistic: western, 210, 211
linguistics, 214; computational, 24, 202, 206; generative, 210; terms common in, 132, 212; theoretical, 136, 181
looking ahead, 15, 135

machine, 2, 3, 6, 7, 14, 23, 26, 116, 169, 207, 209-211; closed, 18, 136, 137; derivational, 5, 16, 17, 111, 118; functioning / running of the, 24, 82, 196, 200; give (input) to the, 117-119
Mahābhāṣya, 5-7, 42, 58, 106, 123, 152, 187, 188, 194, 195, 214
mechanism, 7, 22, 23, 136, 141, 180, 196, 201
mechanistic, 5, 7, 14, 17, 212
metarule, 2-8, 15-17, 22, 29-31, 69, 70, 73-75, 88, 143-148, 150, 151, 203; category of rule, 141; do not accept this, 74; external, 23, 68, 202; governed by, 120, 147, 148; internal / Pāṇinian 23, 104; mind-bending, 205; purpose of writing, 13. *See also paribhāṣā*
morphophonological, 2, 17
mutual opposition, 24, 27, 31, 32, 121, 140, 141

Nāgeśa Bhatta, 6, 16, 69
Natural Language Processing (NLP), 210
natural language, 207, 208; complexity, 24
niravakāśa, 39, 201. *See also anavakāśa*
nonblocking, 53
nonconflict, 32-37, 40, 48-50, 52-54, 86, 99, 134
nondeterministic, 210
nonlinguistic, 142
non-Pāṇinian, 6, 7, 195
Nyāsa, 65, 80, 123, 152, 153, 156, 172

ontological, 201, 202
ontology, 201, 202
operand, 23, 26, 27, 29, 30, 31, 55, 63, 65, 66, 84, 103, 104, 145, 146, 169, 186, 205, 206; LHS, 23, 109, 135, 140; RHS, 23, 87, 109, 135, 140
operational rule, 2, 25, 31, 55, 105, 120, 141, 145-151, 203. *See also vidhi sūtra*

Pāṇinian studies, 24, 121, 198-202, 213
Pāṇinian studies, 24, 121, 198-202, 213, 217
Pāṇinian tradition, 133, 177, 178, 201, 211; evolution of, 179; history of 4; and non-Pāṇinian, 7; path of, 213; texts of, 6
Pāṇinīya, 6, 13-14, 69, 205, 213; their approach to the *Aṣṭādhyāyī*, 11; later, 123; the practice of, 16
para sūtra, 10, 39, 193, 203, 204
paradigm, 7, 136, 137, 185, 201, 202, 212
paribhāṣā / Pbh 38, 9, 10, 13, 15, 17, 203
paribhāṣā rule / *sūtra*, 2, 5, 7, 17, 24, 31, 32, 105, 120, 121, 141, 142
paribhāṣā, 6-10, 13-15, 17, 69-71, 87, 88, 92, 131-133, 146, 187, 205, 213; *anitya*, 71; post-Pāṇinian, 14, 23, 202; texts / literature, 6, 8, 195, 199, 200; traditional inventory of, 212. *See also paribhāṣā* rule / *sūtra* and metarule
Paribhāṣenduśekhara, 6, 9, 10, 12, 13, 15-17, 23, 38, 69, 87, 125, 126, 187, 203

passive, 29, 90, 93, 116-118, 157, 230, 235
pedagogical, 4, 199, 202
philological, 23
philosophical, 180, 199, 201
philosophy, 24, 198, 199, 202
phonological, 107, 140, 212
phonology, 24, 210
Pontillo, T., 26
post-Pāṇinian, 13, 14, 23, 32-37, 40, 41, 54, 68, 111, 177, 201, 202, 213
Pradīpa, 42, 187
prakriyā, 2
prakṛti, 177
prātipadika, 92, 180
Prātiśākhya, 4
pratyaya, 82, 118, 177
primary derivative, 24, 68, 82, 92, 104
problem, 63, 82, 88, 90, 106, 145, 156, 198, 201, 202, 205; circumvent, 71; contain, 13; create, 112, 116; face, 125; deal with, 47, 139, 173; overcome, 66, 91, 115, 168, 171, 204; (re) solve, 50, 73, 75, 92, 115, 147, 156, 172, 175, 213; tackle, 87, 148, 159
problematic, 156; not, 131
pūrva sūtra, 10, 39, 186, 193, 203, 204
pūrvavipratiṣiddha (*vārttika*), 38, 39, 45, 50, 187, 193, 201, 206

right-hand side, 22, 28, 29, 139, 140, 145, 149, 205
right-most, 51, 53, 54, 72, 74, 76, 78, 79, 85, 115
Roodbergen, J. A. F., 3, 15, 17, 18, 63, 176
rule conflict resolution, 9, 14, 17; influence, 123; methods of, 22; *nitya* tool / *nityatva* for, 133, 181; procedure / process of, 42, 122; tool for, 187, 190. *See also* conflict resolution
rule conflict, 3, 6-8, 11, 15, 125, 142, 192, 196, 197, 212; existing understanding of, 1; instances / occasions of, 18, 201; not as, 27; have not used the term, 40; solving / tackling / dealing with / resolution of, 13, 14, 17, 22, 42, 123, 133, 136, 181, 186, 187, 190, 202, 203, 213; traditional understanding of, 202; types / classification of, 22, 23; with respect to Vedic forms and accentuation, 122. *See also* *vipratiṣedha*, *tulyabalavirodha*, and mutual opposition
rule order(ing), 212

samāhāra, 1
samāsa, 68, 80, 81, 106, 110
Same Operand Interaction, 23, 26
Same Step Rule Interaction (SSRI), 25, 30-32, 37, 116, 122, 131, 134, 135, 141, 203, 205, 209, 212
saṁjñā sūtra, 2, 17, 31, 141. *See also* definition rule
sandhi, 4, 7, 59, 61, 63, 81, 92, 106, 137, 162
sapādasaptādhyāyi, 87, 90, 166
śāstrāsiddhi, 152-155, 161, 163
sāvakāśa, 13, 39, 42, 58, 178, 179, 194. *See also* *niravakāśa* and *sāvakāśa*
secondary derivative, 24, 68, 141
self-sufficient, 23
semantically sufficient, 117
sentence-level, 156
serial order (of the *Aṣṭādhyāyī*), 17, 29; that comes earlier in the, 38, 45, 46, 67, 92, 162, 163, 186; that comes later in the, 8, 10-12, 17, 29, 37, 38, 42, 44, 47, 59, 61, 144, 153, 158, 159, 163, 177, 178, 186, 194, 204, 205
Sharma, R. N., 5, 6, 82
siddha principle, 105, 131-135, 197
Siddhāntakaumudī, 7, 16, 44, 69, 70, 144, 152-154
Singh, U., 1
SOI-L, 55, 58, 62, 63, 65, 66, 67, 102
SOI-M, 55, 60, 62, 64, 101, 102, 206
student, 4, 6, 19, 20, 76, 140, 196, 198-200, 205, 211, 213, 214
subrule, 56-60, 206
subset, 55, 56, 58, 60-62, 205-207
substitution, 52, 53, 73, 88, 89, 110, 113, 126, 132, 137-139, 171, 175, 182, 189, 190, 192; LHS, 145, 146; RHS, 145, 146
suspended, 18, 24, 29, 132, 133, 152-155, 171, 162, 175
sūtra style, 2; a feature of / inherent to, 23, 26, 31, 54, 119, 121, 141, 160
svarita, 123-125
symmetrical (blocking), 34, 35

taddhita, 13, 68, 73, 74, 75, 77-81, 110, 111, 120, 121, 127, 161, 179, 191
theoretical, 2, 24, 136, 181, 210
tripādī, 87, 90, 157
tulyabala, 11, 13, 18, 22, 179, 189, 194, 195
tulyabalavirodha, 10, 38
Type 0, 207, 208

Type 1, 25, 26, 30, 31, 54, 207, 208, 210
Type 2, 25, 26, 30, 30, 31, 207, 208, 210
Type 2a (DOI conflict), 40, 42-45, 47, 48, 50, 53, 77, 79, 95, 112, 113, 115
Type 2b (DOI nonconflict), 40, 48-50, 53, 86
Type 3, 207, 208, 210

udātta, 91, 122-125
Uddyota, 42
Uṇādi, 127
unequal strength, 10, 38
utsarga sutra, 10, 17, 61

Vāmana, 7
vārttika, 5, 6, 14, 23, 39, 45, 46, 50, 67, 126, 144, 147, 148, 151, 159, 166, 172, 175, 177-189, 192-194, 199, 200, 214; ad hoc, 173; on the basis of, 132; comments on, 128; interpret, 133. *See also pūrvavipratiṣiddha* (*vārttika*)
Vasu, S. C., 8, 9
Vedic, 14, 97,112, 113, 121-123, 169, 184
Vergiani, 1
vidhi sūtra, 2, 5, 25, 31, 120, 121, 141. *See also* operational rule
vikaraṇa, 15, 82-84, 91, 92, 108, 119, 123, 125,
vipratiṣedha, 8, 10, 11, 13, 27, 38, 39, 41, 58, 177-179, 187, 188, 197; in the event / case of, 8, 11, 39, 140, 188, 193, 194; scope / ambit / jurisdiction / domain of, 22, 179, 189, 194, 195
vṛtti, 7
vyākaraṇa, 14

Western, 1, 32, 124, 200, 210-212
word-level, 156.